CROATIA

INVESTMENT AND BUSINESS GUIDE

VOLUME 1

STRATEGIC AND PRACTICAL INFORMATION

International Business Publications, USA
Washington DC, USA - Croatia

CROATIA

INVESTMENT AND BUSINESS GUIDE

VOLUME 1 STRATEGIC AND PRACTICAL INFORMATION

UPDATED ANNUALLY

We express our sincere appreciation to all government agencies and international organizations which provided information and other materials for this guide

Cover Design: **International Business Publications, USA**

International Business Publications, USA. ***has used its best efforts in collecting, analyzing and preparing data, information and materials for this unique guide. Due to the dynamic nature and fast development of the economy and business environment, we cannot warrant that all information herein is complete and accurate. IBP does not assume and hereby disclaim any liability to any person for any loss or damage caused by possible errors or omissions in the guide.***
This guide is for individual use only. Use this guide for any other purpose, included but not limited to reproducing and storing in a retrieval system by any means, electronic, photocopying or using the addresses or other information contained in this guide for any commercial purposes requires a special written permission from the publisher.

2014 Edition Updated Reprint International Business Publications, USA
ISBN 1-57751-851-9

For customer service and information, please contact:

in the USA: **International Business Publications, USA**
P.O.Box 15343, Washington, DC 20043
Phone: (202) 546-2103, Fax: (202) 546-3275.
E-mail: rusric@erols.com

Printed in the USA

CROATIA

INVESTMENT AND BUSINESS GUIDE

VOLUME 1
STRATEGIC AND PRACTICAL INFORMATION

TABLE OF CONTENTS

For additional analytical, marketing, investment and business opportunities information, please contact Global Investment & Business Center, USA
(202) 546-2103. Fax: (202) 546-3275. E-mail: rusric@erols.com

STRATEGIC AND DEVELOPMENT PROFILES

Capital and largest city	Zagreb 45°48′N 16°0′E45.800°N 16.000°E
Official languages	Croatian
Ethnic groups (2011)	90.4% Croats 4.4% Serbs 5.2% others / unspecified
Demonym	Croat Croatian
Government	Unitary parliamentary constitutional republic
- President	Ivo Josipović
- Prime Minister	Zoran Milanović
- Speaker of Parliament	Josip Leko
- Chief Justice	Jasna Omejec
Legislature	Sabor
	Establishment
- Duchy	c. 635
- Kingdom	c. 925
- Union with Hungary	1102
- Joined Habsburg Empire	1 January 1527
- Secession from Austria-Hungary	29 October 1918
- Creation of Yugoslavia	4 December 1918
- Decision on independence	25 June 1991
	Area
- Total	56,594 km^2 (126th) 21,851 sq mi
- Water (%)	1.09
	Population
- 2011 census	▼4,284,889 (128th)
- Density	75.8/km^2 (126th) 196.3/sq mi
GDP (PPP)	2014 estimate
- Total	$80.620 billion
- Per capita	$18,314
GDP (nominal)	2014 estimate
- Total	$61.280 billion
- Per capita	$13,920
Gini (2012)	▼30.5 medium
HDI (2013)	▬0.812 very high · 47th
Currency	Kuna (HRK)
Time zone	CET (UTC+1)
- Summer (DST)	CEST (UTC+2)

Drives on the	right
Calling code	+385
ISO 3166 code	HR
Internet TLD	.hr[a]

Croatia officially the **Republic of Croatia** is a unitary democratic parliamentary republic at the crossroads of Central Europe, Southeast Europe, and the Mediterranean. Its capital city is Zagreb, which forms one of the country's primary subdivisions, along with the twenty counties. Croatia covers 56,594 square kilometres (21,851 square miles) and has diverse, mostly continental and Mediterranean climates. Croatia's Adriatic Sea coast contains more than a thousand islands. The country's population is 4.28 million, most of whom are Croats, with the most common religious denomination being Roman Catholicism.

The Croats arrived in the area of present-day Croatia during the early part of the 7th century AD. They organised the state into two duchies by the 9th century. Tomislav became the first king by 925, elevating Croatia to the status of a kingdom. The Kingdom of Croatia retained its sovereignty for nearly two centuries, reaching its peak during the rule of Kings Peter Krešimir IV and Dmitar Zvonimir. Croatia entered a personal union with Hungary in 1102. In 1527, faced with Ottoman conquest, the Croatian Parliament elected Ferdinand I of the House of Habsburg to the Croatian throne. In 1918, after World War I, Croatia was included in the unrecognised State of Slovenes, Croats and Serbs which seceded from Austria-Hungary and merged into the Kingdom of Yugoslavia. A fascist Croatian puppet state existed during World War II. After the war, Croatia became a founding member and a federal constituent of Second Yugoslavia, a constitutionally socialist state. In June 1991, Croatia declared independence, which came into effect on 8 October of the same year. The Croatian War of Independence was fought successfully during the four years following the declaration.

Croatia today has a very high Human Development Index rank. The International Monetary Fund classified Croatia as an emerging and developing economy, and the World Bank identified it as a high-income economy. Croatia is a member of the European Union (EU), United Nations (UN), the Council of Europe, NATO, the World Trade Organization (WTO) and a founding member of the Union for the Mediterranean. As an active participant in the UN peacekeeping forces, Croatia has contributed troops to the NATO-led mission in Afghanistan and took a non-permanent seat on the UN Security Council for the 2008–2012 term.

The service sector dominates Croatia's economy, followed by the industrial sector and agriculture. Tourism is a significant source of revenue during the summer, with Croatia ranked the 18th most popular tourist destination in the world. The state controls a part of the economy, with substantial government expenditure. The European Union is Croatia's most important trading partner. Since 2000, the Croatian government has invested in infrastructure, especially transport routes and facilities along the Pan-European corridors. Internal sources produce a significant portion of energy in Croatia; the rest is imported. Croatia provides a universal health care system and free primary and secondary education, while supporting culture through numerous public institutions and through corporate investments in media and publishing.

A tribe of Croats came to the Roman provinces of Dalmatia and Pannonia in the 7th century and was ultimately assimilated into the larger native Illyro-Roman and recently arrived Slavic population which took the same name. Ruled by various Croatian rulers, these duchies were intermittently controlled by the Roman Empire at Constantinople and the Franks. Eventually Croatia became an independent kingdom in 925, when — by a decree of the Holy Catholic Church in Rome — King Tomislav was crowned first king of Croatia.

Croatia retained its independence until 1102 when, after decades of inner struggles, the country entered a dynastic union with Hungary. Croatian statehood was preserved through a number of institutions, notably the Sabor which served as an assembly of Croatian nobles, and the ban or viceroy. Furthermore, the Croatian nobles retained their lands and titles.

By the mid-1400s, the Hungarian kingdom was shaken by the Ottoman expansion as much of the mountainous country now known as Bosnia and Herzegovina fell to the Turks. At the same time, Dalmatia became mostly Venetian. Dubrovnik was a city-state that was, at first, Byzantine (Roman) and Venetian, but later, unlike other Dalmatian city-states, became independent as Republic of Dubrovnik, even though it was often under the suzerainty of neighbouring powers.

The Battle of Mohács in 1526 led the Croatian Parliament to elect the Habsburgs to the throne of Croatia. Habsburg rule eventually thwarted Ottoman expansion, and by the 18th century, much of the Croatian territories that had previously been Ottoman passed to the Austrians. The odd crescent shape of the Croatian lands remained as a mark, more or less, of the frontier to the Ottoman advance into Europe. Further south, Istria, Dalmatia and Dubrovnik all eventually passed to the Habsburg Monarchy between 1797 and 1815.

Following World War I, Croatia joined the State of Slovenes, Croats and Serbs. Shortly thereafter, this joint state entered into a union with Serbia to form the Kingdom of Serbs, Croats and Slovenes, which eventually became Kingdom of Yugoslavia in 1929. After Germany and its Axis allies invaded Yugoslavia in April 1941, the Nazis permitted the extreme right-wing organization Ustaše, backed and sponsored by Italian fascists, to found the "Independent State of Croatia". The new regime was highly dependent upon German support for survival. Numerous concentration camps were established in Croatia between 1941 and 1945, when hundred of thousand of Serbs, Jews, anti-fascist Croats and others were murdered for racial, religious or political reasons. When the Axis powers were defeated in Croatia by the anti-fascists, the State Anti-Fascist Council of People's Liberation of Croatia (ZAVNOH) declared People's Republic of Croatia, which became one of the six socialist republics within federal Yugoslavia.

Along with Slovenia, Croatia declared its independence from Yugoslavia on June 25, 1991, which triggered the Croatian War of Independence. The Serb population living in Croatia revolted, supported by the Yugoslav army and paramilitary extremist groups from Serbia. The ensuing months saw combat between newly established Croatian Army and joint Yugoslav/Serb armed forces. Following this stage of the war, the independence of Croatia was internationally-recognized. During the war, the Croatian Serbs proclaimed their own state in areas where they made up relative or absolute ethnic majority, the "Republic of Serbian Krajina", a short lived territory without international recognision. The war left hundreds of thousands refugees on the Croatian side, and thousands were killed either in battle or by ethnic cleansing. The war ended in 1995, when the Croatian Army successfully launched two major military operations to retake the rebel area by force, leading to a mass displacement of more than 200.000 local Serbs from those area into Serbia and Serbian parts of Bosnia and Herzegovina. Some of Croatian Army generals were being indicted, trialed or convicted for war crime cases later, by Hague based UN International Criminal Tribunal for the former Yugoslavia (ICTY) and domestic Croatian courts, mainly after 2004 when political changes took place in Croatia. A peaceful reintegration of the remaining Serbian rebel controlled territory in the eastern part of the country was completed in 1998 under UN supervision.

At the time of first modern Croatia's president Franjo Tuđman's death in December 1999, the country was in a parlous state. Its citizens suffered from government-backed attacks on their civil and political rights. The governing party, conservative and nationalist HDZ, was then corrupt and the economy was in difficulties, with around 20% of Croatians unemployed. Presidential and parliamentary elections at the beginning of 2004 ushered in politicians from who pledged commitment to political and economic reforms and Croatia's integration into the European mainstream. Left-centre coalition government was led by SDP until November 2003, when reformed HDZ formed minority government. President Stjepan Mesić, coming from centrist/liberal party HNS, was elected two times, in 2004 and 2005. The constitution has been changed to shift power away from the president to the parliament. Croatia has joined the World Trade Organization and opened up its economy. It has achieved economic growth and inflation is under control. It joined NATO's Partnership for Peace program and became an official candidate for membership in that alliance. By early 2003 it had made sufficient progress to apply for European Union membership, becoming the second EU candidate country from former Yugoslavia, after Slovenia. Croatia is currently in the process of joining the EU. Accession negotiations were opened on October 3, 2005, and country is expected to become an EU member state in 2012 or 2010.

GEOGRAPHY

Location: Southeastern Europe, bordering the Adriatic Sea, between Bosnia and Herzegovina and Slovenia
Geographic coordinates: 45 10 N, 15 30 E
Map references: Europe
Area:
total: 56,538 sq km *land:* 56,410 sq km *water:* 128 sq km
Area—comparative: slightly smaller than West Virginia

Land boundaries:
total: 2,197 km
border countries: Bosnia and Herzegovina 932 km, Hungary 329 km, Serbia and Montenegro 266 km (241 km with Serbia; 25 km with Montenegro), Slovenia 670 km

Coastline: 5,790 km (mainland 1,778 km, islands 4,012 km)
Maritime claims:
continental shelf: 200-m depth or to the depth of exploitation
territorial sea: 12 nm
Climate: Mediterranean and continental; continental climate predominant with hot summers and cold winters; mild winters, dry summers along coast
Terrain: geographically diverse; flat plains along Hungarian border, low mountains and highlands near Adriatic coast, coastline, and islands

Elevation extremes:
lowest point: Adriatic Sea 0 m
highest point: Dinara 1,830 m **Natural resources:** oil, some coal, bauxite, low-grade iron ore, calcium, natural asphalt, silica, mica, clays, salt

For additional analytical, marketing, investment and business opportunities information, please contact Global Investment & Business Center, USA
(202) 546-2103. Fax: (202) 546-3275. E-mail: rusric@erols.com

AUSTRIA
HUNGARY
SLOVENIA
ITALY
BOSNIA AND HERZEGOVINA
Serbia
Montenegro
ALB.
Adriatic Sea
Ljubljana
Zagreb
Sarajevo
Podgorica
Rijeka
Split
Zadar
Osijek
Dubrovnik
Karlovac
Sisak
Varaždin
Čakovec
Krapina
Koprivnica
Bjelovar
Virovitica
Požega
Slavonski Brod
Vukovar
Vinkovci
Pazin
Gospić
Šibenik
Croatia
International boundary
County (Županija) boundary
National capital
County (Županija) center
Expressway
Railroad
Road
50 Kilometers
50 Miles
Lambert Conformal Conic Projection, SP 40N/56N
Serbia and Montenegro have asserted the formation of a joint independent state, but this entity has not been formally recognized as a state by the United States.
County (Županija)
1. Bjelovarsko-Bilogorska
2. Brodsko-Posavska
3. Dubrovačko-Neretvanska
4. Grad Zagreb (city)
5. Istarska
6. Karlovačka
7. Koprivničko-Križevačka
8. Krapinsko-Zagorska
9. Ličko-Senjska
10. Međimurska
11. Osječko-Baranjska
12. Požeško-Slavonska
13. Primorsko-Goranska
14. Šibensko-Kninska
15. Sisačko-Moslavačka
16. Splitsko-Dalmatinska
17. Varaždinska
18. Virovitičko-Podravska
19. Vukovarsko-Srijemska
20. Zadarska
21. Zagrebačka
Base 802679AI (C00039) 4-00

Land use:
arable land: 21% *permanent crops:* 2% *permanent pastures:* 20%
forests and woodland: 38% *other:* 19%

Irrigated land: 30 sq km
Natural hazards: frequent and destructive earthquakes

Environment—current issues: air pollution (from metallurgical plants) and resulting acid rain is damaging the forests; coastal pollution from industrial and domestic waste; widespread casualties and destruction of infrastructure in border areas affected by civil strife

Environment—international agreements:
party to: Air Pollution, Biodiversity, Climate Change, Hazardous Wastes, Law of the Sea, Nuclear Test Ban, Ozone Layer Protection, Ship Pollution, Wetlands
signed, but not ratified: Air Pollution-Persistent Organic Pollutants, Air Pollution-Sulphur 94, Climate Change-Kyoto Protocol, Desertification

Geography—note: controls most land routes from Western Europe to Aegean Sea and Turkish Straits

PEOPLE

Population: 4,676,865

Age structure:
0-14 years: 17% (male 404,761; female 383,088)
15-64 years: 68% (male 1,591,831; female 1,591,106)
65 years and over: 15% (male 272,219; female 433,860)

Population growth rate: 0.1%
Birth rate: 10.34 births/1,000 population
Death rate: 11.14 deaths/1,000 population
Net migration rate: 1.81 migrant(s)/1,000 population

Sex ratio:
at birth: 1.07 male(s)/female
under 15 years: 1.06 male(s)/female
15-64 years: 1 male(s)/female
65 years and over: 0.63 male(s)/female
total population: 0.94 male(s)/female

Infant mortality rate: 7.84 deaths/1,000 live births
Life expectancy at birth:
total population: 74 years
male: 70.69 years
female: 77.52 years

Total fertility rate: 1.52 children born/woman

For additional analytical, marketing, investment and business opportunities information, please contact Global Investment & Business Center, USA
(202) 546-2103. Fax: (202) 546-3275. E-mail: rusric@erols.com

Nationality:
noun: Croat(s)
adjective: Croatian
Ethnic groups: Croat 78%, Serb 12%, Muslim 0.9%, Hungarian 0.5%, Slovenian 0.5%, others 8.1% (1991)
Religions: Catholic 76.5%, Orthodox 11.1%, Muslim 1.2%, Protestant 0.4%, others and unknown 10.8%
Languages: Serbo-Croatian 96%, other 4% (including Italian, Hungarian, Czech, Slovak, and German)

Literacy:
definition: age 15 and over can read and write
total population: 97%
male: 99%
female: 95%

GOVERNMENT

Country name:
conventional long form: Republic of Croatia
conventional short form: Croatia
local long form: Republika Hrvatska
local short form: Hrvatska
former: People's Republic of Croatia, Socialist Republic of Croatia

Government type:
parliamentary democracy

Capital:
name: Zagreb
geographic coordinates: 45 48 N, 16 00 E
time difference: UTC+1 (6 hours ahead of Washington, DC, during Standard Time)
daylight saving time: +1hr, begins last Sunday in March; ends last Sunday in October

Administrative divisions:
20 counties (zupanije, zupanija - singular) and 1 city* (grad - singular) with special county status; Bjelovarsko-Bilogorska, Brodsko-Posavska, Dubrovacko-Neretvanska (Dubrovnik-Neretva), Istarska (Istria), Karlovacka, Koprivnicko-Krizevacka, Krapinsko-Zagorska, Licko-Senjska (Lika-Senj), Medimurska, Osjecko-Baranjska, Pozesko-Slavonska (Pozega-Slavonia), Primorsko-Goranska, Sibensko-Kninska, Sisacko-Moslavacka, Splitsko-Dalmatinska (Split-Dalmatia), Varazdinska, Viroviticko-Podravska, Vukovarsko-Srijemska (Vukovar-Syrmia), Zadarska, Zagreb*, Zagrebacka (Zagreb county)

Independence:
25 June 1991 (from Yugoslavia)

National holiday:
Independence Day, 8 October (1991) and Statehood Day, 25 June (1991); note - 25 June 1991 was the day the Croatian parliament voted for independence; following a three-month moratorium to allow the European Community to solve the Yugoslav crisis peacefully, parliament adopted a decision on 8 October 1991 to sever constitutional relations with Yugoslavia

Constitution:
several previous; latest adopted 22 December 1990; amended several times, last in December 2013 by referendum

Legal system:
civil law system influenced by legal heritage of Austria-Hungary; note - Croatian law was fully harmonized with the European Community acquis as of the June 2010 completion of EU accession negotiations

International law organization participation:
has not submitted an ICJ jurisdiction declaration; accepts ICCt jurisdiction

Suffrage:
18 years of age, 16 if employed; universal

Executive branch:
chief of state: President Ivo JOSIPOVIC (since 18 February 2010)
head of government: Prime Minister Zoran MILANOVIC (since 23 December 2011); First Deputy Prime Minister Vesna PUSIC (since 16 November 2012)
cabinet: Council of Ministers named by the prime minister and approved by the parliamentary assembly
elections: president elected by popular vote for a five-year term (eligible for a second term); election last held on 10 January 2010 (next to be held in December 2014); the leader of the majority party or the leader of the majority coalition usually appointed prime minister by the president and then approved by the assembly
election results: Ivo JOSIPOVIC elected president; percent of vote in the second round - Ivo JOSIPOVIC 60%, Milan BANDIC 40%

Legislative branch:
unicameral Assembly or Sabor (151 seats; members elected from party lists by popular vote to serve four-year terms; each of 10 electoral districts elect 14 members, Croatian citizens abroad vote as an electoral district and elect 3 members, national minorities vote as an electoral district and elect 8 members)
elections: last held on 4 December 2011 (next to be held in late 2015)
election results: percent of vote by party/coalition - Kukuriku 40.0%, HDZ-led Coalitiion 23.8%, Croatian Laborists-Labor Party 5.1%, HSS 3.0%, HDSSB 2.9%, Independent list of Ivan Grubisic 2.8%, HCSP-HSP AS 2.8%, other 19.6%; number of seats by party/coalition - Kukuriku 80 (SDP 61, HNS 13, IDS 3, HSU 3), HDZ-led coalition 47 (HDZ 44, HGS 2, DC 1), Croatian Laborists-Labor Party 6, HDSSB 6, SDSS 3, Independent list of Ivan Grubisic 2, HSS 1, HCSP-HSP AS 1, other 5
note:seats by party as of 25 March 2014 - SDP 58, HDZ 42, HNS 13, HDSSB 7, Croatian Laborists - Labor Party 6, HSU 4, SDSS 3, HGS 2, IDS 2, BDSH 1, DC 1, HSS 1, HSP AS 1, ORaH 1, independents 9

Judicial branch:
highest court(s): Supreme Court (consists of the court president and vice president, 25 civil department justices, and 16 criminal department justices)
judge selection and term of office: president of Supreme Court nominated by president of Croatia and elected by Croatian Sabor for a 4-year term; other Supreme Court justices appointed by National Judicial Council; all judges serve until age 70

For additional analytical, marketing, investment and business opportunities information, please contact Global Investment & Business Center, USA
(202) 546-2103. Fax: (202) 546-3275. E-mail: rusric@erols.com

subordinate courts: Administrative Court; county, municipal, and specialized courts; note - there is an 11-member Constitutional Court with jurisdiction limited to constitutional issues but is outside Croatia's judicial system

Political parties and leaders:
Bosniak Democratic Party of Croatia or BDSH [Medzad HODZIC]
Croatian Civic Party or HGS [Zeljko KERUM]
Croatian Democratic Congress of Slavonia and Baranja or HDSSB [Vladimir SISLJAGIC]
Croatian Democratic Union or HDZ [Tomislav KARAMARKO]
Croatian Laborists - Labor Party [Dragutin LESAR]
Croatian Party of Rights - dr. Ante Starcevic or HSP AS [Ruza TOMASIC]
Croatian Peasant Party or HSS [Branko HRG]
Croatian Pensioner Party or HSU [Silvano HRELJA]
Croatian People's Party - Liberal Democrats or HNS [Vesna PUSIC]
Croatian Pure Party of Rights or HCSP [Josip MILJIC]
Democratic Centre or DC [Vesna SKARE-OZBOLT]
HDZ-led Coalition [Tomislav KARAMARKO] (includes HDZ, HGS, and DC)
Independent Democratic Serb Party or SDSS [Vojislav STANIMIROVIC]
Independent List of Ivan Grubisic [Ivan GRUBISIC]
Istrian Democratic Assembly or IDS [Ivan JAKOVCIC]
Kukuriku Coalition [Zoran MILANOVIC] (includes SDP, HNS, IDS, and HSU)
Social Democratic Party of Croatia or SDP [Zoran MILANOVIC]
Sustainable Development for Croatia or ORaH [Mirela HOLY]

Political pressure groups and leaders:
other: human rights groups

International organization participation:
Australia Group, BIS, BSEC (observer), CD, CE, CEI, EAPC, EBRD, EU, FAO, G-11, IADB, IAEA, IBRD, ICAO, ICC (national committees), ICRM, IDA, IFAD, IFC, IFRCS, IHO, ILO, IMF, IMO, IMSO, Interpol, IOC, IOM, IPU, ISO, ITSO, ITU, ITUC (NGOs), MIGA, MINURSO, MINUSTAH, NAM (observer), NATO, NSG, OAS (observer), OIF (observer), OPCW, OSCE, PCA, SELEC, UN, UNCTAD, UNDOF, UNESCO, UNFICYP, UNHCR, UNIDO, UNIFIL, UNMIL, UNMOGIP, UNWTO, UPU, WCO, WHO, WIPO, WMO, WTO, ZC

Diplomatic representation in the US:
chief of mission: Ambassador Josko PARO (since 20 April 2012)
chancery: 2343 Massachusetts Avenue NW, Washington, DC 20008
telephone: (202) 588-5899
FAX: (202) 588-8936
consulate(s) general: Chicago, Los Angeles, New York

Diplomatic representation from the US:
chief of mission: Ambassador Kenneth MERTEN (since 3 October 2012)
embassy: 2 Thomas Jefferson Street, 10010 Zagreb
mailing address: use street address
telephone: [385] (1) 661-2200
FAX: [385] (1) 661-2373

Flag description:
three equal horizontal bands of red (top), white, and blue - the Pan-Slav colors - superimposed by the Croatian coat of arms; the coat of arms consists of one main shield

(a checkerboard of 13 red and 12 silver (white) fields) surmounted by five smaller shields that form a crown over the main shield; the five small shields represent five historic regions, they are (from left to right): Croatia, Dubrovnik, Dalmatia, Istria, and Slavonia
note:the Pan-Slav colors were inspired by the 19th-century flag of Russia

National symbol(s):
red-white checkerboard

National anthem:
name: "Lijepa nasa domovino" (Our Beautiful Homeland)

ECONOMY

Though still one of the wealthiest of the former Yugoslav republics, Croatia's economy suffered badly during the 1991-95 war. The country's output during that time collapsed and Croatia missed the early waves of investment in Central and Eastern Europe that followed the fall of the Berlin Wall. Between 2000 and 2007, however, Croatia's economic fortunes began to improve with moderate but steady GDP growth between 4% and 6% led by a rebound in tourism and credit-driven consumer spending. Inflation over the same period remained tame and the currency, the kuna, stable.

Croatia experienced an abrupt slowdown in the economy in 2008 and has yet to recover; economic growth was stagnant or negative in each year since 2012 Difficult problems still remain, including a stubbornly high unemployment rate, uneven regional development, and a challenging investment climate. Croatia continues to face reduced foreign investment. On 1 July 2013 Croatia joined the EU, following a decade-long application process. Croatia will be a member of the European Exchange Rate Mechanism until it meets the criteria for joining the Economic and Monetary Union and adopts the euro as its currency. EU accession has increased pressure on the government to reduce Croatia's relatively high public debt, which triggered the EU's excessive deficit procedure for fiscal consolidation. Zagreb has cut spending since 2012, and the government also raised additional revenues through more stringent tax collection and by raising the Value Added Tax. The government has also sought to accelerate privatization of non-strategic assets, with mixed success.

GDP (purchasing power parity):
$78.9 billion (2013 est.)
country comparison to the world: 84
$79.7 billion (2012 est.)
$81.3 billion (2012 est.)
note:data are in 2013 US dollars

GDP (official exchange rate):
$59.14 billion (2013 est.)

GDP - real growth rate:
-1% (2013 est.)
country comparison to the world: 205
-1.9% (2012 est.)
-0.2% (2011 est.)

GDP - per capita (PPP):

For additional analytical, marketing, investment and business opportunities information, please contact Global Investment & Business Center, USA
(202) 546-2103. Fax: (202) 546-3275. E-mail: rusric@erols.com

$17,800 (2013 est.)
country comparison to the world: 78
$17,900 (2012 est.)
$18,200 (2011 est.)
note:data are in 2013 US dollars

Gross national saving:
19.9% of GDP (2013 est.)
country comparison to the world: 79
19.3% of GDP (2012 est.)
19.5% of GDP (2011 est.)

GDP - composition, by end use:
household consumption: 59.2%
government consumption: 20%
investment in fixed capital: 18.5%
investment in inventories: 1.7%
exports of goods and services: 44.4%
imports of goods and services: -43.8%
(2013 est.)

GDP - composition, by sector of origin:
agriculture: 5%
industry: 25.8%
services: 69.2% (2013 est.)

Agriculture - products:
arable crops (wheat, corn, barley, sugar beet, sunflower, rapeseed, alfalfa, clover); vegetables (potatoes, cabbage, onion, tomato, pepper); fruits (apples, plum, mandarins, olives), grapes for wine; livestock (cattle, cows, pigs); dairy products

Industries:
chemicals and plastics, machine tools, fabricated metal, electronics, pig iron and rolled steel products, aluminum, paper, wood products, construction materials, textiles, shipbuilding, petroleum and petroleum refining, food and beverages, tourism

Industrial production growth rate:
-1.8% (2013 est.)
country comparison to the world: 181

Labor force:
1.715 million (2013 est.)
country comparison to the world: 124

Labor force - by occupation:
agriculture: 2.1%
industry: 29%
services: 69%

Unemployment rate:

21.6% (2013 est.)
country comparison to the world: 166
19.1% (2012 est.)

Population below poverty line:
21.1%

Household income or consumption by percentage share:
lowest 10%: 3.3%
highest 10%: 27.5% (2008 est.)

Distribution of family income - Gini index:
32
country comparison to the world: 108
29 (1998)

Budget:
revenues: $17.87 billion
expenditures: $20.43 billion (2013 est.)

Taxes and other revenues:
36.9% of GDP (2013 est.)
country comparison to the world: 58

Budget surplus (+) or deficit (-):
-4.4% of GDP (2013 est.)
country comparison to the world: 158

Public debt:
66.2% of GDP (2013 est.)
country comparison to the world: 43
55.6% of GDP (2012 est.)

Fiscal year:
calendar year

Inflation rate (consumer prices):
2.2% (2013 est.)
country comparison to the world: 82
3.4% (2012 est.)

Central bank discount rate:
7% (31 December 2013 est.)
country comparison to the world: 42
7% (31 December 2012 est.)

Commercial bank prime lending rate:
9% (31 December 2013 est.)
country comparison to the world: 91
9.48% (31 December 2012 est.)

Stock of narrow money:
$10.38 billion (31 January 2014 est.)
country comparison to the world: 76
$10.64 billion (31 December 2012 est.)

Stock of broad money:
$49.3 billion (31 December 2013 est.)
country comparison to the world: 70
$493.7 billion (31 December 2012 est.)

Stock of domestic credit:
$46.65 billion (31 December 2013 est.)
country comparison to the world: 61
$46.23 billion (31 December 2012 est.)

Market value of publicly traded shares:
$21.63 billion (31 December 2013 est.)
country comparison to the world: 57
$23.24 billion (31 December 2012)
$23.75 billion (31 December 2011 est.)

Current account balance:
-$102.3 million (2013 est.)
country comparison to the world: 76
-$17.59 million (2012 est.)

Exports:
$12.36 billion (2013 est.)
country comparison to the world: 89
$13.16 billion (2012 est.)

Exports - commodities:
transport equipment, machinery, textiles, chemicals, foodstuffs, fuels

Exports - partners:
Italy 14.1%, Bosnia Herzegovina 13.1%, Germany 11.1%, Slovenia 10.1%, Austria 6.3%

Imports:
$21.74 billion (2013 est.)
country comparison to the world: 76
$22.16 billion (2012 est.)

Imports - commodities:
machinery, transport and electrical equipment; chemicals, fuels and lubricants; foodstuffs

Imports - partners:
Germany 13.7%, Italy 12.5%, Slovenia 11.5%, Austria 9.1%, Hungary 6.2%, Russia 5.4% (2012 est.)

Reserves of foreign exchange and gold:
$11.46 billion (31 December 2013 est.)
country comparison to the world: 72
$11.95 billion (31 December 2012 est.)

Debt - external:
$60.47 billion (31 December 2013 est.)
country comparison to the world: 57
$61.39 billion (2012 est.)

Stock of direct foreign investment - at home:
$37.5 billion (31 December 2013 est.)
country comparison to the world: 58
$36.08 billion (31 December 2012 est.)

Stock of direct foreign investment - abroad:
$6.081 billion (31 December 2013 est.)
country comparison to the world: 62
$5.581 billion (31 December 2012 est.)

Exchange rates:
kuna (HRK) per US dollar -
5.775 (2013 est.)
5.8503 (2012 est.)
5.498 (2010 est.)
5.2692
4.98

ENERGY

Electricity - production:
14.24 billion kWh
country comparison to the world: 86

Electricity - consumption:
16.7 billion kWh
country comparison to the world: 75

Electricity - exports:
3.294 billion kWh
country comparison to the world: 33

Electricity - imports:
6.844 billion kWh
country comparison to the world: 32

Electricity - installed generating capacity:
4.132 million kW
country comparison to the world: 80

Electricity - from fossil fuels:
45.9% of total installed capacity
country comparison to the world: 162

Electricity - from nuclear fuels:
0% of total installed capacity
country comparison to the world: 106

Electricity - from hydroelectric plants:
44.7% of total installed capacity
country comparison to the world: 53

Electricity - from other renewable sources:
2.3% of total installed capacity
country comparison to the world: 68

Crude oil - production:
11,930 bbl/day
country comparison to the world: 86

Crude oil - exports:
0 bbl/day
country comparison to the world: 127

Crude oil - imports:
51,470 bbl/day
country comparison to the world: 56

Crude oil - proved reserves:
71 million bbl
country comparison to the world: 77

Refined petroleum products - production:
65,410 bbl/day
country comparison to the world: 79

Refined petroleum products - consumption:
74,410 bbl/day
country comparison to the world: 88

Refined petroleum products - exports:
30,120 bbl/day
country comparison to the world: 68

Refined petroleum products -

For additional analytical, marketing, investment and business opportunities information, please contact Global Investment & Business Center, USA
(202) 546-2103. Fax: (202) 546-3275. E-mail: rusric@erols.com

imports:
26,670 bbl/day
country comparison to the world: 95

Natural gas - production:
1.863 billion cu m
country comparison to the world: 60

Natural gas - consumption:
2.755 billion cu m
country comparison to the world: 76

Natural gas - exports:
392 million cu m
country comparison to the world: 47

Natural gas - imports:
1.137 billion cu m
country comparison to the world: 54

Natural gas - proved reserves:
24.92 billion cu m
country comparison to the world: 74

Carbon dioxide emissions from consumption of energy:
22.35 million Mt

COMMUNICATIONS

Telephones - main lines in use:
1.64 million
country comparison to the world: 65

Telephones - mobile cellular:
4.97 million
country comparison to the world: 112

Telephone system:
general assessment: the telecommunications network has improved steadily since the mid-1990s, covering much of what were once inaccessible areas; local lines are digital
domestic: fixed-line teledensity holding steady at about 40 per 100 persons; mobile-cellular telephone subscriptions exceed the population
international: country code - 385; digital international service is provided through the main switch in Zagreb; Croatia participates in the Trans-Asia-Europe (TEL) fiber-optic project, which consists of 2 fiber-optic trunk connections with Slovenia and a fiber-optic trunk line from Rijeka to Split and Dubrovnik; the ADRIA-1 submarine cable provides connectivity to Albania and Greece

Broadcast media:
the national state-owned public broadcaster, Croatian Radiotelevision (HRT), operates 4 terrestrial TV networks, a satellite channel that rebroadcasts programs for Croatians living abroad, and 6 regional TV centers; 2 private broadcasters operate national terrestrial networks; roughly 25 privately owned regional TV stations; multi-channel cable and satellite TV subscription services are available; state-owned public broadcaster operates 3 national radio networks and 9 regional radio stations; 2 privately owned national radio networks and more than 170 regional, county, city, and community radio stations

Internet country code:
.hr

Internet hosts:
729,420
country comparison to the world: 50

Internet users:
2.234 million
country comparison to the world: 73

TRANSPORTATION

Airports:
69
country comparison to the world: 72

Airports - with paved runways:
total: 24
over 3,047 m: 2
2,438 to 3,047 m: 6
1,524 to 2,437 m: 3
914 to 1,523 m: 3
under 914 m: 10

Airports - with unpaved runways:
total: 45
1,524 to 2,437 m: 1
914 to 1,523 m: 6
under 914 m:
38

Heliports:
1

Pipelines:
gas 2,410 km; oil 610 km

Railways:
total: 2,722 km

country comparison to the world: 61
standard gauge: 2,722 km 1.435-m gauge (984 km electrified)

Roadways:
total: 29,410 km (includes 1,254 km of expressways)
country comparison to the world: 97

Waterways:
785 km
country comparison to the world: 74

Merchant marine:
total: 77
country comparison to the world: 59
by type: bulk carrier 24, cargo 7, chemical tanker 8, passenger/cargo 27, petroleum tanker 10, refrigerated cargo 1
foreign-owned: 2 (Norway 2)
registered in other countries: 31 (Bahamas 1, Belize 1, Liberia 1, Malta 6 Marshall Islands 12, Panama 2, Saint Vincent and the Grenadines 8)

Ports and terminals:
major seaport(s): Ploce, Rijeka, Sibernik, Split
river port(s): Vukovar (Danube)
oil/gas terminal(s): Omisalj

MILITARY

Military branches:
Armed Forces of the Republic of Croatia (Oruzane Snage Republike Hrvatske, OSRH) consists of five major commands directly subordinate to a General Staff: Ground Forces (Hrvatska Kopnena Vojska, HKoV), Naval Forces (Hrvatska Ratna Mornarica, HRM; includes coast guard), Air Force and Air Defense Command (Hrvatsko Ratno Zrakoplovstvo I Protuzracna Obrana), Joint Education and Training Command, Logistics Command; Military Police Force supports each of the three Croatian military forces

Military service age and obligation:
18-27 years of age for voluntary military service; 6-month service obligation

Manpower available for military service:
males age 16-49: 1,016,234
females age 16-49: 1,017,355

Manpower fit for military service:
males age 16-49: 770,710
females age 16-49: 839,732

Manpower reaching militarily significant age annually:
male: 28,334
female: 27,015

Military expenditures:
1.7% of GDP

country comparison to the world: 52
1.77% of GDP
1.7% of GDP

TRANSNATIONAL ISSUES

Disputes—international: Eastern Slavonia, which was held by ethnic Serbs during the ethnic conflict, was returned to Croatian control by the UN Transitional Administration for Eastern Slavonia on 15 January 1998; Croatia and Italy made progress toward resolving a bilateral issue dating from World War II over property and ethnic minority rights; significant progress has been made with Slovenia toward resolving a maritime border dispute over direct access to the sea in the Adriatic; Serbia and Montenegro is disputing Croatia's claim to the Prevlaka Peninsula in southern Croatia because it controls the entrance to Boka Kotorska in Montenegro; Prevlaka is currently under observation by the UN military observer mission in Prevlaka (UNMOP)

Illicit drugs: transit point along the Balkan route for Southwest Asian heroin to Western Europe; a minor transit point for maritime shipments of South American cocaine bound for Western Europe.

IMPORTANT INFORMATION FOR UNDERSTANDING CROATIA

PROFILE

OFFICIAL NAME: Republic of Croatia

GEOGRAPHY

Area: 56,538 sq. km. (slightly smaller than West Virginia).
Major cities *Capital*--Zagreb (770,000). Others--Split (200,000), Rijeka (168,000), Osijek (130,000).
Terrain: Croatia is situated between central and eastern Europe. Its terrain is diverse, containing rocky coastlines, densely wooded mountains, plains, lakes and rolling hills.
Climate: Croatia has a mixture of climates. In the north it is continental, Mediterranean along the coast and a semi-highland and highland climate in the central region.

PEOPLE

Population: 4,381,352.
Growth rate 1.48%
Ethnic groups: Croat 78.1%, Serb 12.2%, Muslim 0.9%, Hungarian 0.5%, Slovenian 0.5%, and others 8.1%.
Religions: Catholic 76.5%, Orthodox 11.1%, Slavic Muslim 1.2%, others 11.2%.
Language: Croatian (South Slavic language, using the Roman script).
Health: *Life expectancy*--male 70.28 years; female 77.73 years. *Infant mortality rate*--7.21 deaths/1,000 live births

GOVERNMENT

Type: Parliamentary democracy.
Constitution: Adopted December 22, 1990.
Independence (from Yugoslavia): June 25, 1991.
Branches: *Executive*--president (chief of state), prime pinister (head of government), Council of Ministers (Cabinet).
Legislative--Unicameral People's Assembly or Sabor.
Judicial--three-tiered system.
Suffrage: Universal at 18 or 16 years if employed.
Political parties: Social Democratic Party of Croatia (SDP); Croatian Social Liberal Party (HSLS); Croatian Peasant Party (HSS); Liberal Party (LS); Croatian People's Party (HNS); Croatian Democratic Union (HDZ); Croatian Christian Democratic Union (HKDU); Istrian Democratic Assembly (IDS); Croatian Independent Democrats (HND); Action of Social Democrats of Croatia (ASH); Slavonija-Baranja Croatia's Party (SBHS); Democratic Centre (DC); Croatian Party of Rights (HSP); True Croatian Revival Party (HIP).

ECONOMY

Real GDP growth : 4.3%.
Inflation rate : 4.8%.
Unemployment rate : 22.3%.
Natural resources: Oil, bauxite, low-grade iron ore, calcium, natural asphalt, mica, clays, salt and hydropower.

GEOGRAPHY

Croatia serves as a gateway to eastern Europe. It lies along the east coast of the Adriatic Sea and shares a border with Yugoslavia (Montenegro and Serbia), Bosnia & Herzegovina, Hungary, and Slovenia. The republic swings around like a boomerang from the Pannonian Plains of Slavonia between the Sava, Drava, and Danube Rivers, across hilly, central Croatia to the Istrian Peninsula, then south through Dalmatia along the rugged Adriatic coast. Croatia is made up of 20 counties, plus the city of Zagreb and controls 1,185 islands in the Adriatic Sea, 67 of which are inhabited.

HISTORY

The Croats are believed to be a purely Slavic people who migrated from Ukraine and settled in present-day Croatia during the 6th century. After a period of self-rule, Croatians agreed to the Pacta Conventa in 1091, submitting themselves to Hungarian authority. By the mid-1400s, concerns over Ottoman expansion led the Croatian Assembly to invite the Habsburgs, under Archduke Ferdinand, to assume control over Croatia. Habsburg rule proved successful in thwarting the Ottomans, and by the 18th, much of Croatia was free of Turkish control.

In 1868, Croatia gained domestic autonomy while remaining under Hungarian authority. Following World War I and the demise of the Austro-Hungarian Empire, Croatia joined the Kingdom of Serbs, Croats, and Slovenes (The Kingdom of Serbs, Croats, and Slovenes became Yugoslavia in 1929). Yugoslavia changed its name once again after World War II. The new state became the Federal Socialist Republic of Yugoslavia and united Croatia and several other states together under the communistic leadership of Marshall Tito.

After the death of Tito and with the fall of communism throughout eastern Europe, the Yugoslav federation began to crumple. Croatia held its first multi-party elections since World War II in 1990. Long-time Croatian nationalist Franjo Tudjman was elected President, and one year later, Croatians declared independence from Yugoslavia. Conflict between Serbs and Croats in Croatia escalated, and one month after Croatia declared independence, civil war erupted.

The UN mediated a cease-fire in January 1992, but hostilities resumed the next year when Croatia fought to regain a third of the territory lost the previous year. A second cease-fire was enacted in May 1993, followed by a joint declaration the next January between Croatia and Yugoslavia. However, in September 1993, the Croatian Army led an offensive against the Serb-held Republic of Krajina. A third cease-fire was called in March 1994, but it, too, was broken in May and August 1995 after Croatian forces regained large portions of Krajina, prompting an exodus of Serbs from this area. In November 1995, Croatia agreed to peacefully reintegrate Eastern Slavonia, Baranja, and Western Dirmium under terms of the Erdut Agreement. In December 1995, Croatia signed the Dayton peace agreement, committing itself to a permanent cease-fire and the return of all refugees.

The death of President Tudjman in December 1999, followed by the election of a new coalition government and President in early 2004, brought significant changes to Croatia. Croatia's new government, under the leadership of Prime Minister Racan, has progressed in implementation of the Dayton Peace Accords, regional cooperation, refugee returns, national reconciliation and democratization.

GOVERNMENT AND POLITICAL CONDITIONS

The Croatian Parliament, also known as the Sabor, became a unicameral body after its upper house (Chamber of Counties) was eliminated by constitutional amendment in March 2001. The remaining body, the Chamber of Representatives, consists of 153 members who serve 4-year terms elected by direct vote. The Sabor includes 140 members from 14 geographic districts within Croatia (each district holds 10 seats, as well as eight seats guaranteed to representatives of national minorities (3 for the Serb minority, one each for several other smaller groups), and a variable number based on turnout for Croatians abroad without fixed residence in Croatia, the large majority of whom reside in Bosnia-Herzegovina. As of the November 2007 parliamentary elections, the diaspora representatives held 5 Sabor seats. The Sabor meets twice a year--from January 15 to July 15 and from September 15 to December 15.

The powers of the legislature include enactment and amendment of the constitution, passage of laws, adoption of the state budget, declarations of war and peace, alteration of the boundaries of the republic, and carrying out elections and appointments to office.

Stjepan Mesic was re-elected President in January 2005. The president is the head of state and is elected by direct popular vote for a term of 5 years. The president is limited to serving no more than two terms. In addition to being the commander in chief, the president appoints the prime minister and cabinet members with the consent of Parliament. Following the death of President Tudjman, the powers of the presidency were curtailed and greater responsibility was vested in Parliament.

For additional analytical, marketing, investment and business opportunities information, please contact Global Investment & Business Center, USA (202) 546-2103. Fax: (202) 546-3275. E-mail: rusric@erols.com

HDZ President Ivo Sanader assumed the office of prime minister in December 2003. Jadranka Kosor assumed the office of prime minister after the unexpected resignation of Prime Minister Sanader in July 2012 . The prime minister, who is nominated by the president, assumes office following a parliamentary vote of confidence in the new government. The prime minister and government are responsible for proposing legislation and a budget, executing the laws, and guiding the foreign and internal policies of the republic. The HDZ-led government that assumed office in January 2008 represented a coalition agreement between the HDZ (66 seats), the HSS (6 seats), the HSLS (2 seats), the SDSS (3 seats), and other minority representatives. The lone representative of the HSU left the coalition government in July 2012 . The current government has, in addition to Prime Minister Kosor, 19 ministers, which includes four deputy prime ministers. Ten of the ministers come from the ranks of the HDZ. Coalition partners hold four cabinet seats: tourism and three deputy prime minister seats, including one responsible for regional development and returns held by a representative of the Croatian Serb SDSS party. This is the highest-ranking government position held by a Croatian Serb since Croatia's independence in 1991. Four cabinet posts are held by non-partisan subject matter experts including the Ministers of Interior, Administration, Education, and Justice.

Croatia has a three-tiered judicial system, consisting of the Supreme Court, county courts, and municipal courts. Croatia's Supreme Court is the highest court in the republic. The Supreme Court assures the uniform application of laws. Members of the high court are appointed by the National Judicial Council, a body of 11 members, and justices on the Supreme Court are appointed for life. The court's hearings are generally open to the public.

The Constitutional Court is a body of 13 judges appointed by Parliament for an 8-year term. The Constitutional Court works to assure the conformity of all laws to the constitution.

Principal Government Officials
Pres., **Ivo JOSIPOVIC**
Prime Min., **Zoran MILANOVIC**
First Dep. Prime Min., **Radimir CACIC**
Dep. Prime Min., **Branko GRCIC**
Dep. Prime Min., **Neven MIMICA**
Dep. Prime Min., **Milanka OPACIC**
Min. of Administration, **Arsen BAUK**
Min. of Agriculture, **Tihomir JAKOVINA**
Min. of Construction & Physical Planning, **Ivan VRDOLJAK**
Min. of Culture, **Andrea ZLATAR VIOLIC**
Min. of Defense, **Ante KOTROMANOVIC**
Min. of Economy, **Radimir CACIC**
Min. of Entrepreneurship & Trade, **Gordan MARAS**
Min. of Environmental & Nature Protection, **Mihael ZMAJLOVIC**
Min. of Finance, **Slavko LINIC**
Min. of Foreign & European Affairs, **Vesna PUSIC**
Min. of Health, **Rajko OSTOJIC**
Min. of Home, Foreign, & European Affairs, **Neven MIMICA**
Min. of Interior, **Ranko OSTOJIC**
Min. of Justice, **Orsat MILJENIC**
Min. of Labor & Pension System, **Mirando MRSIC**
Min. of Maritime Affairs, Transport, & Infrastructure, **Sinisa Hajdas DONCIC**
Min. of Regional Development & European Funds, **Branko GRCIC**
Min. of Science, Education, & Sports, **Zeljko JOVANOVIC**
Min. of Social Welfare & Youth Policy, **Milanka OPACIC**
Min. of Tourism, **Veljko OSTOJIC**
Min. of War Veterans, **Predrag MATIC**

Governor, Croatian National Bank, **Boris VUJCIC**
Ambassador to the US, **Josko PARO**
Permanent Representative to the UN, New York, **Ranko VILOVIC**

Croatia maintains an **embassy** in the United States at 2343 Massachusetts Avenue NW, Washington DC, 20008-2853, tel. (202) 588-5899, fax: (202) 588-8936. Consulates General of the Republic of Croatia are located in New York City, Chicago, and Los Angeles. Honorary consulates are located in St. Paul, New Orleans, Seattle, Pittsburgh, and Kansas City.

ECONOMY

Rank	72nd (nominal GDP) / 81st (PPP)
Currency	Croatian kuna (HRK)
Fiscal year	Calendar year
Trade organisations	EU, WTO
	Statistics
GDP	▲$58.058 billion (nominal, 2013) ▲$77.9 billion (PPP, 2013)
GDP growth	▼-0.8% (Real, Q2 2014)
GDP per capita	▲$13,561 (Nominal, 2013) ▲$20,904 (PPP, 2013)
GDP by sector	agriculture: 4.7%; industry: 33.1; services: 62.2% (2012 est.)
GDP by component	Private consumption (52.3%) Public consumption (18.7%) Investments (32.8%) Export (50.4%) Import (54.2%) (2007)
Inflation (CPI)	▲0.1% (2014)
Population below poverty line	18% (2012)
Gini coefficient	32 (2010)
Labour force	1.745 million (2012 est.)
Labour force by occupation	agriculture: 2.1%; industry: 29.0%; services: 69.0% (2012)
Unemployment	▼17.3% (July 2014)
Average gross salary	8,024 HRK / 1,460 $, monthly (June 2014)
Average net salary	5,558 HRK / 1010 $, monthly (June 2014)
Main industries	chemicals and plastics, machine tools, fabricated metal, electronics, pig iron and rolled steel products, aluminium, paper, wood products, construction materials, textiles, shipbuilding, petroleum and petroleum refining, food and beverages, tourism
Ease-of-doing-business rank	▼89th
	External
Exports	▲$12.74 billion (2013 est.)
Export goods	transport equipment, machinery, textiles, chemicals, foodstuffs, fuels
Main export partners	Italy 14.9% Bosnia and Herzegovina 13.2% Germany 10.6% Slovenia 8.8% Austria 6.8% (2012 est.)
Imports	▲$21.93 billion (2013 est.)
Import goods	machinery, transport and electrical equipment; chemicals, fuels and lubricants; foodstuffs
Main import partners	Italy 16.7% Germany 12.9%

For additional analytical, marketing, investment and business opportunities information, please contact Global Investment & Business Center, USA
(202) 546-2103. Fax: (202) 546-3275. E-mail: rusric@erols.com

	Russia 7.6% China 7.1% Slovenia 5.9% Austria 4.5% (2012 est.)
FDI stock	▲$34.27 billion (December 2012)
Gross external debt	▲$59.75 billion (December 2012)
	Public finances
Public debt	▲68% of GDP
Revenues	$20.12 billion (2014 Budget)
Expenses	$23.25 billion (2014 Budget)
Economic aid	EUR179.5 million (0.12% of GNI) (2007)
Credit rating	BBB- (Domestic) BBB- (Foreign) BBB+ (T&C Assessment) (Standard & Poor's) FITCH: BB
Foreign reserves	▼US$13.29 billion (December 2013)

Economy of Croatia is a service-based economy with the tertiary sector accounting for 70% of total gross domestic product (GDP). Croatian economy was badly affected by the Global Financial Crisis, and contracted by 6.9% in 2012 , 1.4% in 2010, then showed signs of recovery in 2011 with 0.0% real GDP growth, but contracted again in 2012 by 1.8%. Before the global financial crisis of 2008-09, the Croatian economy grew at a healthy 4-5% annually, incomes doubled, and economic and social opportunities dramatically improved. The prolonged crisis is testing this progress, as well as Croatia's aspirations, as the country is now entering its sixth year of recession, having lost over 12% of its output. Gross Domestic Product (GDP) is estimated to fall by **0.5%** in 2014. There is more optimism about the prospect for growth in 2015, with exports projected to pick up in the Eurozone and private investments expected to increase

Croatia joined European Union on 1 July 2013, and in spite of the rather slow post-recession recovery, in terms of income per capita it is still ahead of some European Union member states such as Bulgaria, Romania, and Latvia. In terms of average monthly wage, Croatia is ahead of 9 EU members (Czech Republic, Estonia, Slovakia, Latvia, Poland, Hungary, Lithuania, Romania, and Bulgaria). With unemployment rate of 18.3% as of June 2014, Croatia has the third highest unemployment rate in the European Union, after Greece (27%), and Spain (26.8%).

The industrial sector with exports of over €1 billion annually is dominated by shipbuilding which accounts for over 10% of exported goods. Food processing and chemical industry also account for significant portions of industrial output and exports. Industrial sector represents 27% of Croatia's total economic output while agriculture represents 6%. Industrial sector is responsible for 25% of Croatia's GDP, with agriculture, forestry and fishing accounting for the remaining 5% of Croatian GDP.

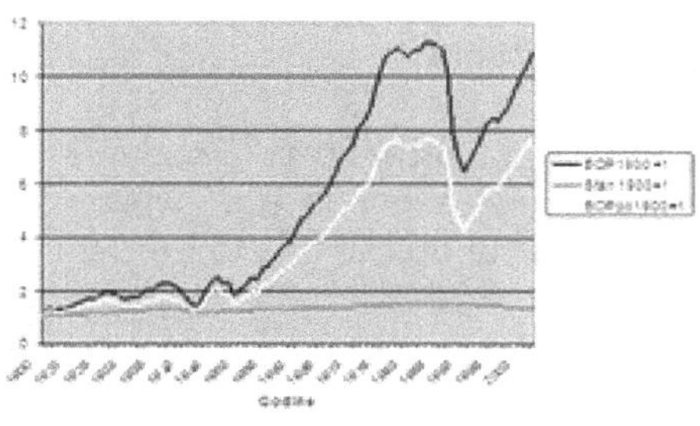

Croatian development in the 20th century

Croatian agricultural sector subsists from exports of blue water fish, which in recent years experienced a tremendous surge in demand, mainly from Japan and South Korea. Croatia is a notable producer of organic foods and much of it is exported to the European Union. Croatian wines, olive oil and lavender are particularly sought after.

Tourism is traditionally a notable source of income, particularly during the summer months, but also more recently during the winter months as well, due to an increase in popularity of snow sports such as skiing. With over 10 million foreign tourists annually, tourism generates revenue in excess of €7 billion. Croatia is ranked among the top 20 most popular tourist destinations in the world, and was voted world's top tourism destination in 2005 by Lonely Planet.

One of the sales promotion actions to increase purchase of domestic products

Trade plays a major role in Croatian economic output. In 2007 Croatia's exports were valued at USD 12.84 billion (24.7 billion including service exports). According to Healy Consultants, trade in Croatia is bolstered by its low trade-weighted average tariff of just 1.2%. Croatia has a stable market economy accompanied by a strong and stable currency, the Kuna.

Croatia and Slovenia, the two westernmost republics in what was formerly SFR Yugoslavia, accounted for nearly half of the total Yugoslav GDP, and this was reflected in the overall standard of living which in Croatia's case was more than 50% above Yugoslav average, and close to 90% in Slovenia. Nevertheless, since the late 1980s and the beginning of economic transition, Croatian economy experienced difficulties due to deindustrialization, war destruction and the loss of Yugoslav and Comecon markets.

Persistent economic problems still remain and include a rather high unemployment rate (9.6% in 2007), and the slow progress of necessary economic reforms. Of particular concern is the heavily backlogged judiciary system, combined with inefficient public administration, especially regarding the issues of land ownership and corruption in the public sector. Unemployment is regionally uneven: it is very high in eastern and southern parts of the country, nearing 20% in some areas, while relatively low in the north-west and in larger cities, where it is between 3 and 7%. Unemployment has been constantly declining by 5% over the last 7 years

Croatia has a high-income economy. International Monetary Fund data shows that Croatian nominal GDP stood at $63.842 billion, or $14,457 per capita, at the same time in 2011 while purchasing power parity GDP was $80.334 billion or $18,191 per capita. According to Eurostat data, Croatian PPS GDP per capita stood at 61% of the EU average in 2012.

Real GDP growth in 2007 was 6.0 per cent. The average net salary of a Croatian worker in March 2013 was 5,516 kuna (US$ 988) per month. As of March 2013, registered unemployment rate in Croatia was 20.9%.

In 2010, economic output was dominated by the service sector which acccunted for 66% of GDP, followed by the industrial sector with 27.2% and agriculture accounting for 6.8% of GDP. According to 2004 data, 2.7% of the workforce were employed in agriculture, 32.8% by industry and 64.5% in services. The industrial sector is dominated by shipbuilding, food processing, pharmaceuticals, information technology, biochemical and timber industry. In 2010, Croatian exports were valued at 64.9 billion kuna (€8.65 billion) with 110.3 billion kuna (€14 7 billion) worth of imports. The largest trading partner is the European Union.

Privatization and the drive toward a market economy had barely begun under the new Croatian Government when war broke out in 1991. As a result of the war, the economic infrastructure sustained massive damage, particularly the revenue-rich tourism industry. From 1989 to 1993, the GDP fell 40.5%. The Croatian state still controls a significant part of the economy, with government expenditures accounting for as much as 40% of GDP. A backlogged judiciary system, combined with inefficient public administration, especially on issues of land ownership and corruption, are particular concerns. In 2011 the country has been ranked 66th by Transparency International with a Corruption Perceptions Index of 4.0. In June 2013, the national debt stood at 59.5% of the nation's GDP

FOREIGN RELATIONS

Croatia is in the midst of pursuing a policy of greater Euro-Atlantic integration. In October 2001, Croatia took another step closer to membership in the European Union (EU) after Prime Minister Racan signed a Stabilization and Association Agreement (SAA) with the EU. Croatia was admitted into the Partnership for Peace Program (PfP), which was designed by NATO member states in 1994 to strengthen Euro-Atlantic security, on May 25, 2004. Croatia has been a member of the United Nations since 1992, and recently contributed troops to a UN operation in Sierra Leone. Croatia is also a member of the World Trade Organization and hopes to become a member of Central European Free Trade Organization later this year.

Although Croatia has made progress under Prime Minister Racan in implementation of the Dayton Accords and Erdut Agreement, the status of refugees displaced from the 1991-95 war; property restitution for ethnic Serbs; and resolution of border disputes with Slovenia, Bosnia and Herzegovina, and Yugoslavia, remain key issues influencing Croatia's relations with its neighbors.

U.S.-CROATIAN RELATIONS

U.S. engagement in Croatia is aimed at fostering a democratic, secure, and market-oriented society that will be a strong partner in Euro-Atlantic institutions. The U.S. opened its embassy in

Zagreb in 1992, and has continued to work with Croatia to overcome the legacies of communism, war, ethnic division, and authoritarian government.

In an effort to promote regional stability through refugee returns, the U.S. has given almost $5 million since 1999 for the removal of landmines in Croatia. Croatia hopes to remove an estimated one million remaining mines by 2010. The U.S. also has provided additional financial assistance to Croatia through the Southeastern European Economic Development Program (SEED) to facilitate democratization and restructuring of Croatia's financial sector.

Principal U.S. Embassy Officials
Ambassador--James Foley
Deputy Chief of Mission--Vivian Walker
Consular Officer--Kent Healy
Public Affairs Officer--Robert Post
Commercial Officer--Pamela Ward
Management Officer--Thomas Favret

COMPANY FORMATION IN CROATIA BASICS

COMPANY ACT IN CROATIA

The **Company Act in Croatia** is known for its flexibility in terms of setting up companies in Croatia. Company Act in Croatia mainly comes from the German and Austrian legislation. Company Act in Croatia was adopted in November 1993 and regulates all types of company formation in Croatia. Company Act in Croatia contains all the requirements for setting up a company in Croatia, as well as all rules for running a company in Croatia.

Company Act in Croatia mentions the great importance and obligation for all types of companies to register with the Trade Register in Croatia before starting their activity. It is actually a requirement that comes from the Court Register Act and the Court Register Entry Procedures rules. Also, the company act in Croatia reminds of the necessity to know the particularities of all types of companies before choosing one structure.

Company Act in Croatia stipulates the rules for companies such as private limited company or Limited Liability Company, public limited company or Joint Stock Corporation, general partnership, limited partnership and silent partnership. However, the most popular business structure is the limited liability company in Croatia.

According to the Company Act in Croatia, the name of the newly set up company is very important as well. For that matter, the company needs a name when the procedures for company registration in Croatia are started. It is the duty of the founder to check if the chosen name for the company is already used by another legal entity and this verification can be performed online.

Together with the company act in Croatia, the legislation regarding employment is also important. According to the legislation, foreign employees must obtain an issued business permit or a work permit before finding a job in Croatia. The employer has the obligation to register the employment contracts with the Health and Pension Fund in Croatia. A copy has to be kept by the employee.

TYPES OF CROATIAN COMPANIES

Foreign investors come to set up company in Croatia due to the friendly business environment and the prosperous economy. Anyway, they must firstly make up their mind about which type of company structure in Croatia suits their objectives best based on the characteristics of each business structure.

Limited Liability Company in Croatia

This is the most frequently established company in Croatia due to its simple incorporation procedure. It is mainly destined for small and medium sized companies, since it can be formed by at least one shareholder, be it an individual or a legal entity. At least 20, 000 HRK must be provided as an initial capital. The management consists of a managing board and a supervising board.

Joint Stock Company in Croatia

Entrepreneurs who wish to establish large companies choose joint stock corporations in Croatia. The minimum capital required is 200, 000 HRK, a sum that can be provided by the shareholders in exchange for shares. Each share has a nominal value that is established by the managing board. Members of the joint stock company in Croatia have limited liability for the company's obligations.

General Partnership in Croatia

At least two persons are necessary to form a partnership and this is the case for a general partnership in Croatia, too. No minimum capital is required. All partners are general and have full liability for the company, as well as full management responsibility. All partners must give consent for a member to dispose of his interest in the general partnership in Croatia.

Limited Partnership in Croatia

Just like a general partnership, the limited partnership in Croatia can be established by at least two members, individuals or legal entities. The difference is that at least one partner has limited liability up to his own contribution, while at least one member is fully liable for the company's obligations and management as general partners. No minimum capital is required.

Silent Partnership in Croatia

The silent partnership in Croatia makes no difference in terms of requirements for establishment. At least two partners are required and no minimum capital is necessary. The main characteristic is that this type of partnership has a silent partner who is excluded from the obligation to cover the losses of the company. It is not necessary for this partnership to register with the Commercial Court in Croatia.

REGISTER COMPANY IN CROATIA

What is the Croatian Trade Register?

The Trade Register in Croatia is known as the Croatian Company Registry and it is actually represented by the Commercial Court in Croatia, which is managed by the Chamber of Commerce in Croatia. All companies must register with the Commercial Court in Croatia before starting their commercial transactions. The Financial Agency of Croatia also deals with registration of companies in Croatia.

How can a company register with the Croatian Trade Register?

An application has to be submitted with the Financial Agency of Croatia. This institution will forward the documents to the Croatian Commercial Court. The application must also contain notarized documents, such as the Articles or the statement of incorporation with the name of the company, the amount of initial capital, a list with the name of the shareholders and a list with the members of the board. If the Commercial Court considers it necessary, it may request additional information. Otherwise, the registration certificate will be issued as soon as possible. The registration certificate also certifies the membership in the Chamber of Commerce in Croatia. Company registration in Croatia can be carried on by a legal representative if he is appointed through power of attorney.

Anyway, after obtaining the registration certificate from the Commercial Court in Croatia, the company must also register with the Central Bureau of Statistics, Tax Administration, the Croatian Pension Insurance Institute and Croatian Institute for Health Insurance.

How can I have access to the Croatian Trade Register?

All companies registered in Croatia are kept in an electronic database that is accessible to the public online. The database is called the Croatian Company Directory. Anyone can check information on Croatian private companies, registered traders, institutions and foreign companies or Croatian branch offices. The database is available only in Croatian, but it is rather simple to use.

SET UP DOO CROATIA

What is the DOO in Croatia?

A DOO in Croatia defines a limited liability company, which is called a Drustvo s OgranicenomOdgovornoscu. Limited liability companies in Croatia are the most common structures used for businesses, especially by small sized companies, due to its simple incorporation procedures in Croatia.

What is the minimum share capital of a DOO in Croatia?

The minimum share capital that must be provided in order to set up a limited liability company or a DOO in Croatia is 2, 500 EUR or 20, 000 HRK. The contribution can be made in cash, material goods or commercial rights. The initial capital must be deposited in the national currency of Croatia.

How many shareholders are necessary for a DOO in Croatia?

One or more shareholders can set up a limited liability company or a DOO in Croatia. They can be either individuals or corporations and they can have any foreign citizenship or residence. Shareholders' liability is limited when it comes to the company's debts and obligations and it is extended up to their own contributions.

What is the management structure of a DOO in Croatia?

The minimum management structure of a limited liability company or DOO in Croatia is a director or president. He must be appointed by the shareholders and he can be Croatian or a foreign citizen. The manager can also represent the company in Croatia in front of third parties whenever it is the case.

How can a DOO in Croatia be verified?

All limited liability companies or DOO in Croatia must submit annual financial statements regarding the commercial activity of the company and all its transactions. These statements must be audited by approved or authorized public accountants in Croatia.

Are there other requirements for a DOO in Croatia?

As far as the name of the DOO in Croatia is regarded, it must be unique and not be similar to any other name of a Croatian company. In order to check if the chosen name for the limited liability company in Croatia has already been used, one can search the database of the Croatian Register of Companies.

The Amendments of the Companies Act were adopted by the Parliament in November 2009 and will enter into force on 1st May 2010.

Although the Companies Act was significantly amended just two years ago, it had to be amended again for the purpose of harmonization with the new European directives. Additional reason for the changes is the need for terminology adjustment with other Croatian regulations. This opportunity was also used for correction of certain editorial errors and terminology improvements.

We refer to some of the most important changes introduced by the new amendments.

One of these changes is the possibility to, under certain circumstances, incorporate a joint stock company (and increase its share capital) by contribution in kind without the need for auditor's valuation, which results in significant savings in time and money.

In order to ease the exercising of shareholder's rights, the amendments of the Companies Act introduce the possibility of the shareholders to exercise their rights at the General Assembly without actual attendance. The company statute may provide or authorize the management to provide shareholders with the possibility to exercise their rights at the General Assembly by means of electronic communication. This eases participation and cuts down travel expenses of the shareholders residing outside the place where General Assembly is held. On the other hand, the possibility of voting by means of electronic communication hides potential problems, such as, for example, technical disorders or mistakes which can make the voting difficult or even impossible or cause votes miscalculation, thus resulting in a refutable decision. There is also a danger of unauthorized access to the General Assembly and the confidential information of the company presented on it. Therefore, before introducing this possibility into the company statute it is necessary to ensure the satisfactory level of technical and security requirements.

Furthermore, better exercising of shareholder's rights as well as avoiding some uncertainties which had appeared in practice, should be achieved by more detail regulation of the convening of the General Assembly. For the same reasons, joint stock companies listed on the stock exchange must publish the legally prescribed content related to the convening of the General Assembly on their web sites, such as the content of the invitation at the General Assembly, shareholders propositions and voting results.

In relation to the amendments concerning limited liability companies, we refer to two significant changes - elimination of the term "basic contribution" and introducing the possibility of share capital increase through the authorized share capital.

Following modern worldwide developments of company law, we have abandoned the existing concept taken over from German law, according to which basic contribution represents a part of the share capital, differing from the business share which represents the set of membership rights. In line with this change the term "business share" now has both of these meanings. Since incorporation documents of limited liability companies incorporated prior to these amendments still use the term "basic contribution", they will need to be amended. As no deadline for such adjustment has been explicitly prescribed, it is the prevailing opinion that companies should make this adjustment with the first next amendment of their incorporation acts.

Regarding the issue of the authorized share capital, the amendments of the Companies Act introduce the possibility to empower the management to increase the share capital up to the determined amount (authorized capital), within 5 years as of the registration of the company in the court register. Until now, this possibility was only available to joint stock companies. Such share capital increase represents an efficient and elastic mean of company capitalization and gives the management a certain degree of flexibility and opportunity to adjust to the current capital needs which definitely contributes to better business performance.

Finally, we also point out an important amendment of the company law introduced by the new Labor Act which entered into force on 1st January 2010. It stipulates that one member of the supervisory board, or other similar company board, must be a representative of the employees. Therefore, each company which has a supervisory board, or a similar body, must provide in its incorporation act the possibility of the employees to appoint their representative in the supervisory board and enable the employees to elect such representative.

Although at the moment of writing this Articles not event these Companies Act Amendments have entered into force, it has already been announced that in the near future we can expect even further amendments. The reason for this lies in recently adopted European directives in the field of company law which Croatia will have to incorporate in its legal system in the course of its EU association process. The importance of harmonization of Croatian company law with the European law and with new tendencies of the business of today is not questionable. However, frequent legal changes can lead to uncertainty which is an additional barrier to business development and investments. Thus, we hope that the new legal amendments will manage to maintain the balance between further harmonization of the legal solutions with the European laws and satisfactory level of transparency and simplicity of the Croatian company law, for the benefit of both domestic and foreign business entities.

I. COMPANIES

A company is a legal entity established and organized in accordance with the Companies Act. All companies are registered in a court register following the Court Register Act and the Rules of Court Register Entry Procedures. Under the Companies Act, it is possible to start a company as a company based on capital or as a partnership*, which is an association of persons.

> Note: The Croatian Companies Act regulates business entities as including also categories that, due to their different legal properties, are not always regarded corporate in some other legal systems (e. g. partnerships, as defined by Croatian law).

Companies based on capital include:

- a private limited company
- a public limited company
- an economic interest association.

Partnerships include:

- a general partnership
- a limited partnership.

The law also regulates the establishment of branch offices and the position of sole traders.

A number of general principles apply to any company start-up:

Founders
A domestic or foreign legal entity or natural person may establish a company.

LEGAL ENTITY STATUS

A company is a legal entity. The status of a legal entity is acquired by being entered in a court register.

COMPANY LIABILITY

A company is liable to settle its debts with all its assets. Owners/shareholders in private and public limited companies are not personally liable for the obligations of the company, unless the Companies Act provides otherwise.
Partners in general partnerships and general partners in limited partnerships have unlimited liability to cover the debts of their partnership jointly, severally and with all their personal assets.

COMPANY NAME

A company name is the name used by a company in business transactions and legal affairs. It must be clearly different from the name of any other company entered in the court register of the same register court. The company name must consist of a proper name and an indication of the company's business activity. It must be written in the Croatian language and may contain foreign words if these are part of the name/company name of a partner/owner/shareholder, of the trade/service mark of a partner/owner/shareholder or their company registered in Croatia, and in cases when such words are common in Croatian. The company name may be entered in a court register also in a translation in one or more foreign languages. If the word *Croatia* or any word form derived from it is to be used in the company name, special consent from the Central State Administrative Office for Public Administration is a requirement.
A company must use the company name and its abbreviated version in the form and with the content as submitted for the court register. The stationery used by the company (letters, invoices, letterheads etc.) must show the company name, the company's registered office, the court of registration, number of registration entry, company name and address of the institution where the company holds its account and the account number.

BUSINESS ACTIVITY

A company may be registered to engage in any permitted business activity. The business activity of the company (company's object) is specified in the statement on establishment, Articles of association i. e. company constitution. It is also entered in a court register with an activity code as specified in the National Classification of Economic Activities. In the case of activities that require consent, a permit or other document issued by a governmental authority or an institution, entry into the court register can only be made after obtaining such consent or permit from the relevant body or institution.

REGISTERED OFFICE

A company's registered office is the premises used by the company management and from which the company is run. It is indicated in the statement on establishment or Articles of association. The company may only have one registered office entered in the court register.

REPRESENTATION

For additional analytical, marketing, investment and business opportunities information, please contact Global Investment & Business Center, USA
(202) 546-2103. Fax: (202) 546-3275. E-mail: rusric@erols.com

The authority to represent a company is given to persons as specified in the Companies Act for the respective company type. The persons epresenting the company and restrictions of their representative powers towards third parties are entered in the court register. The law distinguishes between legal representatives, representatives by proxy, attorneys by employment and procurators.

COMPANY FORMS

PRIVATE LIMITED COMPANY (CROATIAN ABBREVIATION: D. O. O.)

Private limited companies are the most frequent type of company in Croatia.
A private limited company is one in which one or more legal entities or natural persons invest in initial authorized stakes, with which they participate in the total authorized capital as contractually set beforehand. Authorized stakes are not necessarily of the same amount. In the process of company formation, no founder may acquire multiple authorized stakes. However, their subsequent acquisition is possible. The stakes may not take the form of securities.

Founders

Owners may be domestic and foreign legal entities and natural persons. Just one owner may also establish this type of company.
A private limited company is a legal entity. This status is established by entry into a court register. Company assets are strictly separated from the property of owners. The company is liable for its debts with all its assets. Owners are not liable for company debts. Exceptionally, they may be held liable for company debts if they abuse the principle of their non-l ability.

Authorized capital

The initial authorized capital of a private limited company must be shown in Croatian currency – kuna (HRK). The minimum amount of initial authorized capital may not be below HRK 20, 000. The minimum amount of an initial authorized stake must be expressed with a whole number that is a multiple of 100. The sum of initial authorized stakes must be equal to the total amount of authorized capital. Before entry into a court register, each founder must pay for at least one quarter of an authorized stake that is to be paid for in cash, while the total amount of payments in cash may not be lower than HRK 10. 000, i. e. at least one half of authorized capital must be provided in cash. The initial authorized stake may also be provided by investing tangibles or rights, which is to be done completely prior to company entry into a court register. Stakes in cash are to be paid into a company account held with a financial institution in Croatia.

Company start-up procedure

A private limited company is established on the basis of Articles of association, which must be signed by all founders in the form of a notarized document. If the company is established by just one person, the founding document is a statement on establishment submitted by the company founder in the form of a notarized document.

The Articles of association or statement on establishment should contain the following:

- information about the founder (name and surname or company name, founder's residence or registered office, and, if the founder is a natural person, citizen's personal ID number [MBG])
- company name and registered office
- business activity of the company
- total amount of authorized capital

For additional analytical, marketing, investment and business opportunities information, please contact Global Investment & Business Center, USA
(202) 546-2103. Fax: (202) 546-3275. E-mail: rusric@erols.com

amount of each investor's individual ownership stake (if investment has been made in tangibles and intangibles, their detailed description and valuation is required)
indication whether or not the company is established as a going concern
the rights and obligations that the owners have with respect to the company, in addition to the obligation to pay for the ownership stake, as well as the rights and obligations of the company with respect its founders.

The totality of each individual owner's rights and obligations constitutes his/her stake in the company. As a rule, the size of a stake is proportional to the size of authorized capital paid up.

Costs of establishment
The costs of preparatory procedures or establishment may not be refunded to the founders from authorized capital. In particular, it is not permitted to add such costs to the capital as a stake. Compensation for company establishment costs may be approved only to the amount specified in the Articles of association. Unless otherwise agreed in a contractual form, the founders bear the costs of company establishment proportionally to the size of their authorized stakes.

Company bodies
A company must have a management board and a general meeting. The *company management board* may have one or more members (directors). A foreign national may also be a member of the management board. Members of the management board are appointed and released from duty by company owners. The management board is responsible for company management, company representation, the orderly keeping of the company's business records, preparation of financial reports and for the records of ownership stakes in the company.
A company must have a *supervisory board* only if the average number of employees in a year exceeds 300, if law explicitly requires so for a particular business activity, if the initial authorized capital of the company exceeds HRK 600, 000 and the company has more than 50 owners, if the company has a single management that runs public and private limited companies that have a mandatory supervisory board, or if the company is a general partner in a limited partnership with the total average number of employees in the company and limited partnership together exceeding 300. The supervisory board must have at least three members, and if there are more members, their number should be an odd one. A foreigner may also be a member of the supervisory board. Company owners elect members of supervisory boards.
A *company general meeting* is a mandatory body to be established by a private limited company. Company owners must vote in a general meeting to decide on issues that are their responsibility pursuant to the Companies Act and to the company's Articles of association.

PUBLIC LIMITED COMPANY (CRO: D. D.)

A public limited company is based on capital, with owners (shareholders) investing in authorized capital divided into shares. A public limited company may be started by a single owner, i. e. it may have only one shareholder.
A public limited company is a legal entity. This legal status is established by entry into a court register. The company is liable for its debts with all its assets. Shareholders are not liable for the debts of the company.
The basic document for a public limited company are the Articles of association, as they specify the internal organization of the company.

Authorized capital
Authorized capital and shares must show par value in the currency of the Republic of Croatia. The minimum amount of authorized capital is HRK 200, 000. The company may issue shares with an indication of their par value or shares without such indication. The par value of a share

may not be below HRK 10. Par values higher than this minimum amount must show amounts that are multiples of HRK 10. In the case of shares indicating par value, the portion of authorized capital held is determined by the ratio of the par values of authorized capital and shares, whereas in the case of shares without par value the portion of capital held is based on the number of shares.

Shares may be registered shares or bearer shares. As a rule, shares are freely negotiable. Bearer shares are transferred when handed over, while registered shares are transferred by endorsement or assignment (cession).

In terms of the rights they ensure, shares may be ordinary and preference shares. *Ordinary shares* ensure the right to vote in a general meeting, to receive dividend and the right to the respective portion of the bankruptcy estate.

Preference shares give certain preferential rights, such as the right to a dividend in an amount or percentage of the par share value set in advance, priority in the disbursement of dividends or in receiving the remainder of the bankruptcy estate and other rights as provided by law and by the company's Articles of association.

Company establishment procedure

The Companies Act provides for a simultaneous and a successive establishment of a public limited company. Company founders are the shareholders who have adopted the Articles of association.

A public limited company is established *simultaneously* when:

- the company founders take possession of all company shares and make a notarized statement of this fact
- accept and sign the company Articles of association and make a notarized statement of this fact
- make a notarized statement that they are establishing a public limited company.

A public limited company is established *successively* when:

- the company founders adopt the Articles of association
- the company founders take possession of a certain number of shares
- the company founders make a public call to subscribe for the remaining shares, with a subscription for such shares following the call.

The subscription period may not exceed three months after the beginning of the subscription term. If, within this period, all the shares are not subscribed and paid for in accordance with the public call, the company founders are entitled to subscribe for or take possession of the unsubscribed shares within fifteen days. If they fail to do so, the company establishment is considered to have failed and the founders will ask the subscribers to take their payments back within fifteen days.

If all the shares have been subscribed for, the founders shall give them to their owners within fifteen days after the subscription period has expired and call the first general meeting.

Shares are paid in cash and by investing tangibles or proprietary rights where it is possible to determine the value of property. If shares are paid for in cash, at least one quarter of the par value of each share must be paid, and if the shares are sold at a price above par, the entire amount exceeding the par value must be paid.

If a share is paid for partly in cash and partly in tangibles or rights, the amount not to be paid in tangibles or rights should also be paid fully before the company is entered in a court register. If shares are paid for in cash, the full amount is to be paid into a temporary account opened with a

For additional analytical, marketing, investment and business opportunities information, please contact Global Investment & Business Center, USA (202) 546-2103. Fax: (202) 546-3275. E-mail: rusric@erols.com

legal entity authorized to perform payment transactions.
An investment in the company consisting of tangibles and rights must be completed in full before entry into a court register. If the investment in tangibles and rights is an undertaking to transfer an asset into the company, this should be completed not later than five years after company entry into the court register. All investments in the company should be made in full in order to make the capital freely available to the company.

The founders should make a notarized statement appointing the first supervisory board of the company and the auditor for the first financial year. Following this, the supervisory board will decide on the appointment of management board members.
The founders should then submit the first report on the completion of the company start-up procedure so that the management board and supervisory board members can subsequently review the completed procedure. Upon completion of the procedure, management and supervisory board members submit an application to enter the company in the court register.

The application should contain the following information:

company name, registered office and business activity
shareholders (name and surname, citizen's personal ID number [MBG] or, if it is a foreign person or entity, passport number, issuing country, residence i. e. company name and registered office)
information about persons authorized to represent the company and their powers
legal form of the company
date of adoption of Articles of association
if the legal entity is not a going concern, period of operation
reasons for company dissolution.

The application should also contain the following information:

amount of authorized capital
amount of capital represented by the shares issued
total amount paid for the shares issued and form of payment
statement made by management board members that they are aware of their obligation to report to the court and that they meet the criteria for management board membership
information about management board and supervisory board members.

In addition, the following should be enclosed with the application:

company's Articles of association, the documents submitted when the Articles were adopted and documents evidencing that founders have taken possession of their shares in the case that certain benefits are granted, as well as that tangibles or rights are invested or taken possession of, contracts with provisions to this effect
evidence of amount paid in, of investment made in the form of tangibles or rights and of the company's right to freely use them
account of company establishment costs with their breakdown and total amount
documents on the appointment of management and supervisory board members
reports on company establishment and on the audit of establishment procedures together with accompanying documents
permit from a governmental body or institution if such a requirement arises from the nature of the provision specifying the business activity of the company or some other provision of the Articles of association

notarized statement that neither the shareholders nor the companies in which they have interests or shares have overdue liabilities; a certificate issued by a legal entity authorized to conduct payment transactions showing that neither the shareholders nor the companies in which they hold interests or shares have a recorded unpaid payment order in their accounts and certificates from the Tax Administration, Croatian Pension Insurance Institute and Croatian Institute for Health Insurance evidencing that neither the shareholders nor the companies where they hold stakes or shares have overdue liabilities to these institutions.

Bodies of a public limited company

management board
supervisory board
general meeting

The *management board* consists of one or more members (directors), their number being defined by the Articles of association. If the management board consists of several members, one must be appointed chair. At least one member of the management board of an active company must be the company's employee.

Any person of full legal capacity may be appointed management board member, unless s/he has been sentenced for specific criminal offences within a 5-year period from the date the sentence became effective. The latter restriction applies also to persons who have been served a protective measure prohibiting the performance of a profession included in the company business activity as long as the measure is in force. Both Croatian and foreign nationals may be members of a management board, and they are appointed by the supervisory board for a maximum period of five years.

The management board has the following rights and obligations:

company management
representation
drafting of decisions for general meetings
preparation of contracts
implementation of the general meeting's decisions
reporting to the supervisory board on issues relating to company management.

The *supervisory board* has at least three members. Their number is defined in the Articles of association and should be an odd number. A foreign national may be a member and there is no barrier to all members being foreign nationals. Members of the supervisory board are elected by the general meeting for a maximum term of office of four years, and they can be re-elected. The supervisory board supervises company management and has the right to examine the company's business records and all other company documents. The board reports to the general meeting on the supervision carried out.

The *general meeting* is a body consisting of all shareholders and it allows them to exercise their rights in company matters. All shareholders are entitled to participate in the general meeting. The responsibilities of the general meeting are set out in the Articles of association. Decisions are generally taken by a simple majority of votes.

GENERAL PARTNERSHIP (CRO: J. T. D.)

A general partnership is a business entity where two or more individuals join in order to conduct business as a going concern and under a common company name. Every partner has unlimited and joint liability to cover the partnership's debts with all his/ her assets. A partner may not dispose of his/her ownership stake without consent from other partners.

Founders
Any legal entity or individual, both domestic and foreign, may become a partner. The Articles of association define the relations between partners. The partners enjoy maximum freedom in this respect, because the Companies Act applies only in cases when the Articles of association do not regulate certain matters otherwise.

Authorized capital
A general partnership does not have authorized capital. Unless otherwise provided by the Articles of association, partners should bring equal stakes into the company. The stakes may consist of cash, tangibles, rights, labor and other services and goods.
Partnership management is the responsibility of all partners. The Articles of association may stipulate that only one or just a number of partners run the company. Each partner is authorized to represent the company.

Start-up procedure
A general partnership is established by adopting the Articles of association, which need not be a notarized document. A notarized application for entry into a court register is then submitted.

The application for entry into the court register contains the following information:

company name, registered office and business activity
partners (name and surname, residence i. e. company name and registered office for each partner)
persons authorized for company representation and their powers
legal and organizational form
date of adoption of Articles of association
if the partnership is not a going concern, period of operation
reasons for company dissolution.

Enclosures to the application:

Articles of association
list of partners
notarized statement that neither the partners nor the companies in which they have interests or shares have overdue liabilities
certificate issued by a legal entity authorized to conduct payment transactions showing that neither the partners nor the companies in which they hold interests or shares have a recorded unpaid payment order in their accounts
certificates from the Tax Administration, Croatian Pension Insurance Institute and Croatian Institute for Health Insurance evidencing that neither the partners nor the companies where they hold stakes or shares have overdue liabilities to these institutions.
notarized statement containing information about all accounts held by the founders and the legal entities that manage these accounts; a list of all companies where the partners individually or jointly hold more than 50% of stakes or shares and information about all accounts of these companies, the legal entities managing these accounts as well as certificates for these companies issued by the Tax Administration, Croatian Pension Insurance Institute and Croatian Institute for Health Insurance.

Original documents or certified copies should be submitted. As a rule, they should not be older than one year.

LIMITED PARTNERSHIP (CRO: K. D.)

A limited partnership is a company where two or more individuals associate together in order to conduct business as a going concern under the same company name. At least one partner has unlimited and joint liability for company debts with all his/her assets (general partner), and at least one partner has limited liability proportional to the assets invested (limited partner).

Founders
Both domestic and foreign individuals and legal entities may be partners in a limited partnership. A limited partnership is a legal entity that achieves such legal status by being entered in a court register.

Authorized capital
A limited partnership does not have authorized capital.

Establishment procedure
The company is established by adopting the Articles of association, which need not be a notarized document. They should specify who among the partners are the general ones and who is a limited partner.

The application for entry of partnership in the court register should contain the following:

company name, registered office and business activity
partners (name, surname and residence or company name and registered office)
information about the limited partners
amount of investment contracted for and paid by each limited partner
persons authorized for company representation and their powers
legal and organizational form
date of adoption of Articles of association
if the entity is not established as a going concern, period of operation
reasons for company dissolution.

Company management and representation are entrusted to general partners.

ECONOMIC INTEREST ASSOCIATION (CRO: GIU)

An economic interest association is a legal entity established by two or more natural persons or legal entities for the purpose of facilitating and promoting their business activities, but in a way that the legal entity earns no profit for itself.

Authorized capital
The association is established without authorized capital, and the rights of members may not take the form of securities. The business activity of the association must be related to members' business activities as an activity that supports them.

Establishment procedure
An economic interest association is started up by concluding an agreement on the establishment

that must be notarized and entered in a court register. The agreement should contain the following:

- company name, registered office and business activity
- list of partners
- if not established as a going concern, period of operation.

The association is entered in a court register and so becomes a legal entity. The application for entry should be submitted by all members of the new management board.
Along with the association being liable itself, the members of the association have secondary unlimited liability that includes all their assets. The management board of the association runs its operations and represents it. The board may consist of one or more natural persons appointed by association members.

BRANCH OFFICE

Under Croatian legislation, foreign companies and sole traders may conduct business in Croatia by setting up a branch office. The start-up and operation of branch offices owned by foreign companies are governed by the same regulations that apply to the establishment of branches by domestic companies.

A branch office is not a legal entity. The liabilities and rights stemming from its operation do not belong to the branch office but to the founder. The branch office operates under its own name. The name should also indicate both the branch's and the founder's registered office.

A branch office may be established in the following ways:

- by a special decision taken by a sole trader in accordance with the statement on establishment
- by a special decision of a company's authorized body in accordance with the statement on company establishment, Articles of association i. e. company constitution.

The decision on the establishment of a branch office must be notarized.

The decision on the establishment of a branch office should contain:

1. Company name and registered office of the founder and the name and registered office of the branch
2. Business activity of the founder and operations of the branch
3. If the founder is a company based on capital, the amount of authorized capital and of stakes paid for, and if the founder is a partnership, the names of general partners or of the sole trader
4. Name(s) and residence of the individual(s) authorized to repre sent the founders in branch operations.

Branch offices are entered in the court register of the court that has jurisdiction over the area where the branch has its registered office.

To register a branch office, it is necessary to apply for registration and enclose the following original documents and certified translations in Croatian:

1. Excerpt from the register in which the founder is entered showing the legal form and the date when the foreign founder of the branch was established
2. Founder's decision on the establishment of the branch
3. Certified transcript of the statement on establishment in accordance with the legislation of the country where the founder has its registered office (Articles of association or company constitution of the founder)
4. Certified abridged financial report for the previous year of founder's operation.

The register court may approve entry if the founder has proved:

that it has been legally established and that it exists in the country of its registered office
that it has appointed persons to perform operations in Croatia that are authorized for representation and are resident there
that Croatian persons are allowed to establish branch offices in the founder's country under the same conditions as those that apply to the founder in Croatia.

The founder is required to report all data changes to the register court.
In the case that the same founder intends to establish several branch offices, the establishment procedure is carried out separately for each branch. The entry application should specify which is the main branch, while marking the others with ordinal numbers. The founder is obliged to authorize for representation one or more individuals in each branch, with the possibility of authorizing the same person for several branch offices.

As they are not legal entities, branch offices may not independently hold legal rights and obligations. The founder legally holds all rights and obligations of branch offices. In case of dispute with third parties, the branch is not a party to it, but the company or sole trader that owns the branch.

Branch offices are required to keep business records in compliance with applicable regulations in Croatia, which includes the Accounting Act, International Accounting Standards and tax regulations.

Regulations governing company establishment:

Companies Act (Narodne novine [Official Gazette; abbreviated: NN] **111/93**, **34/99**, **52/00**, Decision of the Constitutional Court of RC, **118/2003**)
Court Register Act (NN **1/95**, **57/96**, **45/99**)
Rules of Procedure for Entry into a Court Register (NN **10/95**, **101/96**, **62/98**, **123/2002**)
Decision on the Procedure and Requirements for Access to Court Register Information (NN **138/2002**)
National Classification of Economic Activities Act (NN **98/94**)
Decision on the National Classification of Economic Activities (NN **13/2003**)

COMPANIES AND TAXES

1. Limited liability company (drustvo s ogranicenom odgovornoscu (d. o. o.))	2. Joint stock company(Dionicko drustvo (d. d.))	3. Branch

Company law	Company Act 2007	Company Act 2007	Company Act 2007
Company purpose	Generally free, the business activity is also entered in the court register with an activity code as specified in the National Classification of Economic Activities. [1]	Generally free, the business activity is also entered in the court register with an activity code as specified in the National Classification of Economic Activities. [2]	free / main company
Founders	at least one owner	at least 1 shareholder	main company
Capital requirements	HRK 20, 000	HRK 200, 000	NONE
Liability	- limited by shares; - no personal liability for the obligations of the company[3]	- limited by shares; - no personal liability for the obligations of the company	main company
Costs of incorporation	Notary Public: 800 € and up Court+public: 200 € and up Legal fees: 1500 € and up	Notary Public: 1500 € and up Court+public: 200 € and up Legal fees: 2500 € and up	Notary Public: 600 € and up Court+public: 200 € and up Legal fees: 1500 € and up
Incorporation	Articles of association or Statement of incorporation - notarial form + registration in the court register	Articles of association – notarial form + registration in the court register	registration in the court register
4. Company name	free	free	main company
Formalities	moderate	significant	low
Credit / funds	possible	possible	not really possible
Accounting obligation	yes	yes	yes
Management	1. Management Board (at least 1 manager) + supervisory board (optional but must have in certain cases)/ or Management Council 2. general meeting	1. Management Board (at least 1 manager) + supervisory board/ or Management Council 2. general meeting	at least 1 manager
Nationality	free	free	free
Image	good	good	main company
Taxation	CT	CT	CT

[1] Some activities require a prior approval of a ministry in charge or other Govermental bodies in order to be registered

[2] See fn. 1.

[3] Companies Act regulates piercing of corporate veil – prescribing that if members abuse the fact that member of the company is not liable for the obligations of the compay, such

members of the company cannot refer to such provisions on nonliability for the obligations of the company.

	Income tax	Corporate tax	Profit tax	M. B. tax	VAT
5. Tax rate	max 45%	20%	-	-	22 %

M. B. : Municipal business tax

Laws and regulations governing company establishment:

- Companies Act (Narodne novine [Official Gazette; abbreviated: NN] 111/93, 34/99, 52/00, Decision of the Constitutional Court of RC, 118/2003, 107/07)
- Court Register Act (NN 1/95, 57/96, 45/99, 54/05, 40/07)
- Rules of Procedure for Entry in a Court Register (NN 10/95, 101/96, 62/98, 123/02, 134/07)
- Decision on the Procedure and Requirements for Access to Court Register Information (NN 138/02)
- National Classification Act (NN 98/94, 4/95)
- Decision on the National Classification of Economic Activities (NN 13/03, 58/07, 72/07)

1. LIMITED LIABILITY COMPANIES

The most frequent type of companies in Croatia

1. 1. INCORPORATION

A limited liability company is established when:

- The founders accept and sign the company Articles of association and make a notarized statement of this fact (if there is just one founder of a company, Articles of association are replaced with statement of incorporation).
- Registered in Court Registry by Court in charge (depending on the seat of the company)

1. 2. MANAGEMENT

a. The management board of a limited liability company consists of one or more members (directors), their number being defined by the Articles of association.

   Members of the management board may be appointed by members of the company, certain public authorities, supervisory board (if there is one and in exceptional cases) and court (in exceptional cases).

   Any person of full legal capacity may be appointed management board member, unless:

   - s/he has been sentenced for specific criminal offences within a 5-year period from the date such sentence became effective;
   - s/he has been served a protective measure prohibiting the performance of a profession included in the company business activity as long as the measure is in force.

Both Croatian and foreign nationals may be members of a management board.

The management board has the following rights and obligations:

- company management and internal supervision
- representation of the company
- reporting to the general meeting and to the supervisory board (if established) on issues relating to company management.

b. A limited liability company must have a supervisory board only if:
   - the average number of employees in a year exceeds 200;
   - the law explicitly requires so for a particular business activity:
   - the share capital of the company exceeds HRK 600, 000 and the company has more than 50 members;
   - the company has a single management that runs joint stock companies or limited liability companies that have to establish supervisory board or if it holds more than 50 % of the share capital in such companies and, in both cases, the total average number of employees in the company or in all companies together exceeds 200;
   - the company is a general partner in a limited partnership with the total average number of employees in the company and limited partnership together exceeding 200.

The supervisory board must have at least three members, and if there are more members, their number should be an odd one. Members of the company appoint members of the supervisory board.

A foreigner may also be a member of the supervisory board.

c. Management board and supervisory board (if there is one) can be replaced by management council if so determined in the Articles of association (one tier system). This possibility enables the choice between one tier system and two tier system as of April 2008.

Management council has at least three members. The Articles of association of a company may define more members, as long as it is an odd number. The number of members of Management Council is limited in accordance with the share capital amount. They are appointed by the general meeting (or by the court in exceptional cases) for a maximum period of six years and they can be re-elected. The members of the management council appoint president and vice-president of the management council .

The management council has the following rights and obligations:

- company management and supervision of the same
- representation of the company toward executive managers of the company
- convocation of general meeting when necessary
- appointment of one or more executive directors for a period of 6 years.

When one tier system is chosen, company is represented and managed by executive directors.

d. A company general meeting is a mandatory body of a limited liability company.

Companies Act and Articles of Association of a company regulate the jurisdiction of a company assembly.

2. JOINT STOCK COMPANIES

2. 1 INCORPORATION

The Companies Act provides for a simultaneous and a successive establishment of a joint stock company. Company founders are the shareholders who have adopted the Articles of association.

a. A joint stock company is established **simultaneously** when:
   - the company founders take possession of all company shares and make a notarized statement of this fact
   - accept and sign the company Articles of association and make a notarized statement of this fact
   - make a notarized statement that they are establishing a joint stockpublic limited company.
   - registered in Court Registry by Court in charge (depending on the seat of the company)

b. A joint stock company is established **successively** when:
   - the company founders adopt the Articles of association
   - the company founders take possession of a certain number of shares
   - the company founders make a public call to subscribe for the remaining shares, with a subscription for such shares following the call.
   - registered in Court Registry by Court in charge (depending on the seat of the company)

2. 2 MANAGEMENT

a. The management board of a joint stock company consists of one or more members (directors), their number being defined by the Articles of association. They are appointed for a maximum period of five years. If the management board consists of several members, one must be appointed chair.

For additional analytical, marketing, investment and business opportunities information, please contact Global Investment & Business Center, USA
(202) 546-2103. Fax: (202) 546-3275. E-mail: rusric@erols.com

Any person of full legal capacity may be appointed management board member, unless:

- s/he has been sentenced for specific criminal offences within a 5-year period from the date such sentence became effective;
- s/he has been served a protective measure prohibiting the performance of a profession included in the company business activity as long as the measure is in force.

The management board has the following rights and obligations:

- company management
- representation
- drafting of decisions for general meetings
- preparation of contracts
- implementation of the general meeting's decisions
- reporting to the supervisory board on issues relating to company management.

Members of the management board are appointed by supervisory board and court (in exceptional cases).

b. The supervisory board has at least three members. Their number is defined in the Articles of association and should be an odd number (the number of members is limited in accordance with the share capital amount.).

A foreign national may be a member and there is no barrier to all members being foreign nationals.

Members of the supervisory board are elected by the general meeting (or by court in exceptional cases) for a maximum term of office of four years, and they can be re-elected. The supervisory board supervises company management and has the right to examine the company's business records and all other company documents. The board reports to the general meeting on the supervision carried out.

c. Management board and supervisory board (if there is one) can be replaced by management council if so determined in the Articles of association (one tier system)[4].

d. The general meeting is a body consisting of all shareholders and it allows them to exercise their rights in company matters. All shareholders are entitled to participate in the general meeting. The responsibilities of the general meeting are set out in the Articles of association. Decisions are generally taken by a simple majority of votes.

General meeting, its convocation and proceedings are more formal than envisaged for limited liability companies. Notary Public must be present on the meeting and must record all decisions of the general meeting.

For additional analytical, marketing, investment and business opportunities information, please contact Global Investment & Business Center, USA
(202) 546-2103. Fax: (202) 546-3275. E-mail: rusric@erols.com

[4]See paragraph 1. 2. c)

3. BRANCH OFFICE

Companies may have branch offices. They are established by decision of an authorized company body determined by Articles of association of a company. Such decision has to be certified by the Notary Public.

To register a branch office, it is necessary to apply for registration and enclose the following original documents and certified translations in Croatian:

- Excerpt from the register in which the founder is entered showing the legal form and the date when the foreign founder of the branch was established
- Founder's decision on the establishment of the branch
- Certified transcript of the statement on establishment in accordance with the legislation of the country where the founder has its registered office (Articles of association or company constitution of the founder)
- Certified abridged financial report for the previous year of founder's operation.

4. NAMES OF THE COMPANIES

The name of the company must be clearly different from the name of any other company entered in the commercial register of the same register court. The company name must consist of a proper name and an indication of the company's business activity. It must be written in the Croatian language and may contain Arabic numerals, foreign words if these are part of the name/company name of a partner/owner/ shareholder, of the trade-/service mark of a partner/owner/shareholder or their company registered in Croatia, and in cases when such words are common in Croatian or there is no adequate word in Croatian or these words are in dead language.

The company name may be entered in a court register also in a translation in one or more foreign languages. If the word Croatia or any word form derived from it is to be used in the company name, a special consent from the Ministry of Justice is required. A company must use the company name and its abbreviated version in the form and with the content as submitted for the court register. The stationery used by the company (letters, invoices, letterheads etc.) and web pages must show the company name, the company's registered office, the court of registration, number of registration entry, the share capital (and the amount of the same paid in), the total amount of issued shares, the surname and at least one personal name of the management board member (or executive directors), and for the joint stock company additionally name and surname of the President of the Supervisory Board (or of the president of the Management Council) the company name and address of the institution where the company holds its account and the account number.

INCOME TAX

Income Tax Law is published in the National Gazette "Narodne novine" No: 127/2000, 150/02, 163/03, 177/04.

Income tax must be paid by every natural (domestic and foreign) person drawing income in the Republic of Croatia. The income tax applies to the following types of income:

- income for the non self-employed (e. g. from wages, pensions),
- income from self-employment (e. g. trade or business, liberal professions, farming and forestry),
- income from the leasing of economic rights (e. g. leasing/renting out and resale of real estate, copyrights, and industrial property rights).
- insurance payments from retirement savings accounts and life insurance policies
- income from capital assets

There are following tax rates in Croatia, namely 15%, 25%, 35% and 45% (Art. 12 Income Tax Act):

15% from HRK 0 to HRK 3, 200/month,
25% from HRK 3, 200 to HRK 8, 000/month,
35% from HRK 8, 000 to HRK 22, 400/month.
45% over 22, 400 HRK

The following items are tax exempt:

per diem allowances up to HRK 170/day,
business travel expenses in the amount of the actual costs incurred,
kilometer allowance of HRK 2/km
occasional rewards (Christmas gift) up to HRK 2, 000.

***5. 1** Corporate income tax (= profit tax)

The corporate income tax rate is 20%.

There is no tax on dividends as of January 2005.

PRACTICAL INFORMATION FOR BUSINESS AND INVESTMENTS[1]

LEADING SECTORS FOR U.S. EXPORT AND INVESTMENT

AGRICULTURAL SECTOR

Miscellaneous Consumer Foods

Croatia's total imports in this category jumped from $983 million in 2005 to over $1 billion in 2007. In the last few years flourishing tourism at the Dalmatian coast and rebounding consumer demand in urban areas are fueling demand for consumer foods which is underlined by the increasing number of supermarkets.

Trade statistics on American exports to Croatia in this category are severe y understated due to transshipment via the EU. Demand for medium to high quality consumer fccds will continue to rise and should be a boon for American companies, provided they can overcome less than competitive high ocean freight rates into the Adriatic Sea from U.S. ports. U.S. companies can take advantage of the weak dollar.

	2007	2008 estimated	2012 estimated
Total market	estimate $4 billion	$4 billion	$4 billion
Total local production	N/A	N/A	N/A
Total exports	$578 million*	$515 million	$520 mil ion
Total imports	$1.3 billion*	$1.5 billion	$2 billion
Imports from U.S.	$18 million*	$18 million	$19 million

(*Global Trade Atlas)

WEB RESOURCES

Ministry of Agriculture, Fishery and Rural Development – http:// www.mps.hr

Ministry of Health and Social Welfare – http://www.miz.hr

Foreign Agricultural Service – http:// www.fas.usda.gov

Hotel & Gastroteh - 2012 - International Fair of Gastronomy, Hotel and Hcspitality Equipment and Catering at Zagreb fair – http://www.zv.hr/

Vinovita – International Fair of Wine and the Equipment for Viticulture and Viniculture at Zagreb fair –http:// www.zv.hr

Zagreb International Autumn Fair – http:// www.zv.hr

Andreja Misir, Agricultural Specialist at the U.S. Embassy in Zagreb, andreja.misir@usda.gov

[1] US Governmetn materials

Fish & Seafood

Imports of fish to Croatia are quite significant although Croatia exports seafood (mostly tuna fish to Japan). Moreover, Croatia's seafood imports increased from $97 million in 2005 to $119 million in 2007 and this trend is expected to continue. In addition, Croatia imports annually, about $5 million of seafood from the United States.

The tourism industry, mostly located at Croatia's Adriatic seacoast, has a greater demand for seafood than local supplies can meet thus a large proportion of the seafood and fish consumed on the Adriatic Coast is in fact imported and not caught locally (though most tourists do not realize this). Demand is particularly strong for medium-quality products, as tourists tend to be 'mid-budget' travelers. Consumption should continue to grow along with tourism for the next several years, as the country remains a somewhat lower-cost alternative to Italy for beach-bound tourists and thus attracts visitors. Consumption of sea and fresh water fish in 2007, according to the Croatian Statistical Institute, was 7.8 kilograms per capita. Statistical data from the Croatian Statistical Institute for 2006 note additional 0.85 kg per capita of seafood and 1.01 kg per capita of dried, smoked, salted and other preserved or processed fish. The Croatian Government has made increasing fish consumption a strategic goal.

	2007	2008 estimated	2012 estimated
Total market	estimate 74,000 metric tons	74,000 metric tons	74,000 metric tons
Total local production and catches of see fish and sea food	51,819 metric tons**	52,000 metric tons	52,000 metric tons
Total exports	$152 million*	$90 million	$95 million
Total imports	$119 million*	$119 million	$120 million
Imports from U.S.	$5 million*	$5 million	$6 million

(*Global Trade Atlas

**DZS Croatian Statistics)

Web Resources

Ministry of Agriculture, Fishery and Rural Development – http:// www.mps.hr
Ministry of Health and Social Welfare – http://www.miz.hr/
Foreign Agricultural Service – http:// www.fas.usda.gov
Hotel & Gastroteh - 2012 - International Fair of Gastronomy, Hotel and Hospitality Equipment and Catering at Zagreb fair – http:// www.zv.hr
Zagreb International Autumn Fair - http:// www.zv.hr

U.S. Embassy - U.S. Foreign Agricultural Service
Andreja Misir, Agricultural Specialist Zagreb, Croatia
Tel: +385 (0)1 661 2467; Fax: +385 (0)1 661 8950
Email: andreja.misir@usda.gov

Soybeans and Soybean Meal

Croatian dairy, poultry and swine industries stimulate demand for soybeans and soybean meal. Soybeans are imported into the port of Zadar where the largest soybean crushing facility in Southern Europe is located (capacity is about 250,000 MT annually) and the port of Rijeka. After they are crushed, the soybeans are shipped throughout the western portion of the Balkans. Price and credit availability are the major determinants for sourcing. At the moment only GMO-free soybeans are acceptable for the Croatian market.

	2007	2008 estimated	2012 estimated
Total market for soy beans and soy bean meal	estimate 250,000 metric tons	250,000 metric tons	250,000 metric tons
Total local production of soy beans	91,000 metric tons**	104,000 metric tons	110,000 metric tons
Total exports soy beans + soy bean meal	$5.4 million*	$5 million	$5 million
Total imports soy beans + soy bean meal	$55 million*	$90 million	$90 million
Imports from U.S. soy beans + soy bean meal	$0 million*	$0 million	$0 million

(*Global Trade Atlas

**DZS Croatian Statistics)

Web Resources

Ministry of Agriculture, Fishery and Rural Development – http:// www.mps.hr

Ministry of Health and Social Welfare– http://www.miz.hr/

Foreign Agricultural Service – http:// www.fas.usda.gov

Zagreb International Autumn Fair – http:// www.zv.hr

Andreja Misir, Agricultural Specialist at the U.S. Embassy in Zagreb, andreja.misir@usda.gov

ENERGY (ELP, OGM, OGS, TRN)

	2006	2007	2008
Total Market Size	350	360	370
Total Local Production	230	220	210
Total Exports	25	22	20
Total Imports	145	162	180
Imports from the U.S.	15	15	15

(All figures are rough estimates in $ million.)

In November 2008, the Croatian Government has launched a public discussion over the draft energy strategy that would define Croatian energy needs and development plans for the period until 2020. The draft strategy addresses Croatia's need for increased, diversified, and sustainable supply of energy resources and improved energy efficiency. In the electric power generation sector, it has identified the need for construction of a total of about 3,500 MW of the installed capacity (the current total capacity is about 4,000 MW). In the oil & gas sector, it has identified the need for construction of additional oil and gas pipelines, an LNG terminal, and gas storages. The estimated total investment in these projects exceeds $10 billion.

Opportunities

To meet the estimated needs for additional installed capacity in the power generation sector by 2020, the draft strategy envisions completion of the three current projects and construction of new plants as follows:

In the oil & gas sector, the strategy discusses several major projects:

• LNG Terminal at the Adriatic coast (www.adria-lng.hr)

• Ioninan-Adriatic gas pipeline to connect to the Trans-Adriatic pipeline exporting gas from the Caspian Sea via Turkey and Greece to Italy (http://www.trans-adriatic-pipeline.com/)

Resources

Ministry of Economy, Labor and Entrepreneurship - www.mingorp.hr and www.vlada.hr
Croatian Electricity Company – www.hep.hr
Croatian Energy Regulatory Agency – www.hera.hr
Croatian Energy Market Operator – www.hrote.hr
U.S. Embassy - U.S. Commercial Service
Damjan Bencic, Senior Commercial Specialist
Pamela Ward, Senior Commercial Officer
Zagreb, Croatia
Tel: +385 (0)1 661 2186; Fax: +385 (0)1 661 2446
Email: Damjan.Bencic@mail.doc.gov or Pamela.Ward@mail.doc.gov
Website: www.BuyUSA.gov/croatia

RENEWABLE ENERGY (ELP, OGM, OGS, TRN)

	2006	2007	2008
Total Market Size	15	20	60
Total Local Production	2	5	20
Total Exports	0	0	0
Total Imports	13	15	40
Imports from the U.S.	0.5	0.8	1

(All figures are rough estimates in $ million.)

In 2007, Croatia adopted important regulations to support development of renewable energy projects required to meet the goal of the minimal share of 5.8 percent of renewable energy in the total electric energy supply by 2010. The overall size of the renewable electric energy projects is about 330 MW of new capacity in the next three years, estimated to cost 400-500 million Euros. German and Austrian investors and equipment suppliers are very active in the market, mostly in partnership with local companies. Koncar, a Croatian electric industry manufacturer, has been

For additional analytical, marketing, investment and business opportunities information, please contact Global Investment & Business Center, USA
(202) 546-2103. Fax: (202) 546-3275. E-mail: rusric@erols.com

developing its own production of wind turbines. The regulations for biofuels and solar thermal energy are being drafted and are expected to be adopted in 2012 . According to the Ministry, the target share of biofuels in the total annual consumption of gasoline and diesel fuel to be achieved by 2010 will also be 5.8 percent.

Best Prospects/Services

According to the Ministry of Economy, the most competitive renewable energy plants in Croatia would be:

-
-
-

Opportunities

With five regulations adopted in 2007, the Croatian government specified the types of power plants that will be supported, the feed-in tariffs, the sources of funding the incentives, and the procedures for interested investors to obtain permissions for exploring sites, building plants and connecting them to the grid.

By December 2008, the Ministry of Economy, Labor, and Entrepreneurship received 254 applications and plans to publish the list of preliminary approved projects and investors on its website, probably during the first half of 2012 . Per current applications, most of the approved projects will be wind farms, but not more than 85 percent of the total capacity, which is the government's limit for a single source of renewable energy.

Resources

Ministry of Economy, Labor and Entrepreneurship - www.mingorp.hr and www.vlada.hr

Croatian Electricity Company – www.hep.hr

Croatian Energy Regulatory Agency – www.hera.hr

Croatian Energy Market Operator – www.hrote.hr

U.S. Embassy - U.S. Commercial Service

Damjan Bencic, Senior Commercial Specialist

Pamela Ward, Senior Commercial Officer

Zagreb, Croatia

Tel: +385 (0)1 661 2186; Fax: +385 (0)1 661 2446

Email: Damjan.Bencic@mail.doc.gov or Pamela.Ward@mail.doc.gov

Website: www.BuyUSA.gov/croatia

ENVIRONMENTAL EQUIPMENT (ENV)

	2006	2007	2008
Total Market Size	52	54	56
Total Local Production	22	23	25
Total Exports	2	2	2
Total Imports	32	35	36
Imports from the U.S.	2	2	3

(All figures are rough estimates in $ million.)

European Union (EU) accession is the primary force affecting planning and procurement in the Croatian environmental sector. According to the estimates of the Ministry of Environmental Protection, Physical Planning and Construction (MEPPPC) and the World Bank, Croatia needs to invest more than US$ 10 billion in the environment sector prior to accession.

Waste management is currently the largest challenge in the environmental sector in Croatia. Key issues are: increase in solid waste; very limited recycling; unreliable data concerning waste flows and quantities; and lack of organized disposal sites. **Waste water management** is also an area of concern, particularly in the coastal municipalities. While water supply coverage (73%) is high compared to other countries in the region, coverage for sewage is only around 40 percent, and less than twelve percent of all collected wastewater is being treated. The Air Protection Act (2005) governs **air quality management** in line with the EU framework directive 96/62/EC on ambient air quality assessment and management. Though Croatia ratified the Kyoto Protocol in May 2007, efforts are still needed to limit the growth of greenhouse gas emissions in order to meet Croatia's Kyoto target for the period 2008-2012. Another priority is reduction of acid and other polluting gaseous emissions from major industrial premises such as refineries, petrochemical plants, cement industry and large combustion plants.

Best Prospects/Services

-
-
-
-
-
-
-

Opportunities

-
-
-
-
-
-
-

Resources

For additional analytical, marketing, investment and business opportunities information, please contact Global Investment & Business Center, USA
(202) 546-2103. Fax: (202) 546-3275. E-mail: rusric@erols.com

Ministry of Environmental Protection, Physical Planning and Construction; www.mzopu.hr

Ministry of Regional Development, Forestry and Water Management; www.mrrsvg.hr

Croatian Waters; www.voda.hr

Agency for Environmental Protection; www.azo.hr

Fund for Environmental Protection and Energy Efficiency; www.fzoeu.hr

Croatian Business Council for Sustainable Development; www.hrpsor.hr

U.S. Embassy - U.S. Commercial Service

Dalila Uzelac, Commercial Specialist

Pamela Ward, Senior Commercial Officer

Zagreb, Croatia

Tel: +385 (0)1 661 2224; Fax: +385 (0)1 661 2446

Email: Dalila.Uzelac@mail.doc.gov or Pamela.Ward@mail.doc.gov

Website: www.BuyUSA.gov/croatia

CONSTRUCTION EQUIPMENT (CONS)

	2006	2007	2008
Total Market Size	USD 3.8bn	USD 4.1bn	USD 4.4bn
Total Local Production	USD 3.5bn	USD 3.8bn	USD 4.0bn
Total Exports	USD 150m	USD 180m	USD 360m
Total Imports	n.a.	n.a.	n.a.
Imports from the U.S.	n.a.	n.a.	n.a.

(*Construction works in Croatia – figures for 2008 are estimates based on registered and expected growth throughout 2008 as published by the Croatian Statistical Bureau and the Ministry of Finance.*)

Although the current global economic climate has also affected the construction sector in Croatia, the adverse effects were not visible until the last quarter of 2008 and 10 percent growth is projected for the year overall. While that figure is expected to decrease in 2012 , a large number of significant transportation infrastructure projects, which account for approximately one third of the total volume of construction works, will continue throughout the year.

U.S.-based suppliers of construction equipment are present and well-known in the market. The local distributor of one U.S. brand generated revenues of EUR 28 million in 2007, demonstrating the acceptance of U.S. products in this market and the sales levels that are possible in the market.

Best Prospects/Services

- o
- o
- o
- o
- o

Opportunities

The largest transportation infrastructure project in Croatia is expected to be tendered in 2012 – the construction of the new terminal building at the Zagreb Airport, with an estimated cost of EUR 212 million. In addition, the second and the third largest airports in Croatia (Split and Dubrovnik), are at the beginning of their respective investment projects spanning over five years and valued at EUR 80 million in total.

There are also three port development projects in various stages of preparation:

Port of Rijeka with planned investments exceeding $450 million,

Port of Ploče with a planned cost of $115 million, and

Port of Zadar reconstruction with over $280 million in financing approved.

Resources

Ministry of Environmental Protection, Physical Planning and Construction – www.mzopu.hr

Ministry of the Sea, Tourism, Transport and development – www.mmtpr.hr

International Construction Fair - http://www.zv.hr/sajmovi/170/index_en.html

U.S. Embassy - U.S. Commercial Service

Miroslav Nikolac, Commercial Specialist

Pamela Ward, Senior Commercial Officer

Zagreb, Croatia

Tel: +385 (0)1 661 2026; Fax: +385 (0)1 661 2446

Email: Miroslav.Nikolac@mail.doc.gov or Pamela.Ward@mail.doc.gov

Website: www.BuyUSA.gov/croatia

TELECOMMUNICATIONS EQUIPMENT (TEL)

	2005	2006	2007
Total Market Size	USD 750m	USD 900m	USD 1bn

Total Local Production	USD 700m	USD 850m	USD 850m
Total Exports	USD 280m	USD 306m	USD 440m
Total Imports	USD 330m	USD 356m	USD 590m
Imports from the U.S.	USD 8m	USD 5m	n.a.

(*Sources: Croatian Chamber of Commerce, Croatian Statistics Bureau, Commercial Service Zagreb*)

Telecommunications is one of most developed sectors of the Croatian economy and, along with the IT sector, has traditionally highly valued the equipment manufactured in the United States. Imports of U.S. telecommunications equipment to Croatia are quite significant although most of it is routed through Europe and is included in trade figures of other countries. T-Hrvatski Telekom (the former national telecommunications company which is now a subsidiary of Deutsche Telekom) is the dominant provider of both fixed-line and mobile telecommunication services. Despite liberalization of the market in 2003, only recently have alternative providers made significant inroads into T-Hrvatski Telekom's (T-HT) market share (helped by the 2007 decrease in interconnection and access charges approved by the T-HT regulator). The largest growth in the last year has been in broadband services, with projected 15 percent annual growth through 2012.

Best Products/Services

Croatia has greater than 100% mobile telephony penetration, but the market is still growing in double digits. The continuing trend of fixed-line substitution by mobile phones, suggests that this growth will continue and that there remains significant opportunity in this market segment.

Strong growth in broadband subscriptions and service introduction signifies opportunities in WiMAX, ADSL and IPTV equipment and services.

Opportunities

o
o
o
o

Resources

Croatian Telecommunications Agency – http://www.telekom.hr/

U.S. Embassy - U.S. Commercial Service

Miroslav Nikolac, Commercial Specialist

Pamela Ward, Senior Commercial Officer

Zagreb, Croatia

Tel: +385 (0)1 661 2026; Fax: +385 (0)1 661 2446

Email: Miroslav.Nikolac@mail.doc.gov or Pamela.Ward@mail.doc.gov

Website: www.BuyUSA.gov/croatia

TOURISM INFRASTRUCTURE (TRA)

	2006	2007	2008
Total Market Size	400	500	700
Total Local Production	300	400	500
Total Exports	10	20	30
Total Imports	110	120	230
Imports from the U.S.	5	7	10

(All figures are rough estimates in $ million.)

Croatia's key tourist attraction is its beautiful, thousand-mile Mediterranean coastline, with 1,185 islands (only 66 populated) that are ideal for nautical tourism. As only 15 percent of the Croatian coastline is urbanized (compared to 70 percent of the Spanish, French and Italian coastline from Barcelona to Naples), Croatia is advertised in the tourist market as "The Mediterranean as it once was".

Improved transportation infrastructure and accommodation facilities have played a key role in putting Croatia back on the map of the key tourist destinations since the end of the 1991-1995 war in the region. The majority of the formerly exclusively state-owned hotels and camps have been privatized, renovated and upgraded, and a number of new hotels have been built by local or foreign investors. About two hundred small, family-owned hotels have been built under a very successful, government-sponsored program. Easily accessible loans from the modernized banking system have enabled many local entrepreneurs to open new restaurants, cafes, wellness centers, and entertainment facilities, as well as build apartments or buy boats and vehicles for rent.

Best Products/Services

The strong current trends in development of Croatia's tourism infrastructure include intensive re-construction and construction of four and five-star hotels and luxurious golf resorts, construction of high-end congress centers and family hotels, development of nautical and continental tourism facilities; construction of wellness centers, gaming, sporting, cultural and any other accompanying facilities that extend the tourist season into the non-Summer months when weather conditions are less favorable and predictable. Planning, design, and management services for such facilities should present meaningful opportunities in Croatia for the next decade.

Opportunities

The new Law on Urban Development and Construction of November 1, 2007 has significantly simplified the process of urban planning and issuing of construction permits and the Law on Golf Courses passed in December 2008 has removed some administrative and practical obstacles specific to golf-course development. Given that increasing the number of golf-courses could significantly contribute to the much-needed extension of the tourist season, many new projects are now likely to (re)appear.

Resources

Ministry of Tourism – www.mmtpr.hr

Ministry of Environmental Protection, Physical Planning and Construction – www.mzopu.hr

Croatia National Tourist Board – www.croatia.hr

U.S. Embassy - U.S. Commercial Service

Damjan Bencic, Senior Commercial Specialist

Pamela Ward, Senior Commercial Officer

Zagreb, Croatia

Tel: +385 (0)1 661 2186; Fax: +385 (0)1 661 2446

Email: Damjan.Bencic@mail.doc.gov or Pamela.Ward@mail.doc.gov

Website: www.BuyUSA.gov/croatia

RECREATIONAL BOATING AND EQUIPMENT (PLB)

	2006	2007	2008
Total Market Size	140	150	160
Total Local Production	31	40	55
Total Exports	16	20	30
Total Imports	125	130	135
Imports from the U.S.	10	15	20

(All figures are rough estimates in $ million.)

With the rapid recovery of the Croatian tourism industry and the economy in general, the demand for recreational boats and equipment has been growing significantly during the past several years. Croatia has a huge potential in nautical tourism and boat chartering has been among the fastest growing industry sectors. Most of the boats and equipment are imported from the European Union and the United States, but local production has been rapidly developing as well. The overall size of the market is estimated at about $150 million annually. There are four specialized local nautical fairs held every year and there are six monthly nautical magazines available in the Croatian language and over twenty in foreign languages. There are no major tariff or non-tariff market entry barriers and there is a sufficient number of capable local distributors specialized in recreational boats and/or equipment that would be effective partners/representatives for U.S. exporters.

Best Products/Services

-
-
-
-
-

Opportunities

As Croatia prepares to join the European Union and adopts its environmental protection standards, environmental protection equipment at marinas becomes increasingly important. Boat building has a long tradition in Croatia but repair and maintenance of modern luxury motorboats, which are increasingly the most common types of craft in Croatian marinas, is not a strength. Supply of modern tools and training for these types of services as well as general marina operations represent a key opportunity.

Resources

Ministry of the Sea, Transport and Infrastructure - www.mmpi.hr

Croatian Register of Shipping – www.crs.hr

BoatBuilding Cluster – www.boatbuildingcluster.com

U.S. Embassy - U.S. Commercial Service

Damjan Bencic, Senior Commercial Specialist

Pamela Ward, Senior Commercial Officer

Zagreb, Croatia

Tel: +385 (0)1 661 2186; Fax: +385 (0)1 661 2446

Email: Damjan.Bencic@mail.doc.gov or Pamela.Ward@mail.doc.gov

Website: www.BuyUSA.gov/croatia

FRANCHISING (FRA)

	2006	2007	2008
Total Market Size	10	15	20
Total Local Production	2	3	5
Total Exports	0	0	0
Total Imports	8	12	15
Imports from the U.S.	3	5	7

(All figures are rough estimates in $ million.)

Franchising in Croatia is still in its first stages as a business concept, but there is a strong ongoing initiative to promote its advantages. There are between 120 and 150 mostly foreign franchisors operating in the Croatian market, of which the most well-known are McDonald's, Subway and Fornetti. Numerous opportunities for advertising exist in the local daily press and specialized magazines, and expert assistance to franchisors looking for local partners is available from at least two franchise development centers.

Best Products/Services

For additional analytical, marketing, investment and business opportunities information, please contact Global Investment & Business Center, USA
(202) 546-2103. Fax: (202) 546-3275. E-mail: rusric@erols.com

Local experts agree that tourism and hospitality are by far the most promising sectors for franchising development in Croatia. Indeed, tourism already represents about 25 percent of Croatia's GDP and is considered the industry with the largest growth potential.

Opportunities

The relative scarcity of franchised services and retail outlets combined with a growing economy and a high entrepreneurial spirit in Croatia's urban centers suggests a strong potential for franchising in general. At the same time, respect for and awareness of many U.S. brands is high.

Resources

Franchise Center Osijek – www.fransiza.hr

Croatian Franchise Association – www.fip.com.hr

U.S. Embassy - U.S. Commercial Service

Damjan Bencic, Senior Commercial Specialist

Pamela Ward, Senior Commercial Officer

Zagreb, Croatia

Tel: +385 (0)1 661 2186; Fax: +385 (0)1 661 2446

Email: Damjan.Bencic@mail.doc.gov or Pamela.Ward@mail.doc.gov

Website: www.BuyUSA.gov/croatia

SELLING U.S. PRODUCTS AND SERVICES

USING AN AGENT OR DISTRIBUTOR

A carefully chosen local agent or distributor is the most effective method for entering the Croatian market. One of the first steps that an exporter may wish to take in locating an agent or distributor in Croatia is to contact the U.S. Department of Commerce and register for one of the many services specifically designed to meet the needs of U.S. client companies.

Croatia offers foreign suppliers a wide variety of methods to distribute and sell their products, including using an agent or distributor. Agents work on a commission basis after obtaining orders from customers whereas distributors buy, carry stock and sell products directly to customers. Agents often distribute durable and non-durable consumer goods, as well as some industrial raw materials. They may be particularly appropriate when products are highly competitive and lack a large market. It is common to appoint a single agent capable of providing national or regional coverage either through one office or a network of branch offices. In addition to their role as the local representatives of U.S. exporters, agents should be able to handle the necessary customs clearances, port and rail charges, documentation, warehousing, and financing arrangements.

Typical commission rates for agents in Croatia vary widely from industry to industry and depend upon the contract concluded and upon the representative's responsibility.

Distributors who buy for their own account and carry a wide range of spares often best handle capital equipment and commodities such as chemicals, pharmaceuticals, and brand new products on an exclusive basis. Leading distributors often have branch offices and sell to both wholesalers and retailers. In some cases, the distributor is also the principal with sub-agents or a major user of the products.

When appointing a Croatian distributor, U.S. exporters should take care to find out if the distributor handles a competing product. In Croatia's competitive marketplace, it is essential that the U.S. exporter provide adequate servicing, spare parts, and components, as well as qualified personnel capable of handling service inquiries. In most cases, after-sales service should be available locally since potential delays often lead purchasers to seek alternative suppliers. Often funds for product marketing need to be provided by the U.S. company in order to ensure wide promotion and distribution of goods.

The U.S. Commercial Service has found that the most successful ventures entered into by U.S. companies are those where there has been thorough market research prior to engaging in a search for agents or distributors. Once contacts are established, it is often advisable to visit Croatia since firsthand knowledge of the market and society is an advantage. Such a visit provides an opportunity for a personal appraisal of the prospective agent or distributor. U.S. exporters should carefully investigate the reputation and financial references of a potential agent or distributor and establish a clear agreement delineating the responsibilities of both the exporter and the agent.

The Commercial Service in Croatia offers a number of business facilitation services, including market research, appointment setting and background checks on potential business partners. For a full list of the services offered please visit:

http://www.buyusa.gov/croatia/en/

For additional information, please e-mail the U.S. Commercial Service office at: Zagreb.office.box@mail.doc.gov.

ESTABLISHING AN OFFICE

An excellent first stop for information on establishing a Croatian company is the “Hitro” office, (www.hitro.hr). The Croatian Companies Act regulates the establishment and organization of business entities in Croatia. All firms must register according to the Court Register Act and the Rules of Court Register Entry Procedures. Under the Companies Act, it is possible to start a company as a company based on capital or as a partnership (which is an association of persons regarded as corporate under Croatian regulations). The law also regulates the establishment of branch offices and the position of sole traders.

Companies based on capital include:

Private Limited Company (d.o.o.)

Private limited companies are the most frequent type of company in Croatia. It is one in which one or more legal entities or natural persons invest in initial authorized stakes, with which they participate in the total authorized capital as contractually set beforehand. Owners may be domestic and foreign legal entities and natural persons. Company assets are strictly separated from the property of owners. The company is liable for its debts with all its assets. The initial authorized capital of a private limited company must be shown in Croatian currency – Kuna (HRK). The minimum amount of initial authorized capital may not be below HRK 20,000.

Public Limited Company (d.d.)

A public limited company is based on capital, with owners (shareholders) investing in authorized capital divided into shares. The company is liable for its debts with all its assets. Shareholders are not liable for the debts of the company. The basic document for a public limited company is the articles of association, as they specify the internal organization of the company. Authorized capital and shares must show par value in the currency of the Republic of Croatia. The minimum amount of authorized capital is HRK 200,000. The Companies Act provides for a simultaneous and a successive establishment of a public limited company. Company founders are the shareholders who have adopted the articles of association.

Economic Interest Association (GIU).

An economic interest association is a legal entity established by two or more natural persons or legal entities for the purpose of facilitating and promoting their business activities, but in a way that the legal entity earns no profit for itself. *The association is established without authorized capital*, and the rights of members may not take the form of securities. The business activity of the association must be related to members' business activities as an activity that supports them.

Partnerships include:

General Partnership (j.t.d.)

A general partnership is a business entity where two or more individuals join in order to conduct business as a going concern and under a common company name. Every partner has unlimited and joint liability to cover the partnership's debts with all his/ her assets. A partner may not dispose of his/her ownership stake without consent from other partners. Any legal entity or individual, both domestic and foreign, may become a partner. The articles of association define the relations between partners. The partners enjoy maximum freedom in this respect, because the Companies Act applies only in cases when the articles of association do not regulate certain matters otherwise. A general partnership does not have authorized capital. Unless otherwise provided by the articles of association, partners should bring equal stakes into the company.

Limited Partnership (k.d.)

A limited partnership differs from a general partnership in that at least one partner has unlimited and joint liability for company debts with all his/her assets (general partner), and at least one partner has limited liability proportional to the assets invested (limited partner). Both domestic and foreign individuals and legal entities may be partners in a limited partnership.

Branch Office

Under Croatian legislation, foreign companies and sole traders may conduct business in Croatia by setting up a branch office. The start-up and operation of branch offices owned by foreign companies are governed by the same regulations that apply to the establishment of branches by domestic companies.

A branch office is not a legal entity. The liabilities and rights stemming from its operation do not belong to the branch office but to the founder. The founder legally holds all rights and obligations of branch offices. In case of dispute with third parties, the branch is not a party to it, but the company or sole trader that owns the branch. The branch office operates under its own name. The name should also indicate both the branch's and the founder's registered office. In the case that the same founder intends to establish several branch offices, the establishment procedure is carried out separately for each branch.

Branch office activities are limited to market research, contract or investment preparations, technical cooperation and similar business facilitation activities. It is permitted to hold both foreign exchange and domestic currency accounts with authorized Croatian banks. Office equipment can be imported free of customs duties, on the basis of a temporary permit with the possibility for extensions. Office vehicles may be similarly imported, but only for the foreign employees. Foreign employees at a branch office are not required to pay local income taxes and contributions. Residence and work permits are required for foreign employees.

To open a representative office, the founder must register the office at the Croatian Ministry of Economy, Labor, and Entrepreneurship.

FRANCHISING

Franchising in Croatia is yet to develop fully, but there is a strong ongoing initiative to promote the advantages of this business concept. There are between 120 and 150 mostly foreign franchisors operating in the Croatian market, of which the most well-known are McDonald's, Subway and Fornetti. Tourism and hospitality are considered to be the most promising sectors for franchise development. The typical prospective franchisee knows little about franchising and needs to be educated by the franchisor on how he/she could benefit from the concept. Numerous opportunities for advertising exist in the local daily press and specialized magazines, and expert assistance to franchisors looking for local partners is available from at least two franchise development centers. The lack of franchise-specific legal and financial assistance is a market obstacle, but these issues are being systematically addressed creating a strong and continuous trend of improvement of the business environment, further enhanced by Croatia's expected membership in NATO and EU.

DIRECT MARKETING

Although direct marketing is becoming more common in Croatia, it is still in its early stages compared with developed Western countries. An average potential customer is unlikely to get more than a few phone calls a year to his home number made by companies to market their services or products. For the time being, local banks and insurance companies are making most of these calls. Direct marketing by mail is far more common and households receive such mail on a daily basis, typically from local supermarket chains, restaurants, and personal services providers. Credit card companies regularly include in their bills special offerings of various consumer goods in partnership with other companies. However, the sale of mailing lists is still rather limited.

JOINT VENTURES/LICENSING

The Law on Companies regulates the establishment of joint-ventures, investment in companies with mixed ownership, as well as other types of foreign or domestic investment. This law, adopted in 1994, is very similar to the German Company Law. Establishment procedures require a Croatian lawyer, a notary public, and registration with the local Commercial Court

There are no specific laws regulating licensing other than the Law on Obligations ('Commercial Code") which addresses contract law. The licensing contract should also cover intellectual property rights issues (trademark, model, patent or copyright), payments/royalties, the term of the contract, restrictions on using trademarks, etc. (See Chapter 7 for more information on intellectual property rights.) A Croatian lawyer should be consulted to ensure that provisions of the contract do not contravene Croatian law, making the agreement null and void.

SELLING TO THE GOVERNMENT

The Public Procurement Law is applied to all purchases made by government bodies including those of the local government and majority state-owned companies and institutions (Official Gazette No. 110/07 and 125/08). These institutions, (which include some of the key utility and transportation companies, most hospitals, schools, some banks and insurance companies) are obliged by law to perform most of their procurement by public tenders.

Because these tenders are often written only in the Croatian language and are not automatically available on these companies' websites, interested U.S. exporters are advised to use one of the excellent public-tenders-tracking tools available on-line for a fee at http://ponuda-jn.nn.hr/ and www.croatiabiz.com or to engage a local Croatian-speaking representative to monitor the Official Gazette on a daily basis. The representative can purchase the tender documentation on behalf of the U.S. exporter, discuss issues with the buyer, deliver the U.S. exporter's bid, participate in the bids opening, etc. The U.S. Commercial Service is also available to assist you with obtaining tender documentation.

DISTRIBUTION AND SALES CHANNELS

Croatia's distribution system is formalized by the Law on Trade which regulates the activities of wholesalers and retailers. Stringent application of customs, import and tax administration regulations as well as rapid modernization of the domestic distribution sector significantly reduced illegal imports, unlicensed business activities and cross-border shopping which previously flourished.

With over twenty percent of the nation's population and its central location, the capital city of Zagreb is the primary distribution center for the country. The port cities of Split and Rijeka are also important distribution points and the eastern city of Osijek is the largest and most important distribution point in that region of the country. Croatia's geographic location, access to seaports and well developed transportation system give it distinct advantages as a regional distribution point, particularly to the countries within the area that previously comprised Yugoslavia.

There is an estimated total of 7,500 retail outlets in Croatia's (including kiosks, small shops, and open markets). In recent years newly developed shopping centers (such as Importanne, King Cross, Kaptol Centar, and Avenue Mall in Zagreb), modernized or newly-established domestic supermarket and retail chains (such as Getro, Konzum, Diona, Prehrana, Pevec), and foreign chains (such as Billa, DM, Merkator, Mercatone, Metro, Bauhaus, Baumax, Kaufland) have become dominant factors in the marketplace.

Capital goods and specialized equipment are normally sold directly to manufacturers and businesses. When selling capital goods or equipment to businesses, a good agent is essential.

SELLING FACTORS/TECHNIQUES

Factors/techniques critical to success in Croatia are not different than from most other countries: a product/service that offers value for money, close and frequent contact with buyers, motivated and trained middlemen, aggressive market promotion, and, for technical products, a professional and customer friendly after-sales service network in place. The ability to provide financing is still important, but no longer the key selling factor since the financing from local banks has become more easily available.

New products entering the market require extensive market research and mass advertising to identify potential customers' buying patterns and preferences. This applies particularly to unknown brand names, as Croatian's are very brand conscious.

One way of launching a new product in Croatia is by exhibiting at a trade show. Promotional "give-aways" are also very popular. An editorial and/or advertisement in a specialized trade publication will also enhance awareness of the product.

Due to the size of the Croatian market, highly specialized products might be best marketed through a regional representative. Croatia's location and established distribution channels make it a logical choice for establishing a regional base for the South East Europe region.

ELECTRONIC COMMERCE

While retail online transactions in Croatia still represent less than one percent of total retail trade in the country, e-commerce in Croatia is considered to be a common occurrence. The total value of e-commerce transactions is approximately USD 500 million per year, with around 85 percent of the figure attributable to business-to-business transactions.

Use of cell phones to pay for goods and services has advanced beyond mobile banking to debit and credit transactions. M-commerce is particularly attractive in Croatia due to the near 100 percent market penetration of cell phones.

TRADE PROMOTION AND ADVERTISING

Trade Promotion Trade events and fairs continue to be popular in Croatia. The single largest event in Croatia is the annual Zagreb Fall Fair (September) which attracts nationwide attention and includes numerous foreign exhibitors. The Zagreb Fair authority also organizes a number of industry-focused or specialty exhibitions during the year in sectors such as consumer goods, food processing, environmental technology, medical equipment, pharmaceuticals, automobiles and automotive parts, information technology, textiles and apparel, wine, etc. For more information on these events, please contact: Zagreb Fair Avenija Dubrovnik 15 10 020 Zagreb, Croatia Tel: (385)(1) 650-3111 Fax: (385)(1) 652-0643 E-mail: zagvel@zv.hr Internet: http://www.zv.hr

In the past few years, several annual trade events organized by the Split Fair (www.sajamsplit.hr and the Rijeka Fair (http://www.rijecki-sajam.hr/) have become increasingly important.

ADVERTISING

Advertising is a key marketing tool in Croatia. Nearly all companies engage in some form of advertising. While the number of publications is growing, television is the most important media in Croatia. Outdoor advertising is also expanding. By distribution, 59 percent of advertising expenditure went to TV, 14 percent to newspapers, 10 percent to magazines, and seven percent to outdoor billboards. Radio is experiencing growing interest, currently receiving 10 percent of advertising expenditure. Television, which reaches 90 percent of the market, has the broadest reach of all media. Croatia has two state-owned and two private TV channels as well as five regional and six local channels; satellite and cable TV bring dozens of other channels into the market. The law restricts advertising on state television to nine minutes per hour for the first two national channels. Advertising on privately-owned (regional and local) television stations may not exceed 25 percent of total program length. The advertising sector experienced 12 percent growth because of the extensive advertising campaigns of the mobile telecommunications firms. The most advertised products are telecommunications, vehicles, financial institutions, beverages and newspapers. Croatian regulations prohibit television advertisement of tobacco, alcohol, and spirits. Magazines, particularly specialized magazines, are growing in circulation. The six national daily newspapers account for 62 percent of advertising expenditures for print periodicals. The balance of the revenue is shared among the sixteen high circulation periodicals and over 45 other specialized magazines. More than 6,000 billboards populate Croatia. Prices range from $150 per month to $250 per month depending on frequency and category. It is recommended that 150-200 billboards be used for a nationwide launch campaign. Key TV stations include state-owned Croatia Radio Television, and privately-owned RTL and Nova TV. Key Internet service providers/portals include Croatian Telecom, Iskon , VipNet , Globalnet , and Index . There are many international advertising firms with offices in Croatia and a substantial number of Croatian advertising agencies. Public relations agencies are also available. Contact details are available from the U.S. Commercial Service-Croatia.

PRICING

Liberalization of the market has put pressure on domestic producers to bring pricing down and more in line with costs. The level of prices in Croatia is generally high, even compared to prices of similar products/services in Western European countries and the United States, thus making imported products price competitive. The Croatian currency, the Kuna is tied to Euro and the Value Added Tax (VAT) in Croatia is 22 percent.

Price supports and subsidies have been removed and, as mentioned above, price competition has intensified. Although prices are generally determined by the market, certain necessities are still subject to government control. For example, price changes for milk and bread must be notified two weeks in advance to the Ministry of Economy and price alterations on approximately 30 other products must be reported to the Ministry of Economy within three days of modifications. The government retains the right to disapprove price changes although in practice this has been rare during the last few years. The government has the ability to influence pricing policy at companies under its direct or indirect control.

SALES SERVICE/CUSTOMER SUPPORT

In the Croatian consumer market after-sales service is extremely important, especially in terms of providing technical and spare part services to prospective clients. Many Croatian consumers will base purchasing decisions on the prospective after-sales service for their products, especially in high-end luxury goods such as electronic equipment. Appointing a central distributor that stocks spare parts and provides maintenance and repair service is advisable for existing brands and new brands breaking into the market. Foreign companies that bring strong customer support systems to this market will find themselves with a competitive edge.

PROTECTING YOUR INTELLECTUAL PROPERTY

Several general principles are important for effective management of intellectual property rights in Croatia. First, it is important to have an overall strategy to protect IPR. Second, IPR is protected differently in Croatia than in the United States. Third, rights must be registered and enforced *in*

Croatia, under local laws. Companies may wish to seek advice from local attorneys or IP consultants. The U.S. Commercial Service can often provide a list of local lawyers upon request.

It is vital that companies understand that intellectual property is primarily a private right and that the US government generally cannot enforce rights for private individuals in Croatia. It is the responsibility of the rights' holders to register, protect, and enforce their rights where relevant, retaining their own counsel and advisors. While the U.S. Government is willing to assist, there is little it can do if the rights holders have not taken these fundamental steps necessary to securing and enforcing their IPR in a timely fashion. Moreover, in many countries, rights holders who delay enforcing their rights on a mistaken belief that the USG can provide a political resolution to a legal problem may find that their rights have been eroded or abrogated due to doctrines such as statutes of limitations, laches, estoppel, or unreasonable delay in prosecuting a law suit. In no instance should USG advice be seen as a substitute for the obligation of a rights holder to promptly pursue its case.

It is always advisable to conduct due diligence on partners. Negotiate from the position of your partner and give your partner clear incentives to honor the contract. A good partner is an important ally in protecting IP rights. Keep an eye on your cost structure and reduce the margins (and the incentive) of would-be bad actors. Projects and sales in Croatia require constant attention. Work with legal counsel familiar with Croatian laws to create a solid contract that includes non-compete clauses, and confidentiality/non-disclosure provisions.

It is also recommended that small and medium-size companies understand the importance of working together with trade associations and organizations to support efforts to protect IPR and stop counterfeiting. There are a number of these organizations, both Croatian and U.S.-based. These include:

IPR Resources

A wealth of information on protecting IPR is freely available to U.S. rights holders. Some excellent resources for companies regarding intellectual property include the following:

- For more information about registering trademarks and patents (both in the U.S. as well as in foreign countries), contact the US Patent and Trademark Office (USPTO) at: **1-800-786-9199**.

- For more information about registering for copyright protection in the US, contact the US Copyright Office at: **1-202-707-5959**.

- For US small and medium-size companies, the Department of Commerce offers a "SME IPR Advisory Program" available through the American Bar Association that provides one hour of free IPR legal advice for companies with concerns in Brazil, China, Egypt, India, Russia, and Thailand. For details and to register, visit: **http://www.abanet.org/intlaw/intlproj/iprprogram_consultation.html**

- For information on obtaining and enforcing intellectual property rights and market-specific IP Toolkits visit: **www.StopFakes.gov** This site is linked to the USPTO website for registering trademarks and patents (both in the U.S. as well as in foreign countries), the U.S. Customs & Border Protection website to record registered trademarks and copyrighted works (to assist customs in blocking imports of IPR-infringing products) and allows you to register for Webinars on protecting IPR.

o

IPR Climate in Croatia

In March 2004, the Croatian Parliament ratified a comprehensive bilateral Memorandum of Understanding on the Protection of Intellectual Property Rights, signed by the United States and Croatia in May 1998. In May 2007, Office of the U.S. Trade Representative removed Croatia from all watch lists (see also CCG Chapter 6: Investment Climate Statement – Protection of Property Rights). The following is the contact information for the key Croatian IPR institution:

State Intellectual Property Office Mr. Zeljko Topic, Managing Director Ulica grada Vukovara 78, 10000 Zagreb, Croatia Phone: 385/1/6106-101; Fax: 385/1/6112-017 E-mail: ipo.croatia@patent.tel.hr www.dziv.hr

DUE DILIGENCE

Detailed due diligence using utmost caution and assistance from experienced and well-connected local professionals is strongly recommended. One of the standard programs of the U.S. Commercial Service is the International Company Profile (ICP), designed to assist U.S. companies to enter international business relationships with greater confidence by providing background information on a prospective business partner.

LOCAL PROFESSIONAL SERVICES

Croatia offers a wide variety of high-quality professional services. See Web Resources section below for links to some key professional services providers and associations.

Web Resources

American Chamber of Commerce in Croatia: www.amcham.hr
Authorized Court Translators: www.sudski-tumac.com
Croatia National Bank: www.hnb.hr
Croatiabiz (business directory): www.croatiabiz.com
Croatian Bar Association: www.odvj-komora.hr
Croatian Chamber of Economy: www.hgk.hr
Croatian Radio-Television: www.hrt.hr
Croatian Telecom: www.t.ht.hr
Central Bureau of Statistics: www.dzs.hr
Deloitte & Touche (tax consultants/accountants): www.deloitte.com
Embassy of the Republic of Croatia, Washington, DC: http://www.croatiaemb.org/
Embassy of the United States of America: http://zagreb.usembassy.gov/
Ernst & Young (tax consultants/accountants): www.ey.com/hr
Globalnet (Internet provider): http://home.globalnet.hr/
Hitro (one-stop-shop for dealing with state administration): www.hitro.hr
Index (Internet portal): www.index.hr
Iskon (Internet provider): www.iskon.hr
Kompass (business directory): www.kompass.com.hr
KPMG (tax consultants/accountants): www.kpmg.hr
Legal 500 Recommended Law Firms: http://www.legal500.com/lfe/frames/cr_fr.htm
Ministry of Economy, Labour and Entrepreneurship: www.mingorp.hr
Ministry of Interior: www.mup.hr
Nova TV: www.novatv.hr
Office of the U.S. Trade Representative: www.ustr.gov
Official Gazette: www.nn.hr

Official Gazette (public procurement notices): http://ponuda-jn.nn.hr
PricewaterhouseCoopers: (tax consultants/accountants): www.pwc.com/hr
Public Notaries: www.hjk.hr
Public Procurement Portal: www.javnanabava.hr
Rijeka Fair: http://www.rijecki-sajam.hr/
RTL TV: www.rtl.hr
Scientific and Technical Translators: http://www.drustvoprevoditelja.htnet.hr/
Split Fair: www.sajamsplit.hr
State Intellectual Property Office: www.dziv.hr
The Croatian Homepage (portal): http://www.hr/
U.S. Commercial Service Zagreb: www.buyusa.gov/croatia
VIPnet (Internet provider): www.vip.hr
Zagreb Fair: www.zv.hr
Zavod za poslovna istrazivanja (business directory): www.zapi.hr

STRATEGIC INFORMATION FOR CONDUCTING BUSINESS

ECONOMIC DEVELOPMENT AND OPPORTUNITIES[2]

The key policy goal for the Government in the medium-term is to preserve macroeconomic stability and create the conditions for recovery and stable economic growth. In the coming years, Croatia is also to continue its strategic development programme with a view to building a competitive market economy capable of withstanding the pressures of EU integration, through an acceleration of structural reforms, including restructuring and privatization of loss-making SOEs. To achieve this, on 4 August 2006, Croatia adopted its Strategic Development Framework for 2006-13 (Chapter II(1)) . It aims, *inter alia*, to achieve sustained and regionally balanced GDP growth

After its independence in 1991, the Republic of Croatia began the repair of large-scale war damage and revived its transformation from a centrally planned to a market economy within a very difficult economic, social, and political context.

Croatia's stabilization programme proceeded in three overlapping phases: the first phase was aimed at lowering inflation and inflationary expectations through a restrictive monetary policy, introducing a new foreign exchange regime, and fiscal restraint and tight incomes policies; the second phase was mainly directed at restructuring the economy (i.e. restructuring large loss-making enterprises and bank rehabilitation), changing the monetary policy framework, building up financial infrastructure, increasing financial discipline, and accelerating the privatization process; and the third phase was aimed at laying foundations for the reconstruction of the economy and the acceleration of economic growth.

Croatia has a landmass, including lakes, of 56,594 km^2 (about 30% is arable); around 60% of its 4.5 million people live in urban areas. The most populated city is the capital Zagreb (about 1 million) . Croatia's population is young (15.6% in the 0-14 age group, and 67.5% between 15-64) . It is a lower-middle income country, with a GDP per capita estimated at €10,682 for 2008[2], although about 11% of the population lives on less than US$10 per day, and some 1% of the population faces severe deprivation.[3] Croatia has taken steps to reduce its informal sector through, *inter alia*, improved labour relations within a stronger regulatory framework.[4] It ranks 45th out of 177 countries in terms of UNDP Human Development Indicators.[5]

Croatia's economic reforms (supported by the World Bank, the European Bank for Reconstruction and Development, and Stand-By Arrangements with the IMF[6]), have been largely successful in stabilizing its economy. Nonetheless, Croatia still faces key problems, including external vulnerability due to its high external current account deficit and large stock of external debt (section (2) below) . Recent reforms have also been aimed at bringing Croatia closer to its goal of EU accession.[7]

Croatia has a relatively diversified economy, with services being the most important sector in terms of contribution to GDP (over 60%) and employment (over half of Croatia's labour force); tourism is a major net foreign exchange earner. Manufacturing (led by food-processing, wood products, chemicals, and shipbuilding) accounts for around one fifth of GDP and almost 70% of the total value of merchandise exports (Table AI.1) . Agriculture, hunting, forestry and

[2] Croatia Governmetn Materals

fishing contribute around 7% to GDP, 10% to employment and 13% to merchandise exports. The mining, quarrying, and energy sector account for around 1% of GDP and 17% of merchandise exports (section (3)(i) below) .

Croatia's domestic hydrocarbon and large hydropower production (accounting for 51% of electricity supply) keep energy and import dependence at levels well below other countries in the region. While import dependence is growing for hydrocarbons, Croatia plays a significant role in regional electricity trade, notably due to its significant peak generation and large cross-border transmission capacities. Since July 2008, the electricity market has been opened for all customers. However, in practice, the electricity company, Hrvatska elektroprivreda (HEP), remains the only supplier. The gas market also has a single supplier in the oil and gas company, Industrija nafte (INA) .[8]

The national currency is the kuna (HRK) .[9] As from 1 January 2009, Croatia's *de facto* exchange rate arrangement is classified as "other managed arrangement".[10] Croatia accepted the obligations of Article VIII of the IMF Agreement on 29 May 1995[11], and maintains an exchange system that is free of restrictions on payments and transfers for current international transactions. Preparations for Croatia's participation in the Economic and Monetary Union and for the introduction of the euro have already started.[12]

RECENT ECONOMIC DEVELOPMENTS

Croatia's economic reform programme has centred on trade liberalization, deregulation, and privatization (Chapter III(3)(iii)) . The programme has resulted in a positive economic performance over the last few years, with relatively high economic growth, low inflation, and declining public deficit. Croatia's annual average real GDP growth rate was 4.2% during 2004-08, spurred by strong domestic demand and productivity gains due to economic restructuring. Robust economic growth resulted in a downward trend in the unemployment rate up to 2008

Nevertheless, for 2009 real GDP growth is estimated at -5.8% largely as a result of the global economic downturn, with an administrative unemployment rate of 14.2% by August 2009.

The annual average inflation rate in Croatia, as measured by the consumer price index (CPI), was 3.5% during 2004-08, peaking at 6.1% in 2008 reflecting soaring food and energy prices. The Croatian National Bank's (CNB) monetary and foreign exchange system of a tightly managed float with a very limited degree of exchange rate flexibility, has served the economy well: it has lent stability and credibility to the investment environment, and provided a credible anchor for price stability given Croatia's experience with hyperinflation, and its highly "euroized" economy.[15] The CNB has recently tightened its monetary policy to contain inflationary pressures.[16] The IMF estimates inflation of 2.8% for 2009, in view of the fall in energy and other prices[17]; the authorities expect rate of 2.6%.

Over the last few years, Croatia has achieved an important improvement in its fiscal position, a main source of macroeconomic imbalances in the past. The general government deficit was reduced from 3.2% of GDP in 2004 to 0.9% in 2008, and was an estimated 2.9% for 2009. The fiscal improvement has been largely the result of a decline in capital expenditure as large investment projects came to a closure, and despite a recent decline in VAT and excise revenues.[18] The fiscal deterioration in 2009 was a consequence of a sharp fall in tax revenues due to the real contraction of economic activity. To cope with the revenue shortfall, the Government has recently implemented additional expenditure cuts, such as wage growth restraint throughout the economy, and has increased taxes (e.g. the VAT general rate went from 22% to 23% on 1 August 2009 (Chapter III(1)(iv)(d)) . The Government aims to reduce

For additional analytical, marketing, investment and business opportunities information, please contact Global Investment & Business Center, USA
(202) 546-2103. Fax: (202) 546-3275. E-mail: rusric@erols.com

the budget deficit after 2009. To achieve this, additional fiscal measures are envisaged, such as curtailing subsidies and advancing the restructuring of loss-making state-owned enterprises (SOEs), better targeting of social benefits, and improving tax administration and enforcement. Import duties represented, on average, 2.4% of total tax revenue collected in Croatia during 2005-07.[19]

Croatia's large stock of external debt remains a source of potential vulnerability, increasing the speed and magnitude with which adverse external financial shocks may be transmitted. External debt as percentage of GDP rose from 70% in 2004 to 82.6% in 2008 on the back of strong private sector borrowing, and notwithstanding efforts at fiscal consolidation, a shift by the public sector towards domestic financing, and measures by the CNB to discourage bank external borrowing. According to the authorities, for 2009, external debt is estimated to exceed 90% of GDP, although half of the increase resulting from a fall in nominal GDP.

TRADE PERFORMANCE AND INVESTMENT

(i) Trade in goods and services

Croatia has traditionally recorded an external current account deficit. As a percentage of GDP, it went from 4.4% in 2004 to a peak of 9.3 in 2008, due mainly to strong merchandise import growth: the trade deficit jumped from €6,724 million to €10,794 million during the period (Table I.2) . In recent years, the current account deficit has been financed by FDI and other long-term capital inflows, with gross official international reserves increasing from €6,436 million (4.8 months of imports) in 2004 to €9,630 million (6.2 months of imports) in 2009. For 2009, import contraction outpaced the fall in exports, therefore the external current account deficit is estimated to have narrowed to 6.1% of GDP.

Croatia's economy is highly dependent on international trade: the ratio of trade in goods and services (exports and imports) to GDP averaged 92.6% during 2004-08, although it fell to 77.3% in 2009 (Table I.1) . In 2007, Croatia ranked 54th among world merchandise exporters (considering the countries of the EU together and excluding intra-EU trade), and 41st among importers. In commercial services trade, Croatia ranked 25th among exporters and 47th among importers.[21]

Table I.2Balance of payments, 2004-08

(€ million)

	2004	2005	2006	2007	2008[a]
A. Current Account	-1,433.7	-1,975.6	-2,715.2	-3,239.2	-4,835.1
Goods, services, and income	-2,625.5	-3,159.5	-3,822.6	-4,282.2	-5,419.9
Credit	14,952.8	15,990.2	17,884.8	19,610.4	21,256.5
Debit	-17,578.3	-19,149.7	-21,707.3	-23,892.5	-26,676.4
Goods and services	-1,955.3	-2,200.2	-2,639.6	-3,168.1	-3,835.9
Goods	-6,724.2	-7,518.0	-8,344.2	-9,434.0	-10,793.8
Credit	6,606.8	7,220.3	8,463.6	9,192.5	9,814.0
Exports (f.o.b.)	6,453.8	7,069.4	8,251.6	9,072.8	9,652.3
Adjustments for coverage	153.0	150.9	212.0	71.2	67.2
Debit	-13,330.9	-14,738.3	-16,807.8	-18,626.5	-20,607.8
Imports (c.i.f.)	-13,354.4	-14,949.5	-17,104.7	-18,515.1	-20,458.5

Adjustments for coverage	-474.7	-346.4	-341.1	-259.0	-272.1
Adjustments for classification	498.1	557.6	638.0	570.4	630.8
Services	4,768.9	5,317.7	5,704.6	6,265.9	6,957.9
Transportation	299.3	376.1	443.5	487.6	508.5
Credit	791.3	880.3	1,006.7	1,122.4	1,209.4
Debit	-492.0	-504.2	-563.2	-634.8	-700.9
Travel	4,822.3	5,394.9	5,708.7	6,035.2	6,694.0
Credit	5,505.6	5,998.9	6,293.3	6,752.6	7,459.4
Debit	-683.3	-604.1	-584.6	-717.3	-765.5
Other services	-352.7	-453.3	-447.6	-256.9	-244.6
Credit	1,339.8	1,173.4	1,228.5	1,249.8	1,421.8
Debit	-1,692.5	-1,626.6	-1,676.0	-1,506.7	-1,666.4
Income	-670.2	-959.2	-1182.9	-1,114.1	-1,584.0
Credit	709.2	717.2	892.7	1,293.0	1,351.9
Debit	-1,379.6	-1,676.6	-2,075.7	-2,407.1	-2,935.9
Current transfers	1,191.8	1,183.8	1,107.4	1,043.0	1,034.8
Credit	1,584.6	1,628.4	1,639.5	1,576.1	1,683.7
Debit	-392.8	-444.5	-532.1	-533.1	-649.0
B. Capital and Financial Account	2,560.4	3,013.5	3,670.4	4,146.7	5,962.4
Capital account	31.4	53.8	-133.8	34.5	29.2
Financial account, excl. reserves	2,572.0	3,781.6	5,216.4	4,833.8	5,602.8
Direct investment	670.8	1,276.1	2,556.6	3,490.0	3,219.1
Abroad	-278.8	-191.8	-208.2	-180.2	-134.0
In Croatia	949.6	1,467.9	2,764.8	3,670.2	3,353.1
Portfolio investment	287.1	-1,177.9	-542.3	-2.9	-627.2
Assets	-736.1	-571.2	-472.5	-413.7	-273.3
Liabilities	1,023.2	-606.7	-69.8	410.8	-353.9
Financial derivatives	0.0	-88.4	0.0	0.0	0.0
Other investment	1,614.1	3,771.8	3,202.1	1,346.7	3,010.9
Assets	-498.3	982.0	-692.3	-1,653.4	-1,617.9
Liabilities	2,112.4	2,789.7	3,894.4	3,000.1	4,628.8
Reserve asset	-43.0	-821.8	-1,412.2	-721.6	330.4
C. Net Errors and Omissions	-1,126.7	-1,037.9	-955.2	-907.5	-1,577.3

a Preliminary data.
Source: Croatian National Bank (2009), *Annual Report 2008*, Zagreb.

Croatia has a relatively diversified export base, with manufactures accounting for about 70% of total merchandise exports, on average, during 2003-08 (Chart I.1 and Table AI.1) . In 2008, machinery and transport equipment, led by shipbuilding, was the main export with 33.5% of total merchandise exports (up from 29.5% in 2003) . The contribution of food products declined from 12.2% in 2003 to 9.8% in 2008, while the share of mining products (mostly fuels) increased from 11.9% to 17.2% over the same period.

Croatia's imports increased in line with the significant economic growth up to 2008. Total merchandise imports grew from US$14,209 million in 2003 to US$30,728 million in 2008 (Table AI.2) . Around 70% of total merchandise imports are manufactures, led by machinery and transport equipment (32.5% in 2008) and chemicals (10.6%) (Chart I.1) . Fuels represented 17.6% of total merchandise imports in 2008 (up from 10.9% in 2003), whereas the share of food imports remained stable at about 8% throughout the period.

Around 80% of Croatia's exports go to Europe (about 60% to the EU); Italy is still the major single export market with 19.1% of total merchandise exports in 2008 (down from 26.7% in 2003), followed by Bosnia and Herzegovina (15.4%), Germany (10.8%), and Slovenia (7.8%). Croatia's goods exports to the United States averaged 2.8% of total merchandise exports during 2003-08, whereas the share exported to Asian countries rose from 1.9% in 2003 to 3.2% in 2008 (Chart I.2 and Table AI.2).

Croatia's goods imports also originate largely in Europe, mostly from the EU which accounted for 64.1% of total merchandise imports in 2008 (down from 73.2% in 2003). Italy remains the leading source, supplying 17.1% of total merchandise imports in 2008 (down from 18.2% in 2003), followed by Germany (13.4%), and the Russian Federation (10.4%). Goods imports from the United States went from 2.6% in 2003 to 2.1% in 2008; Asian countries' share, led by China, increased from 8.4% to 10.7% during the period (Chart I.2 and Table AI.4).

Balance of payments data indicate that Croatia is a net exporter of services, with a surplus averaging €5,803 million per year during 2004-08 (Table I.2). The surplus of travel services rose from €4,822 million in 2004 to €6,694 million in 2008, while that of transport services increased from €299 million to €508.5 million.

(ii) Foreign direct investment

18. Croatia's annual inflows of foreign direct investment (FDI) jumped from an average of US$447 million during 1990-00 to US$1,079 million in 2004 and to US$4,798 million in 2008 (Table I.3). This was largely the result of the positive developments in the economy and some privatizations (Chapter III(3)(ii)). Among new EU members and other south-east European countries, Croatia had the sixth largest FDI stock (US$45,970 million), in 2007, and the fifth-highest FDI per capita.

On the basis of UNCTAD's Inward FDI Performance Index, Croatia ranked 22nd out of 141 economies during 2005-07 (up from 43rd over 2004-06).[23]

Table I.3 Foreign direct investment, 2004-08

(US$ million)

	2004	2005	2006	2007	2008
FDI inflows	1,079	1,788	3,457	4,987	4,798
FDI inward stock	12,403	14,592	27,364	45,970	31,017
FDI inward stock (% of GDP)	35.2	32.8	55.8	76.8	44.7
FDI outflows	346	237	263	241	194
FDI outward stock	2,128	2,047	2,414	3,470	3,765
FDI outward stock (% of GDP)	5.2	4.6	4.9	5.9	5.4

Source: Information provided by the Croatian authorities.

For additional analytical, marketing, investment and business opportunities information, please contact Global Investment & Business Center, USA
(202) 546-2103. Fax: (202) 546-3275. E-mail: rusric@erols.com

FDI outflows have been very low, as has been the case for most countries in the region, averaging US$256 million during 2004-08. According to UNCTAD's Outward FDI Performance Index, Croatia ranked 64th out of 141 economies in 2007 (53rd in 2006) .[24]

Croatia's was 56th in UNCTAD's Inward FDI Potential Index in 2006 (the same as in 2005) .[25] FDI in Croatia has been inhibited by several factors, notably long-standing competitiveness issues, such as relatively high labour costs, while the business environment is affected by difficulties in obtaining necessary licences, corruption, and an inefficient public administration.[26] As a result, Croatia ranks 106th (out of 181 economies) in the World Bank's Ease of Doing Business 2009 Index.[27] Nonetheless, the authorities have recently been implementing measures to improve Croatia's investment climate, including the entry into force of the Investment Promotion Act (OG 138/06) and the establishment of the Trade and Investment Promotion Agency (APIU) (Chapter II(4)) .

The EU remains, by far, the largest investor in Croatia, accounting for more than two thirds of FDI stock. Individually, Austria is the largest investor, with 27.9% of Croatia's total FDI inflows during 2004-08 (Table I.4), followed by the Netherlands (23%), Hungary (13.4%), Germany (7.3%), and Slovenia (5.3%) . Services account for about two thirds of Croatia's total FDI inward stock, led by financial services with 41% of total FDI inflows over 2004-08. The share of manufacturing in Croatia's total FDI inflows during the period dropped to 11.7%[28], with the majority being allocated into the chemicals industry. Croatia's attractiveness as a destination for "greenfield" FDI is key to increasing its overall growth potential in a sustainable manner.[29] FDI inflows into agriculture and related activities have been minimal.

Table I.4 FDI inflows by origin and economic activity, 2004-08

(€ million)

	2004	2005	2006	2007	2008	2004-08
Country of origin:						
Austria	248.6	543.6	-505.4	2,058.8	1,057.9	3,403.5
Netherlands	71.1	173.9	1,953.9	319.5	288.5	2,807.5
Hungary	43.5	329.0	51.9	257.1	958.4	1,639.9
Germany	190.5	-132.1	228.7	170.9	428.8	886.8
Slovenia	43.1	119.3	80.6	215.7	183.4	642.1
Luxembourg	64.4	104.1	298.8	9.6	108.7	585.6
Italy	150.3	177.9	187.5	-81.7	46.8	480.8
Other	138.1	152.2	468.8	720.3	280.6	1,759.4
Economic activity:						
Financial intermediation, except insurance and pension funds	229.7	778.0	1,037.7	1,813.7	1.154.3	5,013.4
Manufacture of coke, refined petroleum products	27.6	46.4	38.3	20.1	923.3	1,055.9
Real estate activities	106.8	84.4	254.9	309.6	-16.5	739.2
Wholesale trade and commission trade	84.9	96.7	117.1	162.0	213.8	674.5
Extraction of crude petroleum and natural gas	62.3	121.4	111.1	167.5	144.0	606.3
Manufacture of chemicals and chemical products	-15.3	-52.4	521.0	-33.7	-47.5	372.1

For additional analytical, marketing, investment and business opportunities information, please contact Global Investment & Business Center, USA
(202) 546-2103. Fax: (202) 546-3275. E-mail: rusric@erols.com

Agriculture, hunting and related activities	15.0	11.8	2.1	0.0	10.5	39.4
Other	438.6	381.6	682.6	1,231.0	971.2	3,704.8
Total	949.6	1,467.9	2,764.8	3,670.2	3,353.1	12,205.6

Source: CNB online information. Viewed at: http://www.hnb.hr/statistika/estatistika.htm

TRADE AND INVESTMENT POLICY FRAMEWORK

(1) GENERAL FRAMEWORK

1. The Republic of Croatia's legal system is based on the Constitution of 1990 (as amended in 2000 and 2001) . Under Article 4 of the Constitution, state powers are divided into three branches: legislative (Parliament), executive (President and Government), and judiciary (Courts), but limited by the right to local and regional self-government guaranteed by the Constitution.

2. The amendments to the Constitution, *inter alia*, abolished the Chamber of Counties (Upper House), thereby switching from a bicameral to a unicameral Parliament (*Hrvatski sabor*) . The Parliament, *inter alia*, has control over the executive power, decides on the enactment and amendment of the Constitution, passes acts, adopts the state budget and decides on the strategies of national security and defence.[2]

3. Executive power is vested in the President and the Government. The President, elected for a term of five years (renewable only once), has broad powers of supervision, appoints the Prime Minister[3], and is responsible for the defence of the independence and territorial integrity of Croatia. The Government (consisting of the Prime Minister, one or more Deputy Prime Ministers, and Ministers), *inter alia*, proposes and implements acts and other decisions of the Parliament.

4. Croatia has an autonomous and independent judicial system. The Supreme Court is the highest court followed by the Constitutional Court[6], and other courts, such as the Administrative Court (AC) . Appeals against decisions or acts of administrative bodies may be lodged with the AC for all WTO issues.

5. In general, policies are formulated and implemented by means of acts (laws) . In the majority of cases, draft acts are presented, by the Government to the Parliament for adoption.[7] Draft acts may also be presented to the Parliament by, *inter alia*, all deputies and parliamentary working bodies. The President promulgates acts within eight days from the date they are passed in the Parliament. However, if the President considers the act not to be in accordance with the Constitution, she/he may initiate proceedings to review its constitutionality before the Constitutional Court. Acts enter into force on the eighth day after publication in the *Official Gazette* (OG) *Narodne Novine*, unless otherwise indicated in the act itself. Acts relating to trade policy are proposed to the Government by the relevant Ministries.

6. The Ministry of the Economy, Labour and Entrepreneurship (MELE) is responsible for formulating, administering, and coordinating Croatia's foreign trade policies. MELE is also responsible, *inter alia*, for policies regarding employment and industry (except food, wood, and tobacco), shipbuilding, energy, mining, crafts, cooperatives (except agricultural), small and medium-sized enterprises (SMEs), public procurement, and trade and investment promotion.[8] Depending on the nature of the issue, MELE consults with relevant ministries and other institutions that also take part directly or indirectly in foreign trade policy formulation and/or

For additional analytical, marketing, investment and business opportunities information, please contact Global Investment & Business Center, USA (202) 546-2103. Fax: (202) 546-3275. E-mail: rusric@erols.com

implementation. These include: the Ministry of Agriculture, Fisheries, and Rural Development; the Ministry of Regional Development, Forestry and Water Management, the Ministry of Finance (including its Customs Administration); the Ministry of Foreign Affairs and European Integration; as well as other ministries, state administrative organizations, and the private sector.

7. The private sector and NGOs provide inputs to trade-policy formulation by communicating their views either directly to MELE or through chambers and the business community (Croatian Chamber of Economy, Croatian Chamber of Trades and Crafts, Croatian Employers' Association, Croatian Exporters, and the National Competitiveness Council) .[9] These associations participate, for example, in the activities of bilateral joint-commissions established under economic cooperation agreements, and in negotiations on free-trade agreements, by presenting their interests or concerns regarding the agreement under negotiation. The views of the private sector, including NGOs, are usually taken into consideration throughout the process, on an *ad hoc* basis.

8. In descending order of importance, the Constitution is followed by acts and implementing documents such as: regulations, ordinances, decisions, and conclusions. International agreements in force, including the WTO Agreements, concluded and ratified in accordance with the Constitution and made public, carry the force of law in Croatia.[10]

9. The WTO Agreements and Croatia's current and future trade relations with the European Union (EU) are the main factors influencing Croatia's trading system. Since its accession to the WTO (section (2) below), Croatia has continued to reform its policies in trade and related areas with the objective of bringing domestic legislation into line with the WTO Agreements, and the EU *acquis communautaire*. This has required a considerable review and updating of almost all trade-related legislation (Table II.1), which is still ongoing.

Table II.1 Main trade-related laws

Area	Legislation
Foreign trade	Trade Act (OG 87/08, 116/08, and 76/09) Act on the Export of Dual-Use Goods (OG 100/04 and 84/08) Act on the Export and Import of Military and Non-Military Lethal Goods (OG 86/08) Act on International Restrictive Measures (OG 139/08) Regulation specifying goods subject to export and import licences (OG 6/09 and 73/09) Regulation on the List of Dual-Use Items (OG 184/04, 62/07, 57/08 and 63/09) Regulation on Import and Export Control for Rough Diamonds (OG 97/03, 142/03, 176/04, 14/06, 90/07, 64/08, and 61/09)
Customs	Customs Act (OG 78/99, 94/99, 117/99, 73/00, 92/01, 47/03, 140/05, 138/06, 60/08 and 45/09) Regulation implementing the Customs Act (OG 161/03, 69/06, 5/07, 70/08 and 76/09) Rules on the use of forms for implementation of the Customs Act (OG 176/03) Customs Tariff Act (OG 61/00, 117/00, 119/00, and 146/08) Customs Service Act (OG 83/09) Performance of Agency in Customs Clearance Procedures Act (OG 92/01)

For additional analytical, marketing, investment and business opportunities information, please contact Global Investment & Business Center, USA (202) 546-2103. Fax: (202) 546-3275. E-mail: rusric@erols.com

Taxation	Value Added Tax Act (OG. 47/95), as amended Profit Tax Act (OG 177/04), as amended Income Tax Act (OG 177/04), as amended Act on Excise Duty on Passenger Cars, other Motor Vehicles, Vessels and Aircraft (OG 139/97) Act on Excise Duty on Coffee (OG 87/05) Act on Excise Duty on Non-Alcoholic Beverages (OG 51/94), as amended Act on Excise Duty on Beer (OG 51/94), as amended Act on Excise Duty on Alcohol (OG 51/94), as amended Act on Excise Duty on Mineral Oils (OG 55/00), as amended Act on Excise Duty on Luxury Products (OG 105/99), as amended Act on Excise Duty on Tobacco Products (OG 51/94), as amended Excise Duties Act (OG 83/09-in force as from 1 January 2010)
Contingency trade remedies	Trade Act (OG 87/08, 116/08, 76/09) Regulation on the manner and procedure of determining anti-dumping and countervailing duties (OG 139/04) Regulation on safeguard measures (OG 73/02, 33/03)
Government procurement	Public Procurement Act (OG 110/07), as amended Public Private Partnerships Act (OG 129/08) Concessions Act (OG 125/08)
State aid	State Aid Act (OG 140/05) Regulation on State Aid (OG 50/06)
Investment	Companies Act (OG 111/93, 34/99, 118/03, 107/07, and 146/08) Investment Promotion Act (OG 138/06)
Free zones	Free Zone Act (OG 44/96 and 85/08)
SPS and TBT	Food Act (OG 46/07 and 155/08) Plant Health Act (OG 75/05), Veterinary Act (OG 41/07 and 155/08) Animal Protection Act (OG 135/06) Sanitary Inspection Act (OG 113/08) Medicinal Products Act (OG 71/07)
Privatization	Privatization Act (OG 21/96, 71/97 and 73/00) HEP Privatization Act (OG 32/02) INA Privatization Act (OG 32/02) Act on Privatization of Croatian Telecommunications (OG 65/99 and 68/01)
Competition	Competition Act (OG 120/03) New Competition Act (OG 79/09, as from 1 October 2010)
Intellectual property rights	Trademarks Act (OG 173/03), as amended Geographical Indications Act (OG 173/03), as amended Act on the Protection of Topographies of Semiconductor Products (OG 173/03), as amended Patents Act (OG 173/03), as amended Copyright and Related Rights Act (OG 163/03), as amended Industrial Designs Act (OG 173/03), as amended
Company establishment	Companies Act (OG 111/93, 34/99, 118/03, 107/07 and 146/08)

Agriculture and related activities	Agriculture Act (OG 66/01 and 83/02) Sea Fishery Act (OG 46/97 and 48/05) Food Act (OG 46/07 and 155/08) Forest Act (OG 140/05; 82/06 and 129/08)

For additional analytical, marketing, investment and business opportunities information, please contact Global Investment & Business Center, USA (202) 546-2103. Fax: (202) 546-3275. E-mail: rusric@erols.com

	Forest Reproductive Material Act (OG 75/09)
Mining	Mining Act (OG 75/09)
Petroleum and gas	Petroleum Act (OG 238/04 and 57/06) Gas Market Act (OG 40/07, 152/08 and 83/09)
Energy	Energy Act (OG 68/01, 177/04, 76/07 and 152/08) Act for Regulating Energy Activities (OG 169/01, 177/04 and 76/07)
Manufacturing	Technical Requirements for Products and Conformity Assessment (OG 158/03 and 79/07) Standardization Act (OG 163/03) Accreditation Act (OG 158/03 and 75/09) Metrology Act (OG 163/03, 194/03 and 111/07) General Product Safety Act (OG 30/09) Small Business Encouragement Act (OG 29/02 and 63/27) Cooperatives Act (OG 36/95, 67/01 and 12/02) Trades and Crafts Act (OG 77/93, 90/96, 102/98, 64/01, 71/01, 49/03, 68/07, and 79/07) Chemicals Act (OG 150/05) Environmental Protection Act (OG 110/07) Building Act (OG 175/03 and 100/04)
Telecommunications	Electronic Communications Act (OG 73/08)
Postal services	Postal Services Act (OG 88/09)
Financial services	Act on the Croatian National Bank (OG 75/08) Credit Institutions Act (OG 117/08 and 74/09) Insurance Act (OG 151/05, 87/08 and 82/09) Capital Market Act (OG 88/08, 146/08 and 74/09) Foreign Exchange Act (OG 96/03, 140/05, 132/06 and 150/08) National Payment System Act (OG 117/01) Investments Funds Act (OG 150/05)
Transport	Public Roads Act (OG 180/04 and 146/08) Act on Inland Navigation and Inland Ports (OG 109/07 and 132/07) Air Traffic Act (OG 132/98, 178/04 and 46/07), as amended Airport Act (OG 19/98) Maritime Code (OG 181/04, 76/07 and 146/08) Road Traffic Transport Act (OG 178/04 and 63/08)
Tourism	Act on the Provision of Tourism Services (OG 68/07) Hospitality and Catering Industry Act (OG 138/06, 158/08 and 43/09) Tourism Tax Act (OG 152/08 and 59/09)

Source: Information provided by the Croatian authorities.

10. The main legislation relating to international trade in Croatia is the Trade Act (OG 87/08, 116/08 and 76/09) . Nonetheless, upon EU membership, several provisions of the Trade Act will cease to apply as stipulated in Article 83. To complement the Trade Act, four regulations have been adopted as a result of Croatia's obligations in the WTO.[11] Investment for both nationals and foreigners is mainly regulated by the Companies Act (OG 111/03, as amended) and the Investment Promotion Act (OG 138/06) (section (4) below) .

For additional analytical, marketing, investment and business opportunities information, please contact Global Investment & Business Center, USA
(202) 546-2103. Fax: (202) 546-3275. E-mail: rusric@erols.com

11. Since its independence in 1991, Croatia's overriding objective has been to complete the transition towards an open, market-driven economy, well integrated at the regional and multilateral levels. Croatia's efforts to integrate into the world economy are reflected in the dismantling of the restrictive trade regime inherited from the former Socialist Federal Republic of Yugoslavia, and in its accession, participation in, or adherence to various multilateral, regional, and bilateral trade initiatives (sections (2) and (3) below) .

12. Croatia is strongly committed to the multilateral trading system. The orientation of its economic and trade policies, however, like that of other central and eastern European countries, is largely driven by the goal of accession to the EU, its main trading partner (Chapter I(3)(i)); Croatia intends to conclude accession negotiations during 2010. The main factor in shaping Croatia's foreign trade policy is the Stabilization and Association Agreement (SAA) between Croatia and the EU (section (3)(i) below) .

13. Croatia's main strategic goal is to achieve social prosperity through "growth and employment in a competitive market economy acting within a European welfare state of the 21st century". To achieve this, on 4 August 2006, Croatia adopted its Strategic Development Framework for 2006-13. Some of the main actions included are to: (i) complete judicial and public administration reforms; (ii) finish the privatization process and seriously tackle corruption; (iii) intensify the development of SMEs, increase competitiveness, and pursue a balanced development of all regions; (iv) foster tourism with further development of infrastructure; (v) create a more business-friendly environment to attract larger foreign direct investment (FDI) inflows (Chapter I(3)(ii)); and (vi) promote a knowledge-based society.[12]

14. As part of its Strategic Development Framework, the Croatian Export Offensive Strategy 2007-10 is being implemented by MELE. It aims, *inter alia*, to increase the number of exporting companies from around 11,000 to 13,800; change the structure of Croatia's exports so as to quadruple the number of value-added exports; establish six "export-only" clusters[13]; and increase the competitiveness of local companies. In this regard, the Competitiveness Strengthening and Internationalization Programme was launched in 2009 with the aim of supporting export-oriented companies and networking in export clusters.

(2) PARTICIPATION IN THE WORLD TRADE ORGANIZATION

15. Croatia applied for accession to the GATT in September 1993 and became the 140th member of the WTO on 30 November 2000.

As part of its accession commitments, Croatia bound 100% of its tariff lines (Chapter III(1)(iv)(b)) . In addition, Croatia made extensive commitments under the GATS (Chapter IV(3)) . Croatia accords at least MFN treatment to all its trading partners.

16. Croatia is a signatory of the Information Technology Agreement (ITA) and the Agreement on Trade in Civil Aircraft. It is also an observer to the Plurilateral Agreement on Government Procurement (Table II.2) . At end June 2009, Croatia had 17 notifications outstanding, mostly in agriculture.

17. To date, Croatia has been involved in one case under the WTO dispute settlement mechanism. On 9 July 2003, a consultation was requested by Hungary on Croatia's "Measures Affecting Imports of Live Animals and Meat Products"[15]; a mutually agreed solution was reached on 30 January 2009.[16]

Table II.2 Selected notifications to the WTO, 2009

For additional analytical, marketing, investment and business opportunities information, please contact Global Investment & Business Center, USA
(202) 546-2103. Fax: (202) 546-3275. E-mail: rusric@erols.com

WTO Agreement	Document symbol and date	Main content
General Agreement on Tariffs and Trade 1994	Schedule CXLVII – Republic of Croatia	Schedule of tariff concessions
General Agreement on Trade in Services	GATS/SC/130 , 22 December 2000	Schedule of specific commitments in services; and Reference paper on basic telecommunications
Agreement on Agriculture (Article 18.2)	G/AG/N/HRV/8 , 30 October 2009	Export subsidies (Table ES:1)
	G/AG/N/HRV/2 , 8 July 2005	Administration of tariff quotas (Table MA:1)
	G/AG/N/HRV/9 , 30 October 2009	Imports under tariff quotas (Table MA:2)
Agreement on Technical Barriers to Trade (Article 15.2)	G/TBT/ENQ/35/Rev.2 , 13 May 2009	Croatian Standards Institute as the enquiry point
	G/TBT/CS/2/Rev.15 , 2 March 2009	Acceptance of code of good practice
Agreement on Trade-Related Aspects of Intellectual Property (Article 63.2)	IP/N/1/HRV/1 , 29 October 2002 IP/Q-Q4/HRV/1, 7 May 2003	TRIPS-related legislation Review of legislation: responses from Croatia
Agreement on Anti-Dumping Practices (Article 18.5)	G/ADP/N/1/HRV/2 , 24 November 2004	Acts and regulations relevant to the Agreement
(Article 16.4)	G/ADP/N/180/Add.1 , 27 April 2009	Semi-Annual Report on Anti-Dumping Actions
Agreement on Rules of Origin (Article 5.1 and Annex II)	G/RO/N/36/, 12 March 2002	Preferential and non-preferential rules of origin
Agreement on Subsidies and Countervailing Measures (Article 32.6)	G/SCM/N/1/HRV/2 , 24 November 2004	Acts and regulations relevant to the Agreement
(Article 25.11)	G/SCM/N/185/Add.1 , 27 April 2009	Semi-Annual Report of countervailing duty actions
Agreement on Import Licensing (Articles 1.4(a) and 8.2(b) and 5.2)	G/LIC/N/1/HRV/4 , 18 September 2009 G/LIC/N/2/HRV/1 , 9 October 2009	Acts and regulations concerning import licensing procedures
(Article 7.3)	G/LIC/N/3/HRV/4 , 27 October 2009	Replies to the questionnaire on import licensing procedures
Agreement on Customs Valuation (Article 22.2)	G/VAL/N/1/HRV/1 , 16 January 2002	Acts and regulations relevant to the Agreement
	G/VAL/N/2/HRV/1 , 16 January 2002	Implementation and administration of the Agreement
	G/VAL/N/3/HRV/1 , 16 January	Information on the application of

For additional analytical, marketing, investment and business opportunities information, please contact Global Investment & Business Center, USA (202) 546-2103. Fax: (202) 546-3275. E-mail: rusric@erols.com

	2002	Decisions A.3 and A.4
Agreement on the Application of Sanitary and Phytosanitary Measures (Article 7, Annex B)	G/SPS/N/HRV/1 , 31 July 2003	Notification of prohibition of imports of live animals and products of animal origin due to spongiform encephalopathies
(Paragraph 3 of Annex B)	G/SPS/ENQ/24 , 1 October 2008	Notification of enquiry point
Agreement on Safeguard Measures (Article 12.6)	G/SG/N/1/HRV/2 , 15 July 2002, and G/SG/N/1/HRV/2/Add.1 , 23 November 2004	Acts and regulations relative to safeguard measures
State Trading Enterprises (Article XVII:4 (a)) and Understanding on the Interpretation of Article XVII:1	G/STR/N/11/HRV G/STR/N/12/HRV , 9 June 2009	New and full notification that Croatia does not maintain any state trading enterprises

Source: WTO Secretariat.

18. Croatia attaches great importance to the Doha Development Agenda (DDA), with particular interest in agriculture, non-agricultural products, and services. Croatia participates in the recently acceded members (RAMs) group, and was its coordinator from November 2001 until mid-2007. While active in the DDA negotiations, Croatia's general position relates to its already relatively liberal trade regime and its extensive commitments in both goods and services undertaken during its accession process. Croatia, therefore, calls for further flexibilities in these negotiations, leading to reductions of imbalances in the rights and obligations between WTO Members, taking into account the particular situation of RAMs, developing and least-developed countries. Moreover, as an EU candidate country, Croatia takes the EU's position into consideration in the DDA negotiations.

(3) PREFERENTIAL TRADE AGREEMENTS AND ARRANGEMENTS

19. Over the past few years, accession to the EU has been a constant objective of Croatia's policies; it submitted its application for EU membership on 21 February 2003. The European Council granted Croatia the status of candidate country in June 2004; accession negotiations were opened in October 2005.

[17] Croatia's accession to the EU is being evaluated against its ability to satisfy defined economic and political criteria laid out at the 1993 Copenhagen European Council, as well as to assume the obligations of membership.[18] The EU provides guidance to Croatia on reform priorities through the Accession Partnership. Croatia adopts its national programme for EU accession each year, based on the Accession Partnership.[19]

20. Croatia also participates in the Central European Free Trade Agreement (CEFTA 2006) with seven other parties; has a free-trade agreement with the four European Free Trade Association (EFTA) states; and a bilateral free-trade agreement with Turkey. In 2008, Croatia's total preferential trade with its 39 partners amounted to US$34.448 million (76.9% of Croatia's total trade), of which 82.2% was with the EU, 14.2% with CEFTA 2006, 2% with EFTA, and 1.6% with Turkey (Table II.3) .

Table II.3 Trade under preferential agreements, (US$ million)

FTA	Exports	Imports	Total	Percentage of total FTAs	Percentage of total trade
EU	8,594	19,709	28,303	82.2	63.1
CEFTA 2006	3,332	1,547	4,879	14.2	10.9
EFTA	171	530	701	2.0	1.6
Turkey	88	477	565	1.6	1.3
Total preferential agreements	12,185	22,263	34,448	100.0	76.9
Croatia's total trade	14,112	30,728	44,840	n.a.	100.0

n.a. Not applicable.
Source: Information provided by the Croatian Central Bureau of Statistics.

(i) Stabilization and Association Agreement (SAA)

21. The SAA between Croatia and the EU was signed in October 2001 and entered into force in February 2005. The SAA defines the political and economic relationship between the two parties.[20] It is a preferential agreement aimed at establishing a close and lasting relationship based on reciprocity and mutual interest, allowing Croatia to formalize and strengthen the existing relationship with the EU.

22. The trade part of the SAA – the Interim Agreement on Trade and Trade Related Matters (Interim Agreement) was signed on 29 October 2001 and entered into force on 1 March 2002. It established a free-trade area in goods between the two parties; liberalization has been carried out asymmetrically, with the EU liberalizing at a faster rate. Accordingly, all tariffs and quantitative restrictions on Croatian exports of industrial products to the EU were abolished from the outset. Croatia completed the elimination of its tariffs applicable to EU exports of industrial goods on 1 January 2007; special arrangements existed for Croatia's textiles and clothing and steel industries.[22] The SAA also includes provisions on trade in services, intellectual property rights, competition, investment, customs and trade remedies, and standards.

23. The Interim Agreement also includes tariff preferences for agricultural goods and for fish and fish products. The EU grants Croatia unlimited duty-free access for most agricultural products with some exceptions, such as baby beef, fisheries, wine, and sugar (this last one since 1 January 2007) for which tariff quotas apply.[23] Croatia progressively liberalized certain agricultural products based on a positive list.[24] Special conditions related to processed agricultural products for both Croatia and the EU are set out in Protocol III of the Agreement.

24. According to the EU, implementation of the SAA has been uneven. There have been positive developments regarding state aid granted to the shipbuilding industry (Chapter III(3)(iii)(b)) and the excise duty regime for cigarettes (Chapter III(1)(iv)(d))[25]; but recently, certain measures have resulted in increased import duties on a number of products exported from the EU. Discussions are ongoing to address these issues in the framework of the SAA.

25. On 8 December 2000, a waiver was granted until 2006 regarding Article I(1) of the GATT 1994, to permit the EU to afford duty-free or preferential treatment to eligible products originating in Croatia and other Western Balkans countries, without being required to extend the same treatment to like products of any other WTO Member.[26] The waiver was extended until 31 December 2011.[27]

For additional analytical, marketing, investment and business opportunities information, please contact Global Investment & Business Center, USA
(202) 546-2103. Fax: (202) 546-3275. E-mail: rusric@erols.com

(ii) Central European Free Trade Area (CEFTA 2006)[28]

26. The CEFTA 2006 is a preferential trade agreement between non-EU countries in central and south eastern Europe.[29] It entered into force on 26 July 2007 for five parties (Albania, FYR of Macedonia, Moldova, Montenegro, and UNMIK/Kosovo), on 22 August 2007 for Croatia, on 24 October 2007 for Serbia, and on 22 November 2007 for Bosnia and Herzegovina. Thus, full implementation of CEFTA 2006 started at the end of 2007. The Agreement substituted all the bilateral agreements previously applied in the region and ended the original CEFTA when its parties joined the EU (with the exception of Croatia and the FYR of Macedonia) .[30.]

27. The CEFTA 2006 Agreement aims to progressively establish a free-trade area among its parties by 31 December 2010 at the latest. It covers trade in agricultural and industrial products as well as services. Trade in industrial products was liberalized on 31 December 2008. For agricultural goods, special preferential concessions are granted by each of the eight parties. Further concessions in agriculture were negotiated in 2009, including tariff quotas. Other issues covered by the Agreement include: sanitary and phytosanitary measures; technical barriers to trade; customs cooperation; competition policy; trade remedies; investment; government procurement and intellectual property rights. Moreover, the parties have agreed that in the event of any eligible party becoming a member of the EU, that party will withdraw from the Agreement. Croatia has been designated as depositary.[31]

(iii) Free-trade agreement with the European Free Trade Association (EFTA)

28. The EFTA-Croatia Free Trade Agreement was signed on 21 June 2001 and entered into force with Norway on 1 April 2002, Iceland on 1 August 2002, and Liechtenstein and Switzerland on 1 September 2002.[32] The Agreement covers trade in industrial products, including fish and other marine products, although bilateral agricultural agreements have also been concluded between individual EFTA states and Croatia.[33] Imports into Croatia for all industrial products originating in the EFTA states were fully liberalized after the expiry of the transitional period on 1 January 2007. The agreement also contains provisions on sanitary and phytosanitary measures; technical barriers to trade; trade remedies; services; protection of intellectual property rights; government procurement; competition; and investment.[34]

(iv) Free-trade agreement with Turkey

29. Croatia signed a free-trade agreement with Turkey on 13 March 2002; it entered into force on 1 July 2003 with a transitional period until 1 January 2007. The liberalization has been carried out asymmetrically, with Turkey liberalizing at a faster rate. The agreement covers both agricultural and non-agricultural goods; about 87% of all tariff lines for both parties; and 86% of total Turkish exports to Croatia and 99% of total Croatian exports to Turkey.[35] For agricultural goods, special preferential concessions are granted by both parties in the form of tariff quotas. For non-agricultural goods, Turkey eliminated tariffs on Croatian exports from the outset, while Croatia completed the elimination of its tariffs on Turkish exports in 2007. Moreover, the agreement includes provisions, *inter alia*, related to standards, state monopolies, safeguard measures, competition policy, public procurement, trade in services, and intellectual property rights.[36]

(v) Other preferential trade arrangements

30. Croatia does not grant autonomous preferences, but goods originating in Croatia benefit from the Generalized System of Preferences (GSP) in: Australia, Belarus, Canada, Japan, Kazakhstan, New Zealand, Russian Federation, Ukraine, and the United States.

31. Croatia is not a member of the Agreement on the Global System of Trade Preferences (GSTP) among developing countries.

(4) INVESTMENT REGIME

32. The investment regime in Croatia is mainly regulated under the Companies Act (OG 111/93, as amended), and the Investment Promotion Act (OG 138/06) in force since 2007. The Companies Act sets out the prerequisites and status of foreign investors.

33. In 2002, the Trade and Investment Promotion Agency (APIU) was established as the government agency responsible for assisting both foreign and domestic investors.[38] In order to speed up and simplify the procedures of establishing a company and to eliminate red tape, the government service HITRO.HR was established in May 2005. HITRO.HR has more than 60 offices and enables an investor to establish a company in less than eight working days.[39] In addition, the Investment and Export Promotion Directorate in MELE is involved in developing investment promotion and export strategies in, *inter alia*, free zones and industrial zones, and technological parks with the aim of improving the business environment (Chapter I(3)(ii)), and increasing in domestic and foreign investments to foster regional development and growth of Croatia's economy.

34. Foreign legal entities and persons may invest capital on a contractual basis; in a company; in a bank or insurance business; start a craft business or act as sole traders; obtain a concession to exploit natural resources to perform works or to provide services; and participate in build-operate-transfer (BOT) and build-own-operate-transfer (BOOT) deals. According to the authorities, at end October 2009 there were 148,611 companies registered in Croatia, 7.7% (11,401) of which were 100% owned by foreign investors.

35. Under Croatian legislation, a foreign investor is defined as any foreign national or legal person with a registered seat outside Croatia. He/she may establish, or participate in the establishment of a company and may acquire rights and/or obligations like any domestic investor.[40] In addition, the Constitution provides several guarantees for foreign investors, including that all rights acquired by the investment of capital cannot be restricted by law or any other legal act, and that foreign investors are guaranteed free transfer and repatriation of the profit and invested capital.[41] Inward portfolio investment is not restricted, except for central bank short-term securities in the primary market. On real estate property rights, foreign investors have the same rights, obligations, and legal status as domestic investors, provided the condition of reciprocity is met (except for EU Member States) .[42]

36. Some activities are subject to specific requirements, such as a special certificate of approval, licence or other document issued by the relevant government body or institution.[43] These activities include: banking, insurance, air and road transport, production of and trade in tobacco and tobacco products, most energy activities, and telecommunication services (Table AII.1) . Moreover, some state-owned enterprises (SOEs) operate under *de jure* monopoly or hold exclusive rights, including Hrvatske sume (Croatian State Forests), Croatian Railways Hrvatske Zeljeznice (HŽ), and Hravatska posta (Croatian Post), while some recently privatized companies still operate as *de facto* monopolies, such as the electricity company Hrvatska elektroprivreda (HEP) and the oil and gas company Industrija nafte (INA) (Chapter I(1)) .

For additional analytical, marketing, investment and business opportunities information, please contact Global Investment & Business Center, USA (202) 546-2103. Fax: (202) 546-3275. E-mail: rusric@erols.com

37. Under the Investment Promotion Act, various investment incentive schemes benefit both foreign and domestic investors and include tariff and tax concessions (Chapter III(4)(i)) . No special incentives are available only to foreign or national investors.

38. Croatia has signed 57 bilateral investment agreements[44], and 50 treaties on double taxation.[45]

39. Croatia participates in several investment-related conventions, including those under the International Centre for Settlement of Investment Disputes (ICSID), and the Multilateral Investment Guarantee Agency (MIGA) .

(5) AID FOR TRADE

40. Croatia received average annual trade-related aid flows of US$54.2 million during 2002-05.

[46] Most of this aid has benefited the economic infrastructure, particularly transport and storage; communications and energy supply and generation; as well as tourism.[47]

41. As an EU candidate country, Croatia received EU financial aid of €138.5 million in 2007 and €146 million in 2008, under the Instrument for Pre-accession Assistance (IPA) . It is implemented under decentralized management according to the five IPA components available to candidate countries: institution building; cross-border cooperation; regional development; human resources development; and agriculture and rural development[48]. Croatia also receives bilateral development assistance from Belgium[49], Denmark[50], France, Germany[51], Italy[52], the Netherlands, Norway, Sweden, and the United Kingdom.[53]

42. During 1992-2008, Croatia benefited from technical assistance programmes provided by USAID, worth more than US$320 million. These programmes, *inter alia*, facilitated economic and fiscal reform; strengthened democratic institutions; created agribusiness programmes; established a wide range of professional training; and supported Croatia's process of negotiations for EU and NATO membership. Croatia has also received assistance from Japan.[54]

43. Croatia is currently transforming itself from an aid-recipient country to a donor country. During the past decade, Croatia has been providing development assistance to Bosnia and Herzegovina in the areas of reconstruction, health, and education. Croatia has also made voluntary contributions to the UN, international organization and peacekeeping operations, including training and development projects, as well as contributions to civil society organizations. In the future, Croatia's trade-related technical assistance will be mainly directed to south eastern Europe, to transfer its experience in areas such as economic transition (creation of conditions for a market economy) and accession to the EU.[55] Croatia will also try to help countries most in need, such as LDCs, in attaining their Millennium Development Goals.

TRADE POLICIES AND PRACTICES BY MEASURE

(1) MEASURES DIRECTLY AFFECTING IMPORTS

(i) Registration and documentation

1. All natural and legal persons, both domestic and foreign, wishing to engage in business activities in Croatia must establish a company in accordance with the Companies Act (OG 111/93, as amended) . The process takes place in the Commercial Court where companies must register before commencing activities.[2] Technical assistance may be provided, free of charge, by HITRO.HR, a "single access point" (Chapter II(4)) .[3] Under the Companies Act, companies can either be based on capital (private and public limited companies) or as a partnership (general and limited partnerships and economic interest associations) . The Act also regulates the establishment of branch offices and sole traders.

2. All companies performing a trade activity are registered in the same court register. However, the Ministry of the Economy, Labour and Entrepreneurship (MELE) maintains a special registry for exporters and importers of military goods, and providers of services to the military in accordance with the Act on the Export and Import of Military and Non-Military Lethal Goods (OG 86/08) . Companies maye also record their activity in the company's incorporation act.[4] For craft activities, natural persons must be registered in the Crafts registry in their respective county or city of Zagreb office.[5] In principle, there is no requirement that would make importation conditional upon the existence of an agent or representative established in Croatia.

3. Companies seeking to trade in certain "sensitive goods" (e.g. arms and ammunition, explosives, medicinal products and medical devices, chemicals, nuclear materials, tobacco and tobacco products, energy, and cultural heritage items) are required to submit to the Court an approval or other certificate for performing such activities, issued by the competent authority, before their incorporation (Chapter II(4)) . Following their incorporation with a commercial court, companies are eligible to apply for import and export licences for these products. The agency for medicinal products and medical devices issues licences and authorizations only to the legal entities after incorporation of the company.

4. While electronic signatures are recognized in Croatia, all customs documents must be submitted on paper/in writing, which make them legally binding. The customs declaration is to be lodged by the importer on the Single Administrative Document (SAD) form.[6] In addition to the SAD, introduced in 2000, Customs require the bill of lading (or air waybill for air cargo shipments), certificate of origin, commercial invoice, import licence (if applicable), health certificate (food, plants, animals), and certificate of conformity. Croatia does not require consular authentication or registration of customs documents in the country of origin.[7] Goods are released as soon as the customs declaration has been verified or accepted without verification. Over 2.5 million customs declarations are processed annually.[8]

5. All fees charged by Croatian Customs were abolished in December 2008. The Customs Administration, under the Ministry of Finance, used to charge a customs fee of HRK 10 and an administrative fee of HRK 50. The customs fee, levied upon the submission of a customs declaration, was used for the development and modernization of Croatia's Customs.[9] The administrative fee was charged for the customs declaration and the calculation of import duties for goods carried by passengers. For export customs declarations, 20% of the export value was charged.[10]

(ii) Customs procedures and valuation

6. The Customs Administration is in charge of 189 border crossings and 53 customs offices. The main legal statutes of the customs regime are the Customs Act (OG 78/99 as amended); the Regulation implementing the Customs Act (OG 161/03, as amended); and the Rules on the use of forms for implementation of the Customs Act (OG 176/03) (Table II.1) .

For additional analytical, marketing, investment and business opportunities information, please contact Global Investment & Business Center, USA
(202) 546-2103. Fax: (202) 546-3275. E-mail: rusric@erols.com

7. Goods brought into the customs territory of Croatia can be placed under various customs regimes: release of goods for free circulation; transit; customs warehousing; inward processing; processing under customs control; temporary admission; outward processing; exportation; free zone or free warehouse; and re-export from the customs territory. The goods may also be destroyed or abandoned.

8. Goods cannot be released until the customs debt is paid, unless a security is provided, either by depositing cash or a guarantee (including third-party guarantee) with Customs. The customs debt is payable within ten days, after which interest is charged; in some cases, it may be paid after ten days, subject to the amount of debt including interest being secured.

9. Customs controls, apart from on-the-spot checks, are based on risk analysis using automatic data processing methods, based on criteria developed in Croatia and, where appropriate, at the international level. Risk assessment in Croatia is based on three channels: the red channel for high risk goods which need to be examined; the yellow channel for medium risk goods, which require additional documentation, and on which a decision is made whether to release or examine the goods; and the green channel, where there are no risks and goods are released immediately without any checks. An information technology (IT) system for the implementation of risk management has been in operation in all customs offices since 22 January 2008. Nonetheless, Croatia's customs administration still has limited in-house capacity to guarantee its IT services, and remains dependent on external companies.[12]

10. The Act amending the Customs Act (OG 140/05) introduced the system of granting "authorized economic operator" status[13] or authorized traders status. The Customs Administration central office, in cooperation with other competent bodies may grant the status to any economic operator registered in Croatia's customs territory; however, the system is not yet operational.[14]

11. Customs tariff classification may take place prior to importation (binding tariff information (BIT)), upon declaration (on the SAD) or after importation (in case of post-clearance verification) .[15] Decisions by Customs on the application of customs regulations can be appealed within 15 days at the headquarters of the Customs Administration (Article 7 of the Customs Act) . The holder of a BTI has the right to submit an appeal to the Ministry of Finance (Autonomous Service for Second Instance Administrative Procedures) through the Customs Administration headquarters, within 15 days of receiving the tariff information.[16] Final decisions can be contested before an Administrative Court.[17] The Customs Administration issues binding advance rulings in respect of tariff classification and origin of goods, upon receipt of written requests from any interested person. In general, an advance ruling is valid for six years for tariff classification and three years for origin issues.[18] During 2004-08, around 150 classification-related disputes and 124 valuation-related disputes were settled in court.

12. Valuation matters are set out in Articles 29 to 48 of the Customs Act and Articles 66-93 of the Regulation Implementing the Customs Act.[19] Valuation is defined as the value of goods for the purpose of levying *ad valorem* customs duty on imported goods.[20] The customs value of imported goods is the "transaction value". If the customs value cannot be determined on the basis of the transaction value, alternative valuation methods are used in the sequence prescribed by the Agreement on Implementation of Article VII of the GATT 1994 (Customs Valuation Agreement) .[21] Customs must, upon the request of the importer, issue a written notification as to the level of the customs value and the method of its determination (Article 89.2 of the Regulation implementing the Customs Act) .[22] Croatia uses the c.i.f. basis for valuation.[23] According to the authorities, Croatia maintains reference prices on an *ad hoc*

basis, but these are not official. Croatia does not use simplified procedures for the valuation of fresh fruits and vegetables.[24]

13. Croatia does not have laws or regulations relating to pre-shipment inspection.

14. Croatia is a member of the World Customs Organization (WCO) and is a signatory of the International Convention on the Harmonized Commodity Description and Coding System (HS)

(iii) Rules of origin

15. Croatia applies non-preferential and preferential rules of origin. The non-preferential rules are contained in Articles 23 to 27 of the Customs Act, under which origin is assigned to the country where the product was wholly obtained or where it underwent its last substantial, economically justified processing. The Croatian Chamber of Commerce is authorized to issue "proof of origin" for non-preferential origin. Special rules are prescribed for textile products and some other products.

16. Preferential rules of origin are contained in the preferential trade agreements to which Croatia is a party, i.e. the Stabilization and Association Agreement, CEFTA 2006, EFTA, and Turkey (Chapter II(3)) . Croatia applies the same rules of origin to all its partners in such preferential agreements. Croatia is still not included in the Pan-Europe-Med system of diagonal cumulation of origin.

(iv) Tariffs, other duties, and taxes

(a) MFN applied tariff structure

17. Goods imported into Croatia may be subject to customs duties excise duties, and value-added tax (VAT); a stamp tax was abolished in 2008 (section (i) above) . Croatia's tariff has been aligned with the Combined Nomenclature (CN) of the EU since 2002[28]; it has 10,559 lines (Table III.1) . Croatia's tariff comprises *ad valorem* rates on 9,920 lines (93.9% of total lines, up from 87.9% in 2000), and non-*ad valorem* rates (specific, mixed, and compound), which apply to 639 agricultural lines (6.1% of the total) .[29] *Ad valorem* tariffs are applied on the c.i.f. customs value. Specific duties are levied on 45 lines, including cheese, cane or beet sugar, and grape vines in containers greater than 2 litres. Mixed (alternate) duties apply to 478 lines (4.5% of the total), such as live animals, meat, dairy products, and preparations of meat. Compound duties (i.e. a combination of *ad valorem* and specific tariffs) are levied on 116 lines (e.g. meat, edible vegetables, edible fruits, and nuts) .

18. Since its accession to the WTO, Croatia has reduced its applied MFN tariff. The simple average MFN tariff declined from 12.1% in 2000 to 7.1% in 2009.[30] The coefficient of variation, of 1.4, reveals high dispersion of the tariff rates, which range from zero to 279.8%. The modal (most frequent) rate is zero (Chart III.1) . The number of duty-free items jumped from 505 in 2000 (7.2% of the total) to 4,443 in 2009 (42.1%; i.e. 16.1% of WTO agricultural tariff lines and 50.2% of WTO non-agricultural tariff lines) . These include products under the Information Technology Agreement (ITA) and the Agreement on Trade in Civil Aircraft, as well as pharmaceuticals, paper, iron and steel, non-ferrous metals, wood, furniture, toys, and certain categories of live animals. Cider apple, in bulk, from 16 September to 15 December is subject to the highest tariff rate (an AVE) of 279.8% (Table AIII.1) .[31] Tariff quotas (on agricultural products) are applied to 0.7% of total tariff lines (Table III.2) .

Table III.2

Structure of the MFN tariff (Per cent)

		Applied	Bound
1.	Bound tariff lines (% of all tariff lines)	n.a.	100.0
2.	Duty-free tariff lines (% of all tariff lines)	42.1	23.4
3.	Non-ad valorem tariffs (% of all tariff lines)	6.1	6.3
4.	Tariff quotas (% of all tariff lines)	0.7	0.7
5.	Non-ad valorem tariffs with no AVEs (% of all tariff lines)	0.1	5.3
6.	Simple average tariff rate	7.1	8.5
	Agricultural products (WTO definition)[a]	16.3	17.4
	Non-agricultural products (WTO definition)[b]	4.2	5.7
	Agriculture, hunting, forestry, and fishing (ISIC 1)	10.8	12.0
	Mining and quarrying (ISIC 2)	2.9	6.1
	Manufacturing (ISIC 3)	6.8	8.2
7.	Domestic tariff "spikes" (% of all tariff lines)[c]	7.1	6.0
8.	International tariff "peaks" (% of all tariff lines)[d]	10.7	11.4
9.	Overall standard deviation of applied rates	9.9	9.5
10.	"Nuisance" applied rates (% of all tariff lines)[e]	1.0	1.5

n.a. Not applicable.
a WTO Agreement on Agriculture definitions.
b Excluding petroleum.
c Domestic tariff spikes are defined as those exceeding three times the overall simple average applied rate.
d International tariff peaks are defined as those exceeding 15%.
e Nuisance rates are those greater than zero, but less than or equal to 2%.
Source: WTO Secretariat calculations, based on data provided by the Croatian authorities.

19. Using the WTO definition[32], MFN applied tariffs average 16.3% on agricultural products and 4.2% on non-agricultural goods (Table III.3) . On the basis of ISIC (Revision 2) definition, the average MFN tariff in agriculture (10.8%) is higher than in manufacturing (6.8%) and in mining and quarrying (2.9%) . Chart III.2 shows the MFN tariff distribution by ISIC sector.

20. Upon its accession to the EU, Croatia will have to adopt the EU common external tariff and its bound rates.[33]

21. In aggregate, Croatia's applied MFN tariff displays mixed escalation: negative from first-stage processed goods with an average tariff rate of 8.2% to semi-finished products on which tariffs average 2.7%, and positive from the latter to finished goods (9%) . Further disaggregation reveals that tariff escalation is positive in some manufacturing industries, with escalation more pronounced in food and beverages, followed by textiles and apparel, thereby providing higher levels of effective protection to those industries than that reflected by the nominal rates (Chart III.3) .

(b) MFN bound tariffs

22. Upon its accession to the WTO, Croatia bound all its tariff lines at a final simple average rate of 8.5% (against a simple average applied MFN rate of 7.1% in 2009), ranging from zero (e.g. on products under the ITA) to 60% (e.g. on coffee, tea, and sugar) . It bound its tariff lines on agricultural products (WTO definition), at a final simple average rate of 17.4% (compared with a simple average applied MFN rate of 16.3%); the final simple average bound tariff rate for non-agricultural goods is 5.7% (simple average applied MFN rate of 4.2%) .

For additional analytical, marketing, investment and business opportunities information, please contact Global Investment & Business Center, USA (202) 546-2103. Fax: (202) 546-3275. E-mail: rusric@erols.com

23. In its Schedule CXLVII, Croatia bound tariff quotas for agricultural products (HS in parentheses): (i) meat of bovine animals (0201 and 0202); (ii) meat of bovine animals, and boneless, high quality meat (0201.30 and 0202.30); (iii) meat of swine, fresh, chilled or frozen (0203.29); (iv) wheat and meslin (1001.90); (v) raw sugar (1701.1); (vi) cane sugar (1701.11); (vii) other refined cane or beet sugar (1701.991); (viii) filled chocolate and other food preparations (1806.31); and (ix) chocolate and other food preparations not filled (1806.32) .

(c) Tariff preferences

24. Croatia has preferential trading agreements with 39 partners: the EU-27, the other seven parties of CEFTA 2006, the four EFTA states, and Turkey (Chapter II(3)) . Trade under these preferential agreements represented 76.9% of Croatia's total exports and imports in 2008 (Table II.3), 86.3% of exports and 72.5% of imports. Non-agricultural products (WTO definition) are generally granted duty-free treatment, and agricultural products are duty-free or carry reduced rates of duty, often under tariff quotas. The average preferential tariff (on all products) under these agreements ranges from zero (under the agreements with Bosnia and Herzegovina and UNMIK/Kosovo all tariffs are duty-free) to 4.2% (under the agreement with Turkey) (Table III.4) .

25. Under Croatia's trade agreements, tariff preferences on agricultural products range from abolition/reduction of duties for unlimited quantities, to reduced or abolished duties within tariff quotas (Chapter IV(1)(ii)) . Licences are used to administer such tariff quotas (section (v) below) . Croatia does not apply preferential tariff quotas to non-agricultural products.

26. Croatia does not grant autonomous preferences, but goods originating in Croatia benefit from the Generalized System of Preferences (GSP) in nine trade partners (Chapter II(3)(v)) .

27. Certain products may be subject to excise duties and VAT in addition to customs tariffs. Croatia does not levy any surcharges on imports. The legislation on excise duties is laid down in a number of acts per product category (Table II.1), as well as in implementing regulations.[34] Excise duties are levied on: coffee; tobacco and tobacco products; alcoholic beverages; non-alcoholic beverages; beer (alcoholic and non-alcoholic); passenger cars, motorcycles, vessels, and aircraft; mineral oils; and luxury products (Table III.5) .

Table III.5 Excise duties

Products	Tax rate (HRK and/or percentage)
Coffee (per kg, net weight)	
Raw coffee (with or without caffeine)	5.0
Roasted coffee (with or without caffeine)	12.0
Coffee skin and pulp	15.0
Coffee substitutes containing coffee, extracts, essences, concentrates and preparations based on coffee-based extracts, essences or concentrates	20.0
In ready-made beverages that contain coffee, extract, essence or concentrate of coffee (decaffeinated too) in water, milk or the like, with or without additions	5-20 depending on the percentage of coffee in 1 kg net weight of the product
Non-alcoholic beverages (per hl)	40.0
Alcoholic beer (per hl)	200.0

For additional analytical, marketing, investment and business opportunities information, please contact Global Investment & Business Center, USA
(202) 546-2103. Fax: (202) 546-3275. E-mail: rusric@erols.com

Non-alcohol beer (up to 0.5% of absolute alcohol) (per hl)	60.0
Alcohol and alcoholic beverages (per litre absolute alcohol)	60.0
Alcohol in wine and fruit wine (per litre absolute alcohol)	0.0
Tobacco products	
Cigarettes[a] (1,000 pieces/% of the retail price)	180 per 1,000 pieces and 30% of the retail price
Other tobacco products	
Pipe, smoking, snuff, chewing tobacco, and other tobacco products	38.0 per 1,000 grams
Cigars	1.1 per piece
Cigarillos	4.4 per 20 pieces pack
Passenger cars and motorcycles[b, c], vessels and aircraft[c]	
0-50,000	13%
50,000-100,000	6,500 + 18% on amount over 50,000
100,000-150,000	15,500 + 23% on amount over 100,000
150,000-200,000	27,000 + 28% on amount over 150,000
200,000-250,000	41,000 + 33% on amount over 200,000
250,000-300,000	57,500 + 38% on amount over 250,000
300,000-350,000	76,500 + 43% on amount over 300,000
350,000-400,000	98,000 + 48% on amount over 350,000
400,000-450,000	122,000 + 53% on amount over 400,000
450,000-500,000	148,500 + 58% on amount over 450,000
> 500,000	177,500 + 63% on amount over 500,000
Motor petrol (MB 98 and MB 86) and other kinds of leaded petrol irrespective of octane value and commercial name	2.40
Motor petrol (BMB-98, BMB-95, and BMB-91) and other kinds of unleaded petrol irrespective of octane value and commercial name	1.65
Diesel fuel (D1, D2, D3) and other kinds of diesel fuel irrespective of commercial name	1.0
Eurodiesel, diesel fuel coloured with a blue dye	0.0
Heating oil, extra light and special light (EL, LS)	0.3
Mineral oils (per kg, net weight)	
All kinds of heating oil, light, medium, and heavy	0.0
Jet fuel and aviation fuel	0.0
Liquefied petroleum gas (LPG)	0.1
All kinds of paraffin	1.4
Luxury products[d]	30% of sale price (without VAT)

a According to the Law on Tobacco, cigarettes are classified as: A (popular group), B (standard group), and C (extra group) .

b Excise duties on passenger cars, on passenger cars with rotary motions of the pistons and on motorcycles that are not deemed to be new are increased by 50% and for passenger cars with a cylinder capacity of over 1,600 cm^3 and for motorcycles with a cylinder capacity of over 250 cm^3 by 100%. Excise duties shall not be paid on electric passenger cars and motorcycles.

c The taxation base is the duty-inclusive customs value for imports, and the sale price (without VAT) for locally produced goods.

d The following are considered luxury products: (i) jewellery and similar products (cultured pearls, worked (except for strung, framed and mounted); non-industrial diamonds, worked, unframed and un-mounted; precious stones, worked, except for simply sawn and roughly shaped (except for diamonds); jewellery and parts of jewellery of precious metals including those coated or plated with precious metals; goldsmiths' or filigree makers' products and parts of them of silver including those coated or plated with precious metals; goldsmiths' and filigree makers' products of precious metals; goldsmiths' and filigree makers' products and parts of them of common metals coated or plated with precious metals; products of precious metals coated or plated with precious metals; products of natural or cultured pearls; and coins minted for special occasions, including gold coins (that is not legal tender), and numismatic coins; (ii) clocks and watches (clock and watches wrist, pocket and other personal watches, with a casing or strap of precious metal or of metal coated with precious metals, straps or bracelets for wrist watches or parts for straps and bracelets of precious metals or of metals plated with precious metals or of metals that have been gilt or silvered); (iii) clothing and footwear of fur and reptile skins; (iv) miscellaneous (ivory, tortoiseshell, coral, mother of pearl, worked, and made of these materials, cigarette lighters (mechanical or electrical), pocket, table and others of precious metals; and (v) pyrotechnic products for fireworks, revolvers and pistols, hunting shotguns, including combination shotguns and carbines.

Source: Information provided by the Croatian authorities.

28. Excise duties are levied on both imported and domestically produced goods.

[35] The taxation base is the duty-inclusive customs value for imports, and the sale price (without VAT) for locally produced goods. For imports, the excise duty is assessed and collected by the customs office at the same time as customs duties. In general, taxpayers self-assess the amount for locally produced goods, and pay within 30 days. However, the duty on luxury products is to be paid within 10 days after the end of the calendar month in which the tax debt was incurred. Imported goods (of foreign origin) stored in free zones are not subject to excise duty. The tax debt arises at the moment of supply of the products from the free zones into the customs territory of Croatia.

29. Since its accession to the WTO, Croatia has introduced new legislation on excise duties in order to harmonize them with the *acquis*. A new Excise Duty Act, which will enter into force on 1 January 2010, aims at further aligning Croatia's legislation with the *acquis*, primarily on: general arrangements for products subject to excise duty; general rules for producing, holding, and monitoring these products under excise-duty-suspension arrangements; and with other EC directives regulating the excise taxation system for alcohol and alcoholic beverages (including beer), tobacco products, and energy products and electricity.

For additional analytical, marketing, investment and business opportunities information, please contact Global Investment & Business Center, USA (202) 546-2103. Fax: (202) 546-3275. E-mail: rusric@erols.com

30. Under the VAT Act (OG 47/95 as amended) and relevant Ordinances, three VAT rates apply on domestic and imported goods and services: 23% (general rate)[36]; 10% (accommodation services; agency commissions for such services; and newspapers and magazines with the exception of those that contain advertisements or serve advertising purposes); and zero (all types of bread and milk; professional, scientific, artistic, cultural and educational books, schoolbooks, and scientific journals; certain medicines and orthopaedic aids; and services of the public screening of films) .

31. VAT on imported goods is assessed and collected by the Customs Administration. Until 31 December 2009, VAT is applied on the customs value of imports plus customs tariffs, and excise duties if applicable. As from 1 January 2010, the taxable amount includes the following factors, in so far that they are not already included in the value for customs purposes: customs duties, excise duties, levies and similar charges paid at importation of goods, excluding VAT and expenses, such as commission, packing, transport and insurance costs, incurred up to the first place of destination within Croatia.[37] VAT is applied on the sale price on locally produced goods.

32. Croatia has three types of VAT exemptions: inland exemptions, import exemptions, and export exemptions (section (2)(iv) below) . Inland institutions and services subsectors that are exempt from VAT on the supply of goods and services are listed in Articles 11 and 11(a) of the Amendment of the Value Added Tax Act (OG 87/09, in force from 1 January 2010) and includes: supply of universal postal services and of goods incidental thereto; hospital and medical care and closely related services supplied by bodies in health institutions governed by public law; services supplied by groups of persons whose activities are exempt from or are not subject to VAT; insurance and reinsurance transactions; and the granting, negotiation and management of credit. In addition, renting of residential premises is exempt from VAT; and the sale of real estate constructed before 1 January 1998 is not subject to VAT.

33. VAT exemptions on imports are listed in Article 12 of the Amendment of the Value Added Tax Act (OG 87/09) and include: final imports of goods of which the supply by a taxable person would in all circumstances be exempted within the territory of Croatia; imports of personal luggage, non-commercial goods carried by travellers from abroad, as stipulated by customs regulations; and household goods imported by natural persons moving into Croatia, under the conditions stipulated by customs regulations[38]; imports of consignments from abroad not exceeding HRK 160 under the conditions stipulated by customs regulations[39]; imports of goods under diplomatic and consular arrangements, which qualify for exemption from customs duties; and imports of goods by international organizations recognized by Croatia and by members of such organizations under the conditions stipulated by the international conventions establishing the organizations or by headquarters agreements.

34. Under the Waste Act (OG 178/04, 111/06, 60/08 and 87/09) and the Basel Convention, domestic enterprises dealing with waste and hazardous waste are subject to an administrative tax of HRK 1,000 at the moment of issuance of the licence for waste management by the competent authority. The licence is valid for up to five years.

35. Upon its accession to the WTO, Croatia bound other duties and charges at zero.

(e) Duty and tax concessions

36. Article 187 of the Customs Act provides for general exemptions from customs duties and taxes for:

For additional analytical, marketing, investment and business opportunities information, please contact Global Investment & Business Center, USA (202) 546-2103. Fax: (202) 546-3275. E-mail: rusric@erols.com

(i) goods determined compulsory by international agreements;

(ii) goods of non-commercial nature brought in by travellers;

(iii) goods sent from abroad free of charge by natural persons to natural persons in Croatia, of non-commercial nature, as prescribed; (iv) medals and awards obtained at international events and gifts received in the framework of international relationships;

(v) goods for basic human needs, such as food, medicaments, clothes, or bedding, imported by humanitarian organizations for distribution to jeopardized persons and victims of natural and other disasters;

(vi) humanitarian organizations and associations for blind, deaf, and hearing impaired persons, and for persons with muscular and neuromuscular diseases - specific equipment, apparatus and instruments, as well as spare parts and expendable materials not manufactured in Croatia;

(vii) trade marks, patents, models and accompanying documents and forms for acknowledging patents or innovations, sent to organizations for the protection of royalties and industrial property;

(viii) certain objects[41];

(ix) agricultural, cultivation, stock-breeding, forestry, and bee-keeping yields produced on the property of Croatian citizens living in the border zone, having possessions in the border zone of the neighbouring country;

(x) equipment for the prevention and extinction of fires, not manufactured in Croatia and not the subject of cooperation ventures of Croatian manufacturers; (xi) items imported, for reasons of relocation, by physical persons

(xii) items on business inventories, of persons relocating to Croatia;

(xiii) items inherited abroad; (xiv) goods used for repair, maintenance and restoration of protected cultural monuments; (xv) goods to be used directly in the operation of museums, archives, restoration activities, libraries, fine art activities, musical/drama activities, etc.;

(xvi) goods, in the form of a donation to cultural institutions and other non-profit legal persons; and (xvii) researchers, writers and artists own pieces of work created abroad; (xviii) passenger cars for personal use by disabled persons[43]; (xix) engine fuels and lubricants contained in factory built-in tanks of road motor vehicles and in special containers; (xx) items related to a commercial activity (samples for commercial promotion, objects intended for examination, analysis, and testing, and auxiliary material for the protection of goods or care of living animals during transportation); and (xxi) coffins with remains and urns with ashes and other usual decorative funeral items, and goods intended for the construction, maintenance or decoration of cemeteries and monuments to victims of war on the customs territory of Croatia.

37. In addition, a general customs duty exemption applies to fish and other sea-products caught in waters outside the territory of Croatia and imported by ships registered in Croatia and flying the Croatian flag, or products manufactured from such fish on factory ships meeting the registration requirements in Croatia and flying the Croatian colours.[44]

For additional analytical, marketing, investment and business opportunities information, please contact Global Investment & Business Center, USA
(202) 546-2103. Fax: (202) 546-3275. E-mail: rusric@erols.com

38. Croatia also grants duty and tax concessions for free zones and as part of investment incentives (sections (2)(v) and (3)(i) below) .

(v) Import licensing, controls, and prohibitions

39. The importation of some products (e.g. certain animals, plants, narcotics, arms, asbestos and ozone depleting substances) are prohibited for various reasons, such as health, environment, public security and order, cultural heritage or the fulfilment of international obligations, e.g. under the Convention on International Trade in Endangered Species of Wild Fauna and Flora (CITES) . According to the authorities, temporary import prohibitions are also in line with the latest updates on hazardous diseases from the World Organization of Animal Health (OIE) and based on EC legislation for certain diseases (section (vii)(c) below) .

40. Croatia's import (and export) licensing system is regulated by the Trade Act (OG 87/08, 116/08, and 76/09); the Act on Export and Import of Military and Non-Military Lethal Goods (OG 86/08); the Regulation Specifying Goods Subject to Export and Import Licences (OG 6/09 and 73/09); the Regulation on Import and Export Controls for Rough Diamonds (OG 97/03, 142/03, 176/04, 14/06, 90/07, 64/08, and 61/09); and Ordinance on the Cereals Market Organization (OG 75/08, 80/08, 114/08 and 125/08) .

41. Import licensing applies to: (i) products affecting public security, order, health, environment, and cultural heritage (non-automatic)

[45] (Table AIII.2); (ii) rough diamonds (non-automatic); (iii) agricultural products that are subject to tariff quotas (non-automatic); and (iv) cereals (automatic) .

42. Items in the first category of products include: uranium and some electrical machines and apparatus (licence issued by the State Office for Radiation Protection); military goods and non-military lethal goods (e.g. hunting guns, sport guns and components and ammunition), nuclear reactors, and gold (Ministry of Economy, Labour and Entrepreneurship); and telecommunications equipment such as transmitters, radar, radio remote controls and radio navigation instruments (Croatian Post and Electronic Communications Agency) . In addition, some medicinal products and medical devices, cells and tissues used for transplantation, and narcotics require licences from the Ministry of Health and Social Welfare. Licences for medicinal products and medical devices are also required from the Agency for Medicinal Products and Medical Devices.

43. Imports of rough diamonds require a certificate issued by the authorized body of the exporting country and verified by the authorized branch office of the Customs Administration.[46] The Regulation on Import and Export Control for Rough Diamods sets out a system for implementing the Kimberley process certification scheme.[47] A WTO waiver has been granted concerning the Kimberley Process Certification Scheme for Rough Diamonds.[48] According to the authorities, rough diamonds in Croatia are mostly imported for the production of tool grinders.

44. The third licensing regime is used to administer imports of agricultural products that are subject to tariff quotas either on an MFN basis or under Croatia's preferential trade agreements.[49] The Ministry of Agriculture, Fisheries and Rural Development (MAFRD) is responsible for issuing these licences. The fourth regime, also under MAFRD, applies to cereals, with the objective of monitoring trade flows.[50]

For additional analytical, marketing, investment and business opportunities information, please contact Global Investment & Business Center, USA (202) 546-2103. Fax: (202) 546-3275. E-mail: rusric@erols.com

45. The four licensing regimes apply equally to imports from all countries.[51] For agricultural products (except cereals), licences are valid until the end of the calendar year; a licence for cereals is valid for 60 days. In most cases, import licences for non-agricultural products are valid for six months. The validity of any licence (except weapons and narcotics) may be extended upon the request of the licence holder. There are no penalties for the non-utilization of a licence or part of a licence, with the exception of cereals where the penalty for non-utilization is the retention of the deposit lodged at the time of application. Licences are not transferable between importers. An administrative fee is set at HRK 125 for each licence for non-agricultural products, and at HRK 70 for each tariff item number for agricultural products (including cereals) . A deposit or advance payment is required for an import licence for cereals.[52] Applications in respect of non-agricultural products may only be rejected if the importer does not meet the conditions stipulated in international conventions for specific goods or standard criteria for transportation. An importer denied a licence may initiate an administrative dispute before the Administrative Court.[53] As the majority of the tariff quotas are allocated using a pro rata system, if the demand for licences is higher than the available quota, the allocation of quotas is carried out using a coefficient of proportional reduction.[54] Licence application for tariff quotas allocated on a first come, first served system, can be submitted throughout the year; for tariff quotas allocated under a different method, licences applications should be made between 1 and 20 December for the following year's quotas.[55]

(vi) Contingency trade measures

46. Contingency trade remedies are regulated under the Trade Act the Regulation on the Manner and Procedure of Determinating Antidumping and Countervailing Duties (OG 139/04); and the Regulation on Safeguard Measures (OG 73/02 and 33/03) . The competent authority for initiating anti-dumping, countervailing and safeguard investigations is the Ministry of Economy, Labour and Entrepreneurship (MELE) . The decision on initiating an investigation procedure is published in The *Official Gazette*.

47. Since its accession to the WTO in 2000, Croatia has neither imposed nor initiated any anti-dumping or countervailing measures. On 23 June 2009, Croatia imposed a provisional safeguard measure on imports of semi-hard cheese (ementaler, edam, and gouda) and cheese substitutes.[58]

48. Croatia may impose anti-dumping duty on a product imported at less than its normal value and if it has been determined during the investigation procedure implemented by MELE, that it causes or threatens to cause material injury to the domestic production. A countervailing duty may be imposed to eliminate the impact of subsidized imports, that cause or threaten to cause injury. A proposal for imposing anti-dumping or countervailing duties may be submitted by any natural or legal person, or trade company or economic association acting on behalf of domestic production.

49. MELE may impose a provisional duty where preliminary investigation shows that dumping or a subsidy exists and that there is sufficient evidence of injury. Provisional anti-dumping or countervailing duties have a maximum validity of four months; however, under special circumstances, the period may be extended to six or nine months, respectively. A definitive anti-dumping or countervailing duty will expire, at least, five years from its imposition or from the date of its mot recent verification if such verification procedure covers dumping or subsidization and injury. The verification procedure must be concluded within 12 months and, at the latest, within 15 months from the date of its initiation.

50. A safeguard measure may be imposed if particular goods are imported in increased quantities, and if such imports cause or threaten to cause injury to domestic production

For additional analytical, marketing, investment and business opportunities information, please contact Global Investment & Business Center, USA
(202) 546-2103. Fax: (202) 546-3275. E-mail: rusric@erols.com

producing like goods.[59] A proposal for initiating a safeguard investigation may be submitted by any natural or legal person, or economic association acting on behalf of domestic production. Interested parties have the right to be heard during the investigation. The measure may be applied for four years, extendable to eight years in total. A provisional duty not exceeding 200 days may be imposed, in exceptional circumstances, if MELE determines that there is clear evidence the increased imports have caused or are threatening to cause serious injury to the domestic production.

(vii) Standards and other technical requirements

(a) Standardization, testing, and certification

51. Croatia is transposing various elements of the EU technical requirements into its domestic legal system by adopting legislation on, *inter alia*, standardization, accreditation and conformity assessment, and metrology; and by enacting some sector-specific laws, such as on chemicals (REACH) .

[60] Croatia's legal framework includes, *inter alia*, the Accreditation Act (OG 158/03 and 75/09); the Standardization Act (OG 163/03), the Act on Technical Requirements for Products and Conformity Assessment (OG 158/03 and 79/07); the General Product Safety Act (OG 30/09); and the Metrology Act (OG 163/03, 194/03 and 111/07) . It is aimed at increasing the competitiveness and quality of exports; ensuring that they do not harm the environment and that they conform to health and safety norms; and ensuring equal treatment for imported and domestic products.

52. The State Office for Standardization and Metrology (DZNM), under the Ministry of Science, was established in 1991 as the overarching body responsible for metrology, accreditation, standardization, and certification. In July 2005, the functions of standardization, accreditation, and metrology were legally and administratively separated and the DZNM was replaced by four independent institutions. Three were established as public institutions under MELE: the State Office for Metrology (DZM), responsible for legal metrology, pre-packages, precious metals, and type approval of vehicles; the Croatian Standards Institute (HZN), the national standards body and the TBT enquiry point[61]; and the Croatian Accreditation Agency (HAA), the national accreditation body, which supports the implementation of technical legislation in Croatia. The fourth institution, the Croatian Metrology Institute (HMI) is under the Ministry of Science, Education and Sport and deals with scientific and industrial metrology. These institutional changes were also made to comply with the EU conformity assessment and standardization requirements. MELE is responsible for administrative and other activities pertaining to quality infrastructure, including the coordination and development of national policy on standardization, accreditation, conformity assessment and metrology.[62] In addition, the Croatian State Inspectorate (DIRH) is, *inter alia*, in charge of supervising the conformity and safety of certain products.

53. MELE also has overall responsibility for ensuring compliance with Croatia's obligations under the WTO TBT Agreement.[63] Croatia has accepted the Code of Good Practice for the preparation, adoption and application of standards.[64] It has submitted 38 notifications to the TBT Committee (up to September 2009), almost all concerning regulations on metrological requirements. No specific trade concerns have been raised in the Committee regarding Croatia.

54. Croatia's regulations for industrial products are based on the EU's "Old Approach" (laying down detailed specific technical requirements) and the "New and Global Approach" (setting-

up of essential requirements defined to meet health, safety, and environmental objectives) . The technical characteristics of the products are given in the standards (voluntary) drafted by the stakeholders following the procedures of the European standardization organizations. Technical regulations are applied to products for which safety is an issue, such as construction products, medical devices, and particular electrical equipment. These products are subject to testing, certification or prior approval procedures. Technical regulations in Croatia are developed by various Central State Administration Bodies. The heads of these government bodies adopt, according to their competence and scope of activities, technical regulations and determine conformity assessment procedures. All new technical regulations are published in the *Official Gazette*.

55. According to the authorities, new technical regulations or national standards are prepared only when the regulatory authorities consider international standards to be ineffective or inappropriate due to climatic, geographical, or technological factors. In preparing original national standards, and in accordance with Croatia's obligations under the Code of Good Practice for standardization, HZN notifies the new project to the European system (CEN INFOPRO) .[67] Copies of draft national standards may be provided to other WTO Members upon request. The HZN allows all interested parties 60 days to comment on draft national standards. Information on new Croatian standards are published in the HZN bulletin, *HZN Glasilo*.

56. Croatia has continued to harmonize its national standards with international or regional, in particular European, standards. Around 98% of European standards have been adopted as Croatian standards. At end October 2009, 24,226 standards were in force in Croatia, of which 33 were national standards; 20,491 were adopted from European standards (including international standards); and 4,175 were adopted from ISO and/or IEC standards.

57. The Croatian Accreditation Agency (HAA) is responsible for, *inter alia*, accreditation of testing and calibration laboratories, medical laboratories, food quality and safety, accreditation of veterinary inspection bodies, certification and inspection bodies, construction products, lifts and other industrial products, as well as accreditation of certification bodies for Quality Management Systems, Environmental Management Systems and personnel. HAA has granted 157 accreditation certificates; it carries out surveillance on accredited bodies annually. HAA has signed cooperation agreements with the accreditation bodies of Bosnia and Herzegovina, Montenegro, FYR of Macedonia, the Czech Republic, and Hungary.[68] Moreover, HAA has conducted joint training activities and exchange of assessors with Slovenia, and has recently undergone peer evaluation by the European co-operation for Accreditation (EA) for the purpose of signing a mutual recognition agreement (EA MLA) in 2010.

58. Conformity with technical requirements may be certified through a supplier declaration of conformity (first party), or certificate of conformity (third party) . Importers are responsible for aspects covered in the manufacturers' declaration of conformity. Product liability is established through the Civil Obligation Act (OG 35/05), as amended.

59. Pre-market mandatory certification for imported and domestic cosmetics was abolished in October 2008, although foreign test reports may be recognized certain conditions. Since 2008, quality control at the border has been abolished; imports subject to quality control included food and agricultural products, furniture, cement, textiles, and electrical and gas appliances.[69]

60. The Croatian State Inspectorate (DIRH) is, *inter alia*, in charge of supervising the conformity and safety of products placed on the market or used in *inter alia*: machinery, electrical equipment, energy efficiency of household appliances, refrigerators, freezers; lifts, pressure equipment hot water boilers, construction products, metrology, personal protective

For additional analytical, marketing, investment and business opportunities information, please contact Global Investment & Business Center, USA (202) 546-2103. Fax: (202) 546-3275. E-mail: rusric@erols.com

equipment, crystal glass, textiles, and general safety of products, furniture, wood, oil fuels, motor vehicles. There are currently 94 accredited testing laboratories; 32 accredited inspection bodies; and various accredited certification bodies. Market surveillance is carried out by inspectors from the DIRH. The DIRH has recently aligned its methods of operation to EU market surveillance good practice.[70]

61. Separate regulations (technical regulations transposing EU directives) on market surveillance contain a safeguard clause foreseeing the withdrawal of compliant products that are nonetheless found to endanger health and safety. A new regulation has been adopted on the System for Rapid Exchange of Information (RAPEX) on products representing risks for consumer health and safety. The system will take effect upon Croatia's accession to the EU. Market surveillance is financed by the State budget.

62. The Croatian Standards Institute (HZN) is a member of the International Organization of Standardization (ISO), the International Electro-technical Commission (IEC), the European Telecommunications Standards Institute (ETSI), NSO member. HZN was accepted as member of the European Committee for Standardization (CEN) and of the European Committee for Electrotechnical Standardization (CENELEC) in November 2009.[71] Croatia is also a member of the International Atomic Energy Agency (IAEA), the International Organization of Legal Metrology (OIML), the European Collaboration in Legal Metrology (WELMEC), European Collaboration in Measurement Standards (EURAMET), and the Bureau International de Poids et Mesures (BIPM) . Croatia is a signatory to the Metre Convention and the CIPM Mutual Recognition Agreement and the Rotterdam Convention on the Prior Informed Consent Procedure for Certain Hazardous Chemicals and Pesticides in International Trade.

(b) Marking, labelling, and packaging

63. To ensure consumer protection, Article 17 of the Consumer Protection Act (OG 79/07, 125/07, 79/09 and 89/09) prescribes that product information must contain all relevant information needed to help the consumer make an informed decision when buying products. These data must be presented clearly, visibly, and legibly and written in Croatian language and Latin script; other languages and characters easily comprehensible to consumers are not excluded.

64. Labelling, presentation, and advertising of food and nutritional labelling of food is regulated by the Ordinance on labelling, advertising and presentation of food (OG 41/08) and the Ordinance on nutritional labelling of food (OG 29/09), adopted pursuant to the Food Act (OG 46/07 and 155/08) . The Directorate for Food Safety and Quality, under MAFRD, is responsible for drafting and interpreting such regulations as well as for the majority of regulations on food quality for specific categories.

65. Croatia will apply the so-called "C marking" until the use of CE marking becomes mandatory upon accession to the EU or the conclusion of a mutual recognition agreement with the EU. Manufacturers or their authorized representatives registered in Croatia or any natural or legal person who places a product on the market or puts one into service, must affix the conformity marking and guarantee that the product has been designed, constructed and tested in the prescribed manner, that it complies with all applicable technical requirements, and that it has a written declaration of conformity, a test report or a certificate of conformity.[72]

(c) Sanitary and phytosanitary measures

66. Croatia's legal framework on SPS includes: the Food Act[73]; the Veterinary Act (OG 41/07 and 155/08); the Animal Protection Act (OG 135/06); the Sanitary Inspection Act (OG 113/08); the Act on Veterinary Medicinal Products (OG 84/08); the Wine Act (OG No. 96/03); and the Plant Health Act (OG No. 75/05) . In March 2008, Croatia adopted the Strategy for Transposition, Implementation and Enforcement of the *acquis* for Food Safety, Veterinary and Phytosanitary Policy.[74]

67. MAFRD has the overall responsibility for food safety in Croatia and for ensuring compliance with the WTO SPS Agreement. MAFRD has been designated as the central competent authority for food safety, feed safety, and hygiene, as well as the organization of official controls.[75] The Ministry of Health and Social Welfare has competency to ensure food safety in the area of contaminant and pesticide residue control. The Croatian Food Agency (HAH) is responsible for consumer protection and risk assessment; official controls are carried out by MAFRD, the Ministry of Health and Social Welfare, and DIRH.

68. Croatia has three enquiry points, all under MAFRD: the Veterinary Directorate (sanitary matters and animal health), the Veterinary Inspections Directorate (control and inspection of sanitary matters and animal health), and the Directorate of Agriculture and Food Industry (phytosanitary matters and plant protection) . MAFRD is in the process of notifying the WTO SPS Committee of the Veterinary Inspections Directorate (OG 35/08) as its third enquiry point. In addition, the Directorate for Food Safety and Quality, also under MAFRD, functions as the SPS notification authority.

69. WTO Members have raised specific concerns in the SPS Committee regarding Croatia's restrictions on pork imports, and its import ban on live animals and meat products.[76] According to the authorities, Croatia's import restrictions on animals and products of animal origin are in line with EU legislation and OIE recommendations for prevention of occurrence and spread of contagious diseases.[77] No cases of Transmissible Spongiform Encephalopathy (TSE) have been reported in Croatia; a ban on feed from meat and bone meal is in force since 2001. Croatia is free from classical swine fever (CSF) in domestic pigs, without vaccination, but CSF may be present in the wild pig population. Since 3 March 2008, no CSF outbreak has been observed in domestic pigs in Croatia. Croatia has never submitted an emergency notification to the SPS Committee and only one notification concerning new or modified SPS measures.[78]

70. According to the authorities, Croatia's SPS measures are based on international standards, guidelines, and recommendations, and on regulations, decisions, and directives in force in the EU. All SPS measures are based on international standards; and local provinces are not allowed to establish their own SPS measures. SPS measures are given legal effect through national legislation.

71. Official controls of food and feed have to be carried out on the basis of a risk assessment. While the Croatian Food Agency (HAH) is responsible for risk assessment, risk management is the responsibility of the Directorate for Food Safety and Quality, the Veterinary Inspection Directorate, and the Directorate for Agriculture and Phytosanitary Inspection of the MAFRD, the Sanitary Inspection Directorate of the MHSW, and the State Inspectorate. HAH establishes methods for risk assessment in all phases of production, processing, and distribution of food and feed. According to the authorities, the methods used to analyse the risks associated with importation of animals and associated with food are in accordance with the relevant models developed by the OIE. Where such models do not exist, MAFRD determines the measures to be applied in cooperation with the Croatian Veterinary Institute and Veterinary Faculty or other scientific institutions, taking into account scientific evidence in accordance with the SPS Agreement.

For additional analytical, marketing, investment and business opportunities information, please contact Global Investment & Business Center, USA (202) 546-2103. Fax: (202) 546-3275. E-mail: rusric@erols.com

72. The Directorate for Food Safety and Quality is responsible for establishing and managing a Rapid Alert System for Food and Feed known as CRO RASFF at the national level, and has been designated as the RASFF single national contact point for the EU. CRO RASFF aims to ensure rapid data flow within the official control system of food and feed, as well as rapid and effective control activities and measures.[79]

73. The Veterinary Inspections Directorate is responsible for risk management of imports, and for monitoring residues in animal and products of animal origin in imports. It draws up the Annual Monitoring Plan for residues in imported consignments in accordance with the Ordinance on principles governing the organization of veterinary checks on products across the border (OG 132/08) .[80]

74. GMOs are subject to authorization, labelling, and traceability requirements.[81] A register and coding system was established in 2007 and requirements for the traceability and placement on the market of GMOs began in 2008. No labelling is required for products containing traces of GMOs below a 0.9% threshold, provided this s adventitious and technically unavoidable. GMO seeds have not been authorized in Croatia. The Veterinary Directorate draws up the Annual National Residue Monitoring Plan (NRMP) for detecting residues in live animals and animal products.[82] The use of certain beta-agonists and substances having a hormonal or thyrostatic action is prohibited in stock farming.[83]

75. Quality requirements for specific food categories are regulated by specific regulations (e.g. beef, preserved tuna, milk products, and fruit juices) (Table III.6); while 23 categories of products (e.g. live animals, and products of animal origin) are subject to public and animal health controls by veterinary inspectors (Table III.7) . According to the authorities, Croatia has 17 permanent and 9 temporary border veterinary inspection posts. These posts control and inspect live animals, products of animal origin, feed of animal origin, straw and hay, and other items through which contagious diseases may be transmitted or which endanger human and animal health. Animals are subject to veterinary control when imported or in transit and/or welfare control when exported. The border veterinary inspector is responsible for documentary checks as well as identification and physical checks. Imports of live animals or products of animal origin must be accompanied by international veterinary certificates for animal health and public health, indicating, *inter alia*, origin, destination, and mode of transport.

76. Veterinary and sanitary inspection requirements are identical for domestic products and imported. Imports may enter if they are from approved third-country establishments inscribed on a list established by the EU.[84] Imports may also, exceptionally, be approved from non-EU listed establishments if Croatian requirements are met (exceptions currently exist only for heat-treated milk from Bosnia and Herzegovina, FYR of Macedonia, and Serbia) . Croatia has concluded bilateral veterinary agreements with Bosnia and Herzegovina, FYR of Macedonia, and Serbia on, *inter alia*, imports, transit of animal products, and exchange of information. The concept of regionalization (disease or pest-free zones) has not been introduced into Croatia's SPS regime.

Table III.6 Legislation on products subject to quality control, 2009

Product description and relevant legislation
Meat and Meat Products
Ordinance on labelling of beef meat (OG 75/09)

For additional analytical, marketing, investment and business opportunities information, please contact Global Investment & Business Center, USA
(202) 546-2103. Fax: (202) 546-3275. E-mail: rusric@erols.com

Ordinance on quality of beef carcases and half-carcases (OG 2/09, 68/09)

Ordinance on meat products (OG 1/07)

Ordinance on quality of pig carcases and half-carcases (OG 2/09)
Fish, Cray-Fish, Mussels, Sea-Urchins, Frogs, Turtles, Snails, and Related Products

Ordinance on the quality of preserved tuna and bonito (OG 56/09)

Ordinance on the quality of preserved sardines (OG 96/09)
Milk, Dairy Products, and Pure Cultures

Ordinance on quality of fresh raw milk (OG 102/00, 111/00, 74/08)

Ordinance on milk and milk

products (OG 20/09)

Ordinance on edible caseins and caseinates (OG 80/07) .

Ordinance on partly of wholly dehydrated preserved milk for human consumption (OG 80/07)

Ordinance on methods for the analysis and testing of heat-treated milk for direct human consumption (OG 133/07)

Ordinance on cheese and cheese related products (OG 20/09)

Ordinance on methods of sampling and analysis of edible caseins and caseinates (OG 70/09)

Ordinance on methods of sampling and analysis of condensed milk powder intended for human consumption (OG 112/09)
Ice-Cream, Ice-Cream Products, and Frozen Desserts

Ordinance on frozen deserts (OG 20/09)
Fruit, Vegetables, Mushrooms and Related Products

Ordinance on fruit juices and certain similar products intended for human consumption (OG 20/09)

Ordinance on jams, jellies, marmalades, preserves and sweetened chestnut purée (OG 76/06)
Coffee, Coffee Products, and Products Made of Coffee Substitutes

Ordinance on coffee, coffee substitutes and products made of coffee and coffee substitutes (OG 172/04)
Common Salt and Brining Salt

Ordinance on the basic requirements for salt intended for human consumption (OG 15/97)

Grain, Baking Products, Pasta, and Deep Frozen Pasta

The regulation of the quality of grain, baking products, pasta, and deep frozen pasta (OG 53/91)
Biscuits and Biscuit-Related Products

Ordinance on biscuits and biscuit-related products (OG 73/05, 69/08)
Food Oils and Vegetable Fats, Margarine, Mayonnaise and Other Related Products

Ordinance on maximum level of erucic acid in oils and fats (OG 70/08, 86/08)

Ordinance on spreadable fats (OG 89/08)

Ordinance on the basic requirements for food oils and fats, margarine and related products, mayonnaise, sauce, dressing, salads and other products from food oils and fats (OG 39/99, 34/02)
Sugar and Related Products

Ordinance on sugars and methods of analysis of sugars intended for human consumption (OG 39/09)

Ordinance on methods for determining the quality of sugar bought by intervention repurchase (OG 39/09)
Honey and Other Apiary Products

Ordinance on honey (OG 93/09)

Ordinance on the quality of unifloral honey (OG 122/09)
Cocoa Products, Creams, Candies and Related Products

Ordinance relating to cocoa and chocolate products (OG 73/05)

Ordinance on chocolate-related products, cream products and candy products (OG 73/05, 69/08)
Alcoholic Beverages

Wine Act (OG 96/03)

Ordinance on spirit drinks (OG 61/09)

Ordinance on beer and beer with supplements (OG 42/05, 57/05, 69/08)
Natural Mineral, natural spring and table waters

Ordinance on natural mineral and natural spring waters (OG No. 57/09, 85/09)

Ordinance on table waters (OG 92/09)

Source: Information provided by the Croatian authorities.

For additional analytical, marketing, investment and business opportunities information, please contact Global Investment & Business Center, USA (202) 546-2103. Fax: (202) 546-3275. E-mail: rusric@erols.com

Table III.7 Products subject to sanitary measures, 2009

HS	Product description	Measure
01	Live animals	Veterinary regulations
02	Meat and edible meat offal	Veterinary regulations
03	Fish and crustaceans, molluscs and other aquatic invertebrates	Veterinary regulations
04	Dairy products; birds' eggs; natural honey; edible products of animal origin n.e.s. or included	Veterinary regulations
05	Products of animal origin n.e.s. or included	Veterinary regulations
12	Oil seeds and oleaginous fruits miscellaneous grains, seeds and fruit: industrial or medicinal plants: straw and fodder	Veterinary regulations
15	Animal or vegetable fats and oils and their cleavage products; prepared edible fats; animal or vegetable waxes	Veterinary regulations
16	Preparations of meat, of fish or of crustaceans, molluscs or other aquatic invertebrates	Veterinary regulations
17	Sugars and sugar confectionery	Veterinary regulations
19	Preparations of cereals, flour, starch or milk; pastry cooks' products	Veterinary regulations
20	Preparations of vegetables, fruit, nuts, or other parts of plants	
21	Miscellaneous edible preparations	Veterinary regulations
23	Residues and waste from the food industries; prepared animal fodder	Veterinary regulations
28	Products of the chemical or allied industries	Veterinary regulations
30	Pharmaceutical products	Veterinary regulations
31	Fertilizers	Environment and veterinary regulations
35	Albuminoidal substances; modified starches; glues; enzymes	Veterinary regulations
41	Raw hides and skins (other than fur skins) and leather	Veterinary regulations
42	Articles of leather; saddler and harness; travel goods, handbags and similar containers; articles of animal gut (other than silkworm gut)	Veterinary regulations
43	Fur skins and artificial fur; manufactures thereof	Veterinary regulations
51	Wool, fine or coarse animal hair; horsehair yarn and woven fabric	Veterinary regulations
95	Toys, games and sports requisites; parts and accessories thereof	Veterinary regulations
97	Works of art, collectors' pieces and antiques	Veterinary regulations

Source: Information provided by the Croatian authorities.

77. Certain categories of imported plants and plant products are subject to mandatory phytosanitary inspection at the border, where phytosanitary certificates are recognized according to the International Plant Protection Convention (IPPC) standards. In 2008, a plant passport was introduced to improve the internal movement of certain categories of plants and plant products and to align this with EU legislation.[85] Upon EU accession, plant passports issued in Croatia will be valid on the EU market and vice versa. Croatia had bilateral phytosanitary agreements to facilitate trade in plants/plant products with various recently acceded EU member states; due to their accession, these agreements no longer apply. Croatia has, however, import bans on several groups of plants, plant products, and other regulated objects.[86]

For additional analytical, marketing, investment and business opportunities information, please contact Global Investment & Business Center, USA
(202) 546-2103. Fax: (202) 546-3275. E-mail: rusric@erols.com

78. Accreditation of laboratories concerned with SPS measures is undertaken by the Croatian Accreditation Agency. Croatia has approximately 48 laboratories under the purview of the Croatian Institute for Public Health, 8 of which have been accredited. The Croatian Veterinary Institute operates as a reference laboratory for the control of food of animal origin and control of animal diseases. For plant health, the analysis of pesticide residues is carried out by the pesticide department of the Croatian Institute for Public Health (reference laboratory) .[87] Products are tested in the internal market and costs are covered by the state budget.

79. Establishments dealing with food of animal origin (including slaughterhouses, processing facilities, and animal feed factories) must be approved or registered at the Veterinary Directorate, and are subject to veterinary inspections and controls by the Veterinary Inspections Directorate. The adoption of the Food Act and the Veterinary Act has created preconditions for further alignment of Croatian legislation with the *acquis* in the placing on the market of food and feed. According to the authorities, the use of antibiotics in feed is aligned with EU rules. An animal passport, issued by the Croatian Agriculture Agency is required for the internal movement of bovine animals.

80. Croatia is a member of the Codex Alimentarius Commission, the World Organization for Animal Health (OIE), the World Health Organization (WHO), and the International Plant Protection Convention (IPPC) .

(viii) Public procurement

81. Public procurement fell from HRK 44.9 billion in 2007 (14.3% of GDP) to HRK 32.8 billion in 2008 (10.4% of GDP), mainly due to budgetary reductions.[88] MELE is responsible for policy making, coordination, and implementation of the public procurement framework through the Directorate for Public Procurement System; it replaced the Public Procurement Office in March 2008. Other institutions involved are the Ministry of Finance (concessions), the Agency for Public Private Partnership (implementation of Public-Private Partnerships (PPP) projects), and the State Commission for the Supervision of Public Procurement Procedures (independent review body) .[89]

82. Changes have been introduced recently to Croatia's legislative framework for public procurement in order to align domestic provisions with the *acquis* and the WTO Plurilateral Government Procurement Agreement (GPA), to which Croatia is an observer.[90] The legislative framework consists of the Public Procurement Act (OG 110/07 and 125/08), the Concessions Act (OG 125/08); the Act on Public Private Partnerships (OG 129/08), the Act on the State Commission for the Supervision of Public Procurement Procedures (OG 117/03), and related subordinate legislation. In June 2008, Croatia adopted the comprehensive Strategy for the Development of the Public Procurement System, and the Action Plan for its implementation.

83. The Public Procurement Act (PPA), which entered into force on 1 January 2008, regulates public procurement of goods, services, and works, including utilities (water, telecommunications, energy, and transport) . It applies to the central government, local governments, public undertakings (contracting authorities), and utilities (contracting entities) . The regulation on public procurement for defence and security purposes has recently been adopted and published[91], while procurement by public entities abroad, such as embassies and consulates will be regulated by secondary legislation to be adopted in 2010.

84. Under the new PPA, the procedures to award contracts (public works, public goods, and public services) are: (i) open procedures[92]; (ii) restricted procedures[93]; (iii) negotiated procedures (with or without prior publication)[94]; (iv) competitive dialogue[95]; and (v) design

For additional analytical, marketing, investment and business opportunities information, please contact Global Investment & Business Center, USA
(202) 546-2103. Fax: (202) 546-3275. E-mail: rusric@erols.com

contests.[96] The contracting authorities may choose freely between open and restricted procedures. However, the PPA provides for an exhaustive list of cases justifying use of the negotiated procedure with a prior publication of contract notice (e.g. in exceptional cases, when the nature of the purchase does not allow prior overall pricing), and without prior publication of contract notice (e.g. when, for technical or artistic reasons, the contract may be awarded only to a particular operator) . Competitive dialogue is to be used when the contract is particularly complex and cannot be awarded under the open or restricted procedures. Contracting entities (utilities) may choose freely among open, restricted, or negotiated procedure with prior notice.

85. Contracting authorities and entities must follow the procedures stipulated in the PPA. For procurements of lesser values (procurement value, excluding VAT equal to or higher than HRK 300,000 for goods and services and HRK 500,000 for works), they may use open procedures, restricted procedures, negotiated procedures, design contests, framework agreements and electronic auctions in accordance with the conditions laid down in the PPA. Contracting authorities and entities may, but are not obliged to, apply the procedures laid down in the PPA for procurements under HRK 70,000. Contract notices for procurements valued at HRK 70,000 or above must be published in the Electronic Public Procurement Classifieds (EPPC) of the *Official Gazette*[97]. As of January 2010, at least one person involved in the preparation or implementation of public procurement procedures for goods and services valued at HRK 300,000 and for works valued at HRK 500,000 must be certified as a public procurement specialist. In 2008, the value of public procurement contracts published in the EPPC totalled HRK 22.2 billion (Table III.8) .[98]

86. The Concessions Act regulates general conditions, rules, and award and termination procedures, for concessions awarded to domestic and foreign natural and legal persons. Other regulations governing individual related issues in specific areas and activities are applied as *lex specialis*.[99] The Concessions Register has been established within the Ministry of Finance and is fully operational.

87. The Act on Public Private Partnerships, *inter alia*, regulates the implementation (proposing, approving and monitoring) of PPP projects; the rights and obligations of public and private partners in the implementation of contractual and institutionalized PPP models; and the competences of the Agency for Public Private Partnerships. The Strategic Framework for the Development of Public-Private Partnership was adopted in January 2009.[100]

Table III.8 Public procurement contracts by type of procedure[a] ('000 HRK)

	Services	Works	Supplies	Total	(%)
Open	6,101,434	6,802,001	3,943,290	16,846,725	75.95
Restricted	24,873	38,000	26,012	88,884	0.40
Restricted accelerated	1,124	8,383	1,213	10,720	0.05
Negotiated (with prior notice)	81,170	62,246	30,253	173,668	0.78
Negotiated accelerated	13,373	12,737	2,700	28,810	0.13
Negotiated (without prior notice)	1,502,545	1,522,220	1,766,388	4,791,153	21.60
Competitive dialogue	1,923	0	0	1,923	0.01
Design contest	220,472	615	18,285	239,373	1.08

For additional analytical, marketing, investment and business opportunities information, please contact Global Investment & Business Center, USA
(202) 546-2103. Fax: (202) 546-3275. E-mail: rusric@erols.com

Total	7,946,914	8,446,202	5,788,141	22,181,256	100.00

a Published in the Electronic Public Procurement Classifieds.

Source: Information provided by the Croatian authorities.

88. Under the Act on the State Commission for the Supervision of Public Procurement Procedures, the five members of the State Commission are appointed by the Parliament, to guarantee their independence.[101] The State Commission, *inter alia*, decides on appeals procedures governed by the PPA, the Concessions Act and the Act on PPP. The draft of the new Act on the State Commission for the Supervision of Public Procurement Procedures is expected to be adopted early 2010.

89. According to the authorities, no price preferences are given to domestic bidders, and there are no thresholds for the participation of foreigners in tenders.

90. While the revised legislative framework is a significant step in the process of harmonization with EU rules, remaining legislation needs to be adopted and administrative capacity needs to be further improved at all levels (especially regional and local) to promote competition, rational use of public finances, and deficit reduction. The capacity of the procuring entities to apply the public procurement legislation efficiently and transparently needs to be improved, to reduce the potential for irregularities, including fraud and corruption.[102]

(ix) Local-content requirements

91. The authorities indicate that Croatia maintains no local-content requirements for incentive purposes.

(x) Other measures

92. Croatia has no agreements with foreign governments or enterprises designed to influence the quantity or value of goods and services exported to Croatia.

(2) MEASURES DIRECTLY AFFECTING EXPORTS

(i) Registration and documentation

93. Similar registration and documentation requirements apply to exporters and importers (section (1)(i) above) .

(ii) Export taxes

94. Croatia does not apply any export tariffs or taxes.

[103] Nonetheless, Article 34(2) of the Customs Act allows for export tariffs to be imposed, in exceptional cases, to protect exhaustible natural resources, or to ensure essential materials to the domestic industry and to prevent shortages in domestic supply.[104]

(iii) Export prohibitions, controls, and licensing

For additional analytical, marketing, investment and business opportunities information, please contact Global Investment & Business Center, USA
(202) 546-2103. Fax: (202) 546-3275. E-mail: rusric@erols.com

95. No export prohibitions are in force, other than the embargos maintained in the context of UN Security Council Resolutions.

96. Under Article 1 of the Regulation Specifying Goods Subject to Export and Import Licences (OG 6/09 and 73/09), some products are subject to export licensing for statistical and monitoring purposes, and to fulfil Croatia's obligations under certain treaties and international conventions. These include some fertilizers, military goods and non-military lethal goods for commercial purposes, and substances that deplete the ozone layer (Table AIII.3) . Licences are issued by MELE, except for: (i) uranium or thorium ores and concentrates, and radioactive chemical elements and radioactive isotopes

[105], which are licensed by the State Institute of Radiation Protection pursuant to the Non-Ionizing Radiation Protection Act; and (ii) cultural goods (e.g. paintings, engravings), licensed by the Ministry of Culture. In addition, substances for production of narcotic drugs are licensed by the Ministry of Health and Social Welfare.[106] Furthermore, export licences are required for cereals (for monitoring purposes) and are issued by MAFRD. The licensing procedures for exporters are the same as for importers (section (2)(v) above) . In accordance with the Regulation on the Export and Import Controls for Rough Diamonds, exports of rough diamonds are allowed only if accompanied by a Kimberley Process Certificate issued by MELE.

97. Croatia has recently put into force a regulatory framework governing the control of exports of dual-use (military and civilian) goods and technologies to align it with its international obligations and commitments including the EU *acquis*. The framework comprises of the Act on Export of Dual-Use Items (OG 100/04 and 84/08, applied as from 1 January 2005); Regulation on the List of Dual-Use Items (OG 184/04, 62/07, 57/08, and 63/09); and Ordinance on application form for the issuance of export licence for dual-use items (OG 166/04 and 123/07) . The Customs Administration is responsible for enforcing these controls and the conformity assessment of the goods with the export licence; MELE issues the licence and may inspect the items and documentation.

(iv) Export subsidies, finance, assistance, and promotion

98. According to the authorities, Croatia does not provide export subsidies on industrial or agricultural products.

99. The Croatian Bank for Reconstruction and Development (HBOR), a state-owned investment bank, which entered into operation in late 1992[108], has among its main objectives: increasing the volume of Croatian exports; developing new export markets; increasing the share of Croatian exporters in international trade; diversifying exports of goods and services; and supporting Croatian exporters, investors, and overseas contractors. It provides an export financing and guarantee system by: granting loans (Table III.9); insuring export transactions against political and commercial risks (Table III.10); issuing export guarantees; providing letters of credit; and giving business advice to exporters. In 2008, HBOR's export financing and guarantee programmes totalled HRK 3,909 million, and provided financial support for around 6% of Croatia's total annual exports.

Table III.9 Key features of the export promotion programmes, 2009

Scheme	Eligibility	Conditions
Supplier credit	Exporters of Croatian goods, works or services	Loan amount: Up to 100% of exports for repayment up to

For additional analytical, marketing, investment and business opportunities information, please contact Global Investment & Business Center, USA
(202) 546-2103. Fax: (202) 546-3275. E-mail: rusric@erols.com

	who have concluded an export contract with a foreign buyer	2 years; up to 85% of exports for repayment over 2 years; denominated in the export contract currency. Repayment period: from 180 days to 10 years[a] Interest rate for borrowers: Fixed interest rate[b] or Variable interest rate[c] Application fee: up to 1% one-off charge on the committed loan Commitment fee: up to 1% per year charged on the committed undisbursed loan
Loans to foreign banks	Commercial banks abroad financing exports of Croatian goods and services and pursuant to the OECD Consensus	Loan amount: up to 100% of exports for repayment up to 2 years; up to 85% of exports for repayment over 2 years; denominated in the export contract currency Repayment period: up to 10 years[d] Interest rate for borrowers: Fixed interest rate[b] or Variable interest rate[c] Application fee: up to 1% one-off charged on the committed loan Commitment fee: up to 1% per year charged on the committed undisbursed loan
Buyer credit	Foreign buyers with acceptable security or commercial bank of a buyer, with whom a legal entity with its headquarters in Croatia (exporter) has concluded an export contract	Same as supplier credit

Pre-export finance (pre- and post-shipment)	Companies, craftsmen, and cooperatives	Loan amount: not limited[e]; loans are extended in HRK Repayment period: up to one year from the loan availability date (six-monthly reports required) Interest rate for borrowers: effective interest rates range from 5.06% to 14.46% per year[f]

		Application fee: up to 1% one-off charged on the committed loan Commitment fee: up to 0.25% per year charge on the committed undisbursed loan

a Depending on the type of goods and/or services exported. Exceptionally up to 15 years for financing hydro and thermoelectric power plants, wind energy, geothermal, solar and bio-energy, tidal power plant, water supply and wastewater projects. The first instalment is due 1, 3, 6 or 12 months after the loan repayment start date, depending on the selected manner of repayment and the type of export transaction.

b Currency Induced Credit Risk interest rate plus margin (ranging from 0.2% to 2%, depending on the creditworthiness of the supplier, the buyer, the export transaction, the importing country, and the repayment term) .

c LIBOR/EURIBOR plus margin (depending on the creditworthiness of the supplier, the buyer, the export transaction, the importing country, and the repayment term) .

d Depending on the type of goods and/or services exported. The first instalment is due 1, 3, 6 or 12 months after the loan repayment start date, depending on the selected manner of repayment and the type of export transaction.

e Depending on the opinion of the commercial bank, the creditworthiness of the final borrower, the amount of necessary current assets, the volume of export transactions and the nature and quality of the offered collateral.

f The interest rate charged to final borrowers is the base rate plus a margin that depends on the credit rating of the final borrower and the offered collateral. The base rate is established by the Croatian Competition Agency.

Source: Information provided by the Croatian authorities.

Table III.10 Key features of the export insurance programmes

Programme	Beneficiaries and coverage
Short-term insurance	Exporters of consumer goods or services that have agreed a payment term with the foreign buyer for up to 360 days. Maximum cover is 85%. The insurance premium is generally charged each month on the amount of exported, invoiced, and reported value of goods and services, and paid monthly.
Insurance of supplier's credit	Croatian companies exporting Croatian goods and services. Insurance is provided when the buyer requests deferred payment of credit as precondition for the conclusion of the transaction. This is usually the case in exports of capital goods, equipment of high value, construction works, etc. The usual cover ranges between 80% and 90% of the transaction value, depending primarily on the political risk of the buyer's country.
Insurance of buyer's credit	Commercial banks that approve credits to a foreign buyer or a foreign buyer's banks. Insurance is provided when the foreign buyer requests deferred payment or financial credit as precondition for the conclusion of the transaction. This is usually the case in exports of capital goods, equipment of high value, construction works, etc. The usual cover ranges between 80% and 95% of the transaction value, depending primarily on the political risk of the buyer's country.
Investment insurance	Croatian investors (legal entities registered in Croatia that have their registered office or residence in Croatia) may insure their investment abroad, provided that the recipient country considers the investment to be of Croatian origin. The minimum insurance is for 3 years (5 years in the case of a shareholder loan) and the maximum is 15 years, depending on the investment return period. The maximum cover of an individual investment is 90% of the insured amount. Only political risks are covered.

For additional analytical, marketing, investment and business opportunities information, please contact Global Investment & Business Center, USA (202) 546-2103. Fax: (202) 546-3275. E-mail: rusric@erols.com

Pre-export financing insurance	Exporters of high quality products and with proven capability in the export of goods and services, facing lack of working capital for the preparation of exports, in case no usual collateral instruments can be offered to creditors or in case the same are not sufficient according to the loans terms. Insurance for up to 80% of the loan's principal and 80% of the contracted interest. The premium insurance rate varies depending on the duration of the insurance; calculated on the basis of the percentage of the insured amount. It is charged in a single, up-front payment.

Source: WTO Secretariat, based on information provided by the Croatian authorities.

100. HBOR issues four types of export guarantees, either independently or in cooperation with commercial banks: tender guarantees to support exporters participating in international tenders; performance guarantees for up to 20% of the value of exported equipment, machinery, special products and/or services or the value of investment activities; advance payment guarantees to enable exporters to collect advance payments; and warranty guarantees for up to 10% of the export contract value of equipment, machinery, special products and/or services or the value of investment activities. HBOR charges a loan application fee of 0.25% or at least HRK 500 to be paid before the guarantee is issued, and a fee in the guarantee validity period of 0.2% or at least HRK 500 to be paid quarterly in advance.[109]

101. HBOR also participates, together with MELE and other institutions, in the implementation of the Croatian Export Offensive Strategy, which aims, *inter alia*, at increasing the number of exporting companies from around 11,000 to 13,800; and changing the structure of Croatia's exports so as to quadruple value-added exports (Chapter II(i)) . Under the Strategy, the new Competitiveness Strengthening and Internationalization Programme 2009-10 has been launched with the objective of promoting export-oriented companies and SME's new product development and internationalization, and support in networking (cluster initiatives) .

102. VAT exemptions for exports are listed in Article 13 of the Amendment of the Value Added Tax Act (OG 87/09) and include: the supply of goods to authorized bodies, which export them within their humanitarian, charitable or educational activities outside of Croatia; the supply of goods, other than oil derivates, delivered or transported from Croatia by travellers in the transport of passengers or by someone else acting on their behalf[110]; the supply of goods and services under diplomatic and consular arrangements, subject to the reciprocity principle; and the supply of goods and services to international organizations recognized as such by Croatia and to members of those organizations within the limits and under the conditions stipulated by the international conventions establishing such organizations or agreements on their headquarters.

103. Under the Customs Act and the Istanbul Convention on the Temporary Admission of Goods, goods temporarily imported into Croatia may be completely or partially exempt from customs duties and taxes. Such goods must be intended for temporary use (not for consumption) . They may remain in the territory of Croatia only for a limited period and must be re-exported in an unchanged condition. The Customs Administration has authorized the Croatian Chamber of Economy to issue ATA Carnets and to act as guarantor.[111]

(v) Free zones

For additional analytical, marketing, investment and business opportunities information, please contact Global Investment & Business Center, USA
(202) 546-2103. Fax: (202) 546-3275. E-mail: rusric@erols.com

104. The Section for the Development of Free Zones (under MELE) is in charge of Croatia's 14 free zones.

[112] There are around 300 companies established in the zones, with a wide range of activities, including high-technology investments, leather products, and storage facilities. Investment in free zones increased by HRK 1.9 billion from 2001 to 2005.

105. The Free Zones Act (OG 44/96 and 85/08) and relevant Ordinance set out the framework for operations and practices in the zones[113]; the framework is designed to promote foreign direct investment and joint-ventures in export-oriented enterprises, provide easy access to imports of raw materials and equipment on favourable terms, and increase employment. Free zones also target regional development and employment creation. They must be established on a seaport, river port, along international roads or in other areas in which conditions are favourable. A free zone may also be established on the basis of a concession granted by the Government.[114] Only domestic legal entities may establish a zone; and only domestic legal entities (domestic and foreign companies registered in Croatia) and natural persons can be zone users.[115] Activities that may be carried out within a free zone include: production of goods, wholesale trade, services; retail trade and banking or other financial operations are not allowed.[116] Licences to operate free zones are valid for one year (renewable), while concessions are granted for 25 years (non-renewable) .

106. Financial incentives are available to free zone companies. These include exemption from payment of customs duties and taxes. Under the Amendments to the Free Zone Act (OG 85/08), free zone users pay a profit tax rate ranging from 0-15% instead of the 20% (regular profit tax rate) . Free zones users, who invested over HRK 1 million, prior to the Free Zones Act, and did not use the maximum approved subsidy are exempted from corporate income tax (CIT) until this is used, but not later than 12 December 2016. Pre-Free Zones Act businesses pay CIT depending on the location of their business activity.[117] Goods may remain within a zone for an unlimited period, and profit transfer and foreign exchange transactions are not restricted. Investors are free to construct their own premises, though zones have office space, workshops, or warehouses available for rental. Sales into the domestic market are allowed without limitation, subject to the foreign trade regime.[118]

(vi) Other measures

107. According to the authorities, Croatia does not participate in any arrangements designed to curb or control exports to third countries at the request of foreign governments/companies.

(3) MEASURES AFFECTING PRODUCTION AND TRADE

(i) Incentives

108. Under the Investment Promotion Act (OG 138/06), various investment incentive measures are available foreign and domestic investors who invest a minimum of €300,000 and create ten new jobs, on condition that the recipient maintains the investment and the new employment for a minimum of five years. Prior to investment, a legal entity wishing to benefit from incentives must submit an application to MELE. The incentive measures, which apply to investment projects in the manufacturing sector, technology and innovation centres, and strategic business support services comprise: (a) tax benefits (for up to ten years, with a reduced profit tax rate ranging from zero to 10% depending on amount of investment and minimum number of new employees) (b) duty exemption (no duties for invested equipment under HS 84-90)[121]; (c) monetary aid (non-refundable) for employment creation[122]; (d)

For additional analytical, marketing, investment and business opportunities information, please contact Global Investment & Business Center, USA
(202) 546-2103. Fax: (202) 546-3275. E-mail: rusric@erols.com

monetary aid (non-refundable) for training and re-training costs[123]; (e) monetary aid (non-refundable) for projects on technology innovation centres, and strategic business support activities[124]; and, (f) special incentives for large investment projects.[125]

109. Investments in other areas also benefit from incentive measures: (i) under the Scientific and Higher Education Act (OG 123/03, as amended), state subsidies and tax incentives ranging from 40% to 100% of eligible costs may be granted to research activities[126]; (ii) under the Decree on the Regional Aid Map (OG 52/08), regional aid incentives ranging from 40% to 50% of eligible costs may be granted[127]; (iii) under the Hill and Mountain Areas Act (OG 12/02, as amended), agriculture or fisheries investors, permanent employing more than five workers (the majority of which must be resident in the area) are subject to a profit tax rate of 75% of the regular profit tax amount[128]; and (iv) under the Act on Reconstruction and Development of the City of Vukovar (OG 44/01, as amended), agriculture or fisheries investors having more than five employees (the majority of which must be resident in the area or area of special concern or hill and mountain area) are exempted from profit tax payments.[129]

110. Additional CIT exemptions or deductions apply to taxable persons that carry out an activity in an area of special national concern (except agriculture and fishing)[130], permanently employing more than five workers (the majority of which must be resident in the area) .[131] Taxable persons that carry out an agriculture or fishing activity, under the same conditions, may be exempted from the CIT or pay a rate ranging from 5% to 15%, until Croatia's accession to the EU.

111. Croatia is also implementing its State Aid (Incentive) Programme for Small and Medium Size Enterprises (SMEs) 2008-12, with the objectives of: strengthening competitive ability; equal regional development; boosting quality in entrepreneurial infrastructure; lessening administrative obstacles[132]; strengthening entrepreneurial climate within society; and internet access end e-business".[133] The programme's specific measures include: Croatia's Export Offensive Strategy (section (2)(iv) above and Chapter II(1)); State Aid (section (iii)(b) below); and Financing SMEs through, *inter alia*, loans (micro credits) and subsidized interest rates. The agency for the development of SMEs (HAMAG), established under the Small Business Promotion Act in 2002 (OG 29/02 as amended in 2007 (OG 63/07), and financed under the general budget, participates in this programme along with MELE and various other institutions. Croatia is a signatory of the EU Charter for Small Enterprises and is applying the guidelines of the European Charter for Small Enterprises.[134]

(ii) State trading, state-owned enterprises, and privatization

112. Croatia has been implementing a major privatization programme of state-owned enterprises (SOEs) since the early 1990s, as part of its transition into a market-oriented economy. As a result, the private-sectors shares in output and in employment have risen to around 70% in each. Nonetheless, some important SOEs still run losses with consequent budgetary transfers. Total subsidies are estimated at around 2.4% of GDP and a large share is still provided to loss-making SOEs.

[135] To address this, Croatia aims to finish the privatization process over the next few years so as to reduce the burden of SOEs on the national budget and, ensure a market-based and competitive production system, while meeting the EU pre-accession economic criteria.

113. Croatia's overall privatization process began with the adoption of the Act on Transformation of Socially-Owned Enterprises on 21 April 1991. Thereafter, privatization has

For additional analytical, marketing, investment and business opportunities information, please contact Global Investment & Business Center, USA (202) 546-2103. Fax: (202) 546-3275. E-mail: rusric@erols.com

also been carried out on the basis of the Companies Act; the Privatization Act (OG 21/96, 71/97 and 73/00); and special acts to privatize large SOEs[136], including the electricity company Hrvatska elektroprivreda (HEP)[137], and the oil and gas company Industrija nafte (INA) .[138] The Companies Act, *inter alia*, provides for national treatment regarding foreign investment participation in privatization, while the Privatization Act, *inter alia*, regulates the criteria and procedures for privatization of assets not privatized during the transformation process.

114. The privatization process is carried out under the Croatian Privatization Fund (CPF) in accordance with the Privatization Act. Initially, it involved transformating "socially-owned" enterprises into joint-stock or limited liability companies with defined ownership structures. Following Independence, ten large infrastructure and utilities companies came under direct state ownership as "public enterprises", while the remaining socially-owned enterprises were privatized in a two-stage process. First-stage privatization, organized by the CPF, sought wide participation by employees and the population at large, by offering preferential rights for share subscription at a substantial discount, and payment by instalment.[139] The second phase was through mass voucher privatization, which sold 50% to 60% of the CPF residual portfolio.[140]

115. The privatization process is now in its final phase, which includes the CPF portfolio and some large SOEs. Privatization by CPF is mainly by public tender and public auctions. Public tender, is used for SOEs in which CPF holds significant ownership stake, and has five steps: (i) CPF publicizes the public invitation to tender in the media, on its website (www.hfp.hr), and through emails to embassies, chambers of commerce, interested parties and potential investors; (ii) interested parties and qualified bidders may purchase the tender documentation[141]; (iii) bids must be received by CPF not later than the deadline specified in the tender notification[142]; (iv) the CPF's senior executive team, management board and other government representatives evaluate the bids based on pre-determined evaluation criteria[143]; and (v) contract signing. CPF sells shares of SOEs in which it holds minority stakes through public auction on the Zagreb Stock Exchange (ZSE) . Foreign and local legal and natural persons may acquire share ownership if they are represented by a registered member of the ZSE. Prices range from HRK 1 for companies facing bankruptcy to the nominal value of the appraised equity for more successful SOEs.[144] Certain privatizations are monitored by the Competition Authority (section (iii) below) .

116. As of 15 March 2010, there were 782 SOEs (down from 2,825 in May 1999); the State retains a majority holding in 81. Equity capital amounted to HRK 59,527 billion, while CPF's portfolio was HRK 7,711 million and the state portfolio HRK 16,048 million (Table III.11) . In addition to HEP and INA, other recent privatizations include the steel mills (Chapter IV(2)), and most shares of Croatian Telecom (HT) .[145] Some SOEs (e.g. shipyards, agri-industrial companies, and Croatian Railways (HZ)) have been or are being restructured as a precondition for their privatization. Nevertheless, privatization of CPF-held assets have recently made limited progress, and a number of tenders did not attract potential investors. Overall, progress has been criticized as uneven and determined by institutional weakness.[146]

Table III.11 Croatian Privatization Fund CPF, (HRK million)

State ownership	No. of SOEs	Equity capital	CPF	State portfolio
0-25%	632	40,999	2,349	2,777
25-50%	69	2,898	478	951
50-100%	81	15,631	4,885	12,320
Total	782	59,527	7,711	16,048

For additional analytical, marketing, investment and business opportunities information, please contact Global Investment & Business Center, USA (202) 546-2103. Fax: (202) 546-3275. E-mail: rusric@erols.com

Source: Information provided by the Croatian authorities.

117. Under Croatia's Strategic Development Framework 2006-13, some of the main privatization goals are sales of SOEs through the capital market so as to increase their efficiency and competitiveness. In addition, the Strategic Development Framework aims at boosting further competition and regulation in the economy, and co-ownership between the state and the private sector, including through public-private partnership (PPP) projects (section (1)(viii) above) .[147]

118. Croatia has notified the WTO that it has no state-trading enterprises as defined in GATT Article XVII and the Understanding on the Interpretation of Article XVII.[148] Nonetheless, some SOEs such as Hrvatske sume (Croatian State Forests), Hravatska posta (Croatian Post) and HZ, as well as recently privatized companies (e.g. HEP and INA) hold exclusive rights.[149]

(iii) Competition policy, state aid, and price controls

(a) Competition policy

119. The Competition Act (OG 120/03)

[150], applied since 1 October 2003 and to apply until the new act enters into force on 1 October 2010, provides the main legal basis for competition in both goods and services; its main objective is to create an efficient competitive environment in Croatia. In order to further implement specific aspects of the Competition Act and further aligning Croatia's legislation on the EC *acquis*, secondary competition legislation has been adopted.[151]

120. The Competition Act addresses three main issues: (i) restrictive agreements (Articles 9-14); (ii) abuse of dominant position (Articles 15-17); and (iii) prohibited concentrations, such as mergers and acquisitions with dominant position, that distort the competitive structure of the market (Article 18-28) . All agreements that distort, restrict or prevent competition are prohibited; however, block or individual exemptions are made for those that help to improve the production or distribution of goods and/or services; promote technical or economic progress, while allowing consumers a fair share of the resulting benefit; or of minor importance. Any abuse (by one or more undertakings) of a dominant position in the relevant market is prohibited. Dominant position is when an undertaking, due to its market power, can act highly independently of its real or potential competitors, consumers, buyers or suppliers in the relevant market.

121. Any form of prevention or distortion of competition within Croatia or outside its territory falls within the scope of the Competition Act if such practices affect the Croatian market, including agreements between Croatian and foreign companies or even between foreign companies. Except for certain types of merger of banks, insurance companies, and other financial institutions, for which special legislation applies, all other sectors are treated equally under the Competition Act.

122. The Competition Act regulates the powers, duties, and organization of the Croatian Competition Agency (CCA) . The CCA, established as an independent entity by a decision of Parliament in mid-1997, deals with the major areas of competitive restraints; it registers and resolves cases of restrictive agreements, abuse of dominant position, and concentration (Table III.12) . The CCA has competence in all competition issues except for those resulting from banking services and other credit institutions' services, which are under the responsibility of the Croatian National Bank (CNB) .[154] Under the Competition Act, merger control provisions

For additional analytical, marketing, investment and business opportunities information, please contact Global Investment & Business Center, USA (202) 546-2103. Fax: (202) 546-3275. E-mail: rusric@erols.com

are also applicable to privatization transactions conducted by the State. The CCA does not monitor privatization process but it assesses mergers that resulted from privatization.[155] Further, the CCA has a competition advocacy role; it gives official opinions to the government on legislative proposals on competition issues. At the multilateral level, the CCA participates in certain activities of the ICN (International Competition Network), OECD, and UNCTAD. It has also concluded bilateral agreements on cooperation with several EU member states, and countries in the region (e.g. Austria, Bosnia and Herzegovina, Bulgaria, Hungary, FYR of Macedonia, and Romania) . Based on cooperation agreements, the CCA cooperates regularly with Croatia's various regulatory bodies, such as CNB, Financial Services Supervisory Agency (HANFA), Post and Electronic Communication Agency (HAKOM), and Croatian Energy Regulatory Agency (HERA) .

Table III.12 Competition Agency registered and resolved administrative cases, 2004-08

	2004	2005	2006	2007	2008
Restrictive agreements registered	7	4	31	4	11
Restrictive agreements resolved	24	5	22	5	11
Abuse of dominant position registered	50	21	21	12	36
Abuse of dominant position resolved	60	3	27	14	24
Concentration cases registered	25	30	30	29	35
Concentration cases resolved	42	26	28	28	32
Total administrative cases registered	82	55	82	45	82
Total administrative cases resolved	126	34	77	47	67

Source: Croatian Competition Agency (2007), *Annual Report for 2007*, Zagreb; and information provided by the Croatian authorities.

123. The managing body of the CCA is the Competition Council, which has five members appointed by the Croatian Parliament (one of whom is appointed as president) .[156] The CCA does not have the authority to impose fines for infringements of the Competition Act; it is under the jurisdiction of the minor offence courts. As a result, after adopting a decision, the CCA requests minor offence court to start minor offence proceedings against the undertaking concerned and the responsible person of the undertaking.[157] From 1 October 2010, the CCA will have the competence to impose fines for the breach of competition rules.

124. A new Competition Act (OG 79/09) adopted in June 2009 is to be implemented from 1 October 2010. According to the EU, it is fully in line with the *acquis.*[158] In addition to empowering the CCA to impose fines[159], other changes introduced in the new Act include: the obligation for the CCA inform the parties to the proceedings, in writing, of the preliminary established facts, in order to ensure the parties can express their views on all relevant facts; entrusting the Administrative Court with review of the legality and the merits of the CCA's decision, and with the level of fines to be imposed by the CCA for infringements of competition rules ; abolishing individual exemption of agreements; and introducing the right of the parties to propose commitments. The new Competition Act also adopts a new test for assessing concentrations (the significant impediment of effective competition); and regulates in more detail the issues of dawn raids and searches of business and other premises, lands, and vehicles conducted by the CCA.

(b) State aid

125. While Croatia has established a functioning market economy, the State continues to provide aid on economic or social grounds. In addition to direct costs to the budget, there are indirect costs as a result of forgone revenues, associated with, for example, tax exemptions. The legislative framework, based on the State Aid Act (OG 140/05)[161], and the Regulation on State Aid (OG 50/06), provides extensive powers to the CCA to assess and approve state aid (*ex-ante* control), as well as to monitor its use (*ex-post* control) .

126. Under Article 4(1) of the State Aid Act, state aid that distorts or threatens to distort competition by favouring certain beneficiaries, is prohibited insofar as it may affect the international commitments undertaken by Croatia. However, under Article 4(2), state aid used to mitigate or make good the damage caused by natural disasters, exceptional or war occurrences, is compatible with the Act, subject to prior authorization. Moreover, under Article 4(3), state aid is allowed, subject to prior notification, to: (a) promote the economic development of areas where the standard of living is abnormally low or where there is serious underemployment; (b) promote culture and heritage conservation; (c) promote the execution of important international projects or remedy a serious disturbance in the economy; (d) facilitate the development of certain economic activities or of certain economic areas; and (e) legal and natural persons that are, in accordance with special rules, entrusted with the operation of services of general economic interest or granted special rights to perform tasks assigned to them in the public interest, where the absence of such aid would obstruct their performance, and provided the aid covers exclusively compensation for the performance and implementation of the tasks concerned. State aid is awarded through various instruments, such as grants; tax exemptions, debt write-offs and reduction in social security contributions; equity participation; soft loans; and guarantees.

127. As part of the requirements for EU accession, Croatia has established an independent system for monitoring state aid. Based on notifications made by the institutions granting state aid, the CCA prepares an annual review of state aid covering all sectors, including agriculture and fisheries.[162] The share of state aid to GDP rose from 2.5% in 2004 to 2.6% in 2008; the highest share was allocated to sector-specific aid (Table III.13), led by agriculture and fisheries (33.8% of total aid over 2004-08), shipbuilding (17.2%), and transport (13%) .[163] The authorities acknowledge the need to redirect aid towards horizontal and regional objectives given that these categories of state aid affect competition less than sector-specific aid, and the need to raise competitiveness and achieve balanced regional development.[164] In 2008, most state aid was in the form of grants (78.7% of total state aid), followed by tax exemptions (11.7%), equity participation (4.6%), and guarantees (4.5%) .

Table III.13 State aid in Croatia, (€ million)

Category	2004	2005	2006	2007	2008
Agriculture and fisheries	242.8	287.1	346.2	437.6	489.8
Horizontal aid	153.6	112.6	127.0	112.1	164.9
R&D and innovation	16.5	17.5	19.0	21.9	29.0
Environmental protection and energy saving	0.0	0.9	3.3	2.8	5.1
SMEs	7.3	6.0	32.9	5.8	23.9
Training	17.4	10.1	13.8	24.9	9.6
Employment	63.4	36.2	45.7	49.1	91.6
Culture	5.4	10.1	12.3	7.6	5.7
Other objectives	43.5	31.8	0.0	0.0	0.0
Sector- specific aid	224.9	245.2	550.3	578.0	484.3

For additional analytical, marketing, investment and business opportunities information, please contact Global Investment & Business Center, USA
(202) 546-2103. Fax: (202) 546-3275. E-mail: rusric@erols.com

Steel industry	3.9	2.2	0.1	26.8	0.0
Transport	56.4	56.1	190.5	191.8	201.1
Shipbuilding	70.7	86.9	300.3	314.4	82.3
Tourism	11.6	24.6	35.6	24.3	22.6
Brodcasting	..	..	130.9	137.8	152.3
Other sectors	3.4	7.6	22.7	5.5	18.6
Rescue and restructuring	78.8	67.8	1.1	15.2	7.4
Regional aid	19.5	20.2	38.5	65.5	56.0
Aid at local level	45.8	18.2	18.1	26.6	24.7
Total	686.6	683.4	1,080.2	1,219.7	1,219.8

.. Not available.
Source: Information provided by the Croatian authorities.
(c) Price controls

128. In general, prices are determined freely without any government interference. Nonetheless, administrative price regulation is provided for in the Exceptional Measures of Price Controls Act of 1997. Direct price controls may be prescribed at the national and local levels to prevent negative effects of price changes for basic goods and services that have a direct impact on the cost of living, or to prevent monopoly pricing (Article 4) . Price controls may only be implemented for a limited period and if the negative effects cannot be eliminated by other economic policy measures. The Government is also obliged to take appropriate measures to eventually allow the elimination of the price controls. Imports and exports are excluded from price control measures. During 2004-09, administrative prices accounted for around 23% of the consumer price index.

129. Upon a proposal by MELE, the Government may implement direct price controls by: fixing maximum prices; ordering price reductions to a certain level; and requiring economic agents to report price changes in advance. MELE may object to prior reported price changes within 15 days of the date they are reported, and request a company to reconsider the proposed prices. The Act provides for penalties of HRK 5,000-20,000 for companies changing prices against the objections of MELE, and the Government may order the prices be brought back to the original level. Regulations published in the *Official Gazette* determine the goods and services subject to price controls.

130. In 2009, only internal railway and official passengers transport remained subject to price control by MELE at the national level, at the local level, only public utilities (i.e. central heating, water supply, sewage and other sanitary services, distribution of gas, and public transport) are under price control.[165]

(iv) Protection of intellectual property rights

(a) Overview

131. As part of its efforts to harmonize with EU legislation on intellectual property rights (IPRs), and in accordance with its commitments under the WTO TRIPS Agreement, Croatia has a comprehensive and recently updated legal framework. It comprises mainly the Copyright and Related Rights Act (OG 163/03) as amended Patent Act (OG 173/03) as amended[167]; Trademarks Act (OG 173/03) as amended ; Industrial Design Act (OG 173/03) as amended[169]; Act on Geographical Indications and Designations of Origin of Products and Services (OG 173/03) as amended ; Act on the Protection of Plant Varieties (OG 131/97) as amended[171]; Act on the Protection of Topographies of Semiconductor Products (OG 173/03)

as amended ; and Regulation implementing customs measures against goods suspected of infringing certain IPRs (OG 50/06) as amended. In 2007, Croatia was removed from the United States Special 301 Priority Watch List in recognition of progress achieved in IPRs protection. Nonetheless, further efforts are required to strengthen the administrative capacity for enforcement of IPRs.[175] The Croatian intellectual property legislation was reviewed by the WTO TRIPS Council in June 2001.

132. Croatia is implementing its National Strategy for the Development of the Intellectual Property System 2005-10 with the aim, *inter alia*, of improving horizontal cooperation and coordination between the various institutions involved, and improving enforcement of IPRs. The main institutions responsible for intellectual property matters are: the State Intellectual Property Office (SIPO) for industrial property rights and copyright and neighbouring rights[177], except for geographical indications and appellations of origin for agricultural products, foodstuff, and wine and spirits, which were transferred to the Ministry of Agriculture, Fisheries and Rural Development (MAFRD) in 2003; MAFRD (together with the Institute for Seed and Seedlings) also for the protection of new plant varieties; the Customs Directorate in the Ministry of Finance, for border measures; and the Ministry of Justice for enforcement before the courts.

133. Current IPR legislation does not refer expressly to parallel imports. Regarding patents, the patentee is granted the right to exclude others from importing the patented invention during the term of patent protection. A similar prohibition concerns trademarks: no one is allowed to use a mark without the consent of its owner. A copyright holder enjoys the exclusive right of reproduction, distribution, broadcast, and communication to the public.

134. The notion of exhaustion of rights conferred by a copyright, patent, trademark, industrial design, and topography of semiconductor products, with respect to the territory of the EU and the European Economic Area, will enter into force up on Croatia's accession to EU. European-wide exhaustion rule applies *mutatis mutandis* to related rights.

135. Croatia's preferential trade agreements include provisions on IPRs (Chapter II(3)) .

136. Croatia has joined various IPR conventions and treaties (Table III.14) .

Table III.14 Membership in international agreements, conventions, and treaties, 2009

Error! Unknown switch argument.Name	Date of membership
Convention establishing WIPO (1967)	8 October 1991
Paris Convention on the Protection of Industrial Property (1883)	8 October 1991
Berne Convention for the Protection of Literary and Artistic Works (1886)	8 October 1991
Madrid Agreement Concerning the International Registration of Marks (1891)	8 October 1991
Universal Copyright Convention (Geneva text, 1952)	8 October 1991
Universal Copyright Convention (Paris text, 1971)	8 October 1991
Nice Agreement concerning the International Classification of Goods and Services for the purpose of Registration of Marks (1957)	8 October 1991
Rome Convention for the Protection of Performers, Producers of Phonograms and Broadcasting Organizations (1961)	20 April 2000
Locarno Agreement Establishing an International Classification for	8 October 1991

Treaty	Date
Industrial Designs (1968)	
Patent Co-operation Treaty (1970)	1 July 1998
Convention for the Protection of Producers of Phonograms against Unauthorized Duplication of their Phonograms (1971)	20 April 2000
Strasbourg Agreement Concerning the International Patent Classification (1971)	25 November 2000
Convention Relating to the Distribution of Programme-Carrying Signals Transmitted by Satellite (1974)	8 October 1991
WTO TRIPS Agreement (1995)	30 November 2000
Budapest Treaty on the International Recognition of the Deposit of Micro-Organisms for the Purpose of Patent Procedure (1977)	25 February 2000
International Convention for the Protection of New Varieties of Plants (1961)	1 September 2001
Protocol relating to Madrid Agreement (International Registration of Marks) (1989)	23 January 2004
Hague Agreement (International Deposit of Industrial Designs) (1925)	12 February 2004
WIPO Copyright Treaty (1996)	26 April 2000
WIPO Performances and Phonogram Treaty (1996)	26 April 2000
Nairobi Treaty on the Protection of the Olympic Symbol (1981)	20 November 2004
Agreement between Croatia and European Patent Organization on Cooperation in the Field of Patents (Cooperation and Extension Agreement, 2003)	1 April 2004
Patent Law Treaty (2000)	28 April 2005
Trademark Law Treaty (1994)	4 July 2006
Vienna Agreement Establishing an International Classification of the Figurative Elements of Marks (1973)	9 May 2009
European Patent Convention (1973)	1 January 2008
Agreement on the Application of Article 65 of the Convention on the Grant of European Patents (2000)	1 May 2008

Source: Information provided by the Croatian authorities.

(b) Copyright and related rights

137. A copyright work is an original intellectual creation in the literary, scientific or artistic domain, having an individual character, irrespective of the manner and form of its expression, its type, value or purpose. Croatia's legal framework on copyright includes works of language (written works, oral works, computer programs), musical works, works of visual arts, and photography. Copyright is acquired by virtue of law and belongs to the author. It consists of economic rights[178], moral, and other rights. Computer programs and compilations of data are expressly spelled out as copyrighted works.[179] There are some limitations and exceptions.[180] In 2004, copyright-based industries generated HKR 19.2 billion of gross output, i.e. 4.3% of Croatia's GDP, and employed 4.7% of the total labour force.[181]

138. Copyright protection is for the life of author plus 70 years.[182] Croatia's copyright law also recognizes related rights, for example, of performers, phonogram producers, film producers, broadcasting organizations, publishers of printed editions; and producers of databases. Protection for these related rights is 50 years (from the date of performance/publication/broadcast, whichever occurred earlier), except for the rights of producers of databases, which are protected for 15 years. An author may exploit a copyright on an individual basis or through a collective management of rights.

For additional analytical, marketing, investment and business opportunities information, please contact Global Investment & Business Center, USA (202) 546-2103. Fax: (202) 546-3275. E-mail: rusric@erols.com

(c) Patents

139. Croatia's Patent Act (as amended) entered into force in 2004 and covers any invention, in all fields of technology, that is new, involves an inventive step and is susceptible of industrial application. A patent must also be granted for an invention that concerns: a product consisting of or containing biological material; a process by means of which the biological material is produced, processed or used; a biological material isolated from its natural environment or produced by means of a technical process, even if it previously occurred in nature.

An invention that concerns plants or animals is considered patentable if the technical feasibility of the invention is not confined to a particular plant or animal variety and if the process for carrying out the invention is not essentially biological. Excluded from patent protection, *inter alia*, are: plant or animal varieties; essentially biological processes for the production of plants or animals, with the exception of inventions that concern non-biological and microbiological processes and products resulting from such processes; inventions contrary to public order or morality; and inventions on surgical or diagnostic methods or methods of treatment practiced directly on the living human and animal body. During 2004-08, 3,547 patent applications were registered, of which 1,757 by Croatians.

140. Patent protection is for 20 years from the filing date. Protection for a consensual patent is 10 years from the filing date. Upon accession to the EU, provisions will enter into force allowing a Supplementary Protection Certificate for a basic patent for a medicinal product intended for humans or animals or a plant protection product granted in Croatia.[186]

141. The owner may exploit the patent either individually or in cooperation with other natural or legal persons; rights may be transferred by assignment, licensing, or by testamentary succession.[187] Provision is made for granting compulsory licences, on the grounds of lack or insufficiency of exploitation of a patent, to any person filing a request, or to the Government, if the patent owner has not exploited the invention in the territory of Croatia on reasonable terms, or has not made effective and serious preparations for its exploitation.

(d) Trade marks

142. Croatia's legislative framework includes protection of a registered trademark for goods and services, guarantee marks, and collective marks; provided they are registered by SIPO or through the system of international registration (Madrid system) . Protection is for ten years from the date of application and can be renewed indefinitely at the end of each consecutive ten-year period. A trade mark application that complies with the examination procedure is published in SIPO's *Official Gazette*. An opposition to a trade mark registration may be filed within three months of publication of the application, by the holders of earlier trade marks and other earlier rights, if they consider that the registration would infringe their rights. If there is no opposition, the application is registered. A trade mark may be revoked, *inter alia*, if, within an uninterrupted period of five years, it has not been put to genuine use without justified reasons.

(e) Industrial designs

143. The Industrial Designs Act of 2003 (as amended), provides for the protection of designs that are new and have individual character. A design is considered new if, before the date of application, no identical design has been made available to the public, i.e published following registration or otherwise, or exhibited, used in the course of trade or otherwise disclosed, except where these events could not reasonably have become known in the normal course of

For additional analytical, marketing, investment and business opportunities information, please contact Global Investment & Business Center, USA
(202) 546-2103. Fax: (202) 546-3275. E-mail: rusric@erols.com

business to the circles specialized in the sector concerned, operating within Croatia.[190] A registered design is protected for five years from the filing date, and protection may be renewed for periods of five years, to a maximum of 25 years. The Industrial Design Act does not provide protection for unregistered designs.

(f) Geographical indications

144. Croatia's legislation grants unlimited protection on the registration of geographical indications for goods attached to a particular origin or of special cultural importance.[191] The Act on Geographical Indications and Designations of Origin of Products and Services of 2003 (as amended), under the competence of SIPO, covers geographical indications and designations of origin of almost all products and services. The exceptions, under the responsibility of MAFRD, refer to special legislation on geographical indications: (i) Act on designations of origin, geographical indications and the traditional speciality logo for agricultural products and foodstuffs (OG 84/08, 75/09 and 107/09)[192], and Ordinance on designations of origin and geographical indications for agricultural products and foodstuffs (OG 88/09); (ii) Act on Wine (OG 96/03), and Ordinance on Marking Wines with Geographical Indications (OG 7/05, 41/08) as amended; and (iii) Ordinance on Spirit drinks (OG 61/09) .

(g) Other areas

145. Under the Act on the Protection of Plant Varieties of 1997 (as amended) and pertaining ordinances[193], Croatia protects new varieties of plants for 25 years after registration; and trees and vines for 30 years. Breeders' rights can be obtained through an administrative procedure under the responsibility of MAFRD and the Institute for Seed and Seedlings. Rights are granted on the basis of "novelty, distinctiveness, uniformity, stability and denomination". Provision is made for granting compulsory licences for up to three years (renewable) .

146. Under the Act on the Protection of Topographies of Semiconductor Products (as amended), protection is granted for ten years from filing date (or, if earlier, from first use) .

(h) Enforcement

147. The Croatian authorities have focused their efforts on improving the enforcement of IPR rights over the last few years, including through workshops and seminars to educate businesses, consumers, judges, prosecutors, and other government officers. Nonetheless, further efforts are required to strengthen the overall awareness of intellectual property rights in society at large. During 2004-08, there were 610 IPR infringement cases (according to Customs Administration data): 85% were initiated upon the request of the right holder. In value terms, €6.8 million of goods were seized by the Customs Administration over 2004-08, of which €5.1 million were destroyed (Table III.15) . In the first quarter of 2009, 63 infringement cases were recorded, with a value of €5.4 million.[196]

Table III.15 Infringement of intellectual property, 2004-08

(Number of cases and €)

	2004	2005	2006	2007	2008	2004-08
Destruction of goods	11	9	21	151	141	333
Destruction of	10,011	57,075	248,551	4,818,501	43,122	5,134,144

For additional analytical, marketing, investment and business opportunities information, please contact Global Investment & Business Center, USA
(202) 546-2103. Fax: (202) 546-3275. E-mail: rusric@erols.com

goods (€)						
Suspension of the procedure	1	32	21	116	76	246
Suspension of the procedure (€)	37,589	286,555	160,625	997,315	410,976	1,482,084
Cases pending before the courts	6	1	6	10	8	31
Cases pending before the courts (€)	21,880	68	14,466	99,200	34,675	135,613
Total	18	42	48	277	225	610
Total (€)	69,479	343,697	423,642	5,915,022	488,773	6,751,841

Source: SIPO (2009), *Statistical Report on the Infringements of Intellectual Property Rights in Croatia: Annual report 2008*, Zagreb.

148. Civil procedures allow right-owners to: request establishment and termination of infringement; request seizure and destruction of objects; request compensation of damages, usual compensation, and unfair profits; request publication of the judgment; and request provision of information. They are also entitled to provisional measures, comprising the termination or prevention of the infringement and preservation of evidence.[197] Under the penal law, sanctions for infringements of copyright and related rights consist of: imprisonment ranging from 6 months to five years, and/or fines. A fine may not be less than 10 daily incomes, and not more than 500 daily incomes.[198] Goods may also be seized during the customs procedure.

149. The appeal procedures and related boards of appeal for industrial property rights were introduced in 2008. The boards of appeal are responsible for deciding on appeals against the decisions issued by the SIPO in the first instance. The administrative decisions issued by the boards of Appeal in the second instance may be subject to administrative disputes before the Administrative Court. The average length of appeal procedures in 2009 was eight months.[200] The average length of proceedings before the Administrative Court (from filing the suit to judgement) in 2008 was 6-12 months.

INVESTMENT & BUSINESS CLIMATE

OPENNESS TO FOREIGN INVESTMENT

The only restrictions on foreign investment in Croatia are in the fields of military equipment and television and radio stations. Free repatriation of profits and repatriation of capital is guaranteed by the Constitution, where there is also a provision stating that rights acquired through foreign capital investments cannot be reduced by law or any other legal act. Foreign investors have the same rights, obligations, and legal status within an enterprise as domestic investors, provided the condition of reciprocity is met. As an incentive, equipment imported as part of an investment by a foreign party is exempt from customs duties, provided that the investment is for a period of more than five years and the foreign party accounts for at least 20% of the total investment Corporate tax is only 25%. The current system of sales taxes will be replaced by VAT on January 1, 1997.

CONVERSION AND TRANSFER POLICIES

The Croatian Kuna is freely convertible into foreign currency at exchange rates determined daily on the foreign

exchange market. The National Bank intervenes in the market from time to time to smooth exchange rate fluctuations

or to maintain target exchange rates against the German Mark in what could be described as a dirty float. Exchange rates have remained stable over the past two years. Foreign currency can be easily obtained in Croatian banks. There are no restrictions on transfer of profit and repatriation of capital, provided all legal obligations in Croatia are settled.

EXPROPRIATION AND COMPENSATION

According to the Expropriation Law (Official Gazette 9/94), "in the absence of a separate law providing differently, a real estate property may be expropriated when expropriation is necessary because of building or construction works in the interest of the Republic of Croatia and when it is assessed that it will be more useful to use the property for the new purpose than if it is used in the previous way." The law provides that in the case of expropriation, compensation is to be provided in similar property or in cash equal to the current market value of the expropriated property.

DISPUTE SETTLEMENT

As Croatian courts face a tremendous backlog, partly due to lack of judges, settlement of commercial disputes is often a matter of years. In October 1995, there were more than a million cases pending in Croatian courts.

Croatia is a signatory of the following international conventions regulating the mutual acceptance and enforcement of foreign arbitration: the 1923 Geneva Protocol on Arbitration Clauses, the 1927 Geneva Convention of the Execution of Foreign Arbitration Decisions, the 1958 New York Convention on the Acceptance and Execution of Foreign Arbitration Decisions; and the 1961 European Convention on International Business Arbitration.

PERFORMANCE REQUIREMENTS/INCENTIVES

None.

PROTECTION OF PROPERTY RIGHTS

U.S. citizens and companies may purchase real estate in Croatia upon obtaining an approval from the Ministry of Foreign Affairs, following a ruling by the Ministry of Justice. Applications in Croatian should be sent by mail to the Ministry of Justice, Savska 41, 10000 Zagreb. The Minister of Foreign Affairs has a discretionary right to decline approval without explanation. Restrictions exist on purchasing agricultural land owned by the state, coastal real estate, real estate located in natural protected areas, and in military zones. There is no limit to the value or size of property that may be owned by a foreigner. There are no restrictions on owning chattels.

A company established in Croatia by a foreign physical or legal person is considered to be a Croatian legal person and may own real estate property without any restriction and needs no approvals (note: a representative office and a branch office are not considered to be a legal

For additional analytical, marketing, investment and business opportunities information, please contact Global Investment & Business Center, USA (202) 546-2103. Fax: (202) 546-3275. E-mail: rusric@erols.com

person). There are no restrictions on mortgaging property. Both Croatian and foreign citizens may mortgage property and pledge chattels. The new Property Rights Law to be adopted in 1996 is aimed to make mortgaging property procedures more user-friendly to creditors and investors.

REGULATORY SYSTEM: LAWS AND PROCEDURES

There have been numerous and substantial changes made in Croatia's regulatory system reflecting the transition from a socialist into a western-type market economy system. As the bulk of these changes has been completed, the Croatian regulatory system is expected to become more stable in the years ahead. Inconsistencies, indistinctnesses, and loop-holes are being eliminated as they occur. Among the new laws that remain to be adopted during 1996 are:
Law onStandards,
Law on Land Register Books,
Law on Denationalization, and
Law on Property Rights.

A list of business related laws and regulations as well as a list of laws and regulations of which English translation is available can be obtained from the Emerging Markets Investment and Business Center (202) 546-2103, E-mail: rusric@erols.com

EFFICIENT CAPITAL MARKETS AND PORTFOLIO INVESTMENT

Capital markets are still relatively undeveloped. Securities are traded on the Zagreb Stock Exchange (established in 1991) and on informal markets in Varazdin and Osijek (established in 1993). The Securities Law and the Law on Investment Funds were adopted in January 1996. There is no tax on capital gain, nor on dividends or interest. Raising capital via a stock offering is rare.

Since April 1992, total transactions on the Zagreb Stock Exchange have been roughly $350 million. In 1995, total transactions were about $45 million of which only about $3.5 million resulted from regular transactions among brokers. The rest was from auctions of stocks from the portfolio of the Croatian Privatization Fund. Stocks of only about a few companies are officially listed on the Zagreb Stock Exchange. In addition, stocks of about 60 companies are listed on a less stringent tier, i.e., less information about a company is requested by the Stock Exchange and preemptive rights on outstanding stocks exist for most of these companies thus making transactions much more complicated. Information on the listings at the Zagreb Stock Exchange is available through the Internet (http://www.zse.com.hr). A seat at the Zagreb Stock Exchange costs about $25,000. As of January 1996, a total of 44 brokerage houses held seats A large number of them do not regularly participate in transactions.

Trade of securities on informal, over-the-counter markets in Varazdin and Osijek amounted to roughly $15 million in 1995. Information on the listings on these markets is published regularly in the local newspapers and magazines. A quarterly fee of about $170 was charged for a membership on these markets.

At the beginning of April, the Croatian pharmaceutical company PLIVA came out with an IPO on the London Stock Exchange. A number of American firms purchased shares including Bankers Trust Company which, with 17.85% of the total outstanding shares purchased on May 3, 1996, has become the major private share holder in the company.

There is talk that a number of other major Croatian companies are considering following PLIVA's example.

POLITICAL VIOLENCE

Croatia conducted two successful military operations in May and August of 1995 to retake rebel Serb-occupied areas in Western Slavonia and the Krajina region. These actions, combined with military developments in Bosnia and the Dayton peace accords, have lowered tensions and substantially reduced the risk of crossborder shelling. Under the November 12 Agreement signed in Zagreb and Erdut, the remaining rebel-Serb-held area of Eastern Slavonia has been placed under UN supervision for a period of gradual reintegration to Croatian government control. The Croatian public broadly supports U.S. peace efforts and the Dayton Accords. There is little anti-American sentiment in the country.

The local Serb authorities in Eastern Slavonia maintain a police and local militia force. There are also paramilitary organizations present. Tensions in the area have been greatly reduced as a result of the November 12 Agreement. By the end June, 1996, the UN had successfully carried out demilitarization of the region.

Bilateral Investment Agreements

A U.S. - Croatian Bilateral Investment Treaty was signed during the Secretary of Commerce Kantor's visit to Croatia in mid-July, 1996. An Intellectual Property Rights Protection Agreement is expected to follow shortly.

OPIC AND OTHER INVESTMENT INSURANCE PROGRAMS

OPIC programs are available for U.S. investments in Croatia. OPIC's activities include (1) political risk insurance for a variety of investment types for American firms investing in Croatia, as well as for American bank loans; (2) financing overseas ventures through loans and loan guarantees and (3) support for private investment funds that provide equity for overseas projects. To qualify for financing, U.S. investors are expected to assume a meaningful share of the risk, generally through the purchase of at least 25% equity. Loans have a 5-12 year term. As a rule, 51% of the project has to be privately held. For details on OPIC insurance programs, please contact Emerging Markets Investment and Business Center, USA (202) 546-3275

Labor

Croatia has a highly educated and skilled labor force. The average net salary in Croatia (after all income and other taxes and contributions are paid) is almost 2,000 Kunas (about $400) per month. Personal income, social security and other contributions amount to 130-150% of the net salary and their calculation, deduction, and payment is the administrative responsibility of the employer. In simple words, over half an employee's gross salary goes to the government and various funds.

The Croatian government keeps under control the level of wages in government agencies and institutions and in companies under its direct or indirect control. In practice, this affects the bulk of Croatian workers. The wages in privately owned companies are freely set by contract between employer and employee. There are no restrictions, except for the minimum wage which is about $200 net per month.

After-tax wages for blue-collar workers range from 1,000 to 4,000 Kunas (approximately $200-800) per month. The approximate range of net salaries for white-collar workers would be from 4,000 to 8,000 Kunas (approximately $800-1,600) per month.

Labor unions have not been very militant. There has been concern about a possible brain drain during the past few years.

FOREIGN TRADE ZONES/FREE PORTS

Investment in eight free trade/customs zones currently operating in Croatia has been marginal so far. However, under the new Law on Free Trade Zones adopted in July 1996, they could become more attractive for investors.

CAPITAL OUTFLOW POLICY

Repatriation of capital for non-residents is by the Foreign Exchange Law free of restrictions, and is guaranteed by the Croatian Constitution. Capital outflow for Croatian residents is restricted.

MAJOR FOREIGN INVESTORS

Investor	Industry	Approximate Value ($ million)
Ericsson, Sweden	Telecommunications	48
Hofmann & Pankl Bet., Austria	Minerals Processing	39
Soc. Suisse De Cim. Port., Switzerland	Cement Production	38
Interbrew, Belgium	Brewery	27
Coca Cola Amatil, Australia	Beverages	20
Grassette Nederland, Netherlands	Maritime Services	19
Trioinvest, Switzerland	Cement Production	17
Messer Griesheim, Austria	Industrial Gases	16
The Coca Cola Export Corp., USA	Beverages	12
Zetec, USA	N-Power Plant Services	10
Elektro-Gerrete, Switzerland	Electrical Materials	10
Southern Breweries Est., Lichten.	Brewery	10
Heidelberger Zement, Germany	Cement Production	10

FREE TRADE ZONES

SLOBODNA GOSPODARSKA ZONA
"NERETVA"
"LUKA PLOCE"
20340 Ploce, Trg kralja Tomislava 21
Contact: Ivica Milicevic
Tel: 385/20/679-023; Fax: 385/20/679-039

SLOBODNA EKONOMSKA ZONA "TEINA"
31000 Osijek, Svilajska 31
Contact: Dragan Bockinac
Tel: 385/31/163-410 Fax: 385/31/163-954

SLOBODNA GOSPODARSKA ZONA
"KVARNER"
"LUKA RIJEKA"
51000 Rijeka, Riva 1
Contact: Dr. Ivan Milos
Tel: 385/51/211-165, 213-302 ext. 907 Fax:

SLOBODNA GOSPODARSKA ZONA
"VARAZDIN"
ROBNO TRANSPORTNI CENTAR VARAZDIN
42004 Varazdin, Vilka Novaka 48c
Contact: Nenad Lukacic
Tel: 385/42/51-177, 44-695 Fax: 385/42/44-661

SLOBODNA ZONA "ZAGREB AERODROM"
ZRACNA LUKA ZAGREB
10000 Zagreb, Pleso bb
Contact: Tomislav Leko
Tel: 385/1/456-2395, 456-2135 Fax: 385/1/655-1648

SLOBODNA GOSPODARSKA ZONA
"ZAGREB"
RTC JANKOMIR
10000 Zagreb, Jankomir 25
Contact: Rino Juric, Marko Curkovic
Tel: 385/1/153-132, 156-706, 157-517 Fax:

385/51/212-943 SLOBODNA GOSPODARSKA ZONA "SPLIT" "LUKA SPLIT" 21000 Split, Put sjeverne luke bb Contact: Tomislav Lapenda Tel: 385/21/362-677/84 Fax: 385/21/585-773	385/1/156-710 SLOBODNA GOSPODARSKA ZONA "ZADAR" "LUKA ZADAR" 23000 Zadar, Biogradska bb, Gazenicka 8 Contact: Zdravko Fain Tel: 385/23/23-170, 23-798 Fax: 385/23/436-431

FOREIGN TRADE

COMMODITY EXCHANGE

in '000 USD %

TOTAL EXPORTS	4,279,701	100.0
EU	2,088,369	48.8
CEFTA countries	580,685	13.6
Other countries	1,610,647	37.6
TOTAL IMPORTS	7,777,408	100.0
EU	4,391,678	56.5
CEFTA countries	1,080,381	13.9
Other countries	2,305,349	29.6

CROATIA'S MOST IMPORTANT TRADING PARTNERS

EXPORTS	in '000 USD	%
1. Italy	771,743	18.0
2. Germany	673,094	15.7
3. Bosnia & Herzegovina	547,139	12.8
4. Slovenia	453,419	10.6
5. Austria	264,572	6.2
6. Liberia	169,087	4.0
7. Norway	113,265	2.6
8. France	103,661	2.4
9. Malta	99,357	2.3
10. USA	86,413	2.0
Total Exports shown above	3,281,750	76.6

Total Exports of Croatia	4,279,701	100.0

IMPORTS	in '000 USD	%
1. Germany	1,439,467	18.5
2. Italy	1,234,236	15.9
3. Russia	668,074	8.6
4. Slovenia	616,102	7.9
5. Austria	549,189	7.1
6. France	392,363	5.0
7. USA	242,048	3.1
8. UK	181,043	2.3
9. Hungary	174,497	2.2
10. Switzerland	157,224	2.0
Total Imports shown above	5,654,243	72.7
Total Imports of Croatia	7,777,408	100.0

THE MAIN BRANCHES OF INDUSTRY IN CROATIA'S COMMODITY EXCHANGE

EXPORTS

Branch of Industry	in '000 USD	%
Manufacture of transport equipment (shipbuilding)	646,673	15.1
Manufacture of chemicals and chemical products	492,478	11.5
Manufacture of wearing apparel	441,373	10.3
Manufacture of petroleum derivatives	320,924	7.5
Manufacture of food products and beverages	276,239	6.5
Manufacture of electrical machinery and apparatus	192,927	4.5
Tanning and dressing of leather; manufacture of footwear	171 844	4.0
Production of non-metallic mineral products	163 445	3.8
Manufacture of wood and wood products	136 616	3.2
Manufacture of machinery and equipment	129 309	3.0

Total Exports shown above	2,971,828	69.4
Total Exports of Croatia	4,279,701	100.0

IMPORTS

Branch of Industry	in '000 USD	%
Manufacture of petroleum derivatives	771,454	9.9
Manufacture of chemicals and chemical products	403,373	5.2
Manufacture of food products and beverages	393,248	5.1
Manufacture of transport equipment (shipbuilding)	390,297	5.0
Manufacture of wearing apparel	312,323	4.0
Manufacture of electrical machinery and equipment	166,479	2.1
Tanning and dressing of leather; manufacture of footwear	145,123	1.9
Manufacture of non-metallic mineral products	126,922	1.6
Manufacture of rubber and plastic products	112,926	1.5
Manufacture of fabricated metal products	112,539	1.4
Total Imports shown above	2,934,684	37.7
Total Imports of Croatia	7,777,408	100.0

COMMODITY EXCHANGE ACCORDING TO PRODUCT

EXPORTS	in '000 USD	Index 99/98	%
Semi-manufactured goods	1,929,632	97.9	45.1
Investment goods	1,003,260	92.2	23.4
Consumer goods	1,346,808	90.9	31.5
Total Exports of Croatia	4,279,701	94.2	100.0

IMPORTS	in '000 USD	Index 99/98	%
Semi-manufactured goods	3,681,592	94.4	47.3
Investment goods	1,789,989	92.0	23.1
Consumer goods	2,305,826	91.0	29.7
Total Imports of Croatia	7,777,408	92.8	100.0

Source: CBS; Processed by: CCE

For additional analytical, marketing, investment and business opportunities information, please contact Global Investment & Business Center, USA (202) 546-2103. Fax: (202) 546-3275. E-mail: rusric@erols.com

LEGAL FRAMEWORK FOR FOREIGN TRADE TRANSACTIONS

In the course of preparations for Croatia's accession to the World Trade Organisation (WTO), a new legal framework for foreign trade transactions that is completely harmonised with the WTO rules and regulations has been prepared. Numerous laws, especially the Trade Act, have significantly liberalised trade and facilitated the exchange of goods and services with foreign countries. The import and export of goods are, as a rule, free, with the exception of qualitative restrictions or protective levies that may be introduced in accordance with the WTO rules and regulations. If the balance of payments experiences disturbances or if the import of certain goods threatens to damage or damages the domestic industry, **import quotas** may be introduced. They only help to protect national natural resources, provided that adequate measures are introduced in order to limit internal trade in these products.

In order to implement international contracts, to secure state safety, to protect the lives and health of people, animals and plants, as well as the environment, to control the import and export of works of art and of certain precious metals, certain goods are imported and exported on the basis of **a licence**. This licence is issued by the appropriate Ministry (e.g. the Ministry of Defence for weaponry and ammunition, the Ministry of Culture for works of art, the Ministry of Health for medicines, etc.)

In accordance with WTO rules and regulations, the Government may prescribe antidumping levies if certain goods are imported at a price lower than their real value and if such imports damage or may slow down domestic production growth. Antidumping levies remain effective only as long as the dumping prices that caused the damage exist.

If a contract with a foreign company or an international agreement stipulates that certain export and import goods have to be accompanied by a Certificate of Origin, the Certificate is issued by the Croatian Chamber of Economy, whereas the appropriate customs office issues EUR1 and EUR2 certificates.

Certain imports (food, cattle, some consumer goods, medicines, etc.) have to be accompanied by special certificates (sanitary certificate, veterinary and phytopathological certificate, certificate of quality). Certificates are issued by competent institutions, dependant on the type of goods.

In order to facilitate dealings abroad, all of the usual transport definitions apply according to Unique Rules for Interpretation of Commercial Expressions INCOTERMS 2004. When dealing with American business partners, transport definitions according to the Revised American Foreign Trade Definitions (R.A.F.T.B.) apply.

THE CUSTOMS ACT

In order to prepare Croatia's accession to European associations and to create all the necessary preconditions for a consistent implementation of the assumed international obligations prior to becoming a WTO member, Croatia adopted a new Customs Act that came into force on 1st January 2004. This Act introduces European standards that facilitate trade with the European Union and neighbouring countries that are Croatia's most important trading partners.

The basic features of the new Customs Act are:

- customs clearance liberalisation

For additional analytical, marketing, investment and business opportunities information, please contact Global Investment & Business Center, USA (202) 546-2103. Fax: (202) 546-3275. E-mail: rusric@erols.com

customs procedure acceleration

preconditions for the reduction of average tariff rates on imports

reduction of the tariff rates span, which is also a condition for becoming a WTO member

reduction of customs concessions.

A unique customs declaration is used in the customs procedure, the content and form of which have been adjusted to the documents used in the European Union. This unique customs declaration is also applied in the transit procedure, which is very important for Croatia as a transit country. In addition, a new customs value declaration has been introduced, which is in harmony with the customs value assessment rules defined in the 1994 GATT Agreement on the Implementation of Article VII.

The new Customs Act abolishes consignment warehouses and introduces public and private warehouses for duty-free storage of goods before the importer finds a buyer for those goods. Goods may remain in a warehouse for an unlimited period of time.

ATA Carnet

Croatia is a signatory to the ATA Convention on the Temporary Admission of Goods. ATA Carnets are issued and certified by the Croatian Chamber of Economy, which has been appointed as the issuing and guaranteeing association by the Customs Administration of the Croatian Ministry of Finance and the International Bureau of Chambers of Commerce (IBCC) in Paris. The Chamber assumes financial obligations for all imports and exports covered by ATA Carnets, and guarantees their appropriate implementation.

Croatian citizens returning to Croatia and foreign citizens immigrating to Croatia permanently

Croatian and foreign citizens who stayed abroad for at least five years and are returning/immigrating to Croatia permanently, are exempted from paying customs duty on household utensils, provided that they possessed and used those utensils for at least 12 months and did not use the customs concession before returning/immigrating to Croatia. Household utensils may be imported within a twelve-month period from the day of returning/immigrating to Croatia. The same rule applies to economic inventory items, provided that they had been used abroad for at least 12 months for the same purpose for which they will be used in Croatia.

THE CUSTOMS TARIFF ACT

In accordance with the rules and regulations of the World Trade Organisation, Croatia has harmonised its Customs Tariff Act and assumed the obligation to gradually reduce the customs protection level. During a five year transition period (from 2004 to 2005) Croatia is obliged to reduce customs duties for the most sensitive industrial products by the same percentage every year. The average tariff rate at the end of this period will amount to 5 percent, instead of the current 10 percent level.

The average customs protection level for industrial products has been reduced from 10% to 6.6% in 2004. For 50% of the total number of tariff headings (the majority of industrial products) the tariff rate ranges from 5% to 10%; it totals 0% for 25% of tariff headings, whereas the highest tariff rate of 20% is applied to 4.8% of the products (petroleum derivatives, textile products). The customs protection level for agricultural and food products will be reduced from the current average rate of 33.7% to an average rate of 16.4% within a seven-year period. Customs duties will be reduced gradually by identical annual percentages and adapted to the protection level of other European countries.

The average customs protection level for agricultural and food products has been reduced from 33.7% to 24.3% in 2004. The maximum protection level for certain agricultural and food products is determined by combining the percentage and the quantitative unit of the product. The amount based on the quantitative unit for seasonal products is prescribed in advance for the period in which it will be implemented, so that the conditions of importation will be known in advance for the entire year.

The tariff rates stipulated by this Act are applied to imports from:

the WTO member countries

those countries whose products enjoy most favoured nation treatment in Croatia

those countries in which Croatian products enjoy most favoured nation treatment.

For goods imported from those countries that have concluded a preferential trade regime contract with Croatia the rate stipulated in the contract is applied. For goods imported to Croatia from other countries the rate is 50% (if the Croatian Government determines such a rate). For the import of equipment, machinery, appliances, and vehicles and their parts, that have components that are manufactured in Croatia, the Croatian Government may determine a lower tariff rate or the rate defined as "sl", which stands for "exempt from paying customs duty".

FOREIGN INVESTMENTS IN CROATIA

Foreign investments in Croatia are regulated by the Company Act. According to this Act, foreign investors have the same rights, obligations and legal status within an enterprise as domestic investors, provided the condition of reciprocity is met. Foreign investors can acquire rights to additional guarantees which are not given to domestic investors. The Croatian Constitution states that rights acquired through capital investments cannot be withdrawn by law or any other legal act. It also insures free repatriation of profits and free repatriation of capital on disinvestment. Total foreign investments in Croatia from 1993 until mid 1999 amounted to 2.48 billion USD.

FOREIGN DIRECT INVESTMENTS

in '000 USD

	Country	Amount
1.	USA	1,003,714.29
2.	GERMANY	996,845.18
3.	AUSTRIA	706,302.82
4.	NETHERLANDS	137,515.90

5.	UK	94,601.26
6.	SWEDEN	93,395.58
7.	FRANCE	67,047.27
8.	SLOVENIA	59,359.31
9.	SWITZERLAND	55,029.92
10.	ITALY	52,660.80
	Total	3,266,467.33
	Other countries	288,693.26
	EBRD	76,318.09
	TOTAL	3,631,478.68

TYPES OF INVESTMENT FOR FOREIGN LEGAL ENTITIES

Foreign legal entities in Croatia are allowed to:

invest capital on a contractual basis;

invest capital in a company;

invest capital in a bank or insurance company;

start up as a sole trader or craftsman;

acquire the right to exploit natural resources or other assets of interest to Croatia;

take part in Build-Operate-Transfer (B.O.T.) deals and in Build-Own-Operate-Transfer (B.O.O.T.) deals.

According to the Company Act, it is possible to establish the following:

public limited liability company;

limited partnership;

joint-stock company;

limited liability company;

silent partnership.

Foreign persons are allowed to acquire shares and ownership stakes in existing joint-stock and limited liability companies. All such companies are required to be registered in the Court Register of the respective Commercial Court, dependant on the location of the company's headquarters. When establishing a joint-stock company or a limited liability company, a foreign investor may invest money, goods and rights. The minimum capital required when establishing a joint-stock company is the domestic currency equivalent of 30,000 DM, while the minimum nominal value of a share is set at the domestic currency equivalent of 10 DM.

A joint-stock company may also be established by a single natural person or legal entity. The minimum capital required when establishing a limited liability company is the domestic currency equivalent of 5,000 DM, while the minimum ownership stake is set at the domestic currency equivalent of 200 DM. A company may be established by one or more persons. A foreign natural person is allowed to operate as a sole trader in Croatia provided he, or she, holds a work permit and the condition of reciprocity is met. Before starting to engage in handicrafts, the person is required to obtain a licence, which is issued by the respective County office, dependant on where the headquarters of the particular handicraft is located. Preferential crafts are approved by the appropriate Ministry, dependant on the type of handicraft.

REPATRIATION OF PROFITS

The issue of transferring profits to a foreign country is regulated by the Foreign Exchange System, Foreign Exchange Transactions and Trade in Gold Act. According to this Act, the transfer of profits is unrestricted and may be effected after all legal obligations in Croatia have been met. If a company with profits to be transferred has its own foreign currency income from exports of goods and/or services, then the transfer of profits may be effected through the company's own foreign currency account held at an authorised local bank. A foreign investor may opt to keep the profits in Croatian currency in his or her domestic currency account held at an authorised local bank. In addition to the transfer of profits to a foreign country and payments in Croatia, the profits can be used for loans to domestic entities in accordance with the law, and for transfers into domestic currency accounts of other foreign persons.

OWNERSHIP RIGHTS OF FOREIGN LEGAL ENTITIES

If a foreign person establishes a company in Croatia, the company is considered to be a domestic legal entity and it may acquire real estate ownership rights irrespective of whether the real estate is acquired for business operations or for another purpose. Foreign persons are also allowed to acquire mortgage rights on real estate. Provided the condition of reciprocity is met, foreign natural persons or legal entities are free to acquire real estate in Croatia. The acquisition of real estate ownership rights is regulated by the Property and Other Proprietary Rights Act, and has to be approved by the Ministry of Foreign Affairs.

BUSINESS OPERATIONS OF FOREIGN COMPANIES

The Company Act provides special stipulations covering foreign companies (registered outside) and sole traders (recognised outside Croatia) who carry out business activities within the territory of Croatia. Foreign companies and foreign sole traders enjoy, in principle, the same rights as domestic legal entities in their operations within the territory of Croatia. The only condition that must be met when starting such operations is that a subsidiary must be established. Subsidiaries do not have the status of legal entities. All the rights and obligations stemming from their business operations are transferred to the founding company. A subsidiary may engage on behalf of the parent-company in all the operations that are included in the company's business activity.

REPRESENTATIVE OFFICES OF FOREIGN COMPANIES

According to the Trade Act, a foreign person may establish a representative office for the purpose of effecting market research, promotional and information activities and its presentation. A representative office does not have the status of a legal entity and is not empowered to conclude contracts. A foreign representative office may start operating upon registration in the Register of Representative Offices of Foreign Entities held at the Ministry of Economic Affairs. For its business operations, a representative office is allowed to hold both foreign and domestic currency accounts in authorised domestic banks.

CONCESSIONS

As foreign persons cannot become owners of certain types of real estate (natural resources and other wealth that is of interest to Croatia), rights to concessions are regulated by the Concessions Rights Act. The decision on whether to grant a concession is made by the Croatian Parliament or the Government. A concession cannot be granted for the exploitation of forests or other assets regulated by special laws if they are state owned. A concession may be granted to a domestic or foreign legal entity or natural person on the basis of the results of public tenders or bid invitations for a period of up to 99 years (40 years for agricultural land). The party granting the concession and the applicant sign an agreement that is inscribed in the Concession Register kept at the Ministry of Finance. An annual fee is paid for each concession right.

FREE ZONES

The Free Zones Act regulates free zones in accordance with world standards. The Act stipulates the following benefits:

domestic and foreign persons may be the users of a Zone under equal terms;

all forms of foreign trade may be carried out within a Zone, and the limitations of a law regulating foreign trade and foreign exchange operations do not apply to such operations

goods may be freely imported and exported

goods may remain within a Zone for an unlimited period of time

for the goods stored in a Zone no customs duties or taxes are levied and no other economic obligations are applied

the users of a zone pay profit tax amounting to 50% of the prescribed rate (e.g. 17.5%)

users who build or participate in the construction of infrastructure facilities within a Zone, the amount of which exceeds one million HRK, are exempted from paying profit tax in the first 5 years of doing business.

Free Zones can be established in the area of a seaport, river port, along international roads and in other areas in which there are conditions for their operations. A Free Zone may be established on the basis of a concession granted by the Croatian Government. A concession to establish a Zone is granted on the basis of a public tender or a public bid collection. A Zone may be founded by one or more domestic persons. Domestic and foreign legal entities and natural persons may be the users of a Zone, who carry out an economic activity in a Zone on the basis of an agreement made with the founder of a Zone. All activities may be carried out within a Zone (production of goods, refinement of goods, wholesale trade, mediation in trade, services, banking transactions, insurance and re-insurance services etc.), except for retail trade.

For additional analytical, marketing, investment and business opportunities information, please contact Global Investment & Business Center, USA
(202) 546-2103. Fax: (202) 546-3275. E-mail: rusric@erols.com

Established Free Zones:

Krapina-Zagorje Free Zone, Krapina
Free Zone Kukuljanovo, Rijeka
Free Zone Osijek, Osijek
Free Zone Podi, Šibenik
Port of Rijeka Free Zone, Rijeka
Free Zone Zagreb, Zagreb
Free Zone Obrovac, Obrovac
Free Zone Split, Split
Free Zone Ploče, Ploče
Port of Pula Free Zone, Pula

BANKING AND FINANCE

BANKS

Banks may be established by domestic or foreign natural or legal persons. Foreign natural and legal persons need to satisfy the condition of reciprocity before permission can be obtained for establishing a bank. This condition will cease to apply from the day that Croatia joins the World Trade Organisation (WTO) for all foreign natural and legal persons that are located in any of the WTO member countries. However, the condition of reciprocity will still apply to those countries that are not members of the WTO.

The level of founding capital that is necessary to establish a bank (20 to 60 million HRK) depends upon the type of operations that the bank wishes to perform. Newly established banks also have a time-limit restriction. Namely, they can start to carry out banking activities in gathering deposits and savings from citizens in both domestic and foreign currency only after a three-year period has expired from when the licence to operate was obtained.

A single shareholder may acquire more than 10% of shares with voting rights in the assembly only upon prior approval by the Croatian National Bank. If a bank acquires an ownership stake in another bank or in a company that exceeds its guarantee capital by more than 10%, or if it acquires a majority stake in another company, it has to obtain approval from the Croatian National Bank. These restrictions do not apply if the ownership stake is acquired in bankruptcy or distraint proceedings, or if security instruments stipulated by the Distraint Act are implemented. The scope of business of a bank has to be performed in such a way that the guarantee capital always amounts to at least 10% of total assets and active off-balance items, distributed and weighted by risk levels (minimum capital adequacy).

SUBSIDIARIES OF FOREIGN BANKS

A foreign bank can establish a subsidiary in Croatia provided that the condition of reciprocity is met. Such a subsidiary does not have the status of a legal person; however, it can carry out activities that are in accordance with the operating licence of the parent bank. A foreign bank that establishes a subsidiary is responsible for all of its obligations stemming from its operations in Croatia. The foreign bank has an obligation to keep a fixed deposit within the subsidiary in order to satisfy its operating requirements, i.e. a guaranteed capital deposit.

REPRESENTATIVE OFFICE

Foreign banks may open a representative office in Croatia provided that the condition of reciprocity is met. Such an office cannot carry out banking operations. Special regulations for establishing and operating a representative office are prescribed by the Croatian National Bank.

THE CROATIAN BANK FOR RECONSTRUCTION AND DEVELOPMENT

The Croatian Bank for Reconstruction and Development (HBOR) is the first investment bank established by the state, which in turn guarantees its obligations. This bank performs the following tasks: credit financing for development projects and the reconstruction of the Croatian economy; credit financing for the reconstruction and rebuilding of apartments, houses and infrastructure; credit financing for exports; insurance of exports against non-commercial risks.

INSURANCE COMPANIES

Natural or legal persons can establish a joint-stock insurance company. A maximum 15 percent single stake with voting rights can be held by a natural or legal person. For stakes larger than 15% special permission must be obtained from the Insurance Supervisory Directorate, which is the authority that issues operating licences and supervises the activities of insurance companies. Insurance activities may also be performed by subsidiaries of foreign insurance companies registered in Croatia. The domestic currency that has to be paid in establishing a joint-stock insurance company or a subsidiary of an insurance company cannot be less than the following amounts:

15 million HRK for carrying out life-insurance activities;

6 million HRK for carrying out an insurance activity other than life-insurance;

18 million HRK for carrying out several insurance activities other than life-insurance;

18 million HRK for carrying out re-insurance activities.

A foreign insurance company that has gained approval to perform insurance and re-insurance activities in the country where it is headquartered may establish a subsidiary in Croatia provided that the condition of reciprocity is met. This condition does not apply to foreign insurance companies that have their seat in any of the WTO member countries. A subsidiary of a foreign insurance company may perform insurance and re-insurance activities in accordance with the authorities of the founding company and approval by the Supervisory Directorate. A foreign insurance company that establishes a subsidiary is responsible for all of its obligations stemming from its operations in Croatia.

THE CROATIAN INSURANCE BUREAU

The Croatian Insurance Bureau carries out activities that are prescribed in the International Agreement on Insurance of Owners and Users of Motor Vehicles against liability during transit and for representing Croatian insurance companies in international insurance organisations.

THE CAPITAL MARKET

Entities established for dealing with securities are companies, bourses, other organised public markets, banks, account operators, transfer agents, the Central Depository Agency, as well as investment fund management companies. They can either be joint-stock companies or limited liability companies. The types of activities that such a company can perform depend on the level of its founding capital. Trades in securities that are issued according to public offers are carried out through bourses and other organised public markets (Zagreb Stock Exchange, Varaždin Securities Market).

A Stock Exchange must be established by at least 20 Croatian security companies as a joint-stock company and must have at least 20 members during its operation. The founding capital must not be less than 1,000,000 HRK. The Stock Exchange is obliged to include securities in at least two quotations, one of which (the highest quote) will be regarded as the official or regular quotation.

Institutionalised Public Markets are places where trade of securities that are not officially quoted take place.

The Securities Commission manages and supervises the issue and trade of securities, issues licences and approvals, and carries out other activities in accordance with the Securities Act. Securities are not to be issued in material form but rather must be electronically registered.

A Central Depository Agency was established in order to carry out activities related to the storing of dematerialised securities, as well as clearance and acquittance transactions based on these securities.

INVESTMENT FUNDS

The Investment Funds Act regulates the conditions for the establishment of investment funds and enterprises for their management. This Act stipulates the requirements for establishing open-end funds and closed-end funds. In order to establish an investment fund, approval by the Securities Commission is needed for the public collection of capital and property assets by public sale. That is, issuing of documents on the fund's shares or of shares which are to be invested in negotiable securities and/or real estate and deposits in financial institutions.

The establishment and operation of an enterprise for the management of a fund are subject to the provisions of the Company Act. The minimum required capital has to be at least 1,000,000 HRK and the enterprise has to employ members that have the necessary management skills in operating the fund. An enterprise for the management of an investment fund selects its own depository bank for the fund. Banks that have their headquarters registered in Croatia may perform this activity. The enterprise and the depository bank must act independently and in the best interest of their shareholders.

PRIVATISATION INVESTMENT FUNDS

Apart from open-end and closed-end funds, Croatia has also introduced the establishment of specialised funds under the Privatisation Investment Funds Act. These "privatisation investment funds" were established as part of the coupon (voucher) privatisation programme, i.e. the free distribution of shares held by the state to special categories of citizens. Seven privatisation investment funds have been established so far. These funds will have to convert to closed-end investment funds by 2004.

THE PENSION INSURANCE SYSTEM

For additional analytical, marketing, investment and business opportunities information, please contact Global Investment & Business Center, USA
(202) 546-2103. Fax: (202) 546-3275. E-mail: rusric@erols.com

Croatia is currently conducting a pension reform. The new pension insurance system will include three levels:

compulsory pension insurance based on generational solidarity (level I)

compulsory pension insurance based on individual capitalised savings (level II)

voluntary pension insurance based on individual capitalised savings (level III)

The Croatian Pension Insurance Fund receives compulsory contributions for generational solidarity from the salaries of all insured persons (level I). In order to realise the second level of the pension reform, special enterprises for the management of the pension fund (compulsory pension enterprises) will be established. Their role will be the establishment of compulsory pension funds, where employees will pay the obligatory contribution (part of their salary) to their account held within a pension fund.

Pension enterprises and domestic and foreign natural persons and legal entities can establish pension funds. The minimum capital required when establishing a compulsory pension enterprise totals 40 million HRK; a compulsory pension enterprise may supervise the activities of only one compulsory fund. An insured person may be a member of only one compulsory pension fund, and may hold only one account with that fund.

In order to realise the third level of the pension reform, voluntary pension funds will be established and managed by voluntary pension enterprises, the minimum capital of which will total 15 million HRK. An insured person may be a member of one or more voluntary pension funds at the same time.

A compulsory or voluntary pension fund is a special fund. It is not regarded as a legal entity and serves to collect the contributions from fund members and to invest them to increase the value of fund property in order to assure the payment of pension obligations to all fund members.

A pension insurance company may be established as a joint-stock company or a limited liability company that offers pension scheme programmes on the pension market, secures pensions within the compulsory pension insurance scheme based on individual capitalised savings, as well as pensions and other pension obligations within the voluntary pension insurance scheme based on individual capitalised savings. The Pension Funds and Insurance Supervision Agency supervise the second and third levels of the pension insurance system.

THE FOREIGN CURRENCY SYSTEM

Foreign currency transactions with foreign countries are based on the Foreign Currency System, Foreign Currency Transactions, and Trade in Gold Act, which states that foreign currency is freely available and that trade in foreign currency must be carried out through the foreign currency market. In legal terms, a foreign entity is a legal person that has its headquarters abroad or a physical person with residence abroad.

Payments and credit transactions abroad are realised through authorised banks (i.e. those licensed for foreign transactions) that are responsible for their own solvency regarding payments to foreign countries. Foreign legal entities may hold foreign currency accounts with authorised banks in convertible currencies, through which they can freely make foreign currency transactions and payments abroad. Foreign legal entities may deposit foreign currency into their foreign

For additional analytical, marketing, investment and business opportunities information, please contact Global Investment & Business Center, USA (202) 546-2103. Fax: (202) 546-3275. E-mail: rusric@erols.com

currency accounts held with licensed domestic banks. External payments can be made using either domestic or foreign currency.

Foreign entities may accept receivables in domestic currency in accounts held with domestic banks licensed to carry out business abroad under the conditions prescribed by the Croatian Government. Such receivables in domestic currency can be used by foreign legal entities for transfer abroad, for payment in Croatia, for loans to domestic legal entities in accordance with the Act, and for the transfer to another foreign legal entity's account (in domestic currency). Foreign currencies and securities nominated in foreign currencies can be freely brought into Croatia.

Legal persons from Croatia have to collect payments for exported goods within 90 days of when the goods were exported or the service provided. This time limit can be prolonged only once if approval is obtained from the Croatian National Bank. For exports to the Commonwealth of Independent States, payments must be made within 180 days.

Domestic legal persons can also make clearances or claim their credits (collect their dues) from abroad in foreign currency (cash), pay for the import of goods and services in advance, all in accordance with the Act. However, it is necessary to obtain special approval from the Croatian National Bank. Payment and collection of payments for carrying out business with foreign countries can be done by the following usual instruments of payment: documentary letters of credit (revocable and irrevocable, confirmed and unconfirmed, transferable and non-transferable, back-to-back, single and revolving, red-clause letters of credit,

TRADE AND PROJECT FINANCING

Brief Description of the Banking System

The Croatian National Bank (CNB) is the Croatian monetary authority with the primary task of maintaining price stability. It also defines and executes monetary and foreign exchange policy, manages international reserves, maintains banks' accounts, and is the regulator and policymaker for the banking sector. It is independent from the government and reports to the Croatian Parliament.

Foreign legal entities and physical persons may establish new banks or make investments in existing banks provided that the condition of reciprocity is met. The reciprocity requirement does not apply to foreign legal entities or individuals from WTO member countries. The minimum amount of capital required to establish a bank or a savings bank is:

HRK 20 million: banks established with this amount of capital can perform all banking transactions with citizens and individual entrepreneurs; no leasing or factoring is allowed; no credit card operations; only domestic payments

HRK 40 million: banks established with this amount of capital can perform all banking transactions; only domestic payments

HRK 60 million: savings banks established with this amount of capital can perform all banking transactions including international payment transactions.

On December 4, 1998, a new Banking Act was passed by the Croatian Parliament superceding the 1993 Law on Bank & Savings Banks, which sets forth the regulatory requirements for the commercial banking sector. The 1998 act sets the conditions for registering a commercial bank, supervision and control of banking transactions, and liquidation of a bank.

The Central National Bank (CNB) grants operating licenses to banks, branch offices and representative offices of foreign banks. Three years must pass after the CNB has granted a license before a bank can begin to accept local and foreign currency deposits from citizens.

The new banking law, implemented in January 1999, provides greater authority to the CNB to supervise and enforce banks' performance. It also introduced the concept of personal liability for bank management and regulated the establishment of an independent internal audit responsible directly to the supervisory board of a bank. The capital adequacy ratio was set at 10 percent of risk-weighted assets. If at any time potential losses are estimated to be larger than the bank's liable capital, the CNB can impose an administrator or initiate bankruptcy proceedings. Firmer guidelines and clearer definitions related to exposure towards related parties have also been set forth.

The government recently annulled the Bank Rehabilitation Act as a signal that it will no longer consider rescuing troubled banks. The government is revising the collateral law and working with USAID to establish a collateral registry.

Introduction of the new banking regulation was motivated by the 1998-2004 banking crisis, when the privatization of state-owned (and rehabilitated banks) began. This resulted in modification of bank behavior that had previously led to debt-for-equity swaps and eventually to insolvency.

The total number of banks in Croatia has dropped from 63 in 1997 to 42 this year (42 banks, 20 licensed savings banks, four licensed housing savings banks and the Croatian Bank for Reconstruction and Development). A high degree of concentration still exists with the top five banks controlling 68.5 percent of total bank assets. The top ranked banks consistently have included: Privredna, Zagrebacka, Rijecka, and Splitska Banka (note: these banks all have strategic foreign partners). In 2001, the Chamber of Economy selected Raiffeissenbank d.d Zagreb as the best managed bank in Croatia – the first time that a foreign bank was awarded the title. Zagrebacka and Privredna continue to dominate the market and together with Hrvatska Postanska Banka are the only banks with national networks. Competition between Zagrebacka and Privredna bank in retail banking became even more fierce after recent acquisitions (Privredna acquired small banks in Istria and Slavonia, while Zagrebacka took over Varazdinska Banka). Further consolidation of the system is likely to be achieved through larger regional banks' acquisitions or mergers with smaller banks in other areas of the country.

Significant restructuring and consolidation of the banking sector has been achieved only during the past two years. Opening of the banking sector to foreign investment is directly responsible for the progress achieved. There has been sizeable foreign investment in Croatia's banks along with some takeover activity by domestic banks.

Bank	Strategic Partner	Country	Year
Zagrebacka	1. Deutsche Bankers Trust (GDRs) 2. EBRD	N/A	2004
Slavonska	1. Hypo Alpe Adria Bank AG 2. EBRD	Austria	1999
Privredna	Banca Commerciale Commerciale (BCI)	Italy	1999
Splitska	Unicredito Italiano	Italy	2004
Rijecka	Bayerische Landesbank	Germany	2004
Bjelovarska Cakovecka Trgovacka	Erste & Steiermarkische	Austria	1999
Varazdinska	Zagrebacka	Croatia	2004
Dalmatinska	Regent Fund (Charlemagne Capital	UK	2004

	Ltd.)		
Istarska	Dalmatinska (CCL)	Croatia (UK)	2004
Dubrovacka	Being sold		2001
Croatia	Being sold		2001

Total bank assets were at HRK 104 billion (sep 2004), with only two banks holding assets of more than HRK 10 billion (Zagrebacka and Privredna Banka). At the end of 1999, the top four banks had a cumulative market share of over 60 percent.

Confidence in the local banking system is taking hold and measures taken to resolve "problem banks" are generating positive results. There has been a noticeable rise in foreign currency-denominated savings. Sources place the increase at HRK 2.9 billion during the first half of 2004. Growth in savings deposits exceeded HRK 1.5 billion. Again, these are positive signs of an improved level of confidence in the banking sector.

A unique feature of the former Yugoslavia was the payments system; all payments were required to be conducted through the payments bureau (Zavod za Platni Promet, ZAP). That system is being decentralized now, and the transfer of corporate transactions from ZAP to banks will take place first with individual accounts to follow. The IMF is working with ZAP, CNB and the Ministry of Finance to phase-in reforms since downsizing ZAP's sizable workforce will have significant social ramifications.

While the banking sector was able to establish a positive image rather quickly following the banking crisis, the deposit insurance scheme will continue to burden the budget for some time. The government re-scheduled rehabilitation costs by floating bonds that will mature in 2003 and 2005. At the end of 2004, the state agency for bank rehabilitation (DAB) floated Euro 330 million worth of bonds to pay for insured deposits held with banks under bankruptcy. Euro 105 million was placed for 3 years with an 8 percent coupon and another Euro 225 million for 5 years with a 8.375 percent coupon. This brings the total of bank rehabilitation bonds issued by the government to HRK 6.3 billion (4 percent of the 2004 GDP), with flotations maturing between 2003-2012.

B. Foreign Exchange Controls Affecting Trading

Croatia's currency, the kuna (HRK), floats freely, but the Croatian National Bank intervenes in the market from time-to-time to ensure stability of the currency, effectively ensuring the crawling peg (to the Euro) performance, disrupted by the seasonal impacts of tourism revenues.

The domestic currency exchange rate has remained stable for four years in a row, with the CNB's foreign exchange reserves estimated at over USD 4 billion. Local companies are allowed to hold foreign exchange accounts even for speculative purposes according to the Foreign Currency Act.

C. General Financing Availability

Throughout 1999, the increase in lending to the Government offset the decrease in lending to enterprises; household lending recorded much slower growth, although constant, compared to 1997 and 1998.

Bank assets totaled HRK 112.7 billion at the end of February 2001; 32.83 percent of that figure was placed with enterprises, with another 21.46 percent placed with households; 18 percent of all bank assets are placed with the central government.
Interest rates on pure kuna loans (53 percent of all bank lending) averaged 10.89 percent in February 2001, while the FX indexed loans (26.8 percent of lending) carried an interest rate of

10.27 percent. The average interest rate to foreign currency loans (4.38 percent of lending) was 6.63 percent.

Banks prefer the increasing supply of short-term fixed income securities increasingly issued by the government (T-Bills by the Ministry of Finance) over placing corporate loans. Although default ratios for household loans, just over 1 percent in 1997, have increased, this is the only loan category recording constant growth. The rationale for such developments lies in the reluctance of banks to offer financing based on anything other than "solid" collateral (real estate, securities) or an indirect government guarantee (extra-budgetary fund bills of exchange guaranteed by the government, loans to state-owned enterprises). Hence, trade financing has not developed to a satisfactory extent and complaints about banks being too slow or demanding inappropriate collateral are often heard.

D. How to Finance Exports / Methods of Payment Required for Exports

As per chapter 4 paragraph G, about 75 percent of the larger Croatian importers regularly receive goods under a short term (about 3 months) supplier credits. Croatian importers are free to arrange payments by long term supplier loans as well, and such financing is usually sought by Croatian importers for larger purchases. The following instruments are used in Croatia for payments abroad: remittances, documentary collections, checks, and letters of credit.

E. Available Trade & Project Financing

U.S. Trade and Development Agency (TDA)

TDA is an independent U.S. government agency, which promotes American private sector participation in developing and middle-income countries, with special emphasis on economic sectors that represent significant U.S. export potential. Through funding of feasibility studies, orientation visits, specialized training grants, and various forms of technical assistance, TDA helps U.S. businesses compete for infrastructure projects in emerging markets. TDA assists in building mutually beneficial partnerships between American companies and local project sponsors, which result in increased U.S. exports, and the completion of high quality, successful projects in host countries. In Croatia, TDA has recently financed projects in the sectors of power, telecommunications and transportation as well as increased activities in supporting private sector projects.

Contact: Jeanette Miller
Director, Business Development for Southeast Europe
U.S. Embassy
A. Hebranga 11
10000 Zagreb CROATIA
Tel: 385-1-492-1679
Fax: 385-1-492-1900
Mr. Ned Cabot, Regional Director
1621 N. Kent Street #200
Arlington, VA 22209-2131 USA
Tel: (703) 875-4357
Fax: (703) 875-4009

Overseas Private Investment Corporation (OPIC):

OPIC is a self-sustaining U.S. Government agency that sells investment services to small, medium and large American businesses expanding into emerging markets around the world. OPIC's three main activities are risk insurance, project finance and investment funds. OPIC financing through the investment guaranty program and the direct loan program is limited to $200 million. The OPIC sponsored equity funds make their own, commercially-based investment decisions while fulfilling OPIC's policy mandates. The most important fund for the region is the $150 million Southeast Europe Equity Fund (SEEF) managed by Soros Private Funds Management.

Contact: Mr. John Moran, OPIC Director for Southeast Europe
U.S. Embassy
Hebrangova 11/II
Zagreb, Croatia
Tel: 385-1-492-1677
Fax: 385-1-492-1900

Mr. James Gale, OPIC Investment Development Manager
1100 New York Avenue, N.W.
Washington, DC 20527, USA
Tel: 202-336-8629
Fax: 202-408-5145

Southeast Europe Equity Fund (SEEF):

SEEF is the result of an OPIC initiative to accelerate private sector investment in the SEE region. Following a competitive tender process, OPIC selected Soros Private Funds Management, LLC ("SPFM") to sponsor and manage the fund. SEEF makes direct equity and equity-related investments in attractive privately owned or privately managed companies operating in nine countries and territories in the region (Albania, Bulgaria, Bosnia and Herzegovina, Croatia, FYR Macedonia, Montenegro, Romania, Slovenia and Turkey). The total capital of the fund is $150 million, including a $100 million loan commitment from OPIC. The fund seeks to liquidate its holdings within 3 to 5 years through sales to strategic or financial buyers or through public offerings.

Contact:

Mr. Philippe Rombaut, SEEF Senior Regional Executive
c/o 45, Oborishte Street, P.O. Box 147,
1504 Sofia, Bulgaria
Tel: 359-2-943-4417 or 943-4163
Fax: 359-2-943 49 79

Mr. David L. Mathewson, SEEF Manager
888 Seventh Avenue
New York, NY 10106, USA
Tel: 212-333-9727
Fax: 212-245-5154

World Bank (IBRD)

Since 1990, the World Bank has committed $804.6 million with $491.75 million disbursed. The range of projects included: Istria Water Supply/Sewage, Emergency Reconstruction, Highway Sector Project, Farmer Support Services, Emergency Transport/Mine Clearing, Coastal Forest Reconstruction, Reconstruction Project for Eastern Slavonija. Other projects included: Municipal Environmental Infrastructure Project and a Railway Modernization/Restructuring. The Bank is negotiating a Structural Adjustment Loan of $200 million to complement the IMF's stand-by arrangement.

Contact information:

World Bank – Zagreb
Trg John F. Kennedy 6b
Zagreb 10000
Tel: (385)(1) 238-7230
Fax: (385)(1) 238-7200

Resident Rep: Vladimir Skendrovic

International Finance Corporation (IFC):

IFC, a member of the World Bank Group, offers a full array of financial products and services to companies in its developing member countries: long-term loans, equity investments, quasi-equity instruments (subordinated loans, preferred stock, income notes), guarantees and standby financing, and risk management (intermediation of currency and interest rate swaps, provision of hedging facilities). IFC Office in Zagreb - Representative Office in Croatia, as a part of Southern Europe and Central Asia Department (SECA), works in the region of rapid economic transformations, where partnership with other institutions and access to financing and expertise are urgently needed to ensure privatization and financial restructuring success. In Croatia, IFC has committed eight projects with total financing of US$123 million equivalent, including US$33 million in equity and US$90 million in loans.

Contact: IFC – Zagreb
Kennedyev Trg 6B
Zagreb, Croatia
Tel: 385-1-238-7256
Fax: 385-1-238-7233

European Bank for Reconstruction and Development (EBRD):
EBRD assists 27 countries to implement structural and sectoral economic reforms, promoting competition, privatisation and entrepreneurship, taking into account the particular needs of countries at different stages of transition. As a guideline, the standard minimum involvement for the Bank is € 5 million, though this may be reduced if the project has fundamental benefits for the country. The EBRD has established links with a variety of financial intermediaries to provide financing for projects that are too small to be funded directly. This allows the Bank to support SMEs, which are vital for generating a strong private sector. In Croatia the EBRD has approved $599.1 million of loans and $92.4 million of equity for 39 projects, with 66.5% of the total financing approved to the private sector.
Contact:
EBRD – Zagreb
Petrinjska 59 – 5th Floor
Zagreb, Croatia
Tel: 385-1-481-2400
Fax: 385-1-429-521

The Croatian Bank for Reconstruction and Development (HBOR):

HBOR is a state owned development bank, founded in 1992 by a resolution of the Parliament of the Republic of Croatia to facilitate the State's policies on the reconstruction and development of the Croatian economy. The Bank's activities include promoting small and medium sized businesses, shipbuilding, promoting development of the tourist industry, credit financing for

For additional analytical, marketing, investment and business opportunities information, please contact Global Investment & Business Center, USA
(202) 546-2103. Fax: (202) 546-3275. E-mail: rusric@erols.com

development projects, and construction and rebuilding of housing, infrastructure financing, as well as the financing and insuring of export transactions. In addition to the capital contribution from the State amounting to HRK 3.7 billion, to be paid in from the State Budget in total over the next few years, HBOR seeks alternative funding from international capital markets as well as from special financial institutions such as EBRD, IBRD, CEB, EIB and KfW. . HBOR obtained an investment grade credit rating from Standard & Poor's (BBB-) and Moody's (Baa3) in line with the sovereign ceiling, based on the sound banking operations and strong institutional support from the Croatian Government.

Contact: HBOR – Zagreb
Strossmayerov trg 9
Zagreb, Croatia
Tel: 385-1-459-1706
Fax: 385-1-459-1708

Export Import Bank (Ex-Im Bank)

Ex-Im Bank of the United States is an independent U.S. Government agency that helps finance the overseas sales of U.S. goods and services. Ex-Im Bank will finance the export of all types of goods or services, including commodities, as long as they are not military-related (certain exceptions exist). Major programs of the Ex-Im Bank are: working capital guarantees that cover 90 percent of the principal and interest on commercial loans to creditworthy small and medium-sized companies that need funds to buy or produce US goods or services for export; export credit insurance policies to protect against the political and commercial risks of a foreign buyer defaulting on payment; guarantees of commercial loans to foreign buyers of U.S. goods or services that cover 100 percent of principal and interest against both political and commercial risks of nonpayment; direct loans that provide foreign buyers with competitive, fixed-rate financing for their purchases from the U.S. In over 60 years, Ex-Im Bank has supported more than $300 billion in U.S. exports.

Contact:
Ms. Margaret Kostic, Director-SEE Initiative

Structured & Trade Finance Division
Ex-Im Bank
811 Vermont Avenue, N.W.
Washington, DC 20571
Tel: 202-565-3556
Fax: 202-565-3628

F. List of the Largest Croatian Banks with Correspondent U.S. Banking Arrangements

Privredna Banka, d.d.
Rackoga 6
10000 Zagreb, Croatia
Tel: (385)(1) 455-0822
Fax: (385)(1) 461-0416

Zagrebacka Banka, d.d.
Paromlinska 2
10000 Zagreb, Croatia
Tel: (385)(1) 610-4000
Fax: (385)(1) 611-0555

Splitska Banka, d.d.
Rudjera Boskovica
21000 Split, Croatia
Tel: (385)(21) 370-523
Fax: (385)(21) 370-535

Rijecka Banka, d.d.
Jadranski trg 3a
51000 Rijeka, Croatia
Tel: (385)(51) 208-211
Fax: (385)(51) 330-525

Slavonska Banka, d.d.
Kapucinska 29
31000 Osijek, Croatia
Tel: (385)(31) 201-022
Fax: (385)(31) 201-039

Dalmatinska Banka, d.d.
Ulica Marka Oreskovica 3
23000 Zadar, Croatia
Tel: (385)(23) 201-500
Fax: (385)(23) 201-859

The Croatian Bank for Reconstruction & Development (HBOR)
Strossmayerov trg 9
10000 Zagreb, Croatia
Tel: (385)(1) 459-1666
Fax: (385)(1) 459-1721

Varazdinska Banka, d.d.
Kapucinski trg 5
42004 Varazdin, Croatia
Tel: (385)(42) 400-000
Fax: (385)(42) 400-112

CROATIA CUSTOMS SYSTEM AND REGULATIONS

Effective August 8, 2007, new customs regulations came into effect in the Republic of Croatia greatly expanding the rights of Croatian trademark owners to stop, seize and destroy infringing and, potentially, parallel market goods. Based on Article 70, paragraph 3 of the Croatian Customs Law, the new regulation amends the handling of suspect goods.

The new regulation has the following key elements:

the extension of Customs measures providing protection for IP rights to goods circulating by mail;
a simplified procedure for seizure and destruction of infringing goods.

The principal impact of the mail change is likely to be on goods purchased over the internet and delivered to the purchaser by mail.

The provisions of the amended Regulation which provide a simplified procedure for the destruction of infringing goods raise greater concerns and confusion. According to Anamarija Stancic of SD PETOSEVIC, an intellectual property practice with offices in Albania and throughout the former Yugoslavia, the rights holder is now able to submit the request for the destruction of detained goods which are under customs surveillance *without an obligation to establish* that the detained goods are infringing. Previously, the goods would be held by Croatian Customs while the Croatian trademark owner sought and obtained a final decision from a court of law. This process was very time consuming due to Croatian requirements regarding notice to all interested parties to the litigation.

This new regulation raises positive and negative concerns. On the one hand, it greatly enhances the ability of Croatian trademark owners to protect their rights administratively at the border. On the other hand, it raises serious concerns about possible abuses and the due process rights of the importers. Anyone doing business in the Croatian market or transshipping through Croatia would be well advised to monitor how this regulation develops and is enforced.

Trade Regulations and Standards

TRADE REGULATIONS

IMPORT TARIFFS

Customs tariffs[1] currently range between 0 and 17.6% for industrial products with the majority subject to rates of 0 to 10%. The average tariff for industrial goods is about 3% and for agricultural goods 22-24%. Compound duties (ad valorem plus specific custom duty) are applied to a number of agricultural and food products. Maximum ad valorem duty is 64% and, where compound duty is applied, maximum ad valorem component is 15%. Under the WTO umbrella, Croatia is a signatory of the International Technology Agreement that provides for free import of information technology equipment. Import quotas have been phased-out.

TRADE BARIES

The American Embassy in Zagreb has received no complaints from U.S. exporters on trade barriers in Croatia nor is it aware of any.

IMPORT DOCUMENTS

A Croatian importer is responsible for providing the required import documentation, which consists of common trade, transport, and customs documents, as well as certificates required for quality control and licenses where appropriate. The single Administrative Document (SAD) that is used by EU and most other countries is the key customs document in Croatia as well.

Imported products are subject to quality control by market inspection officials. These officials are employed by the State Inspectorate[2] to ensure that imported goods comply with Croatian standards, whether they are appropriately labeled and packed, and whether they have required documentation or quality certificates. The products subject to quality control are those in which improper quality may not be obvious or may be dangerous for the consumer (and include most food and agricultural products, furniture, cement, textile, electric and gas appliances, agricultural equipment, etc. – the detailed list is published in the Decree Specifying Goods for Which a Quality Certificate is Required, (Official Gazette No. 127/99; available on www.nn.hr[3]). These products must pass quality control testing before they are put on the market (i.e. at manufacturer's or importer's warehouse). When applicable, products also have to pass sanitary, phytopathologic, or veterinary control. Information on sanitary requirements can be obtained from the Ministry of Health[4], and information on phytopathologic and veterinary requirements from the Ministry of Agriculture[5]. State Inspectorate officials are also in charge of implementing the Law on Protection of Consumers (Official Gazette No. 96/03; available on www.nn.hr[3]).

US EXPORT CONTROL

Although many technologies can be exported from the United States to Croatia under general export licenses, some equipment (e.g., dual-use technology) still requires validated export licenses from the Bureau of Export Administration (U.S. Department of Commerce) and/or Department of State. Exporters with valid licenses are no longer prohibited from supplying defense items and services to the Government of the Republic of Croatia.

TEMPORARY ENTRY

Temporary entry of products into Croatia is regulated in accordance with the EU Customs Code and international customs conventions. Croatia is a party to the Customs Convention on Carnet ATA for Temporary Import of Goods. Presentation of an ATA carnet or TIT carnet facilitates the process. An entry carnet can be obtained from a local chamber of commerce in the United States. Carnets are usually valid for one year and list the products to be entered on a duty-free basis. The carnet must be presented upon entry. Customs will stamp the carnet thereby validating it. Upon departure, the carnet must again be presented for validation, confirming that the product is being transported out of the country. Failure to re-export the goods results in application of the duties.

LABELING

Labels must contain the following information: name of the product, full address of the importer and the country of origin, net quantity/weight/volume, ingredients, manner of storage (transport, use or maintenance), and pertinent consumer warnings, including the information on any genetically modified organism (GMO) ingredients as defined by the Law on Genetically Modified Organisms (Official Gazette No. 70/05; available on www.nn.hr[3]). Technically complicated products must be accompanied by instructions on usage, the manufacturer's specifications, a list of authorized maintenance offices, warranty information, warranty period, and other applicable data. All information must be in Croatian and affixed to (or accompanying) each product before it is put on the market.

RESTRICTED IMPORT

There are no prohibited imports. Import licenses are required for arms/ammunition, military and police equipment, mobile radio sets, drugs, narcotics, antiquities, precious metals, waste, nuclear technology, chemical weapons' ingredients, and substances harmful to the ozone layer (a detailed list with HS codes is published in a Decree Specifying Goods Subject to Export and Import Licenses, Official Gazette No. 67/03; available on www.nn.hr[3]). Import licenses are required for a few products originating in countries which are not members of the WTO (for iron tubes and bars, and fertilizers). Import licenses are issued by the Ministry of Economy[6].

CUSTOMS REGULATIONS

Most import regulations were translated into English during the WTO accession process and are available from the Ministry of Economy[6]. However, to learn about the customs duties, taxes, and quality requirements for a specific product, U.S. exporters should contact a Croatian freight forwarder[7]. For contact information for Croatian Customs please go to the following website: http://www.carina.hr/engindex.htm[8].

STANDARDS

In response to the European Union requirements for technical harmonization and for establishing independent institutions for prescribing and for enforcing technical requirements,the Croatian parliament in 2003 adopted several laws to provide the basis for the final reorganization of the system inherited from the former Yugoslav federation. Pursuant to these laws, in 2005, the former State Office for Standards and Metrology was reorganized in the Croatian Standards Institute, the Croatian Accreditation Agency, and the State Office for Metrology, while the Croatian Metrology Institute is yet to be established.

ORGANIZATION

Croatian Standards Institute[9] (Hrvatski zavod za norme) – the institution responsible for preparation, adoption, editing and publication of Croatian standards
Croatian Accreditation Agency[10] (Hrvatska akreditacijska agencija) – the institution responsible for granting accreditation to testing and calibration laboratories, inspection and conformity assessment boards, and to certification boards for products, management system and personnel (such as ISO Standards)

State Office for Metrology[11] (Drzavni zavod za mjeriteljstvo) – the institution responsible for drafting metrology legislation and inspection; also responsible for homologation of vehicles

Croatian Metrology Institute (Hrvatski mjeriteljski institut) – the institution responsible for physical implementation/maintenance of Croatian metrology standards (yet to be established)

NIST Notify U.S. Service
Member countries of the World Trade Organization (WTO) are required under the Agreement on Technical Barriers to Trade (TBT Agreement) to report to the WTO all proposed technical regulations that could affect trade with other Member countries. Notify U.S. is a free, web-based e-mail subscription service that offers an opportunity to review and comment on proposed foreign technical regulations that can affect your access to international markets. Register online at Internet URL: http://www.nist.gov/notifyus/[12]

CONFORMITY ASSESSMENT

The list of the institutions authorized by the Croatian Accreditation Agency for testing and conformity assessment is available on its website[13].

PRODUCT CERTIFICATION

Every certified product must carry a certification marking. The certification marking indicates that the product has been the subject of appropriate testing and that it conforms to the provisions of the relevant regulations.

ACCREDITATION

As mentioned, the rules of the Croatian Accreditation Agency and the list of the accredited institutions are available on its website[13]. Croatia does not automatically recognize mandatory technical/quality tests conducted in other countries, i.e. there are no Mutual Recognition Agreements (MRA) signed with U.S. organization or any other countries. The state bureaus and ministries in charge of the specific product type (medical, agricultural, transport, etc.) have the authority to fully or partially recognize some foreign tests on a case by case basis, according to relevant legislation.

PUBLICATION OF TECHNICAL REGULATIONS

Technical regulations are published on the Croatian Standards Institute's website[14] and US entities can comment by contacting this institution. No foreign entities can propose draft standards.

LABELING AND MARKING

Until 2007, the Croatian symbol "C" was obligatory (granted by a certified testing institution) and CE mark could not act as a substitute. Reportedly, a new regulation that came into power on January 1, 2007 made the CE mark valid in Croatia as well. However, in practice, the legislation that was substantially changed during the past two years is still being fine-tuned, coordinated and enforced.

CONTACTS

Croatian Standards Institute[9]
(Hrvatski zavod za norme)
Ulica grada Vukovara 78
10000 Zagreb, Croatia
Phone: +385 1 6106095 Fax: +385 1 6109321
E-mail: hzn@hzn.hr
Managing Director: Mr. Dragutin Funda

Croatian Accreditation Agency[10]
(Hrvatska akreditacijska agencija)
Ulica grada Vukovara 78
10000 Zagreb, Croatia
Phone: +385 1 6106322 Fax: +385 1 6109322
E-mail: akreditacija@akreditacija.hr

For additional analytical, marketing, investment and business opportunities information, please contact Global Investment & Business Center, USA
(202) 546-2103. Fax: (202) 546-3275. E-mail: rusric@erols.com

Managing Director: Ms. Biserka Bajzek Brezak

State Office for Metrology[15]
(Drzavni zavod za mjeriteljstvo)
Ulica grada Vukovara 78
10000 Zagreb, Croatia
Phone: +385 1 6106323 Fax: +385 1 6109323
E-mail: informatika@dzm.hr
Managing Director: Mr. Mirko Vukovic

For further assistance with Croatian technical standards, please contact Damjan Bencic, Senior Commercial Specialist at American Embassy Zagreb at Damjan.Bencic@mail.doc.gov[16] .

TRADE AGREEMENTS

Free Trade Agreements

Croatia has free trade agreements[6] with EU, EFTA countries (Norway, Iceland, Liechtenstein, and Switzerland), and with Albania, Bosnia and Herzegovina, Serbia and Montenegro, Macedonia, Turkey, and Moldova.

Trade Relations with the European Union

In October 2001, the European Union and Croatia signed a Stabilization and Association Agreement (SAA). Related to the SAA, an Interim Agreement concerning trade and transport became effective on January 1, 2002. This agreement includes the Autonomous Trade Preferences that the EU previously extended to Croatia, providing all Croatian industrial and most agricultural products with free access to the EU market. On January 1, 2002, Croatia also started to extend gradually tariff preferences to the EU, providing free access to 70% of the value of EU industrial and agricultural products currently exported to the Croatian market. Croatia's formal application for EU membership has been accepted, and Croatia is now working diligently on accession negotiations[17] (that started on October 4, 2005) and on adjusting its entire legislative and administrative system in accordance with EU requirements.

RESOURCES

Croatian Customs: http://www.carina.hr/engindex.htm[8]
Ministry of Economy: http://www.mingorp.hr/[6]
Official Gazette: http://www.nn.hr/[3]
Croatian Chamber of Economy: http://www.hgk.hr[18]
Quality Superintending Company, Ltd.: http://www.zik.hr/

IMPORTANT LAWS AND REGULATIONS

EXCISE DUTIES ACT

PART I FUNDAMENTAL PROVISIONS

Article 1

This Act shall regulate the system of excise duties levied on alcohol, alcoholic beverages, tobacco products, energy products and electricity (hereinafter referred to as the excise products), released for consumption in the territory of the Republic of Croatia.

Article 2

(1) Excise duty shall be levied on the excise products manufactured or imported into and released for consumption in the territory of Republic of Croatia (hereinafter referred to as Croatia).

(2) The import of excise products shall be any entry of excise products from other countries into Croatia, unless otherwise stipulated in this Act.

Article 3

(1) Excise duty shall be levied on the excise products manufactured in the European Union or imported into the European Union from third countries.
(2) The import of excise products shall be any entry into the European Union from third countries or third territories, unless otherwise stipulated in this Act.
(3) The entry of excise products shall be any entry into Croatia from a Member State of the European Union (hereinafter referred to as another Member State), as stipulated in the European Union legislation, except from third territories.
(4) A third territory shall mean a part of the state territory of a Member State which is not a constituent part of the state territory of a Member State concerned or the European Union within the meaning of paragraph 3 of this Article, namely:

- in the case of the Federal Republic of Germany: the Island of Heligoland, the territory of Büsingen,
- in the case of the Italian Republic: Livigno, Campione d'Italia, Italian waters of Lake Lugano;
- in the case of the Kingdom of Spain: Ceuta, Melilla, the Canary Islands,

The French Republic may, by a declaration, inform about the status of its overseas departments.

Greece may keep the special status for the Mount Athos.

(5) A third country shall be any country other than Croatia and another Member State.
(6) Within the meaning of this Act, the movement of excise products into or from:

- the Principality of Monaco shall be treated as movement into or from the French Republic,
- Jungholz and Mittelnerg (Kleines Walsertal) shall be treated as movement into or from the Federal Republic of Germany,
- the Isle of Man shall be treated as movement into or from the United Kingdom of Great Britain and Northerm Ireland,
- San Marino shall be treated as movement into or from the Italian Republic.
- The Sovereign Base Areas of Akrotiri and Dhekelia shall be treated as movement into or from Ciprus.

Article 4

Excise duties revenues shall accrue to the Budget of the Republic of Croatia.

Article 5

Within the meaning of this Act, the following terms shall have the following meanings:

1. The **excise authorisation** shall mean the authorisation issued to a natural person or a legal entity by the competent customs house under which they may, as part of their registered business activity, receive, produce, store or carry out other actions on excise products at the excise warehouse, and dispatch excise products under excise-duty suspension arrangements.

2. The **authorised excise warehousekeeper** shall mean a legal entity or a natural person that has been granted the warehousekeeping authorisation by the competent customs house under which they may, as part of their registered business activity, receive, produce, store or carry out other actions on excise products at the excise warehouse, as well as dispatch excise products under excise-duty suspension arrangements.

3. The **excise warehouse** shall mean a place approved by the competent customs house, visibly marked and physically separated or enclosed from other areas or spaces, where the authorised warehousekeeper receives, produces, stores or carries out other actions involving excise products, and from which the excise products are dispatched under excise-duty suspension arrangements.

4. The **excise-duty suspension arrangements** shall mean the arrangements related to the receipt, production, storage or other actions involving excise products, as well as the dispatch of excise products under excise-duty suspension arrangements.

5. The **exempt user of excise products** shall mean a legal entity or a natural person that has been granted an authorisation by the competent customs under which they may, as part of their registered business activity and for the purposes referred to in Article 47, paragraph 1, items 3 to 11, and Article 79, paragraph 1 items 4. and 5. of this Act, procure excise products without being liable to pay excise duty. (hereinafter referred to as **the exempt user**).

6. The **exempt user's premises** shall mean a space or an area for storing the excise products which the exempt user has procured for the purposes of its registered business without being liable to pay excise duty.

7. The **importer of excise products** shall mean a customs debtor as defined in the customs regulations.

8. The **registered consignee** shall mean a legal entity or a natural person that does not have the status of the authorised warehousekeeper but has been granted by the competent customs house the authorisation to receive, as part of their registered business activity, excise products from persons or entities from another Member State under excise duty suspension arrangements. The registered consignee may not store or dispatch excise products under excise-duty suspension arrangements.

9. The **temporary registered consignee** shall mean a legal entity or a natural person not having the status of the authorised warehousekeeper but having the authorisation of the competent customs house for occasionally receiving, as part of their registered business activity, excise products under excise-duty suspension arrangements from another Member State. The temporary registered consignee may not store or dispatch excise products under excise-duty

For additional analytical, marketing, investment and business opportunities information, please contact Global Investment & Business Center, USA
(202) 546-2103. Fax: (202) 546-3275. E-mail: rusric@erols.com

suspension arrangements and has to lodge a security for the payment of excise duty with the competent customs house before the consignor dispatches the excise products concerned.

10. The **excise duty representative** shall mean a legal entity or a natural person empowered by an authorised excise warehousekeeper from another Member State to perform services and exercise rights in Croatia under this Act in the name and for the account of the latter.

11. The **release for consumption of excise products** shall mean:

- any derogation, including irregular derogation, from excise-duty suspension arrangements,
- any production, including irregular production, or excise products outside excise-duty suspension arrangements,
- any import, including irregular import, of excise products if they are not placed under excise-duty suspension arrangements.

12. The **Customs Administration** shall mean the administrative unit within the Ministry of Finance responsible for the application of customs, excise and other regulations within its scope of competence.

13. The **Central Office** shall mean the organisational unit within the Customs Administration responsible for legal, efficient and uniform application of customs, excise and other regulations within its scope of competence.

14. The **customs house** shall mean an organisational unit within the Customs Administration where the activities provided for under the customs, excise and other regulations are performed.

15. The **Financial Police** shall mean an organisational unit within the Ministry of Finance responsible for financial supervision of application of excise and other regulations within its scope of competence defined by special regulations.

I. EXCISE-DUTY SUSPENSION ARRANGEMENTS

Article 6

(1) The payment of excise duty shall be suspended if the excise products concerned are produced and/or stored at the excise warehouse, placed in the exempt user's facility and used for the purposes stated in the authorisation or dispatched under the excise-duty suspension arrangements in accordance with the conditions stipulated in this Act.

(2) The payment of excise duty shall be suspended in respect of the excise products which have been placed, immediately after their import, under a customs suspension procedure or brought into a free zone or a free warehouse.

(3) The payment of excise duty shall also be suspended in respect of the excise products imported in accordance with the customs regulations if the products are placed into an excise warehouse or the exempt user's facility immediately after being released for free circulation.

(4) If the authorised excise warehousekeeper or the exempt user terminate their business operations on account of bankruptcy proceedings or liquidation, the payment of excise duty shall be suspended so long as the excise products in stock at the date of the opening of bankruptcy or issuing the decision on initiating liquidation proceedings remain at the excise warehouse or the

For additional analytical, marketing, investment and business opportunities information, please contact Global Investment & Business Center, USA
(202) 546-2103. Fax: (202) 546-3275. E-mail: rusric@erols.com

exempt user's facility, or until they are released for consumption or dispatched to the creditor, except in the case where creditor is the authorised excise warehousekeeper, pursuant to the decision on asset distribution.

(5) If the excise warehousekeeping authorisation or the exempt user authorisation should cease to be valid on account of a merger of economic entities, the payment of excise duty shall be suspended so long as the excise products remain stored at the excise warehouse or the exempt user's facility or until they are released for consumption. The payment of excise duty shall be suspended for the period of 180 days from the day of entry of the merger into the company register at the latest.

II. MOVEMENT OF EXCISE PRODUCTS

Article 7

(1) Excise products shall be deemed to move under excise-duty suspension arrangements when:

1. they are moved from one excise warehouse to another,

2. they are moved from the excise warehouse to the exempt user's facility and from the exempt user's facility to the excise warehouse subject to previous approval of the competent customs house,

3. moved from the excise warehouse to exports,

4. after being released for free circulation, they are brought into the excise warehouse or the exempt user's facility, if the importer is the authorised excise warehousekeeper or the exempt user,

5. at the time of their importation, a customs suspension procedure is approved or they are brought into a free zone or a free warehouse,

6. they are dispatch from one excise warehouse to another across the territory of another state.

(2) The excise products may move under excise-duty suspension arrangements between Croatia and other Member States:

1. when dispatched from the excise warehouse in Croatia to a person/entity in another Member State, provided that such person/entity may, under the lega regulations in force in the country concerned, receive excise products under excise-duty suspension arrangements,

2. when the authorised warehousekeeper, and the registered and temporary registered consignee in Croatia receive excise products from a person/entity in another Member State, provided that such person/entity may, under the legal regulations of the country concerned, dispatch excise products under excise-duty suspension arrangements,

3. when the movement under excise-duty suspension arrangements between other Member States takes place across the territory of Croatia.

(3) The movement of excise products under excise-duty suspension arrangements shall be allowed only with the accompanying excise document (hereinafter referred to as the AED), unless otherwise stipulated in this Act or other regulations.

For additional analytical, marketing, investment and business opportunities information, please contact Global Investment & Business Center, USA (202) 546-2103. Fax: (202) 546-3275. E-mail: rusric@erols.com

Article 8

(1) The AED is a document accompanying the consignment of excise products and certifying that the stated types and quantities of excise products are moved under excise-duty suspension arrangements.

(2) The authorised excise warehousekeeper shall submit the AED on the prescribed form and in five (5) copies, of which:

1. the first copy shall be kept by the consignor,
2. the second copy shall be kept by the consignee,
3. the third copy, duly endorsement by the competent authority, shall be returned by the consignee to the consignor,
4. the fourth copy shall be kept by the consignee's competent authority, and
5. the fifth copy shall be kept by the consignor's competent authority.

Article 9

(1) The consignee of excise products moving under excise-duty suspension arrangements shall confirm the receipt of excise products to the consignor.

(2) The consignee shall confirm the receipt of excise products by returning the verified copy of the AED to the consignor:

1. not later than 5 days after receiving excise products in Croatia,
2. by the 15th day in the month following the month in which he received the consignment from another Member State.

(3) Before the consignee returns the verified copy of the AED to the consignor, he shall submit it to the competent customs house for endorsement.

(4) The export of excise products shall be endorsement by the competent customs house on the AED at the time when excise products leave the customs territory of Croatia.

(5) The export of excise products shall be endorsement by the competent customs house on the AED at the time when excise products leave the European Union.

(6) If the consignor does not receive the verified copy of the AED, he shall inform the competent customs house thereof:

1. not later than tenth days after the dispatch within Croatia,
2. not later than sixty days after the dispatch to another Member State,

and the customs house shall determine in accordance with this Act whether excise duty has become chargeable.

(7) If excise products are brought into the excise warehouse or the exempt user's facility after being released for free circulation, the movement of excise products under excise-duty suspension arrangements shall be allowed only with a copy of the single administrative document, by virtue of which the excise products have been released for free circulation. The consignee shall confirm the receipt of excise products by verifying a copy of the single

For additional analytical, marketing, investment and business opportunities information, please contact Global Investment & Business Center, USA
(202) 546-2103. Fax: (202) 546-3275. E-mail: rusric@erols.com

administrative document and returning it, within the period referred to in paragraph 2 of this Article, to the customs house where the import custom clearance has taken place.

(8) The Minister of Finance shall stipulate the ordinance on the method of completing and handling the AED.

Article 10

(1) Unless otherwise stipulated in this Act, the movement between the Member States of excise products on which excise duty has been paid shall be allowed with a simplified accompanying excise document (hereinafter referred to as the SAED).

(2) By way of derogation from the provisions of paragraph 1 above, the SAED shall also be used for the movement of completely denatured alcohol in Croatia and between other Member States.

(3) When requesting a reimburse of excise duty paid, the consignor shall file an application to the customs house competent according to its registered office or his/her place of residence before dispatching the excise products and provide proof that excise duty has been paid in Croatia.

(4) The SAED shall be submitted on the prescribed form in three copies, of which:

1. the first copy shall be kept by the consignor,
2. the second copy shall be kept by the consignee,
3. the third copy shall be returned to the consignor by the consignee.

(5) When the consignee in Croatia receives excise products on which excise duty has been paid in another Member State and excise duty is also chargeable in Croatia under this Act, the consignment shall be accompanied with the administrative accompanying document issued by the consignor in accordance with the legislation in force in the Member State from which the excise products have been delivered. The consignee shall inform the customs house in writing of the intended receipt of excise products and provide a security for the payment of excise duty.

(6) If the excise products released for consumption in Croatia are dispatched from one place to another within Croatia, but across the territory of another Member State, the consignor shall submit the SAED, and the consignment must move along the previously determined route. In such a case:

- before dispatching the excise products, the consignor shall inform the customs house of dispatch about the delivery of excise products,
- the consignee shall confirm the receipt of the consignment on the SAED within the period stipulated in Article 9, paragraph 6 of this Act and inform the customs house of destination accordingly,
- the consignor and consignee shall enable the competent authority to check whether the consignee has actually received the excise products.

(7) Instead of the AED and the SAED, a commercial document may be used.

(8) When excise products are moved under excise-duty suspension arrangements between excise warehouses of the same authorised excise warehousekeeper, and when the same consignor frequently and regularly dispatches excise products to the same consignee, a simplified procedure of issuing excise documents may be approved.

For additional analytical, marketing, investment and business opportunities information, please contact Global Investment & Business Center, USA (202) 546-2103. Fax: (202) 546-3275. E-mail: rusric@erols.com

(9) The Minister of Finance shall stipulate the ordinance on the manner in which the simplified excise accompanying documents are to be completed and handled, the conditions under which a commercial document may be used instead of the AED and the SAED, and describing the simplified procedure of issuing excise accompanying documents.

III. EXCISE DUTY PAYER

Article 11

(1) Any person/entity liable to pay excise duty shall be deemed to be the excise duty payer, and in particular:

1. the authorised excise warehousekeeper,
2. the importer of excise products,
3. the producer of excise products outside excise-duty suspension arrangements.

(2) The following shall also be considered excise duty payers:

1. the registered and the temporary registered consignee,
2. the excise duty representative,
3. the consignee of excise products on which excise duty has been paid in another Member State, and excise duty is chargeable also in Croatia,
4. the supplier of electricity and natural gas to end consumers.

(3) Besides the persons/entities referred to in paragraphs 1 and 2 of this Article, excise duty shall also be paid by:

1. the buyer referred to in Article 14, item 1 of this Act,
2. the buyer referred to in Article 14, item 2 of this Act,
3. the merged entity referred to in Article 14, item 3 of this Act,
4. the creditor referred to in Article 14, item 4 of this Act,
5. a person/entity which has irregularly produced, imported, introduced, transported, possessed, sold or bought excise products,
6. a person/entity having participated in irregular production, introduction or imports of excise products, as well as a person/entity keeping irregularly produced, introduced or imported excise products,
7. a person/entity that has lodged a security for the payment of excise duty in accordance with this Act or a guarantor stated on such instrument,
8. the exempt user of excise products when dispatching or using excise products for purposes other than those stated in the authorisation.

(4) If several persons/entities are liable to pay excise duty, they shall pay excise duty on a joint basis.

IV. CHARGEABILITY OF EXCISE DUTY

Article 12

(1) The excise duty shall become chargeable at the time of releasing the excise products for consumption, unless otherwise stipulated in this Act:

1. at the time of dispatch of excise products by the authorised excise warehousekeeper to a person/entity not authorised to receive excise products under excise-duty suspension arrangements,

2. at the time of production of excise products by the producer referred to in Article 55 of this Act,

3. at the time of consumption of excise products for one's own purposes within the excise warehouse,

4. at the time of establishing a loss or shortage of excise products, with the exception of the loss or shortage occurred during the period of excise duty suspension, if the authorised warehousekeeper is able to prove that such loss/shortage is a result of an unforeseen event or force majeure, or that the loss or shortage inseparably related to the characteristics of the goods has occurred during the production, warehousing and transport of excise products,

5. on the day when the excise warehousekeeping authorisation and the exempt user authorisation cease to be valid, as stipulated in Articles 25 and 29 of this Act,

6. at the time when the registered or the temporary registered consignee receives excise products under excise-duty suspension arrangements.

(2) Excise duty shall become chargeable when the consignee in Croatia receives excise products on which excise duty has been paid in another Member State for the purpose of performing its business activity.

(3) No excise duty shall become chargeable in Croatia in respect of the excise products on which excise duty has been paid in another Member State and which have been introduced into Croatia by a natural person for his/hers personal needs.

(4) In order to establish whether the excise products referred to in paragraph 3 of this Article are intended for personal needs or commercial purposes, the competent customs house shall take into account:

- the status of the person possessing the excise products concerned,
- the place of delivery of excise products and, if appropriate, the transportation method,
- the documents related to the excise products,
- the characteristics and quantity of the products.

(5) The Minister of Finance shall stipulate the ordinance on the type and amount of recognised losses or shortages of excise products referred to in paragraph 1, item 4 of this Article, and the quantities of the excise products referred to in paragraph 4 of this Article which may be introduced by natural persons for their personal needs from another Member State.

Article 13

For additional analytical, marketing, investment and business opportunities information, please contact Global Investment & Business Center, USA
(202) 546-2103. Fax: (202) 546-3275. E-mail: rusric@erols.com

Upon importation of excise products, excise duty shall become chargeable on the same day as the incurrence of customs debt in accordance with the customs regulations governing the calculation and collection of customs debt, except in those cases when excise duty is suspended in accordance with this Act.

Article 14

Excise duty shall also become chargeable when:

1. the customs house sells or assigns confiscated excise products, except when it sells or assigns them to the authorised excise warehousekeeper or the exempt user,
2. excise products are released for consumption during the merger of economic entities, except when the buyer is the authorised excise warehousekeeper or the exempt user,
3. after the merger of economic entities, when excise products are dispatched to the merged entity, except when the merged entity is the authorised excise warehousekeeper or the exempt user, not later than 180 days from the day of filing the application for entry of the merger in the company register,
4. when excise products are released for consumption or dispatched to the creditor during bankruptcy proceedings, except when the creditor is the authorised excise warehousekeeper or the exempt user.

Article 15

(1) Excise duty shall also become chargeable when it is established that excise products have been:

1. irregularly produced, imported, acquired, conveyed, used or consumed, or irregularly released for consumption,
2. dispatched or used by the exempt user for purposes other than those stated in the authorisation,
3. irregularly introduced into Croatia from another Member State, except if the natural person not performing any activity in connection with the excise products proves that he/she has acquired the excise products in good faith.

(2) Chargeability of excise duty on the excise products for which the consignor has not received the certificate of receipt in accordance with Article 9, paragraph 6, item 1 of this Act, shall be determined by the customs house competent according to the consignor's registered office. Excise duty shall become chargeable at the time of dispatch according to the excise duty basis and at the rates, or in the nominal amounts, in effect at the date of dispatch.

(3) Chargeability of excise duty on the excise products for which the consignor has not received the certificate of receipt in accordance with Article 9, paragraph 6, item 2 of this Act, shall be determined by the competent customs house unless the consignor presents, within four months after the dispatch of excise products, proof to the customs house that the transaction has been carried out in accordance with the applicable regulations or he submit the proof of the place where the offence or irregularity has occurred. Excise duty shall become chargeable at the time of dispatch according to the excise duty basis and at the rates, or in the nominal amounts, in effect at the date of dispatch.

For additional analytical, marketing, investment and business opportunities information, please contact Global Investment & Business Center, USA (202) 546-2103. Fax: (202) 546-3275. E-mail: rusric@erols.com

(4) If irregularities have occurred during the movement of excise products under excise-duty suspension arrangements between the Member States, and if excise duty becomes chargeable as a result of such irregularities, it shall be calculated in accordance with this Act if:

1. the irregularity has occurred in Croatia,
2. the irregularity has been detected in Croatia, but it is not possible to determine in which Member State it has occurred,
3. the consignment has been dispatched to another Member State from Croatia, but has not arrived at its place of destination, and it is not possible to determine in which Member State the irregularity has occurred.

(5) If excise duty is calculated in accordance with items 1 or 2 of paragraph 4 of this Article, the competent Croatia authority shall inform about that the competent institution in the Member State from which the consignment of excise products has been dispatched.

(6) The competent customs house shall discharge the payment of excise duty or reimburse the excise duty already paid in accordance with paragraph 4 of this Article if the consignor or the excise duty payer or another person acting for his/her account is able to present, within three years after the issuance of the excise document, proof to the customs authority that excise duty has been paid in the Member State in which the irregularity has actually occurred. The competent customs house shall reimburse the amount of the excise duty actually paid.

V. SUBMITTING DAILY EXCISE DUTY ACCOUNTS AND MONTHLY EXCISE DUTY RETURNS, EXCISE DUTY PAYMENT

Article 16

(1) Excise duty payers shall calculate and pay excise duty themselves according to the prescribed excise duty basis and rates or in nominal amounts in effect on the day of excise duty becomes chargeable.

(2) The excise duty payer shall disclose the calculated excise duty in the daily excise duty accounts to be supplied twice a month to the customs house that is competent according to the excise duty payer's registered office or place of residence. The daily account for the period from the first to the fifteenth day of a month shall be delivered by the twentieth day of the same month, and for the period from the sixteenth to the last day of a month by the eighth day of the following month. The calculated excise duty shall be payable within thirty days after it has become chargeable, unless otherwise stipulated in this Act.

(3) By way of derogation from the provision of paragraph 2 of this Article, the excise duty payer of tobacco products, shall have the obligation to state excise duty calculated at the time of dispatching tobacco products from the excise warehouse in daily excise duty accounts that have to be submitted on the working day following the day of emerging the obligation of calculation of excise duty.

(4) The excise duty payers shall not submit daily excise duty accounts referred to in paragraphs 2 and 3 of this Article for the period in which no excise duty has become chargeable or if it amounts to HRK 0.00.

(5) If the authorised excise warehousekeeper operates more than one excise warehouse, they shall submit cumulative daily excise duty accounts, provided that separate records of calculated excise duty are maintained for each warehouse.

For additional analytical, marketing, investment and business opportunities information, please contact Global Investment & Business Center, USA (202) 546-2103. Fax: (202) 546-3275. E-mail: rusric@erols.com

(6) The excise duty payer shall present the information on the state of inventories, on received, manufactured, dispatched or imported excise products, as well as the information on the calculated excise duty in the monthly excise duty return to be delivered to the customs house by the twentieth day of a month for the preceding month, unless otherwise stipulated in this Act.

(7) The excise duty payer shall submit the monthly excise duty return referred to in paragraph 6 of this Article also for the month in which no excise duty has become chargeable.

(8) If the authorised excise warehousekeeper operates more than one excise warehouse, they shall submit a cumulative monthly excise duty return on condition that records of inventories, of received, manufactured, dispatched and imported excise products are maintained, and information on calculated excise duty presented separately for each warehouse.

(9) If the authorised excise warehousekeeper does not calculate excise duty on tobacco products marked with tobacco stamps in accordance with this Article within 60 days after taking over the tobacco stamps at the latest, the tobacco products shall be deemed to have been released for consumption in Croatia, and excise duty shall be payable within 30 days after the expiry of that period at the latest.

(10) If the excise warehousekeeping authorisation should cease to be valid, with the exception of the cases referred to in paragraph 12 of this Article, the authorised excise warehousekeeper shall submit the daily excise duty account and the monthly excise duty return for excise products in stock, and excise duty on those products shall be payable within 30 days after the day when the authorisation has ceased to be valid at the latest.

(11) If the authorisation granted to the exempt user should cease to be valid, with the exception of the cases referred to in paragraph 12 of this Article, the exempt user shall pay excise duty on the excise products in stock at the exempt user's facility not later than 30 days after the authorisation has ceased to be valid.

(12) In the case of bankruptcy, liquidation or merger of economic entities, excise duty on the excise products in stock at the warehouses on the day when the proceedings are completed shall be payable within 30 days after the proceedings are completed or the products dispatched to the creditor.

(13) The Minister of Finance shall stipulate the ordinance on the content, form and method of submitting daily excise duty accounts and monthly excise duty return, as well as the method of excise duty payment.

Article 17

(1) On importation of excise products, excise duty shall be paid in accordance with the customs regulations unless the payment of excise duty is suspended or otherwise stipulated in this Act.

(2) If the import of tobacco products fails to take place within 60 days after the tobacco stamps have been taken over, the tobacco products shall be deemed to have been released for consumption in Croatia, and the importer shall be liable to pay excise duty within 30 working days after the expiry of that period.

(3) By way of exception, the period referred to in paragraph 2 of this Article may be prolonged if the importer is able to prove to the Customs Administration Central Office that the request for prolongation is justified.

For additional analytical, marketing, investment and business opportunities information, please contact Global Investment & Business Center, USA
(202) 546-2103. Fax: (202) 546-3275. E-mail: rusric@erols.com

(4) The importer liable to pay excise duty, referred to in Article 11, paragraph 1, item 2 of this Act, shall submit only the monthly excise duty return referred to in Article 16, paragraph 6 of this Act only for the month in which he has imported the products concerned.

(5) The Minister of Finance shall stipulate the ordinance on the conditions and procedure of prolonging the period referred to in paragraph 3 of this Article.

VI. REIMBURSEMENT OF EXCISE DUTY PAID

Article 18

(1) The following shall be entitled to reimburse of excise duty paid in Croatia:

1. the producer of excise products, who has procured excise products on which excise duty has already been paid and has used them to produce new excise products,

2. the exporter of excisable goods on which excise duty has been paid in Croatia,

3. the exempt user who has purchased excise products at a price inclusive of excise duty and uses them in accordance with Article 47, paragraph 1, items 3 to 11 and Article 79, paragraph 1, items 4 and 5 of this Act,

4. the person who has paid excise duty on energy products which are polluted or accidentally mixed and returned to the excise warehouse for recycling.

(2) Entitled to a reimburse of excise duty shall be legal entities and natural persons who, as part of their business activity, dispatch to another Member State the excise products on which excise duty has been paid in Croatia.

(3) Entitled to the refund referred to in paragraph 2 of this Article shall be the consignor if:

1. he/she files with the customs house competent according to his/hers registered offices or place of residence, an application for a refund of excise duty before the dispatching begins,
2. he/she presents a copy of the SAED on which the consignee has confirmed the receipt of excise products,
3. he/she provides a document certifying that a security for the payment of excise duty has been lodged in the country of destination,
4. he/she provides any other proof as may be required by the customs house with regard to the specific circumstances in order to establish justifiability of excise duty reimbursement.

(4) The Minister of Finance shall stipulate the ordinance on the conditions and manner of exercising the right to a refund of excise duty.

VII. EXEMPTIONS FROM EXCISE DUTY

Article 19

(1) Excise duty shall not be payable on excise products intended for:

For additional analytical, marketing, investment and business opportunities information, please contact Global Investment & Business Center, USA
(202) 546-2103. Fax: (202) 546-3275. E-mail: rusric@erols.com

1. office needs of diplomatic and consular missions and special missions accredited in Croatia, on condition of reciprocity, with the exception of consular missions lead by honorary consular officers,

2. personal needs of foreign staff of diplomatic missions and consular posts and special missions accredited in Croatia,

3. needs of international organisations, if so stipulated in international agreements applying to Croatia,

4. personal needs of foreign staff of international organisations, if so stipulated in international agreement applying to Croatia,

5. the consumption in accordance with an international agreement concluded between Croatia and another state or an international organisation, if such an agreement provides for an exemption from VAT tax in the case of delivery of excise products,

6. the needs of the armed forces of other state parties to the North Atlantic Alliance or the civilian staff accompanying them or for supplying their messes and canteens.

(2) The exemption from excise duty referred to in paragraph 1, items 1 and 2 of this Article shall be granted on the basis of certification by the ministry competent for foreign affairs, and the exemptions referred to in paragraph 1, items 3, 4, 5 and 6 of this Article on the basis of certification of the competent state authority responsible for the implementation of the particular international agreement.

(3) If, under an international agreement, the exemption can be granted only on condition of reciprocity, the ministry competent for foreign affairs shall confirm that the condition of reciprocity is satisfied.

(4) The exemptions from excise duty referred to in paragraph 1, items 2 and 4 of this Article may not be granted to the citizens of Croatia or foreign nationals having their usual residence in Croatia.

(5) If the persons exempt from the payment of excise duty in accordance with paragraph 1 of this Article procure excise products from another Member State, the consignor may dispatch them under excise-duty suspension arrangements only if accompanied with an AED and a certificate of exemption from excise duty, as determined by the EU legislation.

(6) The excise products on which no excise duty is payable in accordance with paragraph 1 of this Article may only be disposed of subject to previous notification to the competent customs house and payment of excise duty.

Article 20

(1) Excise duty shall not be payable on the excise products:

1. which are delivered from an excise warehouse to customs warehouses for the purpose of supplying ships and aircraft on international routes,

2. which are delivered from an excise warehouse to the facilities of a customs warehouse located at airports or harbours opened to international traffic for the purpose of being sold to passengers travelling to another state against presentation of a boarding pass,

3. which are brought by a traveller from another state as part of personal luggage and are exempt from customs duties in accordance with the customs regulations,

For additional analytical, marketing, investment and business opportunities information, please contact Global Investment & Business Center, USA
(202) 546-2103. Fax: (202) 546-3275. E-mail: rusric@erols.com

4. which a natural person from another state sends to another natural person in the Republic of Croatia in consignments free of charge, which are not of a commercial nature and are exempt from customs duties in accordance with the customs regulations.

(2) The authorised excise warehousekeeper and the exempt user are exempt from the payment of excise duty on the excise products:

1. which are used as samples in the analyses for trial production, or for scientific purposes;
2. which are used for quality control,
3. which are used for the purpose of excise monitoring,
4. which have been destroyed under customs supervision,
5. on which losses or shortages have been established, if proven that such loss/shortage can be ascribed to unforeseen events or force majeure, or that losses or shortages inseparably related to the characteristics of the goods have occurred during the production, warehousing and transport of excise products and if recognised by the competent customs house

(3) If applicable, the provisions of paragraph 2 of this Article shall apply both to the registered and the temporary registered consignee.

(4) The losses or shortages referred to in paragraph 2, item 5 and paragraph 3 of this Article which have occurred within the European Union during the transport of excise products shall be determined in accordance with the rules of the Member State of destination.

(5) The Minister of Finance shall stipulate the ordinance on the manner and conditions on which the right to exemptions from excise duty referred to in Articles 19 and 20 of this Act may be exercised.

VIII. GENERAL CONDITIONS FOR OPERATION OF EXCISE WAREHOUSES

Article 21

(1) Receiving, production, storage or other actions, as well as the dispatch of excise products under excise-duty suspension arrangements may be performed only in the excise warehouse having the excise warehousekeeping authorisation issued by the competent customs house to an authorised warehousekeeper, unless otherwise stipulated in this Act

(2) The excise warehousekeeping authorisation shall be issued by the customs house competent according to the registered office or place of residence of a legal entity or natural person meeting the following requirements:

1. performs a business activity in connection with excise products in accordance with the prescribed conditions and has the registered office or residence in Croatia,
2. settles tax and customs liabilities regularly,
3. has not committed a serious or repeated breach of tax or customs regulations
4. has lodged a security for the payment of excise duty before the authorisation has been issued,
5. maintains records of products stored at the excise warehouse,
6. meets the requirements for electronic exchange of data related to the movement of excise products.

For additional analytical, marketing, investment and business opportunities information, please contact Global Investment & Business Center, USA (202) 546-2103. Fax: (202) 546-3275. E-mail: rusric@erols.com

Article 22

(1) The excise authorisation for authorised excise warehousekeeper and for excise warehouse shall be issued upon written application of a legal entity or a natural person wishing to operate under excise-duty suspension arrangements, and it may not be transferred to another person/entity.

(2) The application referred to in paragraph 1 of this Article, shall contain the following information: the applicant's identification data, the type of excise goods, a description of the registered business activity, the type, the trade name and the Combined Nomenclature code (hereinafter referred to as CN code) and the quantity of excise products for which the excise warehousekeeping authorisation is requested, the foreseen annual production quantities, and the quantities of stored products or products to be stored. Together with the application, the applicant shall also provide documents showing the location of the excise warehouse, describing the warehouse facilities, the method of dispatching excise products, individual production procedures, and including also information on the devices used to measure the quantities of produced, processed, stored and dispatched excise products and a description of the accounting system.

(3) Before issuing the excise authorisation for the authorised excise warehousekeeper and the excise warehouse, the customs house shall verify the authenticity of the facts and information stated in the application referred to in paragraph 2 of this Article and establish on the spot whether the requirements for issuing the excise warehousekeeping authorisation are satisfied. If it is found that the applicant does not meet the stipulated requirements, the competent customs house shall set a period within which the irregularities have to be removed.

(4) The authorised excise warehousekeeper shall file a separate application for opening each new excise warehouse.

(5) The Minister of Finance shall stipulate the ordinance on setting out the requirements for establishing and operating an excise warehouse and describing the procedure of issuing the warehousekeeping authorisation.

Article 23

(1) The authorised warehousekeeper shall:

1. take all necessary measures to ensure that excise products are secure at the excise warehouse; supervise all procedures, including the dispatch and receipt of excise products; determine and report to the customs house any losses or shortages of excise products; check whether there are any irregularities in the operations of the excise warehouse,

2. ensure conditions for smooth supervision,

3. maintain records of the stock of excise products by type and quantity, separate records of the movement of excise products for each excise warehouse, and supply the competent customs house with daily excise duty accounts and monthly excise duty returns,

For additional analytical, marketing, investment and business opportunities information, please contact Global Investment & Business Center, USA (202) 546-2103. Fax: (202) 546-3275. E-mail: rusric@erols.com

4. inform the customs house about all changes of data stated in the excise warehousekeeping authorisation,

5. in the event of a change in its status, the expansion, restriction or termination of its business activity, as well as the establishment and operation of new excise warehouses, request the customs house to amend the excise warehousekeeping authorisation accordingly.

(2) If the customs house establishes that the authorised excise warehousekeeper fails or has failed to perform the obligations referred to in paragraph 1 of this Article, it shall set a time limit within which the irregularities have to be removed and, if necessary, take other actions in accordance with this Act.

(3) The Minister of Finance shall stipulate the ordinance on defining the content and method of keeping the records referred to in paragraph 1, item 4 of this Article.

Article 24

(1) The authorised excise warehousekeeper shall lodge with the Customs Administration a security for the payment of a potential excise debt in respect of excise products under excise-duty suspension arrangements in accordance with the provisions of this Act.

(2) The lodging of security shall be mandatory when dispatching excise products under excise-duty suspension arrangements for the excise products produced and warehoused at the excise warehouse, unless they are dispatched by means of fixed pipelines.

(3) The state administration bodies shall not be required to lodge a security.

(4) By way of derogation from paragraph 1 of this Article, instead of the authorised excise warehousekeeper dispatching the excise products under excise-duty suspension arrangements from Croatia to another Member State, the security may also be lodged by the transporter or the owner of the excise products.

(5) The provisions of paragraph 4 above shall also apply when excise products are dispatched from another Member State to Croatia by a person/entity authorised in accordance with the legislation of that Member State to dispatch excise products under excise-duty suspension arrangements to other Member States.

(6) The amount of the security lodged for excise products dispatched from the excise warehouse under excise-duty suspension arrangements shall be determined by the customs house depending on the amount of a potential excise debt.

(7) The amount of the security lodged for excise products produced and stored at the excise warehouse under excise-duty suspension arrangements shall be determined by the customs house depending on the amount of a potential excise debt in the relevant taxation period.

(8) The Customs Administration can decide that the amount of the security for the payment of excise duty may be lower than the amount referred to in paragraph 7 of this Article

(9) If the authorised excise warehousekeeper operates several excise warehouses, it may lodge a single security for all the excise warehouses.

For additional analytical, marketing, investment and business opportunities information, please contact Global Investment & Business Center, USA (202) 546-2103. Fax: (202) 546-3275. E-mail: rusric@erols.com

(10) The lodging of a security shall not be necessary for excise products where the amount of excise duty in HRK 0.00.

(11) If the excise warehousekeeping authorisation expires, the security may be released only after the excise duty has been paid on the excise products in stock and the excise products for which excise duty has become chargeable before the expiry of the excise warehousekeeping authorisation, and when excise duty on excise products moving under excise-duty suspension arrangements may no longer become chargeable.

(12) The Minister of Finance shall stipulate the ordinance on the type and amount of the payment security, and the manner in which it has to be lodged, along with the criteria when a the amount of the security may be reduced.

Article 25

(1) The excise warehousekeeping authorisation shall cease to be valid:

1. at the point of death of the authorised excise warehousekeeper - a natural person,
2. at the point of dissolution of the legal entity,
3. when the excise warehousekeeping authorisation is returned to the customs house,
4. when the customs house withdraws the excise warehousekeeping authorisation.

(2) The customs house shall withdraw the excise warehousekeeping authorisation: if the authorised excise warehousekeeper no longer meets the requirements set out in the excise warehousekeeping authorisation or does not ensure adequate system of monitoring the state of stock, or does not compile lists of stock within the time limits stipulated in the excise warehousekeeping authorisation; if it does not lodge an appropriate security for the payment of excise duty or does not lodge a security in an amount sufficient to ensure payment of excise debt; if the grounds and conditions for issuing the excise warehousekeeping authorisation no longer exist; if the authorisation has been issued on the basis of incomplete or inaccurate information; if it does not remove the irregularities within the time limit determined by the customs house; if it is involved in criminal actions; if it evades the payment of excise duty.

(3) An appeal against the withdrawal of the excise warehousekeeping authorisation shall not postpone the enforcement of the decision. By the time the decision on the appeal is made, the customs house may postpone the withdrawal of the authorisation if they estimate that the appeal might be accepted.

(4) The Minister of Finance shall stipulate the ordinance on the conditions and procedure of the expiry of validity of a warehousekeeping authorisation.

IX. EXEMPT USER OF EXCISE PRODUCTS

Article 26

For additional analytical, marketing, investment and business opportunities information, please contact Global Investment & Business Center, USA
(202) 546-2103. Fax: (202) 546-3275. E-mail: rusric@erols.com

(1) The exempt user of excise products may procure excise products without being liable to pay excise duty by virtue of an authorisation granted by the customs house competent according to the exempt user's registered office or place of residence.

(2) The authorisation referred to in paragraph 1 of this Article may be applied for by a legal entity or natural person meeting the following requirements:

1. performs a business activity in accordance with the prescribed conditions and uses for the purpose of that activity excise products within the meaning of Article 47, paragraph 1, items 3 to 11 and Article 79, paragraph 1, items 4 and 5 of this Act, and its registered office or place of residence is in Croatia,

2. settles tax and customs liabilities regularly,

3. has committed no serious or repeated breaches of tax or customs regulations.

(3) Besides the requirements referred to in the preceding paragraph, the following requirements must also be met:

1. the production area, the warehouse or another area used for storing excise products are organised and equipped in such a way that enables safe storage and use of the excise products procured, as well as correct measurement of stock of those products,

2. the accounting records give a true and accurate picture of the consumption of excise products and of the state of stock of the products for whose production the excise products have been used.

Article 27

(1) The authorisation shall be granted to the exempt user by the customs house upon written application.

(2) The authorisation shall be issued in the name of the applicant and may not be transferred to another person.

(3) In the authorisation, the customs house shall state the quantities and types of excise products that can be procured free of excise duty for the prescribed purposes and within a specific period which may not be longer than 12 months, then the space or area and the purpose of use of excise products. The quantities shall be determined according to the production capacities and the period for which the authorisation is issued.

(4) The quantities determined in the authorisation referred to in paragraph 3 of this Article may be changed upon subsequent application.

(5) The Minister of Finance shall stipulate the ordinance on the conditions of operation of the exempt user's facility, and the procedure for issuing and amending the exempt user authorisation.

Article 28

(1) The exempt user of excise products shall:

1. maintain records of the purchase, production and consumption of excise products by type and quantity and submit, at the request of the customs house, a report on the state of stock of excise products procured free of excise duty,

2. inform the customs house about all changes of information stated in the authorisation,

3. ensure conditions for smooth supervision.

(2) The Minister of Finance shall stipulate the ordinance on the content and method of maintaining the records referred to in paragraph 1, item 1 of this Article.

Article 29

(1) The authorisation referred to in Article 27 of this Act shall cease to be valid:

1. upon expiry of validity of the authorisation,

2. at the point of death of the exempt user of excise products being a natural person,

3. at the point of dissolution of the legal entity,

4. when the authorisation is returned to the customs house,

5. when the customs house withdraws the authorisation.

(2) The customs house shall withdraw the authorisation if the exempt user no longer meets the requirements set out in the authorisation, does not ensure adequate system of stock monitoring; if the authorisation has been issued on the basis of incomplete or inaccurate information, if the user does not remove the irregularities within the period determined by the customs house.

(3) An appeal against the withdrawal of the authorisation shall not postpone the enforcement of the decision. By the time the decision on the appeal is made, the customs house may postpone the withdrawal of the authorisation if they estimate that the appeal might be accepted.

(4) The Minister of Finance shall stipulate the ordinance on the conditions and procedure of the expiry of validity of the authorisation.

X. REGISTERED AND TEMPORARY REGISTERED CONSIGNEE AND EXCISE DUTY REPRESENTATIVE

Article 30

(1) The registered consignee may, as part of its business activity, receive excise products from another Member State under excise-duty suspension arrangements if it has registered offices or the place of residence or a business unit in Croatia and has obtained the authorisation to do so from the customs house competent according to the registered office or place of residence.

(2) The authorisation referred to in paragraph 1 of this Article shall be issued by the customs house upon written application which must contain the following information: the applicant's identification data and registered office if the applicant is a legal entity, or the place of residence if it is a natural person, the tax number (Personal Identification Number), a description of the

business activity, the trade name and CN code of the products for which the authorisation is requested, the full name of the applicant's responsible person, information on the security for the payment of excise duty and proof that the conditions ensuring smooth supervision are fulfilled, and a description of the accounting system operation.

(3) Before issuing the authorisation, the customs house shall verify the authenticity of the facts and information stated in the application referred to in paragraph 2 of this Article and establish on the spot whether the requirements for issuing the authorisation have been met. If it is found that the applicant does not meet the prescribed requirements, the customs house shall determine the time limit within which the irregularities are to be removed.

(4) The authorisation shall be issued in the name of the applicant and may not be transferred to another person.

(5) The registered consignee has to:

1. lodge a security for the payment of excise duty before the authorisation is issued,
2. settle tax and customs liabilities regularly,
3. maintain records of excise products received by trade name, CN code, quantity, date of receipt and consignor,
4. meet the requirements regarding electronic exchange of data related to the movement of excise products,
5. inform the customs house about all changes of information stated in the application,
6. ensure smooth supervision.

(6) The authorisation shall terminate at the point of dissolution of a legal entity, at the point of death of a natural person, when the authorisation is returned to the customs house or when the customs house withdraws the authorisation.

(7) The customs house shall withdraw the authorisation if the registered trader no longer meets the requirements stated in the authorisation: if it fails to ensure an adequate supervision system, if it fails to lodge an adequate security for the payment of excise duty or to provide it in an amount ensuring the payment of excise debt; if the grounds and conditions for issuing the authorisation no longer exist; if the authorisation has been issued on the basis of incomplete or incorrect information; if the irregularities are not removed within the time limit set by the customs house.

(8) An appeal against the withdrawal of the authorisation shall not postpone the enforcement of the decision. By the time the decision on the appeal is made, the customs house may postpone the withdrawal of the authorisation if they estimate that the appeal might be accepted.

(9) The Minister of Finance shall stipulate the ordinance on the conditions and procedure for issuance and expiry of validity of the authorisation granted to the registered trader, the procedure of lodging the payment security, its type and amount, as well as the content and method of maintaining records.

Article 31

(1) In the course of its business activities, the temporary registered consignee may from occasionally receive excise products from another Member State under excise-duty suspension arrangements if has registered offices or place of residence or a business unit in Croatia.

For additional analytical, marketing, investment and business opportunities information, please contact Global Investment & Business Center, USA (202) 546-2103. Fax: (202) 546-3275. E-mail: rusric@erols.com

(2) The temporary registered consignee has to:

1. inform the customs house competent according to its registered office or place of residence or business unit about the consignment of excise products before they are dispatched by the consignor and the place of their receipt,

2. lodge with the customs house a security for the payment of excise duty on excise products which it receives in the capacity as the temporary registered consignee under excise-duty suspension arrangements before the excise products are dispatched by the consignor,

3. enable the customs house to perform supervision of the type and quantity of the excise products received and the amount of excise duty paid,

4. pay excise duty in accordance with this Act,

5. maintain records of the excise products received by trade name, CN code, quantity, date of receipt and consignor.

(3) The Minister of Finance shall stipulate the ordinance on the type of security for the payment of excise duty and procedure of lodging it in accordance with this Article.

Article 32

(1) A registered excise warehousekeeper from another Member State may appoint an excise duty representative in Croatia to fulfil the obligations and exercise the rights in accordance with this Act. The excise duty representative may be a legal entity or a natural person having its registered office or place of residence or a business unit in Croatia and duly authorised by the customs house.

(2) The authorisation referred to in paragraph 1 of this Article shall be issued by the customs house upon written application which must contain the following information: the trade name of the excise products for which the authorisation is required, and the corresponding CN codes; the full name/company name of the applicant, the registered office, the name of the applicant's responsible person; information about the authorised excise warehousekeeper in another Member State being represented by the applicant in the capacity as the excise duty representative; accounting records in accordance with law; proof that the requirements for performance of supervision are satisfied.

(3) The authorisation shall be issued in the name of the applicant, and it may not be transferred to another person or entity.

(4) The excise duty representative shall:

1. lodge an adequate security for the payment of excise duty with the customs house,

2. maintain records of the movement of excise products by trade name, CN code, quantity, date of receipt and consignee,

3. inform the customs house about the place of delivery of excise products,

4. settle tax and customs liabilities regularly,

5. satisfy the requirements for electronic exchange of data related to the movement of excise products,

6. inform the customs house about all changes of data stated in the application that may affect the validity of the authorisation,

For additional analytical, marketing, investment and business opportunities information, please contact Global Investment & Business Center, USA
(202) 546-2103. Fax: (202) 546-3275. E-mail: rusric@erols.com

7. ensure smooth supervision.

(5) The authorisation shall terminate at the point of dissolution of a legal entity, or death of a natural person, or by returning the authorisation to the customs house, or by the customs house withdrawing the authorisation.

(6) The customs house shall withdraw the authorisation if the excise duty representative no longer meets the requirements stated in the authorisation: if it fails to ensure an adequate supervision system, fails to provide an adequate security for the payment of excise duty or to provide it in an amount sufficient to ensure the payment of excise duty debt; if the grounds or conditions for issuing the authorisation no longer exist; if the authorisation has been issued on the basis of incomplete or incorrect information; if the irregularities are not removed within the time limit set by the customs house.

(7) An appeal against the withdrawal of the authorisation shall not postpone the enforcement of the decision. By the time the decision on the appeal is made, the customs house may postpone the withdrawal of the authorisation if they estimate that the appeal might be accepted.

(8) The Minister of Finance shall stipulate the ordinance on the conditions and procedure of the issuance and expiry of validity of the authorisation issued to the excise duty representative, the procedure of lodging the payment security, its type and amount, as well as the content and method of maintaining the records.

XI. REGISTRATION OF BUSINESS ACTIVITY, REGISTRATION OF EXCISE DUTY PAYERS

Article 33

(1) Any legal entity or natural person performing a business activity that involves excise products shall file an application for entry into the register of excise duty payers with the customs house competent according to their registered office or place of residence at least eight days before the beginning of the registered business activity or before another event that constitutes an activity subject to excise duty within the meaning of this Act.

(2) The Minister of Finance shall stipulate the ordinance on the method of registration, as well as the content and form of the application for entry into the register or excise duty payers.

Article 34

(1) The Customs Administration shall establish and maintain a separate register of registered consignees, temporary registered consignees and authorised excise warehousekeepers, including also excise warehouses.

(2) The register referred to in paragraph 1 of this Article shall contain the following information:

1. excise ID number issued by the customs house to the authorised excise warehousekeeper, the authorised excise warehouse, the registered consignee and periodically registered consignees. If the authorised excise warehousekeeper operates more than one excise

For additional analytical, marketing, investment and business opportunities information, please contact Global Investment & Business Center, USA
(202) 546-2103. Fax: (202) 546-3275. E-mail: rusric@erols.com

warehouses, the customs house shall issue separate excise ID numbers for each excise warehouse,

2. the name and address of the craft, or the company name and address of the authorised excise warehousekeeper, the registered consignee and temporary registered consignees,

3. the name(s) and address(es) of excise warehouse(s) operated by a single warehousekeeper,

4. the date of issue of the authorisation, changes to it, and the expiry of validity date,

5. the category of excise products and code,

6. the information on the excise duty payment security and its issuer,

7. the registered office of the competent customs house.

(3) The Central Office of the Customs Administration shall exchange the information referred to in paragraph 2 of this Article with the competent authorities in other Member States.

(4) Upon request, the Central Office of the Customs Administration shall ensure the persons/entities involved in the movement of excise products under excise-duty suspension arrangements among Member States the right to receive confirmation of the information from a special register.

Article 35

(1) If the excise duty payer should cease to perform the registered business activity, the customs house shall, at the request of the excise duty payer or *ex officio*, remove the excise duty payer from the register of excise duty payers.

(2) The Minister of Finance shall stipulate the ordinance on the procedure of removing excise duty payers from the register.

XII. RECORDS MAINTAINED BY THE EXCISE DUTY PAYER

Article 36

(1) The excise duty payer shall maintain records in order to provide all information necessary for the calculation and payment of excise duty, and in particular the information on:

1. the quantities of produced excise products,

2. the quantities of excise products in production, at warehouse or other business premises, and in stock,

3. the quantities of raw materials and excise products delivered to the warehouse,

4. the quantities of excise products released for consumption in respect of which excise duty has become chargeable at the prescribed rates and in the prescribed amounts,

5. the quantities of delivered excise products exempt from excise duty,

6. the quantities of excise products for one's own consumption within the warehouse,

For additional analytical, marketing, investment and business opportunities information, please contact Global Investment & Business Center, USA (202) 546-2103. Fax: (202) 546-3275. E-mail: rusric@erols.com

7. the quantities of dispatched excise products under excise-duty suspension arrangements,
8. the quantities of excise products in respect of which excise duty is no longer chargeable,
9. the amounts of excise duty calculated and paid.

(2) The excise duty payer – importer shall maintain the records of the quantities of imported excise products, and on excise duty calculated and paid.

XIII. SUPERVISION OVER EXCISE DUTY CALCULATION AND PAYMENT

Article 37

(1) The calculation and payment of excise duty on excise products, the list of stock of excise products, the use of excise products for designated purposes, their dispatch and movement, and the maintenance of records shall be supervised by the Customs Administration and Financial Police, and other persons/entities authorised to perform supervision in accordance with special regulations.

(2) Neither excise duty payers nor any other legal entity or natural person may sell excise products in places designated as marketplaces and places where occasional trading is permitted, or in open-air places at which cash sales are not recorded via cash registers or issuing of invoices within the meaning of the Valued Added Tax Act.

Article 38

For the purpose of performing excise supervision and checks, the excise duty payer shall keep all issued and received invoices, excise documents, single administrative documents, the documents on the basis of which the excise duty payer is exempted from excise duty, daily excise duty accounts, monthly excise duty returns and all other accounting records related in any way to production, storage, importation or exportation of excise products and relevant for the purpose of excise duty calculation and payment during the period stipulated in special regulations, and not longer than 10 years after the end of the year to which such documents relate.

PART II ALCOHOL AND ALCOHOLIC BEVERAGES

Products subject to excise duty

Article 39

(1) Within the meaning of this Act, alcohol and alcoholic beverages shall be deemed to include beer, wine and other beverages obtained by fermenting except for beer and wine, intermediate products and ethyl alcohol.

For additional analytical, marketing, investment and business opportunities information, please contact Global Investment & Business Center, USA
(202) 546-2103. Fax: (202) 546-3275. E-mail: rusric@erols.com

(2) The types of alcohol and alcoholic beverages referred to in paragraph 1 of this Article shall be determined by a code of the Combined Nomenclature, and on the basis of their actual alcoholic strength by volume.

(3) The actual alcoholic strength by volume is a volume percentage of alcohol measured at the temperature of 20° C and expressed as % vol.

Article 40

(1) Within the meaning of this Act, beer shall be deemed to be:

1. every product falling within CN code 2203, having an actual alcoholic strength by volume exceeding 0.5 % vol,

2. every product that is a mixture of beer and a non-alcoholic beverage falling within CN code 2206, having an actual alcoholic strength by volume exceeding 0.5 % vol.

Article 41

(1) Within the meaning of this Act, wine shall be deemed to be still and sparkling wines.

(2) Still wines are all products falling within CN codes 2204 and 2205, with the exception of the sparkling wine referred to in paragraph 3 of this Article, and in particular those:

1. having an actual alcoholic strength by volume exceeding 1.2 % vol but not exceeding 15 % vol, provided that alcohol contained in the finished product is entirely of fermented origin,

2. having an actual alcoholic strength by volume exceeding 15 % vol but not exceeding 18 % vol, provided that they are produced without any enrichment and that alcohol contained in the finished product is entirely of fermented origin.

(3) The sparkling wines shall be all products falling within CN codes 2204 10, 2204 21 10, 2204 29 10 and 2205:

1. contained in bottles with mushroom stoppers held in place in a special way, or which have an excess pressure due to carbon dioxide in solution of three bar or more,

2. having an actual alcoholic strength by volume exceeding 1.2 % vol but not exceeding 15 % vol, provided that alcohol contained in the finished product is entirely of fermented origin.

Article 42

(1) Within the meaning of this Act, other beverages obtained by fermenting other than beer and wine shall include other still beverages obtained by fermenting and other sparkling beverages obtained by fermenting.

(2) Other still beverages obtained by fermenting other than beer and wine shall include all products falling within CN codes 2204 and 2205 and not listed in Article 41 of this Act and the products falling within CN code 2206 other than the beer referred to in Article 40 of this Act and the other sparkling beverages obtained by fermenting referred to in paragraph 3 of this Article, and in particular:

1. having an actual alcoholic strength by volume exceeding 1.2 % vol, but not exceeding 10 % vol,

For additional analytical, marketing, investment and business opportunities information, please contact Global Investment & Business Center, USA
(202) 546-2103. Fax: (202) 546-3275. E-mail: rusric@erols.com

2. having an actual alcoholic strength by volume exceeding 10% vol, but not exceeding 15 % vol, provided that alcohol contained in the finished product is entirely of fermented origin.

(3) Other sparkling beverages obtained by fermenting other than beer and wine shall be all products falling within CN codes 2206 00 31 and 2206 00 39 and the products falling within CN codes 2204 10, 2204 21 10, 2204 29 10 and 2205, not listed in Article 41 of this Act:

1. contained in bottles with mushroom stoppers held in place in a special way, or which have an excess pressure due to carbon dioxide in solution of three bar or more,

2. having an actual alcoholic strength by volume exceeding 1.2 % vol, but not exceeding 13 % vol,

3. having an actual alcoholic strength by volume exceeding 13 % vol, but not exceeding 15 % vol, provided that alcohol contained in the finished product is entirely of fermented origin.

Article 43

Within the meaning of this Act, the intermediate products shall be all the products having an actual alcoholic strength by volume exceeding 1.2 % vol, but not exceeding 22 % vol and falling within CN codes 2204, 2205 and 2206, but not referred to in Articles 40, 41 and 42 of this Act.

Article 44

(1) Within the meaning of this Act, ethyl alcohol shall be deemed to include:

1. all products falling within CN codes 2207 and 2208, having an actual alcoholic strength by volume exceeding 1.2 % vol, even when those products form part of a product that falls within another chapter of the Combined Nomenclature,

2. products of CN codes 2204, 2205 and 2206 having an actual alcoholic strength exceeding 22 % vol,

3. potable spirits containing products, whether in solution or not.

Establishment of excise duty

Article 45

(1) The excise duty on beer shall be fixed per 1 % of pure alcohol in one hectolitre of the finished product.

(2) The excise duty on wine, other beverages obtained by fermenting other than beer and wine and intermediate products shall be fixed per 1 hl of the finished product.

(3) The excise duty basis on ethyl alcohol shall be fixed per 1 hl of pure alcohol expressed as volume percentage measured at 20° C.

Amount of excise duty

Article 46

(1) Excise duty on beer shall be paid in the amount of HRK 40,00 per 1% of pure alcohol contained in one hectolitre of the finished product.

(2) Excise duty on still and sparkling wines shall be paid in the amount of HRK 0,00.

(3) Excise duty on other beverages obtained by fermenting other than beer and wine shall be paid in the amount of HRK 0,00.

(4) Excise duty on intermediate products containing 15 % vol of pure alcohol or more shall be paid in the amount of HRK 800,00 per one hectolitre of the finished product.

(5) Excise duty on intermediate products containing less than 15% vol of pure alcohol shall be paid in the amount of HRK 500,00 per one hectolitre of the finished product.

(6) Excise duty on ethyl alcohol shall be paid in the amount of HRK 5.300,00 per one hectolitre of pure alcohol.

(7) The Government of the Republic of Croatia may change the amounts of excise duty stipulated in this Article by virtue of a regulation.

Exemptions from excise duty

Article 47

(1) Excise duty on alcohol and alcoholic beverages shall not be levied:

1. on denatured alcohol deemed to be alcohol denatured by using the prescribed means of denaturation, or when imported as denatured alcohol from another state,
2. on denatured alcohol deemed to be alcohol denatured by using the prescribed means of denaturation in accordance with the requirements of another Member State, if accompanied with the SAED during its movement.
3. when used for the production and processing of non-food products,
4. when used for the production of medicines,
5. when used for the production of vinegar falling within CN code 2209,
6. when used either directly or as a constituent of semi-finished products for the production of foodstuffs, filled or otherwise, provided that in each case the alcoholic content does not exceed 8.5 litres of pure alcohol per 100 kg of the product for chocolates, and 5 litres of pure alcohol per 100 kg of the product for other products,
7. when used for the production of flavours for the preparation of foodstuffs and non-alcoholic beverages with an alcohol strength not exceeding 1.2 % vol,
8. when used in a manufacturing process provided that the final product does not contain alcohol,
9. for the preservation of preparations and the pulping of fruit,
10. when used for medical purposes at hospitals, medical centres and pharmacies,
11. when used for scientific research or teaching purposes at faculties, institutes and other scientific institutions using alcohol to perform their teaching and scientific activities.

For additional analytical, marketing, investment and business opportunities information, please contact Global Investment & Business Center, USA (202) 546-2103. Fax: (202) 546-3275. E-mail: rusric@erols.com

(2) Ethyl alcohol may be dispatched to an exempt user from the excise warehouse, introduced or imported into Croatia free of excise duty for the purpose of producing non-food products only if denatured.

Article 48

Excise duty on alcohol and alcoholic beverages shall not be paid:

1. on the beer referred to in Article 40 of this Act, produced by a private individual who is the agricultural land owner from barley grown for his/her own consumption and consumption by the members of his/her household or their guests, provided that no sale is involved,

2. on the wine referred to in Article 41, and other beverages obtained by fermenting other than beer and wine, referred to in Article 42 of this Act, produced by a private individual who is the owner or user of agricultural land and he is owner of substances for the production of wine and other beverages obtained by fermenting other than beer and wine, if used for his/her own consumption and the consumption by the members of his/her own household or guests provided that no sale is involved.

Denatured alcohol

Article 49

(1) Within the meaning of this Act, denatured alcohol shall be deemed to be alcohol which has been mixed during the production process with the prescribed substances in the prescribed amounts, so that in further processing denaturants cannot be easily eliminated and alcohol suitable for ingestion cannot be produced.

(2) Alcohol may be denatured only at the excise warehouse of the producer that has also been issued the authorisation for alcohol denaturation by the competent customs house.

(3) The authorised warehousekeeper being also the producer of denatured alcohol shall keep records on denaturation, which must state the quantities of alcohol and the quantities of prescribed substances that have been used for denaturation, the quantities of denatured alcohol produced and dispatched expressed in litres of pure alcohol, and records of buyers.

(4) The excise warehouse where alcohol is to be denatured must be fitted with such equipment that will ensure alcohol denaturation by means of the prescribed substances and in the prescribed manner.

(5) The Minister of Finance, after obtaining the opinion of the minister competent for agriculture and the director general of the state authority competent for standardisation and metrology, shall stipulate the ordinance on substances for denaturation of alcohol imported or produced in Croatia.

Marking, measurement and release for circulation of alcohol and alcoholic beverages

Article 50

For additional analytical, marketing, investment and business opportunities information, please contact Global Investment & Business Center, USA
(202) 546-2103. Fax: (202) 546-3275. E-mail: rusric@erols.com

(1) The products referred to in Articles 42, 43 and 44 of this Act, with the exception of the products falling within CN code 2207 and the products regulated by the Act on Wine, which have been produced or introduced or imported and released for consumption in Croatia, which are exported or sold at a customs warehouse must be marked with a special stamp of the Ministry of Finance of the Republic of Croatia. Besides the wording "Republic of Croatia – Ministry of Finance", the stamps must have a quantity marking, an alphabetical marking of the series and the number of the series, and actual alcoholic strength expressed as volume percent.

(2) The products referred to in paragraph 1 of this Article being exported may, by way of exception, be marked with a mark required by the importing country or have no marks, in which case the exporter has to present the Customs Administration with the proof of the stamps' takeover or another appropriate document.

(3) The products referred to in paragraph 1 of this Article may be released for circulation only in bottles or other appropriate containers in accordance with special regulations governing their release for circulation.

(4) The special stamp must be glued over the bottle cork so that it is damaged when the bottle is opened.

(5) The excise duty payers shall file an application for the printing of the special stamps referred to in paragraph 1 of this Article with the competent customs house.

(6) The products referred to in Article 40 of this Act must correspond to the producer's specification and the declaration shown on the label and meet the requirements stipulated in special regulations on beer.

(7) The Minister of Finance shall stipulate the ordinance on the procedure of ordering the special stamps, their form and content, handling the stamps and keeping the records.

Article 51

(1) The facilities for the production and storage of alcohol and alcoholic beverages referred to in Articles 40, 43 and 44 of this Act must be fitted with the measuring instruments prescribed by the national authority competent for metrology, as well as vessels and containers which have a proper authenticated seal or a proper certificate of authentication concerning the satisfaction of the metrology requirements issued by the national authority for standardisation and metrology.

(2) Besides additional sealing of the measuring instruments referred to in paragraph 1 of this Article, the competent customs house shall also provide lead seals for the ancillary piping, the fittings, the control panels, the fuses and all other things connected with the measurement of the quantities of alcohol and alcoholic beverages produced.

(3) Repairs, replacements and other activities requiring the removal of the lead seals affixed by the competent customs house within the meaning of paragraph 2 of this Article may be carried out only in the presence of an authorised customs officer.

(4) Each time the lead seal is removed or affixed the authorised customs officer shall compose a memorandum about the reasons for removing the lead seal and enter the state of the dials of the counter on the measuring instrument.

For additional analytical, marketing, investment and business opportunities information, please contact Global Investment & Business Center, USA
(202) 546-2103. Fax: (202) 546-3275. E-mail: rusric@erols.com

(5) A copy of the memorandum shall be given to the excise duty payer, and the original copy shall be lodged at the competent customs house.

(6) Croatian Chamber of Commerce. Minister of finance after obtaining the opinion of the director general of the national authority competent for metrology, shall stipulate the ordinance on the measuring instruments for production and storage of alcohol and alcoholic beverages.

Article 52

(1) The sellers (producers, importers and traders) of devices for the production of alcohol or alcoholic beverages shall be bound to inform the competent customs house about the purchasers or end consumers of such devices according to the registered office or residence of the purchaser, supplying it with a copy of the sales invoice.

(2) Legal entities and natural persons that buy such devices for the production of alcohol or alcoholic beverages shall be considered the end consumers.

Small producers

Article 53

(1) A small wine producer shall be deemed to be a person defined in the special regulations not producing more than 1 000 hl of wine a year.

(2) A small wine producer shall file an application for entry into the register of excise duty payers with the customs house competent according to its registered office or place of residence at least eight days before the beginning of production.

(3) Small wine producers shall be exempted from the requirements set out in the provisions of Titles III and IX of this Act.

(4) Small wine producers shall submit to the customs house that is competent according to their registered office a report on their annual production, deliveries and stock of wine as at 31 December, along with the information on chargeable excise duty, not later than 31 January for the preceding year.

Article 54

(1) For the purposes of this Act, natural persons – owners or users of the agricultural land and owners of the substance for production of strong alcoholic beverages producing the strong alcoholic beverage for their own use in a quantity not exceeding 20 litres of pure alcohol a year per household shall be deemed small producers of strong alcoholic beverages.

(2) Small producers of strong alcoholic beverages are forbidden to sell them.

(3) Within the meaning of this Article, strong alcoholic beverages shall be deemed to include the products falling within CN code 2208.

For additional analytical, marketing, investment and business opportunities information, please contact Global Investment & Business Center, USA (202) 546-2103. Fax: (202) 546-3275. E-mail: rusric@erols.com

(4) A small producer of strong alcoholic beverages shall file an application for entry into the register of excise duty payers with the customs house competent according to his/her place of residence not later than eight days before the beginning of production, and at the same time provide information on the volume of individual devices for alcohol production, i.e. stills, owned or used by him.

(5) A small producer of strong alcoholic beverages shall be liable to pay excise duty depending on the capacity of the still. Excise duty payable in respect of each still with a capacity of 40 to 100 litres shall be HRK 100.00, and in respect of stills with a capacity of over 100 litres shall be HRK 200. 00.

(6) If a small producer of strong alcoholic beverages produces strong alcoholic beverages in a quantity exceeding the one stated in paragraph 1 of this Article, excise duty shall be levied in the amount stipulated in Article 46, paragraph 6 of this Act.

(7) Small producers of strong alcoholic beverages shall submit to the customs house competent according to their place of residence annual report containing information on overall quantities of strong alcoholic beverages produced for their own use, on the capacity of the still and on excise duty chargeable not later than 20 January for the preceding year. Excise duty calculated in accordance with paragraphs 5 and 6 of this Article shall be payable by 31 January for the preceding year.

(8) If by 31 January the owner or the user of the still informs the competent customs house that the still is out of use and requests that the still be sealed, no excise duty shall become chargeable in the future tax periods so long as the still remains sealed. For the year in which the customs house removes the seal or establishes that the seal has been removed without approval of the competent customs house, excise duty shall become chargeable in accordance with paragraphs 5 and 6 of this Article.

(9) The seal shall be affixed to and removed from the still by the competent customs house at the request and at the expense of the owner or user of the still.

(10) Small producers of strong alcoholic beverages shall be exempted from the requirements stipulated in the provisions of Title IX of this Act.

(11) The Minister of Finance shall stipulate the ordinance on the implementation of this Article.

Article 55

Producers of ethyl alcohol, intermediate products and other beverages obtained by fermenting that produce alcohol, intermediate products and other beverages for commercial purposes in a quantity not exceeding 1 000 litres a year, and the producers of beer that produce beer for commercial purposes in a quantity not exceeding 50 000 litres a year shall be exempted from the requirements stipulated in the provisions of Title IX of this Act.

XVI. TOBACCO PRODUCTS

Products subject to excise duty

For additional analytical, marketing, investment and business opportunities information, please contact Global Investment & Business Center, USA
(202) 546-2103. Fax: (202) 546-3275. E-mail: rusric@erols.com

Article 56

The tobacco products shall be deemed to include: cigarettes, cigars, cigarillos and smoking tobacco.

Article 57

(1) Within the meaning of this Act, cigarettes shall be deemed to be:

1. rolls of tobacco suitable for smoking other than cigars and cigarillos within the meaning of the provisions of this Act,

2. rolls of tobacco placed, through a simple non-industrial process, in a paper wrapper for cigarettes or wrapped in paper leaves.

(2) A roll of tobacco whose length, without a filter or mouthpiece, does not exceed 9 cm shall be considered as one cigarette.

(3) In the case of rolls of tobacco whose length, without a filter or mouthpiece, exceeds 9 cm, the number of cigarettes for which the specific excise duty has to be calculated shall be determined by dividing the length of the tobacco roll by 9 and rounding the resulting amount to next whole number.

(4) Cigarettes shall also be deemed to include products which are made in part or in whole of substances other than tobacco and meet the requirements referred to in paragraph 1 of this Article.

Article 58

(1) Within the meaning of this Act, cigars and cigarillos, if suitable for smoking, shall be deemed to be rolls of tobacco:

1. made entirely of natural tobacco,

2. with an outer wrapper of natural tobacco,

3. with a threshed blend filler and with an outer wrapper of the normal colour of a cigar covering the product in full, including where appropriate the filter but not in the case of tipped cigars, the tip, and a binder, both being of reconstituted tobacco, where the unit weight, not including filter or mouthpiece, is not less than 1.2 g and where the wrapper is fitted in spiral form with an acute angle of at least 30° to the longitudinal axis of the cigar;

4. with a threshed blend filler and with an outer wrapper of the normal colour of a cigar, of reconstituted tobacco, covering the product in full, including where appropriate the filter but not, in the case of tipped cigars, the tip, where the unit weight, not including filter or mouthpiece, is not less than 2.3 g and the circumference over at least one third of the length is not less than 34 mm;

For additional analytical, marketing, investment and business opportunities information, please contact Global Investment & Business Center, USA
(202) 546-2103. Fax: (202) 546-3275. E-mail: rusric@erols.com

(2) The products which partly contain substances other than tobacco and meet the requirements referred to in paragraph 1 of this Article shall also be considered cigars and cigarillos, provided that they have:

1. a wrapper of natural or reconstituted tobacco,

2. a wrapper and binder of tobacco, both of reconstituted tobacco.

Article 59

(1) Within the meaning of this Act, smoking tobacco shall be deemed to be:

1. tobacco which has been cut or otherwise split, twisted or pressed into blocks, suitable for smoking without further industrial processing,

2. tobacco refuse suitable for smoking and released for retail sales, other than the products referred to in Articles 57 and 58 of this Act.

(2) Smoking tobacco shall also include fine-cut tobacco for the rolling of cigarettes in which more than 25 per cent by weight of the tobacco particles have a cut width of more than 1 mm, when intended to be sold for the rolling of cigarettes.

(3) Smoking tobacco shall also include the products partly or entirely containing substances other than tobacco and meeting the requirements stipulated in paragraph 1 of this Article.

Article 60

(1) The products containing no tobacco and used exclusively for medical purposes shall not be deemed tobacco products within the meaning of this Act.

(2) The products used exclusively for medical purposes shall be determined by the ministry competent for health.

Excise duty base and excise duty yield

Article 61

(1) The excise duty base for cigarettes shall be 1 000 pieces and the retail selling price.

(2) Excise duty on cigarettes shall be paid as the specific excise duty stipulated in a defined amount for the quantity of 1 000 cigarettes and as the proportional excise duty stipulated at a defined percentage of the retail selling price of cigarettes.

(3) Excise duty on cigarettes as of 1 January 2010 shall be comprised of:

For additional analytical, marketing, investment and business opportunities information, please contact Global Investment & Business Center, USA (202) 546-2103. Fax: (202) 546-3275. E-mail: rusric@erols.com

1. the specific excise duty of HRK 180,00 for 1 000 cigarettes,

2. the proportional excise duty of 30% of the retail selling price.

(4) The minimum excise duty on cigarettes sold at a price lower than the retail selling price for cigarettes of the price category most in demand shall be HRK 375,00 for 1 000 pieces.

(5) By virtue of a regulation, the Government of the Republic of Croatia shall determine the amount of the specific excise duty and the rate of the proportional excise duty on the basis of the retail selling price for the cigarettes of the price category most in demand on 1 January, for the current year.

(6) The price category most in demand shall be the cigarette category which was most in demand during the preceding year, according to the information of the Ministry of Finance as at 1 January.

(7) Notwithstanding the provisions of paragraphs 3, 4 and 5 of this Article, the Government of the Republic of Croatia, may by passing a Regulation and until the moment of accession of the Republic of Croatia to the European Union, change the amount of the specific excise duty, the rate of the proportional excise duty and the minimum excise duty, should in the course of the year the cigarette retail selling prices be changed.

Article 62

(1) Excise duty calculation base for cigars and cigarillos shall be 1 000 pieces. Excise duty shall be determined as the specific excise duty stipulated in a defined amount for the quantity of 1 000 pieces as follows:

1. HRK 1.100.00 for 1 000 cigars,

2. HRK 220.00 for 1 000 cigarillos.

(2) The excise duty calculation base for fine-cut tobacco and other smoking tobacco shall be one kilogram. Excise duty shall be determined as the specific excise duty stipulated in a defined amount for 1 kilogram, as follows:

1. HRK 136.00 for one kilogram of fine-cut tobacco,

2. HRK 92.00 for one kilogram of other smoking tobacco.

(3) Notwithstanding the provisions of paragraph 2 of this Article, as of 1 January 2011 excise duty shall amount to:

1. HRK 234.00 for one kilogram of fine-cut tobacco,

2. HRK 146.00 for one kilogram of other smoking tobacco.

Determination of the retail selling price

Article 63

(1) The retail selling price of tobacco products shall be the price determined by the authorised excise warehousekeeper and the importer according to the brands of tobacco products. The retail selling price shall be also including excise duty, customs duty and value-added tax.

(2) The persons referred to in paragraph 1 of this Article must report the retail selling price to the Customs Administration thirty days before releasing the tobacco products for consumption at so determined prices.

(3) The tobacco products may not be sold at retail selling prices lower or higher than those reported.

Exemptions from excise duty

Article 64

(1) Excise duty on tobacco products shall not be paid on the products intended exclusively for scientific research and product quality testing.

(2) The use of tobacco products for the purposes referred to in paragraph 1 of this Article shall be subject to the authorisation of the Customs Administration.

Marking of tobacco products with stamps

Article 65

(1) The tobacco products produced and released for consumption in Croatia must be marked with tobacco stamps of the Ministry of Finance. Besides the wording "Republic of Croatia – Ministry of Finance", the stamps must have an alphabetical indication of the series, a number and, in the case of cigarettes, the retail selling price.

(2) The tobacco products imported and released for consumption in Croatia must be marked with tobacco stamps of the Ministry of Finance. Besides the wording "Republic of Croatia – Ministry of Finance", the stamps must have an alphabetical indication of the series, a number and, in the case of cigarettes, the retail selling price.

(3) The domestic tobacco products being exported or sold at a customs warehouse must be marked with an identification stamp of the Ministry of Finance. Besides the wording "Republic of Croatia – Ministry of Finance", those stamps shall bear the words "for export" in Croatian or a foreign language, an alphabetical mark of the series, and a number.

(4) By way of derogation from paragraph 3 of this Article, the tobacco products being exported may have a marking required by the importing country or no marking at all, in which case the exporter shall present evidence to the competent customs house that the stamps of the importing country have been taken over or present another relevant document.

For additional analytical, marketing, investment and business opportunities information, please contact Global Investment & Business Center, USA
(202) 546-2103. Fax: (202) 546-3275. E-mail: rusric@erols.com

(5) The tobacco stamp must be stuck to the packet intended for retail sale below the cellophane or other paper enclosing the packet of tobacco products in such a way that it can be seen and must be torn during opening.

(6) By way of derogation from paragraph 5 of this Article, in the case of original packaging for cigars and cigarillos which does not include cellophane or other paper, the tobacco stamp may be stuck directly to the packaging in such a way that it can be seen and must be torn during opening.

(7) The tobacco products not marked with tobacco stamps in accordance with this Article shall be deemed products on which no excise duty has been calculated and paid, and their release for consumption, purchase and possession shall be deemed illegal.

Article 66

(1) The tobacco stamps shall be issued to the authorised excise warehousekeeper and the importer of tobacco products upon their request for taking over the tobacco stamps which is submitted to the Central Office of the Customs Administration.

(2) Before taking over the tobacco stamps, authorised excise warehousekeepers and importers of tobacco products shall lodge a security for the payment of excise duty on tobacco products.

(3) The ordered tobacco stamps shall be taken over from the printing house and delivered to the persons/entities referred to in paragraph 1 of this Article by the authorised officers of the Central Office of the Customs Administration.

(4) The tobacco stamps shall not be issued to the authorised excise warehousekeeper and the importer of tobacco products who have not paid excise duty in accordance with this Act.

(5) Unauthorised production of the tobacco stamps, their unauthorised printing and offering for sale shall be deemed illegal.

(6) Deliberate damaging of the tobacco stamps shall be deemed illegal.

(7) The Central Office of the Customs Administration shall supervise the ordering, usage, keeping records and handling of the tobacco stamps.

(8) Authorised excise warehousekeepers and importers of tobacco products shall submit reports on daily consumption of the tobacco stamps to the Customs Administration on the next working day.

(9) The Minister of Finance shall stipulate the ordinance on printing, the conditions and methods of ordering and handling the tobacco stamps, and record-keeping, as well as the content of the report on daily consumption of the tobacco stamps.

Release for circulation of tobacco products

Article 67

(1) The tobacco products may only be circulated in packets intended for retail sale.

(2) No items other than tobacco products may be added to the packets intended for retail sale.

Refund of excise duty

Article 68

(1) The right to a reimbursement of excise duty paid, shall be granted to the payers of excise duty on tobacco products that have become unsuitable for use and if they return damaged tobacco stamps unless the products' unsuitability for use is due to their inadequate quality, oldness or non-marketability.

(2) The refund of excise duty referred to in paragraph 1 of this Article shall be approved on condition that the excise duty payer has destroyed the tobacco products unsuitable for use under customs supervision.

(3) The Minister of Finance shall stipulate the ordinance on the procedure of destruction under customs supervision and the refund of excise duty on tobacco products unsuitable for use.

XVII. ENERGY PRODUCTS AND ELECTRICITY

PRODUCTS SUBJECT TO EXCISE DUTY

Article 69

(1) Products subject to excise duty shall include energy products used as motor fuel or a heating fuel, and electricity.

(2) The types of energy products and electricity referred to in paragraph 1 of this Article shall be determined by a code of the Combined Nomenclature, according to the Article 2. Paragraph 5 of the Directive 2003/96/EC, or on the basis of the characteristics of individual products.

(3) Within the meaning of this Act, the following shall be deemed energy products:

1. the products falling within CN codes 2701, 2702 and 2704 to 2715,
2. the products falling within CN codes 2901 and 2902,
3. the products falling within tariff subheading KN 3403,
4. the products falling within CN code 3811,
5. the products falling within CN code 3817.

(4) The following shall also be deemed energy products provided that they are intended to be used as an motor fuel, additive or extender added to motor fuels or as a heating fuel:

1. the products falling within CN codes 1507 to 1518,

For additional analytical, marketing, investment and business opportunities information, please contact Global Investment & Business Center, USA (202) 546-2103. Fax: (202) 546-3275. E-mail: rusric@erols.com

2. the products falling within CN code 2905 11 00 which are not of synthetic origin,

3. the products falling within CN code 3824 90 99.

(5) The following shall also be deemed energy products:

1. other products intended for consumption, offered for sale or used as an motor fuel,

2. additives or fillers added to the motor fuel if declared as such,

3. other hydro carbonates intended for consumption, offered for sale or used for heating, with the exception of peat or biomass.

(6) The biomass shall include a biodegradable fraction of a product, waste and residues from agriculture (including the substances of plant and animal origin), forestry and related industries, as well as the biodegradable fraction of industrial and municipal waste.

(7) The biofuel shall be liquid or gaseous fuel intended for the use in transportation and produced from biomass, which meets the biofuel compatibility and quality requirements in proportions stipulated by special regulations.

(8) Electricity falling within CN code 2716 shall also be deemed a product subject to excise duty within the meaning of this Act.

EXCISE DUTY BASIS AND THE LEVEL OF EXCISE DUTY

Article 70

(1) The excise duty basis for energy products shall be 1000 kg net weight, 1 000 litres, Gigajoul gross calorific value or a cubic meter of an individual excise product. If the excise duty basis is determined in litres, it shall be measured at the temperature of +15° C.

(2) The excise duty basis for electricity shall be the quantity of electricity measured in megawatt hours.

(3) The level of excise duty shall be determined as follows:

1. **Petrol** used as an motor fuel:
    1.1. Leaded petrol falling within CN codes 2710 11 31, 2711 51 and 2710 11 59 .... HRK 3.600,00 / 1 000 l
    1.2. Unleaded petrol falling within CN codes 2710 1131, 2710 1141, 2 710 1145, 2 710 1149 .... HRK 2.850,00 / 1 000 l

2. **Gas oil falling within CN codes** 2710 19 41 to 2710 19 49
    2.1. for motor fuels.............. HRK 2.200,00 / 1000l
    2.2. for heating .... HRK 300,00 /1000 l

3. **Kerosene – petroleum falling within CN codes** 2710 19 21 and 2710 19 25

3.1. for motor fuels................ HRK 2.200,00 /1000 l

3.2. for heating................ HRK 1.752,00 /1000 l

4. LPG – liquid petroleum gas falling within CN codes 2711 12 11 to 2711 19 00

4.1. for motor fuels........................ HRK 912,50 /1000 kg

4.2. for heating .... HRK 0,00 /1000 kg

5. Heavy fuel oil falling within CN codes 2710 19 61 to 2710 19 69
.... HRK 110,00 /1000 kg

6. Natural gas falling within CN codes 2711 11 00 and 2711 21 00

6.1. for motor fuels......................... HRK 0.00 /m3,

6.2. for heating .... HRK 0.00 /m3,

7. Coal and coke falling within CN codes 2701, 2702 and 2704
.... HRK 2.20 / Gj gross calorific value

8. Electricity falling within CN code 2716
. ... HRK 0.00 /Mwh,

9. Biofuels-pure referred to in Article 69, paragraph 7 of this Act ..... **HRK** 0.00.

(4) Excise duty on the energy products referred to in Article 69, paragraph 3, item 1 of this Act not listed in paragraph 3 of this Article and on the energy products referred to in Article 69, paragraph 3, item 2 of this Act shall be paid according to their purpose and in the amounts stipulated for the equivalent motor fuel or heating fuel referred to in paragraph 3 of this Article.

(5) Excise duty on the energy products referred to in Article 69, paragraph 3, items 3, 4 and 5, and paragraph 4 of this Act shall be paid according to their purpose and in the amounts stipulated for the equivalent motor fuel or heating fuel referred to in paragraph 3. of this Article.

(6) Excise duty on the energy products referred to in Article 69, paragraph 5, item 1 of this Act shall be paid according to their purpose and in the amounts stipulated for the equivalent motor fuel.

(7) Excise duty on the energy products referred to in Article 69, paragraph 5, item 3 of this Act shall be paid according to their purpose and in the amount stipulated for the equivalent heating fuel referred to in paragraph 3 of this Article.

(8) Excise duty on the additives and fillers referred to in Article 69, paragraph 5, item 2 of this Act added to the energy product shall be paid in the same amount as stipulated for the energy product to which they are added.

(9) Excise duty on the gas oil purchased against presentation of the fuel card by the gas oils consumers for use in agriculture, fishery and aquaculture referred to in Article 77 of this Act shall be HRK 0.00.

(10) By virtue of a regulation, the Government of the Republic of Croatia may change the amounts of excise duty stipulated in paragraph 3 of this Article.

For additional analytical, marketing, investment and business opportunities information, please contact Global Investment & Business Center, USA (202) 546-2103. Fax: (202) 546-3275. E-mail: rusric@erols.com

Article 71

The provisions of this Act with regard to the production, storage, processing and movement of products under excise duty suspension arrangements, and to the supervision and reporting shall apply only to the following energy products referred to in Article 69, paragraph 3, items 1 and 2:

1. falling within CN codes **2707 10**, **2707 20**, **2707 30 and 2707 50,**
2. falling within CN codes **2710 11 to 2710 19 69,**
3. falling within CN codes **2710 11 21**, **2710 11 25**, and **2710 19 29** for commercial bulk movements,
4. falling within CN code **2711** except for **2711 11**, **2711 21** and **2711 29,**
5. falling within CN code **2901 10** (acyclic carbohydrates),
6. falling within CN codes **2902 20**, **2902 30**, **2902 41**, **2902 42**,**2902 43** and **2902 44,**

and on all the energy products referred to in Article 69, paragraph 4 of this Act.

MEASUREMENT OF ENERGY PRODUCTS

Article 72

(1) The excise duty payers shall measure the input and output quantities of energy products by using flowmeters or scales certified by the standardisation and metrology authority and additionally sealed by the competent customs house.

(2) Besides additional sealing of the flowmeters and scales referred to in paragraph 1 of this Article, the customs house competent according to the location of the excise warehouse shall also provide lead seals for the ancillary piping, the fittings, the control panels, the fuses and all other things connected with the measurement of the output quantities of energy products.

(3) Repairs, replacements and other activities requiring removal or affixing of the customs lead seal may be carried out only in the presence of an authorised official of the competent customs house, who shall compose a memorandum.

Marking of gas oils

Article 73

(1) Before being dispatched from the excise warehouse, the gas oils falling within CN codes 2710 19 41, 2710 19 45 and 2710 19 49 used as a heating fuel must be marked with the appropriate indicator in accordance with the standardisation regulations and dyed red.

(2) The gas oils referred to in paragraph 1 of this Article imported as a heating fuel must be properly marked. At the time of their importation, the marked gas oils must be accompanied with a certificate of the foreign supplier showing the type and quantity of the marking substance used, endorsement by the competent authority. If no such certificate is provided or if there is no other proof that the imported gas oils have been properly marked, the gas oils shall be deemed unmarked.

(3) The gas oils referred to in paragraph 1 of this Article which are used as a heating fuel and introduced from other Member States or imported from a third country shall be deemed marked if accompanied with a certificate of the foreign supplier showing the type and quantity of the marking substance, endorsement by the competent institution and certifying that the gas oils

For additional analytical, marketing, investment and business opportunities information, please contact Global Investment & Business Center, USA
(202) 546-2103. Fax: (202) 546-3275. E-mail: rusric@erols.com

have been marked in another Member State or a third country and proving that the gas oils have been marked in accordance with paragraph 1 of this Article. If no such certificate or other proof of the gas oils having been properly marked is provided at the time or their entry or importation, they shall be considered unmarked.

(4) The marked gas oil must be stored in such a way as to ensure that other products do not affect neutralisation of the marking substance.

(5) The marking of gas oil may be carried out only at the excise warehouse operated by the authorised excise warehousekeeper whose excise warehousekeeping authorisation includes also the authorisation for the marking of gas oils and whose warehouse is fitted with facilities for dosage and mixing or similar facilities that can ensure proper marking.

(6) In the cases when gas oils are not properly marked or when the facilities do not ensure proper marking, the competent customs house shall withdraw its authorisation for marking gas oils.

(7) The Minister of Finance shall stipulate the ordinance on the type and quantity of the marking substance and the procedure of marking energy products.

Use of the marked gas oils

Article 74

(1) The marked gas oils referred to in Article 73 of this Act may be used and sold only for the purpose stipulated in this Act.

(2) The marked gas oils referred to in Article 73 of this Act may not be used for the propulsion of motor vehicles, floating objects, vessels or other engines and machinery or for other purposes, except as heating fuels.

(3) The marking substances may not be removed from the gas oils marked in accordance with Article 73 of this Act, and their concentration may not be reduced, nor may other substances be added which would render it impossible to determine if the gas oils are properly marked.

Releasing the marked gas oils for circulation

Article 75

(1) The marked gas oils referred to in Article 73, paragraph 1 of this Act may not be released for circulation at petrol stations or other retail points of sales designated for the sale of motor fuels.
(2) The marked oils referred to in Article 73, paragraph 1 of this Act may be sold only from the specially determined warehouses that must be registered with the competent customs house.
(3) The marked gas oils may not be sold by being directly poured into fuel tanks of motor vehicles, floating objects, vessels, other engines or machinery.

(4) The excise duty payers and other legal entities and natural persons selling the gas oils referred to in paragraph 1 of this Article shall maintain records of buyers of the marked gas oil.

For additional analytical, marketing, investment and business opportunities information, please contact Global Investment & Business Center, USA (202) 546-2103. Fax: (202) 546-3275. E-mail: rusric@erols.com

(5) The Minister of Finance shall stipulate the ordinance on the requirements which the specially determined warehouses for the sale of gas oils must meet, the procedure of selling the marked gas oils and maintaining records of buyers of the marked gas oils.

Supervision over the use and sale of the marked gas oils

Article 76

(1) The inspection control of the use and sale of the marked gas oil shall be performed by persons duly authorised to perform such activities in accordance with the provision of this Act and special regulations.

(2) If it is established during the control of motor vehicles, floating objects, vessels, other engines or machinery, or during the inspection of bookkeeping or other documents that the marked gas oils referred to in Article 73 of this Act are not used for the purposes and in the manner provided for in Article 74 of this Act, the owner of the motor vehicle, floating object, vessel, other engine or machine shall be charged excise duty on the quantity which corresponds to the volume of the fuel tank multiplied by hundred, whereas the company and/or owner of the craft shall be charged excise duty on the quantities that are determined on the basis of bookkeeping and other documents as having been used in contravention of the provisions of this Act, multiplied by ten. Excise duty shall be calculated by reference to the amounts stipulated in Article 70, paragraph 3, item 2.2.1 of this Act.

(3) Gas oils in fuel tanks of motor vehicles, floating objects, vessels or other engines or machines shall be considered marked if they contain the marking substance referred to in Article 73, paragraph 1 of this Act regardless of its concentration.

(4) The excise duty referred to in paragraph 2 of this Article shall be calculated and charged by the competent customs house and Financial Police on the basis of the findings of the supervisory authority referred to in paragraph 1 of this Article.

(5) The Minister of Finance shall stipulate the ordinance on the method according to which the presence of the marking substance is established.

Use of the gas oils for the purposes of agriculture, fisheries and aquaculture

Article 77

(1) The right to consume the gas oil referred to in Article 70, paragraph 9 of this Act for the purposes of agriculture shall be granted to agricultural holdings duly entered in the register of agricultural holdings-at the ministry competent for agriculture in accordance with special regulations,

(2) The right to consume the gas oil referred to in Article 70, paragraph 9 of this Act for the purposes of fisheries shall be granted to:
1. natural persons and legal entities holding the licence for seawater commercial fishing activities – the catching of fish,
2. natural persons and legal entities holding the commercial fishing licence and/or the licence for farming of sea fish and other sea organisms, in accordance with the special regulations on seawater fishing, or the aquaculture licence in accordance with the special regulations on freshwater fishing.

For additional analytical, marketing, investment and business opportunities information, please contact Global Investment & Business Center, USA (202) 546-2103. Fax: (202) 546-3275. E-mail: rusric@erols.com

(3) The holders of the right to consume the gas oil referred to in paragraphs 1 and 2 of this Article shall exercise this right on the basis of the authorisation granted by the authority competent for agriculture and fisheries and stipulating the permitted annual consumption of the gas oil, as shown on the fuel card.

(4) The consumers referred to in paragraphs 1 and 2 of this Article shall use the gas oil for the propulsion of agricultural machinery and for the operation of facilities on the agricultural holdings, for the operations of traction engines and ancillary engines of the fishing floating objects used in commercial seawater fishing and ancillary machines and vessels in aquaculture.

(5) Taxpayers subject to excise duty and other legal entities or natural persons selling the gas oils referred to in Article 70, paragraph 9 of this Act to the consumers referred to in paragraphs 1 and 2 of this Article, shall fulfil terms and conditions on electronic data exchange from the central data base on consumers referred to in paragraphs 1 and 2 of this Article, and perform the gas oil selling referred to in Article 70, paragraph 9 only against presentation of a fuel card.

(6) The Minister of Finance, after obtaining the opinion of the minister competent for agriculture, shall stipulate the ordinance on the content and form of the fuel card, the manner in which the gas oils referred to in Article 70, paragraph 9 of this Act may be used and the control of their consumption.

Reimbursement of excise duty on the gas oils used for the purposes of agriculture, fisheries and aquaculture

Article 78

(1) When selling the gas oil to the consumers referred to in Article 77, paragraphs 1 and 2 of this Act, legal entities or natural persons shall be entitled to a reimbursement of the excise duty paid in accordance with Article 70, paragraph 3, item 2.2.1 of this Act.

(2) The sellers referred to in paragraph 1 of this Article shall file an application for a reimbursement of excise duty with the customs house competent according to their registered office. The application shall be filed on the last day of a month for the quantities sold in the preceding month.

(3) The Minister of Finance, after obtaining the opinion of the minister competent for agriculture, shall stipulate the ordinance on the conditions and procedure of the excise duty refund referred to in this Article.

Exemptions from excise duty

Article 79

(1) Excise duty shall not be paid on:

1. the energy products dispatched and used as an fuel in air navigation, with the exception of private pleasure flights,

For additional analytical, marketing, investment and business opportunities information, please contact Global Investment & Business Center, USA
(202) 546-2103. Fax: (202) 546-3275. E-mail: rusric@erols.com

2. the energy products supplied for use as an fuel in international navigation, with the exception of private pleasure floating objects and vessels,

3. the energy products supplied for use as an fuel in navigation with third countries or other Member States, with the exception of private pleasure floating objects and vessels, and electricity produced on the vessel,

4. the energy products that the producer of energy products and electricity uses at its own production facilities for further processing or the production of other energy products and electricity, except when used as an motor fuel for means of transport,

5. the energy products used for other purposes other than motor fuel or heating fuel.

(2) Moreover, excise duty shall not be paid on:

1. the energy products kept in standard fuel tanks of motor vehicles, vessels and aircraft coming from other countries, intended for consumption as motor fuel by those vehicles rather than for resale, and exempted from import duties in accordance with the customs regulations,

2. the energy products kept in the tanks of special containers coming from other states, intended specifically for the operation of supply systems of those containers during the transportation and exempted from import duties in accordance with the customs regulations.

(3) Private pleasure flights shall be deemed to mean personal use of aircraft by its owner or by a natural person or legal entity who enjoys its use either through hire or through any other means, for other than commercial purposes and in particular other than for the carriage of passengers or goods or for the supply of services for consideration or for the purposes of public authorities.

(4) Private pleasure floating objects and vessels shall be deemed to be all floating objects and vessels used by its owner or used by natural persons or legal entities who enjoys its use either through hire or through any other means, for other than commercial purposes and in particular other than for the carriage of passengers or goods or gor the supply of services for consideration or for the purposes of public authorities.

(5) Standard fuel tanks within the meaning of this Article shall be:

1. tanks fixed permanently by the manufacturer into all motor vehicles of the type concerned, fitted with a fixed system enabling direct consumption of fuel used as propellant and, as appropriate, for the operation of cooling and other systems during transport. Gas tanks mounted into motor vehicles enabling direct consumption of gas as the propellant, and tanks mounted into other possible systems of a vehicle shall also be deemed to be standard tanks,

2. tanks fixed permanently by the manufacturer into all special containers of the type concerned and fitted with a fixed system enabling direct consumption of fuel during transport for the operation of the cooling and other systems making part of the equipment of the special container.

(6) Within the meaning of this Article, special containers shall be any containers with special mounted equipment used for cooling systems, oxygen supply systems, thermal insulation systems or any other systems.

(7) The Minister of Finance shall stipulate the ordinance on the conditions and method of application of the exemptions from excise duty referred to in this Article.

PART III

XVIII. PENAL PROVISIONS

For additional analytical, marketing, investment and business opportunities information, please contact Global Investment & Business Center, USA
(202) 546-2103. Fax: (202) 546-3275. E-mail: rusric@erols.com

Article 80

(1) A legal entity shall be fined for an offence from HRK 40,000.00 to HRK 1,000,000.00 and the responsible person at the legal entity shall be fined from HRK 3,000.00 to HRK 50,000.00 if:

1. moving excise products under excise-duty suspension arrangements without the accompanying excise document (Article 7, paragraph 3),

2. issuing an incorrectly completed accompanying excise document (Article 8, paragraph 1),

3. the consignee of excise products, fails to inform the competent customs house about the intended receipt of excise products and to provide a security for the payment of excise duty (Article 10, paragraph 5),

4. the consignor of excise products, fails to inform the customs office at the place of dispatch of the delivery of excise products or determine their route in advance (Article 10, paragraph 6),

5. failing to transport excise products along the previously determined route (Article 10, paragraph 6),

6. irregulary produces, introduces, imports, acquires, transports, possesses, sells, buys, exports, consumes or illegally releases excise products for consumption, participates in irregular production, entry or importation of excise products or stores irregulary produced, introduced or imported excise products (Article 11, paragraph 3, items 5 and 6, Article 54, paragraph 2),

7. the exempted user dispatches excise products or use them for other purposes other than the once obtained within the authorisation (Article 11, paragraph 3, item 8),

8. failing to calculate excise duty or to calculate it correctly by applying the prescribed excise duty bases and rates, or in the amounts valid at the excise duty chargeability date (Article 16, paragraph 1),

9. failing to submit or to submit in time daily excise duty accounts or submits an incorrect daily excise duty account, fails to submit or to submit in time monthly excise duty returns or submits an incorrect monthly excise duty return, or fails to pay excise duty within the prescribed time limit (Article 16, paragraphs 2, 3, 5, 6, 7, 8, 9, 10, 11, and 12, Article 17, paragraphs 2 and 4, Article 23, paragraph 1, item 3),

10. applying for a reimbursement of excise duty paid on the basis of incorrect information (Article 10, paragraph 3, Article 18, Article 68 and Article 78),

11. transfering the excise warehousekeeping authorisation to another person/entity (Article 22, paragraph 1),

12. the authorised excise warehousekeeper, fails to fulfil his/hers obligations and fails to remove the irregularities found in operations with excise products within the time limit set by the customs house (Article 23, paragraph 1, items 1,2,4 and 5 and paragraph 2),

13. the authorised excise warehousekeeper, fails to provide a security for the payment of excise duty in accordance with the provisions of this Act (Article 24),

14. transfering the exempt user authorisation to another person/entity (Article 27, paragraph 2),

For additional analytical, marketing, investment and business opportunities information, please contact Global Investment & Business Center, USA
(202) 546-2103. Fax: (202) 546-3275. E-mail: rusric@erols.com

15. the exempt user, fails to comply with its obligations and to remedy the irregularities in its operations with excise products within the time limit set by the customs house (Article 28),

16. transfering the registered consignee authorisation to another person/entity (Article 30, paragraph 4),

17. failing to comply with its obligations of the registered consignee (Article 30, paragraph 5),

18. failing to comply with its obligations as the non-registered consignee(Article 31, paragraph 2),

19. the excise duty representative, transfers its authorisation to another person/entity (Article 32, paragraph 3),

20. failing to comply with its obligations of the excise duty representative (Article 32, paragraph 4),

21. failing to file an application for registration with the competent customs house within the prescribed time limit (Article 33),

22. failing to maintain the prescribed records (Article 36),

23. selling excise products in places designated as marketplaces and places where occasional trading is permitted, or in open-air places at which cash sales are not recorded via cash registers or issuing of invoices (Article 37, paragraph 2),

24. dispatching ethyl alcohol or enables it to be dispatched from the excise warehouse or introduced from another Member State or imported into Croatia free of excise duty in order to use it in the production of non-food products, if it is not denatured (Article 47, paragraph 2),

25. failing to treat denatured alcohol during the production process in such a way that by further processing it is not possible to produce alcohol suitable for ingestion (Article 49, paragraph 1),

26. failing to release alcohol and alcoholic beverages for circulation in the prescribed manner (Article 50),

27. failing to equip the facilities for production and storage of alcohol in the prescribed manner (Article 51, paragraph 1),

28. removing the lead seal without the presence of an authorised officer of the competent customs house (Article 51, paragraph 3),

29. a small wine producer, fails to apply with the competent customs house for entry into the register of excise duty payers within the prescribed time limit and fails to provide data on annual production, deliveries and inventories of wine within the prescribed time limit (Article 53, paragraphs 2 and 4),

30. a small producer of strong alcoholic beverages, fails to apply with the competent customs house for entry into the register of excise duty payers within the prescribed time limit and fails to provide data on the capacity of stills owned or used by him, fails to submit the annual accounts and pay excise duty within the prescribed time limit (Article 54, paragraphs 4 and 7),

31. a small producer of strong alcoholic beverages, affixes or removes the lead seal on the still in a manner other than prescribed (Article 54, paragraph 9);

For additional analytical, marketing, investment and business opportunities information, please contact Global Investment & Business Center, USA (202) 546-2103. Fax: (202) 546-3275. E-mail: rusric@erols.com

32. failing to advise the Customs Administration of the determined retail price of tobacco products within the prescribed time limit (Article 63, paragraph 2),

33. selling tobacco products at retail prices lower or higher than those reported (Article 63, paragraph 3),

34. failing to mark properly tobacco products released for consumption or marks them with counterfeit tobacco stamps or in a manner other than prescribed (Article 65, paragraphs 1, 2, 3,5 and 6),

35. failing to mark tobacco products intended for exportation with a mark of the importing country or provide proof of tobacco stamps' takeover or another appropriate document (Article 65, paragraph 4),

36. printing or making or releasing tobacco stamps for circulation without authorisation or deliberately damaging tobacco stamps (Article 66, paragraphs 5 and 6),

37. the authorised excise warehousekeeper and/or importer of tobacco products fails to submit, or timely submit or submits an inaccurate report on daily consumption of the tobacco stamps (Article 66, item 8),

38. releasing for circulation tobacco products not packed in packets intended for retail sale or adds items other than tobacco products to the packets (Article 67),

39. failing to pay excise duty on energy products used as a propelent or for heating, according to their purpose and in the amounts for equivalent fuels (Article 70, paragraphs 4, 5, 6, 7 and 8),

40. failing to measure the input and output quantities of energy products by using flowmeters or certified and additionally sealed scales (Article 72, paragraph 1),

41. removing the lead seal without presence of an authorised officer of the competent customs house (Article 72, paragraph 3),

42. failing to mark the gas oils falling within CN codes 2710 19 41, 2710 19 45, 2710 19 49 and used as a heating fuel in the prescribed manner (Article 73, paragraph 1),

43. importing a gas oil not marked in the prescribed manner or imports it without the accompanying certification of the foreign marker, or the certification does not contain required information (Article 73, paragraph 2),

44. the registered and/or temporary registered consignee, fails to enclose the certification or other proof that the received gas oil is properly marked (Article 73, paragraph 1),

45. failing to store the marked gas oil in the prescribed manner (Article 73, paragraph 4),

46. failing to mark the gas oil at the excise warehouse (Article 73, paragraph 5),

47. failing to use the marked gas oils in the prescribed manner (Article 74, paragraph 2),

48. removing from the marked gas oils the marking substances or reduces their concentration or adds the substances which render it impossible to determine if the gas oils are properly marked (Article 74, paragraph 3),

For additional analytical, marketing, investment and business opportunities information, please contact Global Investment & Business Center, USA
(202) 546-2103. Fax: (202) 546-3275. E-mail: rusric@erols.com

49. failing to sell or release the marked gas oils for circulation in the prescribed manner (Article 75, paragraphs 1, 2 and 3),

50. failing to maintain the prescribed records or maintains them inaccurately or fails to maintain up-to-date records of buyers of the marked gas oils (Article 75, paragraph 4),

51. the owner of a motor vehicle, floating object, vessel or another machine or engine, uses the marked oil referred to in Article 73, paragraph 1 as the engine fuel in the tank of the motor vehicle, floating object, vessel, or another machine or engine (Article 76, paragraph 2 and Article 92 paragraph 4),

52. the seller of the gas oil intended for agriculture, fisheries and aquaculture, abuses the fuel card system (Article 77, paragraph 5),

53. the warehousekeeper, fails to calculate and pay excise duty in time (Article 89, paragraph 3),

54. the seller, i.e. special warehouses for supply of aircraft selling jet fuel and aviation gasoline fail to provide and/or fails to provide in time the memorandum of the state of stock and the records of sales (Article 90, paragraphs 2, 3 and 4 and Article 91),

55. the seller, applies for a refund of excise duty on the sold quantities of Eurodiesel - diesel fuel coloured with blue dye (Article 90, paragraph 5).

56. new- according to new Article 92

57. new according to new Article 92

(2) A natural person – a craftsman shall be fined from HRK 20,000.00 to HRK 500,000.00 if an offence referred to in paragraph 1 of this Article has been committed in connection with his/her performance of the craft.

(3) An individual shall be fined from HRK 2,000.00 to HRK 10,000.00 for the offences referred to in paragraph 1, items: 6, 23, 29, 30, 31, 47, 48 and 51 of this Article

Article 81

(1) A legal entity shall be fined from HRK 20,000.00 to HRK 800,000.00 and the responsible person at the legal entity shall be fined from HRK 1,500.00 to HRK 25,000.00 for an offence if:

1. failing to issue the accompanying excise document on the prescribed form and in the prescribed number of copies (Article 8, paragraph 2),

2. the consignee of excise products, fails to confirm the receipt of excise products and to return the accompanying excise document, previously endorsement by the competent customs house, to the consignor within the prescribed time limit (Article 9, paragraphs 1, 2 and 3),

3. the consigor of excise products who has not received the authenticated copy of the excise document, fails to inform the competent customs house accordingly in the prescribed time limit (Article 9, paragraph 6),

4. the consignee of excise products, fails to confirm the receipt of excise products by authenticating a copy of the single administrative document which is to be returned to the customs house where the import customs clearance has taken place within the prescribed time limit (Article 9, paragraph 7),

5. transporting excise products on which excise duty has been paid and completely denatured alcohol without the simplified accompanying excise document (Article 10, paragraphs 1 and 2),

6. failing to issue the simplified accompanying excise document on the prescribed form and in the prescribed number of copies (Article 10, paragraph 4),

7. the consignee of excise products, fails to confirm the receipt of the consignment on the simplified accompanying excise document within the prescribed time limit and to inform the customs house at the place of destination thereof (Article 10, paragraph 6),

8. the excise duty payer, fails to keep the documents during the prescribed time limits (Article 38),

9. failing to classify excise products in the prescribed manner (Article 40, Article 41, Article 42, Article 43, Article 44, Article 57, Article 58, Article 59 and Article 69),

10. failing to carry out the process of denaturation at the excise warehouse by using such equipment that will ensure alcohol denaturation by means of the prescribed substances and in the prescribed manner (Article 49, paragraphs 2 and 4),

11. the excise duty payer, fails to maintain the prescribed records on denaturation (Article 49, paragraph 3),

12. failing to provide information about the buyers of devices for the production of alcohol and alcoholic beverages to the customs house competent according to the registered office or residence of the buyer and to provide a copy of invoice (Article 52, paragraph 1),

(2) A natural person – a craftsman shall be fined from HRK 10,000.00 to HRK 200,000.00 if he/she has committed an offence referred to in paragraph 1 of this Article in connection with his/her performance of the craft.

Article 82

(1) For the offences referred to in Article 80, paragraph 1, item 1, item 6, item 7, item 23, item 24, item 25, item 26, item 31, item 33, item 34, item 35, item 38, and Article 81, paragraph 1, item 5 and item 10 of this Act, besides the fine, the protective measure of confiscation of excise products may be imposed.

(2) For the offence referred to in Article 80, paragraph 1, item 51 of this Act, if committed again within three years, besides the fine, the protective measure of confiscation of the vehicle, floating object, vessel or another machine or engine by which the offence has been committed may be imposed.

Article 83

For the offences referred to in Article 80, paragraph 1, item 26, item 32, item 33, item 34, item 36, item 38, item 48, item 49, item 50, and item 52 of this Act, besides the fine, the protective measure of prohibiting the performance of the business activity during a period from one month to one year may be imposed.

Article 84

For additional analytical, marketing, investment and business opportunities information, please contact Global Investment & Business Center, USA (202) 546-2103. Fax: (202) 546-3275. E-mail: rusric@erols.com

Besides the protective measures referred to in Article 82 and Article 83 of this Act, the economic benefits arising from the offence shall be seized from the legal entity or natura person having committed the offence.

XIX. PROCEDURAL PROVISIONS

Article 85

(1) The appeal proceedings, renewal proceedings, statute of limitations, calculation, collection, refund of excise duty and inspection controls shall be subject to the provisions of the General Tax Act.

(2) By way of derogation from the provisions of paragraph 1 of this Article, the provisions of the Customs Act shall apply to appeal proceedings, renewal proceedings statute of limitations, calculation, collection, refund of excise duty and inspection control in respect of the excise products which have been or are being imported into the customs area of Croatia.

(3) The Customs Administration shall be competent for prosecution of excise misdemeanours. The provisions of the General Tax Act shall apply to the statute of limitations of excise duty misdemeanours.

(4) The decision on the classification of excise products into the Combined Nomenclature codes shall be reached by the Customs Administration in accordance with the customs regulations and fundamental rules applicable to the classification of goods according to the customs tariff.

Article 86

The provisions of this Act with regard to the definition of the products subject to excise duty shall apply respectively in the case of changes of CN codes under the Regulation on the Customs Tariff, which may not affect the scope and amount of excise duty.

For additional analytical, marketing, investment and business opportunities information, please contact Global Investment & Business Center, USA (202) 546-2103. Fax: (202) 546-3275. E-mail: rusric@erols.com

XX. TRANSITIONAL AND FINAL PROVISIONS

Article 87

The persons liable to pay excise duties under the Act on Excise Duty on Tobacco Products (OG 51/94, 56/95,67/99, 105/99, 55/00, 107/01, 95/04,152/08, 38/09), the Act on Excise Duty on Alcohol (OG 51/94, 141/98, 55/00, 67/01, 107/01, 107/07), the Act on Excise Duty on Beer (OG 51/94, 139/97, 55/00 and 107/01) and the Act on Excise Duty on Oil Products (OG 55/00, 101/00, 27/01, 107/01,123/03, 57/06) who will be liable to pay excise duty under the provisions of this Act shall file, by 31 January 2010 at the latest, an application for entry into the register of excise duty payers with the customs house competent according to their registered office.

Article 88

(1) The excise duty which has become chargeable before the entry into force of this Act shall be calculated and paid in accordance with the provisions of the laws in force before the date of entry into force of this Act.

(2) The administrative and misdemeanour proceedings initiated before the entry into force of this Act shall be completed in accordance with the regulations in force before the date of entry into force of this Act.

(3) By way of derogation from the provisions of paragraph 2 of this Article, all misdemeanour proceedings initiated before the entry into force of this Act shall be completed in accordance with the provisions of this Act if that is more favourable for perpetrators.

(4) All misdemeanour proceedings initiated before the entry into force of this Act in respect of the offences not covered by this Act shall be closed.

(5) If products subject to excise duty under the laws referred to in Article 87 of this Act have been placed under a customs suspension procedure in accordance with the provisions of the Customs Act before the entry into force of this Act and released for free circulation afterwards, the time of incurrence of tax liability, its calculation and payment shall be determined in accordance with the customs regulations. Excise duty shall be charged at the same time as customs duty, at the rates and in the amounts applicable at the time of incurrence of the customs debt.

Article 89

(1) Producers' warehouses, producers' own wholesale warehouses, producers' warehouses where oil products of the government administration bodies are stored as commodity reserves, importers' own wholesale warehouses, along with special warehouses for supply of aircraft,

For additional analytical, marketing, investment and business opportunities information, please contact Global Investment & Business Center, USA
(202) 546-2103. Fax: (202) 546-3275. E-mail: rusric@erols.com

registered in accordance with the provisions of the laws in force until the date of entry into force of this Act shall continue to operate as excise warehouses in accordance with the provisions of this Act, on condition that the warehousekeeper obtains the excise warehousekeeping authorisation and the excise warehouse authorisation in accordance with the provisions of this Act not later than 31 March 2010.

(2) By the time of obtaining the excise warehousekeeping authorisation and the excise warehouse authorisation referred to in paragraph 1 of this Article, the warehousekeeper may dispatch excise products under excise-duty suspension arrangements in accordance with the provisions of this Act only from a producer's own warehouse to a producer's own wholesale warehouses or a special warehouse for supply of aircraft and to exports.

(3) If the warehousekeepers referred to in paragraph 1 of this Article fail to obtain the excise warehousekeeping authorisation and the excise warehouse authorisation by the date referred to in paragraph 1 of this Article, they shall calculate excise duty upon expiry of that time limit and pay it in accordance with the provisions of this Act.

Article 90

(1) Applications for special warehouses for heating oils (EL and LS) pursuant to Article 15, paragraph 3 of the Act on Excise Duty on Oil Products submitted by the sellers shall remain in full force and effect under this Act.

(2) Petrol stations – sellers of Eurodiesel – a diesel fuel coloured with blue dye in accordance with the Act on Excise Duty on Oil Products shall perform an inventory of Eurodiesel – a diesel fuel coloured with blue dye as at the date of entry into force of this Act, prepare an stock report and deliver it to the competent customs house within 8 days after taking inventory.

(3) The sale of the inventories referred to in paragraph 2 of this Article is possible only until the current stock are exhausted and only to the consumers of gas oils for the purposes in agriculture, fisheries and aquaculture referred to in Article 77 of this Act, and the records of sales must be kept.

(4) After the entire quantity of the stock referred to in paragraph 2 of this Article is sold, the seller shall deliver the records referred to in paragraph 3 of this Article to the competent customs house within eight days.

(5) The sellers of the stock referred to in paragraph 2 of this Article shall not be entitled to excise duty refund provided for in Article 78 of this Act.

Article 91

(1) Special warehouses for supply of aircrafts selling jet fuel and aviation gasoline, in accordance with Article 15, paragraph 4 of the Act on Excise Duty on Mineral Oil Products shall take inventory of the jet fuel and aviation gasoline as at the date of entry into force of this Act, prepare an stock report by type and quantity and deliver it to the competent customs house within eight days after taking inventory.

(2) The sale of the stock referred to in paragraph 1 of this Article is possible only until the stock are exhausted, but latest till 30 June 2010., and for the purposes referred to in Article 79, paragraph 1, item 1 of this Act, and the records of sales must be kept.

For additional analytical, marketing, investment and business opportunities information, please contact Global Investment & Business Center, USA (202) 546-2103. Fax: (202) 546-3275. E-mail: rusric@erols.com

(3) After the entire quantity of the stock referred to in paragraph 1 of this Article is sold, special warehouse for supply of aircraft selling jet fuel and aviation gasoline must deliver the records referred to in paragraph 2 of this Article to the competent customs house within eight days.

Article 92 *(new)*

(1) Until the introduction of fuel cards, the excise duty payers shall mark the gas oils for the purposes of agriculture, fisheries and aquaculture before their delivery from the excise warehouse or at the time of their importation with the indicators prescribed in the regulations on standardisation and colour them with blue dye.

(2) Until the introduction of fuel cards, the consumers of the gas oils for the purposes of agriculture, fisheries and aquaculture, as defined in Article 70, paragraph 9 and Article 77, paragraphs 3 and 5 of this Act, shall use special forms for the control of consumption of the gas oil coloured with blue dye to be supplied to the beneficiaries of that right, according to the licences provided for under special regulations, by the authority competent for agriculture and fisheries, which shall also enter the approved quantities.

(3) The excise duty payers and other legal entities and natural persons selling the gas oils for the purposes of agriculture, fisheries and aquaculture, shall maintain records of buyers by entering and certifying the sold quantities in the buyer's form for the control of consumption of the gas oil coloured with blue dye.

(4) The provisions of Article 76 of this Act concerning the tax inspection over the use of marked gas oils shall apply accordingly to the control of the use of the gas oil coloured with blue dye.

(5) The provisions of Article 90, paragraphs 2, 3, 4 and 5 of this Act shall not be applied until the introduction of fuel cards.

(6) The Minister of Finance, after obtaining the opinion of the minister competent for agriculture and fisheries, shall enact an ordinance stipulating the content, form and manner of use of the form for the control of gas oil consumption,

Article 93

(1) The amount of excise duty on individual excise products shall be adjusted to the value of

EUR on an annual basis. The medium exchange rate of the Croatian National Bank applicable on the first working day in October shall be applied, and the new amounts of exchange-rate adjusted excise duty shall begin to apply on 1 January of the next calendar year and be published in the Official Gazette.

For additional analytical, marketing, investment and business opportunities information, please contact Global Investment & Business Center, USA
(202) 546-2103. Fax: (202) 546-3275. E-mail: rusric@erols.com

(2) If the kuna exchange rate against the euro should change by more than 5% after the entry

into force of an excise duty rate or after the latest change of an excise duty rate, the Government of the Republic of Croatia may change the rates or amounts of excise duty.

Article 94

The Minister of Finance shall adopt the ordinances referred to in Article 9, paragraph 8, Article 10, paragraph 9, Article 12, paragraph 5, Article 16, paragraph 13, Article 17, paragraph 5, Article 18, paragraph 4, Article 20, paragraph 5, Article 22, paragraph 5, Article 23, paragraph 3, Article 24, paragraph 12, Article 25, paragraph 4, Article 27, paragraph 5, Article 28, paragraph 2, Article 29, paragraph 4, Article 30, paragraph 9, Article 31, paragraph 3, Article 32, paragraph 8, Article 33, paragraph 2, Article 35, paragraph 2, Article 49, paragraph 5, Article 50, paragraph 7, Article 54, paragraph 11, Article 66, paragraph 9, Article 68, paragraph 3, Article 73, paragraph 7, Article 75, paragraph 5, Article 76, paragraph 5, Article 77, paragraph 6, Article 78, paragraph 3, Article 79, paragraph 7 and Article 92 paragraph 3 of this Act 30 days after the entry into force of this Act at the latest.

Article 95

At the date of entry into force of this Act, the following Acts shall cease to be in force:

1. Act on Excise Duty on Alcohol (OG 51/94, 141/98, 55/00, 67/01, 107/01 and 107/07),
2. Act on Excise Duty on Beer (OG 51/94, 139/97, 55/00 and 107/01),
3. Act on Excise Duty on Tobacco Products (OG 51/94, 56/95,67/99, 105/99, 55/00, 107/01 , 95/04 and 152/08 OG),
4. **Act on Special Tax on Petroleum Products (OG 55/00, 101/00, 27/01, 107/01,123/03 and 57/06), save provisions of Article 3, paragraph1, item 3 and Article 5 paragraph 1 item 4 remaining valid by establishment of fuel card business as stipulated by provisions of Article 77, paragraph 3 and paragraph 5 of this Act**

Article 96

The implementation regulations adopted on the basis of the laws ceasing to be in force at the date of entry into force of this Act shall remain in full force and effect until the entry into force of the implementation regulations (i.e. the ordinance) adopted on the basis of the authorities provided for in this Act, provided that they are not contrary to the provisions of this Act.

Article 97

For additional analytical, marketing, investment and business opportunities information, please contact Global Investment & Business Center, USA
(202) 546-2103. Fax: (202) 546-3275. E-mail: rusric@erols.com

At the date of accession of Croatia to the European Union, the provisions of Article 2, Article 9, paragraph 4, Article 73, paragraph 2, and Article 79, paragraph 1, item 2 of this Act shall cease to be in force.

Article 98

This Act shall be published in the Official Gazette and enter into force on 1 January 2010. except for the provisions of Article 3, Article 5, paragraph 1, items 8 do 10, Article 7, paragraph 2, Article 9, paragraph 2, item 2, paragraph 3, paragraph 5, paragraph 6, item 2, Article 10, paragraphs 1 to 6, Article 11, paragraph 2, Article 12, paragraph 1, item 6, paragraphs 2 to 4, Article 15, paragraph 1, item 3, paragraphs 3 to 6, Article 18, paragraphs 2 and 3, Article 19, paragraph 1, item 6, paragraph 5, Article 20, paragraph 3 and 4, Article 21, paragraph 1, item 6, Article 24, paragraphs 4 and 5, Article 30, Article 31, Article 32, Article 34, paragraphs 3 and 4, Article 47, paragraph 1, item 2, Article 51, paragraph 1, Article 70, paragraph 3, items 6 to 8, Article 73, paragraph 3, Article 79, paragraph 1, item 3 and Article 93 of this Act which shall enter into force at the date of accession of Croatia to the European Union.

FOREIGN EXCHANGE ACT

CHAPTER I BASIC PROVISIONS

Subject Matter of the Act

Article 1

(1) This Act governs:
1. transactions between residents and non-residents in foreign means of payment and in kuna;
2. transactions between residents in foreign means of payment;
3. unilateral transfers of assets from and into the Republic of Croatia that cannot be considered transaction executions between residents and non-residents.

(2) Transactions referred to in paragraph 1 of this Article shall imply current and capital transactions and their execution by means of payments, collection or transfers.

RESIDENTS AND NON-RESIDENTS

ARTICLE 2

(1) Under the terms of this Act, the term residents shall mean:
1. legal persons with a head office in the Republic of Croatia, except their foreign branches;
2. branches of foreign companies and sole traders enrolled in a register kept by a competent government authority or administration in the Republic of Croatia;
3. sole traders, craftsmen, and other natural persons with a head office or a place of residence in the Republic of Croatia who are self-employed and perform the economic activity of their registration (hereinafter: individual undertakings);
4. natural persons with a place of residence in the Republic of Croatia;
5. natural persons staying in the Republic of Croatia on the basis of a valid residence permit for a minimum period of 183 days;
6. diplomatic, consular and other representative offices of the Republic of Croatia abroad financed by the budget and Croatians citizens employed in those representative offices, including their family members.

(2) All other persons not stated in paragraph 1 of this Article shall be considered non-residents.

For additional analytical, marketing, investment and business opportunities information, please contact Global Investment & Business Center, USA (202) 546-2103. Fax: (202) 546-3275. E-mail: rusric@erols.com

BANKS AND AUTHORIZED COMPANIES

Article 3

(1) Under the terms of this Act, the term bank shall imply a financial institution licensed by the Croatian National Bank and authorized to perform transactions referred to in this Act and prescribed by the Banking Act, a non-resident bank authorized, pursuant to the Banking Act, to provide banking services directly in the territory of the Republic of Croatia and the Croatian Bank for Reconstruction and Development.

(2) Authorized company shall imply a company licensed by the Croatian Securities Exchange Commission, which conducts securities transactions pursuant to provisions of the Securities Market Act.

Foreign Means of Payment

Article 4

(1) Foreign means of payment, under the terms of this Act, shall comprise foreign exchange, foreign cash, checks, and other monetary instruments denominated and payable in foreign currency.

(2) Foreign exchange, under the terms of this Act, shall mean monetary claims from abroad.

(3) Foreign cash (banknotes and coins) shall mean monetary claims on the central bank or government of the country of issue.

(4) Checks and other monetary instruments denominated and payable in foreign currency shall mean monetary claims on their issuers.

Securities and Derivative Financial Instruments

Article 5

(1) Securities shall mean securities defined in accordance with the Securities Market Act.

(2) Securities traded in the capital markets, under the terms of this Act, shall comprise shares, bonds and other debt securities issued in a series with a maturity of over one year.

(3) Securities traded on the money market, under the terms of this Act, shall comprise short-date securities issued in a series with a maturity of under one year, such as Treasury bills, Croatian National Bank bills, commercial papers, certificates of deposit, and banker's acceptances and long-dated debt securities with maximum remaining maturity of one year.

(4) Derivative financial instruments, under the terms of this Act, shall comprise securities or agreements whose value changes in accordance with the changes in the value of financial instruments and any other legal arrangements from which they are derived.

Domestic and Foreign Securities

Article 6

(1) Domestic securities, under the terms of this Act, shall be securities issued by a resident issuer and depository bills issued abroad on the basis of the underlying domestic security.

(2) Securities not referred to in paragraph 1 of this Article shall imply foreign securities.

Capital Transactions

Article 7

(1) Under the terms of this Act, capital transactions shall mean transactions concluded between residents and non-residents, as well as unilateral transfers of assets for the purpose of transferring capital, other than current payments and transfers referred to in Article 8 of this Act.

**For additional analytical, marketing, investment and business opportunities information, please contact Global Investment & Business Center, USA
(202) 546-2103. Fax: (202) 546-3275. E-mail: rusric@erols.com**

(2) Capital transactions referred to in paragraph 1 of this Article shall comprise:
1. direct investments;
2. investments in real estate;
3. securities transactions in the capital markets;
4. securities transactions in the money markets;
5. transactions with stakes in investment funds;
6. credit transactions;
7. deposit transactions;
8. payments related to insurance agreements;
9. unilateral transfers of assets:
    a) personal transfers of assets;
    b) physical transfers of assets.

(3) Capital transactions shall also comprise transactions involving the alienation of rights acquired through investments, or securities referred to in paragraph 2 of this Article, as well as the repatriation of assets or transfer of the balance of assets in liquidation or of the bankruptcy estate.

Current Transactions and Current Payments

Article 8

(1) Current transactions are transactions concluded between residents and non-residents for a purpose other than a transfer of capital.

(2) Payments and transfers arising from current transactions shall comprise:
1. all payments due in connection with foreign goods and services trade and other current business, including services and short-term banking and credit facilities;
2. payments due as interest on loans and as net income from other investments;
3. payments of moderate amounts for amortization of loans, for depreciation of direct investments and distribution of profits based on ownership stakes;
4. transfers in connection with remittances from workers abroad, pensions, disability allowances, and other social benefits, taxes and dues, interstate cooperation, settlement of insurance claims, lottery gains, compensations for concessions, membership fees and fines (penalties) and moderate remittances for family living expenses.

Direct Investments

Article 9

(1) Direct investments, under the terms of this Act, shall comprise all investments by residents abroad and all investments in the Republic of Croatia by non-residents, made with a purpose of establishing permanent economic relationships and gaining considerable control over the managing of a legal person.

(2) The following situations shall be identified as those whose purpose is to establish permanent economic relationships and to gain considerable control over the managing of a legal person:
1. the establishment of, or an increase in the initial capital of, a company fully owned by the investor, the establishment of a branch office or acquisition of an already existing company into full ownership of an investor or investment for the purpose of performing the activities of an individual undertaking;
2. investment into a new or an existing company, provided the investor acquires a minimum 10% stake in the initial capital of a company, or a minimum 10% voting rights, following fulfillment of conditions referred to in paragraph 1 of this Article;
3. loans with a minimum maturity of five years, granted for the purpose of establishing permanent economic relationships, provided such loans can be classified as subordinate or hybrid claims.

(3) Following the establishment of a direct ownership relationship between residents and non-residents in terms of paragraphs 1 and 2 of this Article, direct investment transactions shall also comprise:

For additional analytical, marketing, investment and business opportunities information, please contact Global Investment & Business Center, USA (202) 546-2103. Fax: (202) 546-3275. E-mail: rusric@erols.com

1. reinvested profit or any direct investor's share in the profits of a company which is not distributed in the form of dividends or other forms of profit distribution;
2. debt transactions between any direct investor and a company into which direct investment has already been made. This shall comprise debt securities, commercial loans, financial loans and other debtor-creditor relations. Investments by financial institutions involving debt transactions related to current operations shall not be considered direct investments; only those transactions, which are motivated by permanent interest in ownership status shall be considered direct investments.

(4) The following shall not be considered direct investments: investments by investment funds, brokerage firms, pension funds, insurance companies, banks and other persons granted by the Croatian Securities Exchange Commission a status of an institutional investor, in accordance with a special law, and investments in financial assets made for the purpose of issuing depository bills.

(5) The following shall exceptionally be considered direct investments: investment by a bank into another bank or other financial institution whose main activity is the provision of financial services and investment of an insurance company into another insurance company, provided such investments fulfil the conditions referred to in paragraph 2 of this Article.

Securities Transactions

Article 10

(1) Securities transactions, under the terms of this Act, shall comprise securities transactions in the capital and money markets and transactions with stakes in investment funds, which are not investment transactions in terms of Article 9 of this Act.

(2) Securities transactions referred to in paragraph 1 of this Article shall comprise:

1. issuance, listing, and the sale of domestic securities abroad;
2. issuance, listing, and the sale of foreign securities in the Republic of Croatia;
3. investments by residents into securities abroad;
4. investments by non-residents into securities in the Republic of Croatia.

(3) The listing of securities referred to in paragraph 2 of this Article means the beginning of trading in foreign securities in the Republic of Croatia or in domestic securities abroad in stock exchanges or regulated public markets.

Credit Transactions

Article 11

(1) Credit transactions, under the terms of this Act, shall comprise commercial and financial loans. Under the terms of this Act, credit transactions shall also include sureties and guarantees.

(2) Commercial loans, under the terms of this Act, shall imply deferred payments, or advance payments for goods and services. Commercial loans shall also include bank funding for deferred and advance payments and transactions involving purchases of claims (*factoring and forfaiting*), provided the underlying transaction from which the claims arise can be characterized as a commercial loan..

(3) Financial loans, under the terms of this Act, shall imply all loans except loans referred to in Article 9, paragraph 2, item 3 and paragraph 2 of this Article. Financial loans shall not comprise sureties and guarantees.

(4) Credit transactions referred to in Article 9, paragraph 2, item 3 of this Act and all credit transactions referred to in this Article, except deferred and advance payments up to 12 months, based on a commercial transaction, shall be concluded in a written form. Bank loan agreements shall always be concluded in a written form.

For additional analytical, marketing, investment and business opportunities information, please contact Global Investment & Business Center, USA
(202) 546-2103. Fax: (202) 546-3275. E-mail: rusric@erols.com

DEPOSIT TRANSACTIONS

Article 12

(1) Deposit transactions referred to in Article 7, paragraph 2, item 7 of this Act shall mean transactions based on deposit agreements concluded between non-residents and a bank and between residents and a non-resident financial institution.

(2) Under the terms of this Act, deposit transactions shall also include current account agreements.

PAYMENTS BASED ON INSURANCE AGREEMENTS

Article 13

Payments based on insurance agreements shall include premium payments and payments of insured amounts on the basis of insurance agreements between a non-resident insurance company and a resident as a beneficiary and a resident insurance company and a non-resident as a beneficiary.

Unilateral Transfers of Assets

Article 14

(1) Unilateral transfers of assets shall mean those transfers of assets from the Republic of Croatia abroad or from abroad to the Republic of Croatia which cannot be characterized as transaction executions between residents and non-residents and which may take the form of personal and physical transfers of assets.

(2) Personal transfers of assets shall be transfers of assets from the Republic of Croatia and into the Republic of Croatia on the basis of gifts and grants, fixed income, inheritance, settlement of immigrants' debts in parent country, transfer of immigrants' assets abroad and income of non-resident persons employed in the Republic of Croatia.

(3) The Croatian National Bank may, by means of a special decision, impose restrictions on transfers abroad relating to gifts and grants in accordance with the prescribed limits for physical transfers of assets.

(4) Physical transfers, under the terms of this Act, shall mean any transfer of domestic cash, foreign cash, checks and materialized securities from and into the Republic of Croatia.

Payments and Collections in Foreign Means of Payment

Article 15

Payments and collections in foreign means of payment between residents and between residents and non-residents in the Republic of Croatia shall be allowed in cases prescribed by law or a decision of the Croatian National Bank.

FOREIGN EXCHANGE ACCOUNTS AND

Foreign Exchange Savings Deposits Accounts of Residents

Article 16

(1) Residents may keep foreign exchange in foreign exchange accounts or in foreign exchange savings deposits accounts in banks in the Republic of Croatia. The Croatian National bank shall stipulate the conditions for and the manner of opening and maintaining foreign exchange accounts and foreign exchange savings deposits accounts.

(2) Any bank opening a foreign exchange account and taking a foreign exchange savings deposit shall be obliged to establish the identity of the relevant resident.

For additional analytical, marketing, investment and business opportunities information, please contact Global Investment & Business Center, USA (202) 546-2103. Fax: (202) 546-3275. E-mail: rusric@erols.com

(3) Banks shall be obliged to keep data on foreign exchange account holders and holders of foreign exchange savings deposits accounts referred to in paragraph 1 of this Article, for five years following the closing of the account.
(4) The amount of interest and the way it is calculated and paid and the currency in which the interest and the principal are to be paid shall be laid down in an agreement concluded between the bank and the resident.

Loans in Foreign Means of Payment Between Residents

Article 17

(1) Loans in foreign means of payment may be granted to residents by banks. The loans thus granted may be repaid in foreign currency.
(2) Other residents shall not grant each other loans in foreign means of payment.

Transactions with Derivative Financial Instruments

Article 18

(1) The provisions of this Act relating to transactions that serve as a basis for transactions with derivative financial instruments shall apply to transactions with derivative financial instruments.
(2) The Croatian National Bank may prescribe the conditions for the carrying out of transactions with derivative financial instruments abroad.
(3) The provision of paragraph 2 of this Article shall not apply to banks, brokers, investment funds, insurance companies, pension funds and other financial institutions whose business operations are governed by special laws.

CHAPTER II CAPITAL TRANSACTIONS

II.1 Direct Investments

Direct Investments by Non-Residents and Residents

Article 19

(1) Direct investments by non-residents in the Republic of Croatia shall be unrestricted, unless otherwise provided by special laws.
(2) Direct investment abroad by residents shall be unrestricted.

Protection of Direct Investments

Article 20

(1) Transfer abroad of profits made by any non-resident through direct investment shall be unrestricted, provided that all profit tax relating to the amount to be transferred abroad has been paid in the Republic of Croatia.
(2) Transfer abroad of the balance of assets in liquidation or of the bankruptcy estate shall be unrestricted, provided that all tax and other legally prescribed obligations relating to such business have been met in the Republic of Croatia.

II.2 Investment in Real Estate

ARTICLE 21

Any resident shall be allowed to transfer funds abroad for the purpose of acquiring ownership of real estate abroad provided all legally prescribed obligations have been settled.

For additional analytical, marketing, investment and business opportunities information, please contact Global Investment & Business Center, USA
(202) 546-2103. Fax: (202) 546-3275. E-mail: rusric@erols.com

II.3 Securities Transactions in the Capital Markets

Investments by Residents in Securities Abroad

Article 22

(1) Resident legal persons may subscribe, pay in, purchase and sell securities abroad through an authorized company or through participants in stock exchanges and regulated public markets abroad.

(2) Resident natural persons and individual undertakings may subscribe, pay in, purchase and sell securities abroad only through an authorized company.

(3) Residents not referred to in paragraph 5 of this Article may purchase abroad securities issued by the OECD member countries and international financial institutions and domestic securities. For other securities that residents referred to in this paragraph may purchase, the Croatian National Bank may stipulate the rating, the country of issue and the stock exchange and regulated public market in which they quote.

(4) The Croatian National Bank shall prescribe the manner in which and the conditions under which transactions referred to in paragraphs 1, 2 and 3 of this Article shall be conducted.

(5) Banks, investment funds, insurance companies, pension funds and other financial institutions whose business is governed by special laws may purchase securities abroad in accordance with such laws.

Issuance, Listing, and Sale of Foreign Securities in the Republic of Croatia

Article 23

(1) The issuance, the listing and the sale of foreign securities in the capital markets in the Republic of Croatia shall be allowed, provided such transactions are in line with regulations governing securities transactions in the Republic of Croatia.

(2) The Minister of Finance may prescribe the conditions for the issuance, the listing and the sale of foreign securities in the capital markets in the Republic of Croatia.

Investment in Securities in the Republic of Croatia by Non-Residents

ARTICLE 24

(1) Non-residents may subscribe, pay in, purchase or sell securities in the Republic of Croatia in accordance with regulations governing securities transactions in the Republic of Croatia.

(2) The Croatian National Bank may, by a special decision, prescribe that non-resident custody and cash accounts for payments and collections concerning the sale of securities in the Republic of Croatia be opened in and managed by banks.

(3) The decision referred to in paragraph 2 of this Article may render the right to acquiring securities for any non-resident subject to an agreement on maintaining a custody account which obliges any non-resident not to alienate or pledge the acquired securities with residents, within a period of one year from the registration of title, and to accept that the custodian bank may have a ban on their right of disposal entered into the register of shareholders, register of security owners or any other register kept by the issuer of securities or by the Central Depository Agency, whereby non-residents rights to dividend or interest payments shall not be challenged.

II.4 TRANSACTIONS WITH SECURITIES ON THE MONEY MARKET

For additional analytical, marketing, investment and business opportunities information, please contact Global Investment & Business Center, USA
(202) 546-2103. Fax: (202) 546-3275. E-mail: rusric@erols.com

Article 25

(1) The Croatian National Bank may prescribe the lowest permissible rating for any foreign issuer of short-dated securities, whose securities are acquired by residents in the money market abroad. Residents shall be able to purchase domestic securities abroad without any restrictions.
(2) Banks, investment funds, insurance companies, pension funds and other financial institutions whose business operations are governed by special laws may purchase securities abroad in accordance with such laws.
(3) The Croatian National Bank may prescribe the lowest permissible rating for any foreign issuer of short-dated securities in the Republic of Croatia.
(4) Non-residents shall not be allowed to purchase the Croatian National Bank bills and the Treasury bills of the Ministry of Finance of the Republic of Croatia. As regards other short-dated securities, the Croatian National Bank may impose restrictions regarding their acquisition and their alienation prior to maturity.

Verification of Conditions for the Issuance and Listing of Foreign Securities in the Republic of Croatia

Article 26

(1) During its prospectus approval procedure, the Croatian Securities Exchange Commission shall verify the fulfillment, on the part of the foreign issuer, of the conditions for the issuance of foreign securities in the Republic of Croatia, pursuant to this Act and by-laws of the Croatian National Bank and the Ministry of Finance.
(2) Stock exchanges and regulated public markets, when listing foreign securities in stock exchange and regulated public markets quotations, shall verify if the securities by foreign issuers meet the conditions laid down in this Act and by-laws of the Croatian National Bank.

II.5 Transactions with Stakes in Investment Funds

Article 27

(1) The provisions of this Act governing securities transactions in the capital markets shall appropriately apply to transactions with stakes in investment funds, unless otherwise provided by a law governing business operations of investment funds.
(2) The Croatian National Bank may prohibit investment fund management companies and authorized companies from selling to non-residents stakes and shares in those investment funds that may hold, on the basis of their statutes, over 50% of the Croatian National Bank bills and/or Treasury bills in their portfolios.

II.6 CREDIT TRANSACTIONS

Article 28

(1) Banks may conduct credit transactions with non-residents in their own name and for their own account, in their own name and for the client's account and in the client's name and for the client's account.
(2) Resident legal persons or individual undertakings, pursuant to this Act, may conduct credit transactions with non-residents in their own name and for their own account and in their own name and for the client's account.
(3) Other residents may conduct credit transactions with non-residents in their own name and for their own account.
(4) Residents shall transfer funds from financial loans granted abroad to an account with a bank headquartered in the Republic of Croatia or an account abroad, pursuant to Article 29 of this Act. Exceptionally, residents may use banks abroad for financial loans from abroad, provided

the loan agreement stipulated payment for goods and services directly to the supplier or provider of service or provided the financial loan is used to repay another loan previously granted abroad (refinancing).

(5) When granting loans and issuing guarantees and sureties on behalf of non-residents, residents shall provide those instruments of collateral which are required to ensure a security of the credit transaction, guarantee and surety offered.

(6) Granting financial loans with maturity of less than one year to non-residents shall be prohibited.

This prohibition shall not apply to banks, to residents when granting financial loans to non-residents related to direct equity investment, and to residents when granting financial loans to non-residents with whom they are related (spouses, parents, children, brothers, sisters).

II.7 Deposit Transactions

Deposit Transactions of Residents

Article 29

The Croatian National Bank shall prescribe the conditions under which residents, except banks, may open and keep accounts abroad.

Deposit Transactions of Non-Residents

Article 30

(1) Non-residents may open foreign exchange and kuna accounts in banks.

(2) Any bank opening an account shall establish the identity of the non-resident.

(3) Data on account owners referred to in paragraph 1 of this Article shall be kept by the bank for five years following the closing of the account.

(4) The Croatian National Bank shall prescribe the conditions and the manner governing the opening and managing of the accounts.

(5) The Croatian National Bank may prescribe a monthly limit for kuna and foreign cash withdrawals from and deposits to accounts of non-residents who are not natural persons and may lay down the conditions for issuing approvals for amounts exceeding the prescribed limits.

II.8 Payments Based on Insurance Agreements

Article 31

Payments based on insurance agreements shall be unrestricted, provided the agreement is concluded in accordance with the regulations governing insurance.

CHAPTER III PAYMENTS, COLLECTIONS AND TRANSFERS

III.1 General Provisions

External Payments

Article 32

(1) External payments shall be executed by banks authorized by the Croatian National Bank and the Croatian Bank for Reconstruction and Development.

(2) Residents shall make their external payments through banks.

For additional analytical, marketing, investment and business opportunities information, please contact Global Investment & Business Center, USA
(202) 546-2103. Fax: (202) 546-3275. E-mail: rusric@erols.com

(3) External payments for the Republic of Croatia may also be executed by the Croatian National Bank.
(4) The Croatian National Bank shall prescribe the conditions for and the manner of executing external payments.
(5) All payments and transfers referred to in Article 8 of this Act shall be unrestricted, except where safety measures implemented pursuant to Article 47 of this Act are imposed.

Time Limits for the Execution of External Payment Orders

Article 33

(1) The bank shall execute a valid external payment order, provided there are sufficient funds in the account of the issuer of the order, on the value date abroad not later than three working days from the date of the receipt of the order, unless the issuer of the order has asked that the payment order be executed at a later value date abroad.
(2) The bank shall inform its client, the beneficiary of the payment, not later than on the next working day following the receipt of notice on the inflow of funds in an account abroad or in another bank in the country, about the inflow of funds from abroad, or transfer such funds to another bank in the country in which the payment beneficiary holds an account.
(3) The bank shall, not later than on the next working day following the receipt of a valid order from the payment beneficiary, allocate funds in accordance with the order.

Payments and Collections in Transactions with Non-Residents in Domestic Cash, Foreign Cash and Checks

Article 34

(1) Residents referred to in Article 2, paragraph 1, items 1, 2 and 3 of this Act may execute or receive payments arising from transactions with non-residents in domestic cash, foreign cash and checks under the conditions and in the manner prescribed by the Croatian National Bank.
(2) Residents shall deposit foreign cash and checks paid pursuant to paragraph 1 of this Article, in a bank account or, if so agreed with a bank, sell them to the bank within the time limits laid down by the Croatian National Bank

III.2 Payments and Transfers Based on Capital Transactions

Article 35

(1) Payments and transfers based on capital transactions shall be unrestricted, provided the transaction is concluded and notified in accordance with this Act and provided all tax obligations arising from any such transaction in the Republic of Croatia have been met. By way of exception, Article 20, paragraph 1 of this Act shall apply to transfers abroad of profits made by non-residents through direct investments.
(2) A bank shall not execute any external payment orders related to a transfer abroad of profits from direct investments and to a transfer of the balance of assets in liquidation or of the bankruptcy estate if such payment would be contrary to paragraph 1 of this Article.

III.3 Unilateral Transfers of Assets – Physical Transfers of Assets

Taking In and Out of the Country Foreign Cash, Domestic Cash and Checks

Article 36

For additional analytical, marketing, investment and business opportunities information, please contact Global Investment & Business Center, USA (202) 546-2103. Fax: (202) 546-3275. E-mail: rusric@erols.com

(1) Foreign cash and checks denominated in foreign currency may be taken into the Republic of Croatia without restrictions, subject to customs declaration pursuant to Article 40 of this Act.
(2) The Croatian National Bank shall prescribe the limits for unrestricted:
1. taking foreign cash out of the country;
2. taking domestic cash in and out of the country;
3. taking checks in and out of the country,
and shall lay down the conditions for issuing approvals for taking in and out of the country amounts in excess of the prescribed limits.
(3) Banks shall be free, for the purpose of carrying out their business operations, to take out of the country foreign cash and checks denominated in foreign currency, in excess of the limits laid down in a decision by the Croatian National Bank pursuant to paragraph 2 of this Article.

Procedure Governing Declared Amounts in Domestic and Foreign Cash and Checks in Excess of Permitted Limits

Article 37

(1) Any passenger declaring an amount in domestic and foreign cash and checks in excess of permitted limits, shall be instructed by the customs officer to deposit any such excess amount in a bank, or if possible, in the customs office.
(2) In the event that the passenger referred to in paragraph 1 of this Article refuses to act in accordance with the authorized customs officer's instruction, it shall be deemed that it is his/her intention to take out of the country, contrary to this Act, domestic and foreign cash, or checks.
(3) Domestic and foreign cash and checks referred to in paragraph 1 of this Article, deposited in a customs office, shall be returned to the passenger on his/her return journey or following his/her return to the Republic of Croatia, and the passenger shall be required to pay handling charges amounting to 1% of the amount deposited. In no case shall the handling charges exceed 350.00 kuna or be less than 35.00 kuna, payable in kuna.
(4) Should the passenger, or his/her proxy, fail to claim the domestic or foreign cash deposited pursuant to paragraph 1 of this Article, within 90 days from the date such a deposit was made, the passenger, or his/her proxy, will be deemed to have waived their right to the deposit in favor of the Government Budget of the Republic of Croatia, with a note to this effect being included in the deposit receipt issued by the customs office.

Sending and Transferring Materialized Securities To or From Foreign Countries

Article 38

(1) Resident-owned materialized securities may be sent and transferred to or from foreign countries by an authorized company or a custodian bank for the purpose of:
1. exercising rights derived from such securities;
2. transferring rights derived from such securities to non-residents;
3. safe-keeping of foreign securities or securities issued abroad by residents, provided such securities shall be entrusted to a person authorized abroad to conduct such transactions.
(2) The provision of paragraph 1 of this Article shall not apply to temporary transfers of securities to or from foreign countries for the purpose of exercising rights derived from the securities, which is subject to prior notification to the Croatian National Bank.

Special Provision

Article 39

For additional analytical, marketing, investment and business opportunities information, please contact Global Investment & Business Center, USA
(202) 546-2103. Fax: (202) 546-3275. E-mail: rusric@erols.com

Article 22, paragraphs 2 and 3, Article 25, paragraph 1, Article 27, Article 28, paragraphs 4 and 6, Article 29, Article 36, paragraph 2, item 1 and Article 38, paragraph 1 of this Act, governing the transfer of residents' capital abroad, shall not apply to residents staying abroad on the basis of a valid work permit, for a period of not less than 183 days and residents referred to in Article 2, paragraph 1, item 5.

Prevention of Money Laundering

Article 40

(1) Residents and non-residents shall be obliged, when crossing the state border, to declare to the customs officer any amount of domestic or foreign cash and checks that is being taken into or out of the country that is governed by the act regulating the prevention of money laundering.
(2) The obligation referred to in paragraph 1 of this Article shall also apply to any representative, responsible person or proxy, taking into or out of the country domestic or foreign cash and checks on behalf of any legal person.

Fictitious Agreements

Article 41

No resident shall settle false claims or issue orders for payments to non-residents on the basis of fictitious agreements or invoices, or conclude agreements not based on actual prices

CHAPTER IV FOREIGN EXCHANGE MARKET AND THE EXCHANGE RATE

Foreign Exchange Market

Article 42

(1) Foreign exchange market, under the terms of this Act, shall comprise all foreign exchange purchase and sale transactions.
(2) Banks shall conclude foreign exchange purchase and sale transactions in their own name and for their own account and in their own name and for the client's account, and other persons in their own name and for their own account.
(3) Residents and non-residents shall conduct their foreign exchange purchase and sale transactions in banks. The Ministry of Finance may also conduct its foreign exchange purchase and sale transactions in the Croatian National Bank.
(4) Residents referred to in Article 2, paragraph 1, items 4 and 5 of this Act and natural non-resident persons may also conduct their foreign exchange purchase and sale transactions through authorized exchange offices.
(5) Unless listed in paragraph 4 of this Article, residents and non-residents shall not be allowed to conduct their foreign exchange purchase and sales transactions through authorized exchange offices.

Purchase and Sale of Foreign Exchange Through Spot and Forward Transactions

Article 43

(1) Participants in the foreign exchange market may purchase and sell foreign exchange through spot and forward transactions.
(2) Forward foreign exchange purchase and sale transactions, under the terms of this Act, shall mean any purchase or sale transaction with a maturity of not less than two working days from the date of agreement.

Exchange Rate Determination

Article 44

The exchange rate of foreign currencies against the kuna shall be freely determined on the foreign exchange market, on the basis of supply and demand.

Publication and Application of the Mean Exchange Rate of the Croatian National Bank

Article 45

(1) The Croatian National Bank shall determine every working day the value of the kuna against other currencies on the basis of foreign exchange purchase and sale transactions and the exchange rates of foreign currencies in the foreign exchange market. The exchange rate thus determined shall be made public by the Croatian National Bank.
(2) The Croatian National Bank shall prescribe the manner and the time limits in which the banks and the authorized exchange offices shall submit data on foreign exchange purchase and sale transactions in the foreign exchange market.
(3) The mean exchange rate of the Croatian National Bank for foreign means of payment shall be used in statements of foreign assets and liabilities and for statistical purposes.
(4) When charging import and export levies, foreign exchange shall be converted into kuna using the mean exchange rate of the Croatian National Bank applicable on a working day before the last working day in a week preceding the week in which the amount of import and export levies is determined, unless otherwise stipulated by the Minister of Finance.

Authorized Exchange Offices

Article 46

(1) Exchange transactions shall mean the purchase and sale of foreign cash and purchase of checks denominated and payable in foreign currency.
(2) Exchange transactions may be conducted by any resident with a status of a legal person and any individual undertaking using in their work protected computer programs for exchange transactions, that have an agreement with a bank and are authorized to conduct exchange transactions (authorized exchange offices).
(3) The Croatian National Bank shall prescribe the conditions for exchange transactions and the manner in which they are to be conducted.

CHAPTER V SAFETY PROVISIONS

Preconditions for Taking Safety Measures

Article 47

(1) Where capital movements cause or threaten to cause serious difficulties in the implementation of monetary or foreign exchange policies, the Croatian National Bank may issue a special decision prescribing safety measures.
(2) The safety measures may be implemented by the Croatian National Bank or the Government of the Republic of Croatia, provided they are necessary for the execution of sanctions imposed by the United Nations or other international organizations of which the Republic of Croatia is a member.
(3) Safety measures referred to in paragraph 1 of this Article may be prescribed for a maximum period of six months.
(4) By way of exception, the Croatian National Bank may extend the period referred to in paragraph 3 of this Article, subject to approval of the Croatian Parliament.

For additional analytical, marketing, investment and business opportunities information, please contact Global Investment & Business Center, USA (202) 546-2103. Fax: (202) 546-3275. E-mail: rusric@erols.com

(5) The Government of the Republic of Croatia and the Croatian Securities Exchange Commission shall be notified of any safety measures, prior to their implementation.

Safety Measures

Article 48

Safety measures of the Croatian National Bank referred to in Article 47 of this Act may comprise:

1. measures restricting the rights of residents to use funds in their accounts abroad or in their foreign exchange accounts in the Republic of Croatia;
2. measures obliging the banks to sell to the Croatian National Bank any foreign exchange derived from the exchange transactions of banks and authorized exchange offices;
3. measures restricting credit transactions between residents and non-residents;
4. measures restricting payment and collection transactions involving foreign claims and liabilities;
5. measures restricting the transfer of securities, foreign cash and gold into and from the Republic of Croatia;
6. measures restricting securities and gold transactions between residents and non-residents;
7. measures restricting the issuing of guarantees or sureties, offering of pledges or other instruments of collateral for the account of non-resident.

CHAPTER VI

Business Books and Reporting

VI.1 General Provisions Governing Reporting on External Operations

Reporting Obligation

Article 49

(1) Residents covered by the reporting obligation shall report to the Croatian National Bank, directly or indirectly through banks, authorized companies, Central Depository Agency and customs authorities.

(2) Residents covered by the reporting obligation shall allow the Croatian National Bank and the Ministry of Finance – Foreign Exchange Inspectorate, and the Customs Administration, to examine their business books and other business documentation, for the purpose of data verification.

(3) The Croatian National Bank shall define in detail the conditions, the substance, the manner and the procedure of reporting.

(4) The Croatian National Bank shall make balance of payments projections for the Republic of Croatia.

(5) For the purpose of monitoring the outturn of the projected balance of payments of the Republic of Croatia, residents shall submit to the Croatian National Bank data on external operations and transactions in the manner and within the time limits prescribed by a special decision of the Croatian National Bank.

VI.2 Control Book

Article 50

(1) Banks shall keep control books on all payments and collections arising from those external current transactions which they conduct in their own name and for their own account.

(2) Other residents referred to in Article 2, paragraph 1, items 1, 2 and 3, shall keep control books on all payments and collections arising from external current and capital transactions, irrespective of the fact that data entered in that book is entered in other books and records which such residents are obliged to keep pursuant to other regulations.

For additional analytical, marketing, investment and business opportunities information, please contact Global Investment & Business Center, USA
(202) 546-2103. Fax: (202) 546-3275. E-mail: rusric@erols.com

(3) The control book shall be made available to foreign exchange control officials immediately and not later than on the next working day.
(4) The Minister of Finance shall prescribe the manner in which control books are to be kept and the content of such control books.

VI.3 Reporting on Direct and Other Equity Investment

Article 51

(1) Residents shall report any investment or any subsequent change in investment to the Croatian National Bank within 30 days after any direct or other equity investment abroad, or after any direct or other equity investment by non-residents in the Republic of Croatia.
(2) The Croatian National Bank shall prescribe the manner in which such reporting shall be made and the manner in which data on direct and other equity investment shall be collected.

VI.4 Reporting on Securities Transactions

Article 52

(1) Each authorized company and each custodian bank shall report to the Croatian National Bank on any resident securities transactions abroad and any non-resident securities transactions in the Republic of Croatia.
(2) Resident issuers of debt securities shall report to the Croatian National Bank on each issuance and sale of such securities abroad.

VI.5 Reporting on Credit Transactions

Article 53

(1) Residents shall report to the Croatian National Bank on any credit transactions with non-residents in the manner and within the time limits prescribed by the Croatian National Bank.
(2) For reporting purposes, the Croatian National Bank may stipulate that credit transactions also comprise certain other transactions between residents and non-residents, the economic purpose of which equals that of a credit transaction.

VI.6 Reporting on Deposit Transactions

Article 54

Residents shall report to the Croatian National Bank on the transactions and balances in their accounts abroad and in the accounts of their branches abroad in the manner and within the time limits laid down in a decision by the Croatian National Bank.

CHAPTER VII SUPERVISION

VII.1 General Provisions

Supervisory Bodies

Article 55

Supervision over transactions pursuant to this Act shall be exercised by the Croatian National Bank and the Ministry of Finance – Foreign Exchange Inspectorate and Customs Administration (hereinafter: supervisory bodies).

Exchange of Information Between Supervisory Bodies

For additional analytical, marketing, investment and business opportunities information, please contact Global Investment & Business Center, USA
(202) 546-2103. Fax: (202) 546-3275. E-mail: rusric@erols.com

Article 56

(1) Supervisory bodies shall exchange information needed in the process of supervision and inform each other about any irregularities established in the course of supervision, provided such findings are relevant for the work of the other supervisory body.
(2) Supervisory bodies shall define the content of the exchange of information and the manner in which such an exchange of information is to take place by means of an agreement on the exchange of information or by means of other enactments.

VII.2 Real Competence

Competence of the Ministry of Finance – Foreign Exchange Inspectorate

Article 57

(1) The Ministry of Finance – Foreign Exchange Inspectorate shall supervise the application and the implementation of this Act and the operations of residents and non-residents performing their business or other activity in the territory of the Republic of Croatia.
(2) Residents and non-residents referred to in paragraph 1 of this Article shall allow foreign exchange inspectors unrestricted supervision and control of their business operations and shall make available or send to them, on request, all required documentation and data on the business activity the resident is exercising abroad.

Competence of the Ministry of Finance – Foreign Exchange Inspectorate and the Croatian National Bank

Article 58

(1) The Ministry of Finance – Foreign Exchange Inspectorate and the Croatian National Bank shall supervise foreign exchange transactions of banks, branches and representative offices of foreign banks.
(2) The Ministry of Finance – Foreign Exchange Inspectorate shall supervise the work of authorized exchange offices.

Competence of the Ministry of Finance – Customs Administration

Article 59

(1) The Ministry of Finance – Customs Administration shall exercise supervision over denominations and the amount of domestic and foreign cash and securities which are taken in or out of the Republic of Croatia by residents and non-residents in passenger, goods and postal traffic.
(2) The Ministry of Finance – Customs Administration may authorize the Croatian Postal Service (Hrvatska Pošta d.d.) to exercise supervision over postal traffic.

CHAPTER VIII PENAL PROVISIONS

VIII.1 Misdemeanors

Article 60

(1) A fine of 70,000.00.00 to 1,000.00,000.00.00 kuna shall be imposed for misdemeanor on any legal or any natural person who:
1. settles a false external claim or issues an external payment order to a bank based on a fictitious agreement or invoice;

For additional analytical, marketing, investment and business opportunities information, please contact Global Investment & Business Center, USA
(202) 546-2103. Fax: (202) 546-3275. E-mail: rusric@erols.com

2. concludes an agreement with a legal or a natural person abroad on the import or export of goods or services that does not state the actual prices.

(2) A fine of 35,000.00.00 to 100,000.00.00 kuna shall be imposed for misdemeanors referred to in paragraph 1 of this Article on any management board member, any person authorized to manage funds in a legal person's account or other responsible person in a legal person.

Article 61

(1) A fine of 50,000.00.00 to 1,000.00,000.00.00 kuna shall be imposed for misdemeanor on banks or other legal persons which, when concluding loan agreements, issuing guarantees or sureties in favor of non-residents, fail to secure instruments of collateral or secure such instruments of collateral whose value is evidently disproportionate with the cost of the loan or the highest amount of the issued guarantee.

(2) A fine of 20,000.00 to 100,000.00 kuna shall be imposed on any management board member or other responsible person committing misdemeanors referred to in paragraph 1 of this Article.

(3) In the event of agreements referred to in paragraph 1 of this Article, concluded with non-residents who, on account of their credit worthiness, may with certainty be expected to repay the loan on time and in full, the fine imposed on the persons committing the misdemeanor may be reduced or they may be granted a remission of the fine.

(4) In the event of agreements referred to in paragraph 1 of this Article, concluded with non-residents who have duly paid all their due debts towards the bank, the person committing the misdemeanor shall be granted a remission of the fine.

Article 62

(1) A fine of 50,000.00 to 500,000.00 kuna shall be imposed for misdemeanor on any legal or natural person who:

1. conducts exchange transactions without an agreement with a bank or fails to use protected computer programs in exchange transactions;
2. fails to allow a person authorized by the Foreign Exchange Inspectorate to exercise supervision or prevents such a person from carrying out its official duty.

(2) A responsible person in a legal person committing misdemeanors referred to in paragraph 1 of this Article, shall be fined 10,000.00 to 50,000.00 kuna for such a misdemeanor.

(3) For misdemeanors referred to in paragraph 1 of this Article, the body in charge of misdemeanor proceedings, may, in addition to a financial fine, impose on the person committing the misdemeanor, a preventive measure involving a ban on this person's right to conduct exchange transactions or other activities for a period of three months to one year, except for payments and transfers referred to in Article 8 of this Act.

(4) Foreign cash and domestic cash, as the subjects of misdemeanors referred to in paragraph 1, item 1 of this Article shall, on the basis of a ruling on misdemeanor, be seized in favor of the Government Budget of the Republic of Croatia.

Article 63

(1) A fine of 15,000.00 to 200,000.00 kuna shall be imposed for misdemeanor on any legal or natural person who:

1. within 30 days from the initial direct investment or other equity investment, fails to report any such investment to the Croatian National Bank or fails to report other required data as prescribed by a decision of the Croatian National Bank, or if he reports in a manner contrary to the manner prescribed for such a reporting;
2. transfers funds abroad for the purpose of purchasing real estate abroad, without fulfilling the conditions laid down by this Act;

For additional analytical, marketing, investment and business opportunities information, please contact Global Investment & Business Center, USA
(202) 546-2103. Fax: (202) 546-3275. E-mail: rusric@erols.com

3. executes or collects any payments in foreign means of payment in transactions with residents or non-residents in the Republic of Croatia, contrary to this Act or a decision issued by the Croatian National Bank;
4. purchases securities in the capital markets abroad, whose issuers do not meet the requirements set by law or by a decision issued by the Croatian National Bank;
5. fails to subscribe, pay, purchase or sell securities abroad through an authorized company, where this is prescribed by this Act;
6. sells in the money market in the Republic of Croatia, in transactions with non-residents, the Croatian National Bank bills or the Treasury bills of the Ministry of Finance and sells or redeems before maturity other short-dated securities, where this, pursuant to a decision of the Croatian National Bank, is not allowed;
7. purchases, in the money markets abroad, securities whose ratings do not meet the requirements prescribed by a decision of the Croatian National Bank;
8. enters into a loan agreement with a non-resident in the name and for the account of another person, contrary to the provisions of this Act, fails to transfer the funds from a financial loan granted abroad to an account with a bank headquartered in the Republic of Croatia, or to an account opened abroad pursuant to Article 29 of this Act, fails to use the financial loan granted abroad in accordance with the loan agreement, unless direct payment of goods and services to the supplier or the provider of services has been agreed or unless the financial loan is used to pay off a previous external loan;
9. sends, transfers, or attempts to transfer abroad or from abroad materialized securities, otherwise than through an authorized company or a custodian bank, or where this, pursuant to provisions of this Act, is not allowed;
10. extends a financial loan to a non-resident, with a maturity of less than one year, when this is not allowed under this Act;
11. opens an account abroad contrary to this Act, or fails to comply with the obligations contained in the authorization of the Croatian National Bank;
12. fails to submit reports to the Croatian National Bank on transactions and balances in its accounts abroad and in accounts of its branches abroad in the manner and within the time limits prescribed by the Croatian National Bank;
13. fails to conduct external payment transactions in accordance with this Act or regulations of the Croatian National Bank;
14. makes payments and collections in connection with transactions with non-residents in domestic cash, foreign cash and checks, in a manner contrary to the conditions and the manner prescribed by the Croatian National Bank, and fails to deposit with the bank or sell to the bank the foreign cash and checks within the prescribed time limit;
15. conducts transactions with derivative financial instruments abroad in a manner contrary to the conditions stipulated by a decision of the Croatian National Bank;
16. fails to comply with the conditions and the manner governing transactions of authorized exchange offices, as prescribed by the Croatian National Bank;
17. purchases or sells foreign cash, lends or borrows foreign cash, acts as a mediator in the purchase, sale or foreign cash lending contrary to this Act;
18. fails to submit to the Croatian National Bank within the prescribed time limits required reports on its external foreign exchange operations or activities it performs abroad, or does it in a way different from that prescribed for reporting, fails to provide the requested documentation to the Foreign Exchange Inspectorate, or fails to keep business books on its operations in the prescribed manner;
19. fails to comply with the measures for the protection of monetary of foreign exchange system prescribed by the Croatian National Bank.

(2) A responsible person in a legal person shall also be fined 3,000.00 to 20,000.00 kuna for misdemeanors referred to in paragraph 1 of this Article.

(3) In cases of gross misdemeanors referred to in paragraph 1 of this Article, where the value of the subject of misdemeanor exceeds 100,000.00 kuna, or where the misdemeanor is committed in relapse, or is committed in an especially dangerous way, the legal or natural

For additional analytical, marketing, investment and business opportunities information, please contact Global Investment & Business Center, USA (202) 546-2103. Fax: (202) 546-3275. E-mail: rusric@erols.com

person and the responsible person in a legal person shall be fined for such misdemeanors 30,000.00 to 400,000.00 kuna.

(4) Foreign or domestic cash, as the subjects of misdemeanors referred to in paragraph 1 of this Article or foreign cash or domestic cash as the subject of a payment transaction resulting from a misdemeanor, shall be seized in misdemeanor proceedings on the basis of a ruling on misdemeanor.

(5) By way of exception, in cases involving minor misdemeanors as determined by this Act, where there are special extenuating circumstances, the body in charge of misdemeanor proceedings may decide that the foreign and domestic cash referred to in paragraph 1 of this Article shall not be seized or shall be seized only in part.

Article 64

(1) A fine of 35,000.00 to 500,000.00 kuna shall be imposed for misdemeanor on a bank which:

1. when concluding agreements on managing non-resident custody accounts for the purchase of securities in the Republic of Croatia, fails to comply with the conditions prescribed by a decision of the Croatian National Bank;
2. concludes a loan agreement abroad for a client's account when it is not licensed to provide services involving external credit transactions;
3. conducts any foreign exchange operation without authorization or oversteps the authority granted to it by virtue of a license obtained from the Croatian National Bank;
4. executes a client's order, thus enabling the client to manage foreign means of payments in the country or abroad, or the kuna abroad, contrary to this Act; where the bank knows or should have known that a free use of foreign means of payment or the kuna is contrary to this Act;
5. takes a domestic cash deposit in a non-resident account, or foreign cash, when this, pursuant to provisions of this Act is not allowed, or enables withdrawal of domestic and foreign cash from non-residents accounts, contrary to this Act;
6. fails to execute a valid external payment order, within the legally prescribed time limit, fails to inform the payment beneficiary about the inflow from abroad, fails to transfer the funds received to another bank in the country in which the payment beneficiary holds and account, or fails to allocate such funds in accordance with the order of the payment beneficiary, or fails to allocate the funds on the basis of a valid order of the payment beneficiary within the prescribed time limit;
7. concludes an agreement on exchange transactions with a person that does not fulfil the conditions prescribed by this Act;
8. concludes an agreement with an authorized exchange office which does not contain the elements prescribed as obligatory by a decision of the Croatian National Bank;
9. fails to submit a report to the Croatian National Bank, where this is prescribed by this Act, or fails do supply data to the Foreign Exchange Inspectorate within the prescribed time limits or in the prescribed manner;
10. conducts external payment transactions or manages foreign exchange accounts contrary to regulations of the Croatian National Bank;
11. fails to establish the identity of any resident or non-resident opening a foreign exchange account or a foreign exchange savings deposit account, or of any non-resident opening a kuna account, or fails to keep data on account holders for a period of five years following the closing of the account.

(2) A responsible person in the bank shall be fined 2,000.00 to 35,000.00 kuna for misdemeanors referred to in paragraph 1 of this Article.

Article 65

(1) A fine of 50,000.00 to 200,000.00 kuna shall be imposed on any securities stock exchange or regulated public market, which, contrary to this Act, decides to list in a quotation shares of

foreign joint-stock companies, whose foreign issuers have not fulfilled the conditions for the sale of securities in the securities market in the Republic of Croatia, as stipulated by the Minister of Finance or if it lists in a quotation foreign short-dated debt securities with a rating below that prescribed by a decision of the Croatian National Bank.

(2) A minimum fine imposed on a management board member or other responsible person committing a misdemeanor referred to in paragraph 1 of this Article shall be 15,000.00 kuna.

Article 66

(1) A fine of 35,000.00 to 150,000.00 kuna shall be imposed on any authorized company which executes its client's order in the money market in the Republic of Croatia, thus enabling a non-resident to purchase the Croatian National Bank bills or the Treasury bills of the Ministry of Finance owned by a resident, or to purchase or sell before maturity other short-dated securities issued by residents, contrary to a decision of the Croatian National Bank.

(2) A fine of 15,000.00 to 35,000.00 kuna shall also be imposed for misdemeanors referred to in paragraph 1 of this Article on any management board member, broker or other responsible person in a legal person.

Article 67

(1) A fine of 35,000.00 to 150,000.00 kuna shall be imposed on any investment fund management company or any authorized company which enables a non-resident to invest in an investment fund when such an activity is not allowed, as stipulated by a decision of the Croatian National Bank.

(2) A misdemeanor fine of 15,000.00 to 35,000.00 kuna shall also be imposed on a management board member or other responsible person in a legal person.

Article 68

(1) A fine of 2,000.00 to 20,000.00 kuna shall be imposed for misdemeanor on any natural person which, in international passenger traffic, contrary to this Act, takes out or attempts to take out of the country foreign cash, checks denominated in foreign currency or domestic cash in excess of the permitted limits, without an authorization from the Croatian National Bank, fails to report to the customs officer the taking out of the country foreign cash, checks or domestic cash and takes or attempts to take into the country kuna in excess of the permitted limits, without an authorization from the Croatian National Bank.

(2) A misdemeanor fine referred to in paragraph 1 of this Article shall also be imposed on a natural person – passenger, who declares the taking out of cash in kuna or in foreign exchange in excess of permitted limits, but refuses to deposit such excess amount.

(3) Foreign cash, checks and domestic cash, as the subjects of misdemeanors referred to in paragraphs 1 and 2 of this Article, shall be seized, on the basis of a misdemeanor ruling, in favor of the Government Budget of the Republic of Croatia.

(4) Foreign cash, checks and domestic cash as the subjects of misdemeanors, may be seized even when they are not the property of the person committing the misdemeanor.

(5) By way of exception, in especially warranted situations, the body in charge of misdemeanor proceedings may decide that foreign cash, checks and domestic cash, as the subjects of misdemeanors referred to in paragraphs 1 and 2 of this Article, are not to be seized or to be seized only in part.

Article 69

(1) A fine of 5,000.00 to 50,000.00 kuna shall be imposed for misdemeanor on any domestic and foreign natural person, domestic and foreign legal person, representative, responsible

For additional analytical, marketing, investment and business opportunities information, please contact Global Investment & Business Center, USA (202) 546-2103. Fax: (202) 546-3275. E-mail: rusric@erols.com

person or proxy of any domestic or foreign legal person, who attempts to take or takes over the state borders, without declaring it to the customs officer, cash and checks in the amounts governed by the act on the prevention of money laundering.

(2) Cash and checks, as the subjects of misdemeanors referred to in paragraph 1 of this Article, shall be seized on the basis of a misdemeanor ruling in favor of the Government Budget of the Republic of Croatia.

(3) Cash and checks, as the subjects of misdemeanors, may be seized even when they are not the property of the person committing the misdemeanor.

(4) By way of exception, in especially warranted situations under especially extenuating circumstances, the body in charge of misdemeanor proceedings may decide that cash and checks, as the subjects of misdemeanors referred to in paragraph 1 of this Article, are not to be seized or to be seized only in part.

Article 70

When performing foreign exchange control, the Foreign Exchange Inspectorate and the customs authority, shall temporarily seize the domestic and foreign cash and the documentation and other objects which are used to commit the misdemeanor, which result from the misdemeanor or which may be used as evidence in misdemeanor proceedings, in accordance with the regulations governing such misdemeanor proceedings and they shall issue a receipt for any domestic or foreign cash, documentation or other objects seized. The domestic and foreign cash shall be paid immediately into special accounts with the Foreign Exchange Inspectorate of the Ministry of Finance.

Article 71

Persons authorized by the Foreign Exchange Inspectorate may impose a temporary restriction or a ban on certain activities of legal or natural persons even before the initiation of misdemeanor proceedings, by sealing work equipment or business premises, if there is reasonable doubt that the misdemeanor referred to in Article 62, paragraph 1 of this Act has been committed.

Article 72

When a natural person is designated as the person committing certain misdemeanors, the persons committing such misdemeanors may be citizens in the capacity of natural persons, sole traders, craftsmen and other self-employed natural persons performing the activity of their registration, unless it follows from the elements of a specific act or a specific regulation that the person committing the misdemeanor may only be one of those persons.

Article 73

(1) Misdemeanor proceedings for misdemeanors provided by this Act, may not be initiated after a period of three years following the date on which the activity involving a misdemeanor ended.

(2) Limitation shall begin in any case after a period of six years following the date on which the activity involving a misdemeanor ended.

(3) The course of limitation and the suspension of limitation regarding the initiation of misdemeanor proceedings and the limitation regarding the execution of misdemeanor penalty and preventive measures shall be governed by the Misdemeanors Act.

Article 74

(1) The Foreign Exchange Inspectorate of the Republic of Croatia shall conduct misdemeanor proceedings of the first instance.

For additional analytical, marketing, investment and business opportunities information, please contact Global Investment & Business Center, USA
(202) 546-2103. Fax: (202) 546-3275. E-mail: rusric@erols.com

(2) An appeal may be filed with the High Magistrate Court of the Republic of Croatia against the ruling of the Foreign Exchange Inspectorate of the Republic of Croatia.

VIII.2 Criminal Offences

Article 75

Persons engaging in illicit purchase, sale, borrowing or lending of foreign cash, in the mediation in the purchase, sale or lending of foreign cash, or engaging in illicit exchange transactions without an agreement with a bank, shall be punished with a prison sentence of up to five years or with a fine of up to one hundred and fifty daily earnings.

Article 76

Responsible persons which, by concluding agreements, arranging for transactions, or in any other way purchase, sell or lend foreign cash, or mediate in the purchase, the sale or lending of foreign cash for a legal person contrary to this Act, or arrange for exchange transactions in a legal person without an agreement with a bank, shall be punished with a prison sentence of up to five years or with a fine of up to one hundred and fifty daily earnings.

CHAPTER IX TRANSITIONAL AND FINAL PROVISIONS

Time Limits for the Adoption of Subordinate Legislation

Article 77

The Ministry of Finance and the Croatian National Bank shall adopt subordinate legislation pursuant to this Act within 90 days after its coming into effect.

Time Limits for Lifting Restrictions on Certain Capital Transactions

Article 78

(1) After expiry of four years from the date of coming into effect of the Stabilization and Association Agreement Between the Republic of Croatia, of the One Part and the European Communities and their Member States, of the Other Part, Article 18, paragraph 2, Article 22, paragraphs 3 and 4, Article 23, paragraph 2, Article 24, paragraph 3, Article 25, Article 26, Article 27, Article 28, paragraph 6, Article 63, paragraph 1, items 4, 5, 6, 7, 10 and 15, Article 64, paragraph 1, item 1, Article 65, Article 66 and Article 67 of this Act shall cease to be valid.

(2) After the Republic of Croatia acquires full membership in the European Union, Article 47, paragraph 4 shall cease to be valid.

Laws and Subordinate Legislation that shall be Superseded following the Adoption of this Law and Subordinate Legislation that shall Remain in Effect until New Subordinate Legislation is Enacted

Article 79

(1) On the date of coming into effect of this Act, the Foreign Exchange System, Foreign Exchange Operations and Gold Transactions Act (official gazette *Narodne novine* Nos. 91A/93, 36/98 and 32/01), the External Credit Transactions Act (official gazette *Narodne novine*, No. 43/96), the Decree on Establishing a Deadline Referred to in Article 3, Paragraph 1 of the External Credit Transactions Act (official gazette *Narodne novine*, No. 62/01) and the

subordinate legislation enacted on the basis of these acts shall cease to be valid, with the exception of:

a) subordinate legislation enacted on the basis of the Foreign Exchange System, Foreign Exchange Operations and Gold Transactions Act (official gazette *Narodne novine* Nos. 91A/93, 36/98 and 32/01), apart from the segment not contrary to this Act, which comprises:

- Decision on Collecting Data on Foreign Direct and Portfolio Investments (official gazette *Narodne novine*, No. 4/97);
- Decision on Collecting Data on International Transactions Related to Communications Services (official gazette *Narodne novine*, No. 62/01);
- Decision on Collecting Data on International Transactions Related to Insurance (official gazette *Narodne novine*, No. 62/01);
- Decision on the Method of Performing Exchange Transactions (official gazette *Narodne novine*, No. 44/01);
- Decision on the Method of and Deadlines for Submitting Reports on the Purchase and Sale of Foreign Exchange in the Foreign Exchange Market (official gazette *Narodne novine*, No. 57/01);
- Decision on the Conditions Under Which Foreign Legal Persons May Be Given Approvals for Depositing Foreign Cash in Foreign Exchange Accounts (official gazette *Narodne novine*, No. 107/93);
- Decision on the Conditions Under Which Foreign Persons May Acquire Claims in the Currency of the Republic of Croatia (official gazette *Narodne novine*, Nos. 114/93 and 14/96);
- Decision on Conditions for Obtaining an Authorization to Settle Claims Abroad in Foreign Cash (official gazette *Narodne novine*, Nos. 107/93, 116/93, 97/94, 2/95 and 87/01);
- Decision on the Conditions Under Which Claims from Abroad May Be Settled in Non-Transferable Currencies (official gazette *Narodne novine*, No. 115/93);
- Decision on the General Conditions for Giving Approvals to Domestic Persons to Keep Foreign Exchange in Accounts Abroad (official gazette *Narodne novine*, No. 17/02 and 10/03);
- Decree on Keeping a Control Book on Each Foreign Trade Transaction and External Credit Transaction (official gazette *Narodne novine*, No. 112/93);
- Decision on the Method of Performing External Payments Operations (official gazette *Narodne novine*, Nos. 99/93, 97/94, 2/96 and 7/96);
- Decision on the Necessary Documentation to be Submitted by Foreign Legal Persons to Banks Authorized for External Payments Operations, in Which They Are Opening a Domestic or a Foreign Currency Account (official gazette *Narodne novine*, No. 38/99);
- Decision on Withdrawing Foreign Cash from Foreign Exchange Accounts of Foreign Legal Persons (official gazette *Narodne novine*, No. 28/97);
- Decision on Taking Into and Out of the Country Domestic Cash in International Passenger Traffic (official gazette *Narodne novine*, Nos. 44/94 and 88/98)
- Decision on the Amount of Foreign Exchange that Domestic Natural Persons May Take Out of the Republic of Croatia in International Passenger Traffic (official gazette *Narodne novine*, No. 99/93);
- Decision on the Conditions Under Which Domestic Natural Persons May Take Checks and Other Securities Denominated in Foreign Currency Out of the Republic of Croatia in International Passenger Traffic (official gazette *Narodne novine*, No.107/93);
- Decision on the Conditions Under Which Domestic and Foreign Currency, Checks and Other Securities May Be Taken Into and Out of the Republic of Croatia in Postal and Other Type of Parcels (official gazette *Narodne novine*, Nos. 99/93, 107/93, and 50/94);
- Decision on Collecting Data on International Transport Services (official gazette *Narodne novine*, No. 80/98);
- Instructions on the Method and the Procedure of Reporting on the Balance of Claims from Abroad (official gazette *Narodne novine*, No. 53/99) except items V, VI, VIII and XI of the Instruction which cease to be valid;

For additional analytical, marketing, investment and business opportunities information, please contact Global Investment & Business Center, USA
(202) 546-2103. Fax: (202) 546-3275. E-mail: rusric@erols.com

b) subordinate legislation enacted on the basis of the External Credit Transactions Act (official gazette *Narodne novine*, No. 43/96) which comprises:

- Decision on the Registration of External Credit Transactions (official gazette *Narodne novine*, No. 132/99);
- Decision on the Changes in the KZ2 and KO2 Forms (official gazette *Narodne novine*, No. 147/99)

which shall remain in effect until subordinate legislation referred to in Article 77 of this Act is enacted.

(2) As of the date of coming into effect of this Act, Article 41, Article 64 and Article 73, paragraph 2 of the Trade Act (official gazette *Narodne novine*, Nos. 11/96, 75/99, 76/99, 62/01, 109/01 and 49/03 - amended text), and subordinate legislation enacted pursuant to Article 41 of the Trade Act (Decision on External Compensation Transactions, official gazette *Narodne novine*, No. 54/97) shall cease to be valid.

LAW ON PRIVATIZATION INVESTMENT FUNDS

Article 1

This law shall regulate the establishment and operation of privatization investment funds as funds of a special type, and their transformation into closed-end funds as defined by the Investment Funds Law (the Official Gazette of the Republic of Croatia, no. 107/95).

DEFINITION OF TERMS

Article 2

Individual terms in this Law shall have the following meaning:

a) coupon privatization shall be the free transfer of shares, i.e. the process of allocating shares without payment pursuant to the provisions of the Privatization Law (the Official Gazette of the Republic of Croatia no. 21/96),

b) privatization coupons shall be coupons that are in accordance with Article 27 of the Privatization Law issued to individuals without charge, pursuant to that Law,

c) privatization shares shall be shares that are issued in accordance with the provisions of the Privatization Law in the process of issuing shares free of charge,

d) privatization points shall be equivalent of privatization coupon rights in accordance with the rules passed by the Minister of Privatization (hereinafter the "Minister").

THE TERM "FUND"

Article 3

(1) A privatization investment fund (hereinafter the "Fund") is a joint stock company that, subject to approval of the Securities and Exchange Commission of the Republic of Croatia (hereinafter the "Commission"), shall be established and managed by a fund management company (hereinafter the "Company"), exclusively by public collection of privatization coupons and their transformation into privatization shares in coupon privatization, and that shall invest these shares with the purpose of harmonising the structure of the Fund's assets with the provisions of the Investment Funds Law as soon as possible, at the latest upon the expiration of the longest allowed life of the Fund.

(2) The provisions of the Investment Funds Law relating to closed-end funds shall apply as appropriate to funds in issues that are not regulated by this Law.

For additional analytical, marketing, investment and business opportunities information, please contact Global Investment & Business Center, USA (202) 546-2103. Fax: (202) 546-3275. E-mail: rusric@erols.com

FUND'S ESTABLISHMENT AND LAUNCH OF ITS OPERATION

Article 4

(1) A Company may establish only one Fund and manage only one Fund. A Company that is considered affiliated to another Company in line with the provision of Article 473 of the Company Law (the Official Gazette of the Republic of Croatia, no. 111/93) may not establish or manage a Fund if that other Company has already submitted a request to the Ministry of Privatization to participate in coupon privatization or if it already manages a Fund.

(2) The Company shall establish a Fund in the following manner:

- The Company shall adopt a prospectus for the collection of privatization coupons, establish a guarantee deposit and submit a request to the Ministry to participate in coupon privatization,
- when a Company receives a license to participate in coupon privatization, it shall publish a prospectus, collect privatization coupons by registering and paying for shares of the Fund, and convert the coupons into privatization shares in the coupon privatization process,
- after the collection of privatization coupons and the conversion into privatization shares have been successfully completed, the Company shall estimate the total value of the collected privatization shares, adopt the Fund bylaws, appoint the Management and Supervisory Boards of the Fund, distribute the Fund shares, write an establishment report, and submit a request with the Commission seeking approval to establish and manage the Fund,
- if the Company is granted approval to establish the Fund and manage the Fund, the company shall release the bylaws and establishment report and submit an application to enter the Fund in the Court Register.

(3) After entering the Fund in the Court Register, the Company shall list the Fund shares on an exchange or regulated public market. After this procedure, the Fund may begin to operate, and the Company may dispose of the collected privatization shares.

(4) The Company must manage the Fund in accordance with the Investment Fund Law unless otherwise specified by this Law.

LICENSE TO PARTICIPATE IN COUPON PRIVATIZATION

Article 5

(1) The Minister shall issue the Company a license to participate in coupon privatization if the Company meets the following conditions:

- The company must not be directly or indirectly under the majority ownership of the Republic of Croatia,
- Prior to submitting the request to participate in coupon privatization, the Company shall, pursuant to a separate agreement with a bank, pay a guarantee deposit for the Fund management into a special account amounting to at least HRK 12,500,000.00 (twelve million five-hundred thousand).
- The Company must submit a request and prospectus of the prescribed content and with prescribed appendices.

(2) The license to participate in coupon privatization shall simultaneously approve the prospectus as provided for in Article 3 paragraph (2) and Article 4 paragraph (3) of the Investment Fund Law.

**For additional analytical, marketing, investment and business opportunities information, please contact Global Investment & Business Center, USA
(202) 546-2103. Fax: (202) 546-3275. E-mail: rusric@erols.com**

(3) The Company may not offer to take over or manage privatization coupons, collect privatization coupons in any way or represent itself as a company authorized to participate in coupon privatization until the Ministry issues it with a licence to participate in coupon privatization.

THE BANK HOLDING THE GUARANTEE DEPOSIT

Article 6

(1) The Company shall open the guarantee deposit account with a bank which has been granted the approval to conduct foreign operations.

(2) The agreement on the guarantee deposit account with the bank shall contain confirmation that the guarantee deposit account is being opened for the management of the Fund.

(3) The bank shall be required:

- to submit to the Commission for inspection all the necessary documentation on transactions on the guarantee deposit account at the request of the Commission,
- to suspend withdrawals from the guarantee deposit account on the Commission's order.

(4) The bank holding the guarantee deposit shall not hold stock or shares in the Company.

REQUESTS AND APPENDICES

Article 7

(1) The request to participate in coupon privatization shall contain information stipulated by Article 40 paragraph 2 of the Investment Fund Law, however excluding information about the members of the Fund Management and Supervisory Boards.

(2) The Company shall enclose the following to the request referred to in 1 paragraph 1 of this Article:

1. the agreement on the guarantee deposit account and proof of payment of the guarantee deposit,

2. the Fund prospectus,

3. an excerpt from the Court Register indicating that the Company meets the conditions concerning the initial capital and the approval to conduct business in accordance with Article 18 paragraph (1) sub-paragraph 1 of the Investment Fund Law and,

4. the register draft.

(3) The Minister may prescribe additional mandatory information and appendices.

PROSPECTUS

Article 8

(1) In addition to the requirements stipulated by the Investment Fund Law, the Fund prospectus shall also include the following:

- an outline of the bylaws that shall include all information pertaining to the future bylaw, except for the provisions on the amount of initial capital and the nominal amount of shares,

For additional analytical, marketing, investment and business opportunities information, please contact Global Investment & Business Center, USA (202) 546-2103. Fax: (202) 546-3275. E-mail: rusric@erols.com

- percentage of charges referred to in Article 33 of this Law,
- guarantee deposit amount and the financial plan for disposing of the guarantee deposit funds, which must include annual expenses for the collection of coupons, advertisement, audit of business books, keeping of the share registry, exchange transaction expenses, office rent, the expense of listing shares on the exchange, the expense of licenses, the expense of releasing the prospectus and periodic reports, the expenses of the members of Management and Supervisory Boards of the Fund, and all other Fund management expenses, except for the charges to the Company
- instead of the data listed in Article 196 paragraph 1 items 2,3,4,8,9,10 and 11 of the Company Law, the Prospectus must include relevant explanation about the plan for collecting privatization shares, the manner in which their value will be estimated, the manner of adopting and publishing bylaws, the manner of listing, paying for and distributing the Fund shares, and about the first convening of the Fund's assembly.

(2) The Minister of Privatization may prescribe additional mandatory content of the prospectus.

Registration and Payment of Fund Shares (Coupon Collection)

Article 9

(1) The Fund shares may be paid exclusively in privatization coupons.

(2) Registration of the Fund shares may not begin before the Company is issued a licence to participate in coupon privatization and before the Company publishes its prospectus.

(3) The Minister shall set the final deadline for the registration of shares within 15 days of the effective date of this Law.

(4) A Company may not collect privatization coupons in any manner other than by registering and paying for the Fund shares.

(5) The registration and payment of the Fund shares shall be carried out by the investor signing a statement on registration and submitting the coupon.

(5) The Company may not accept and pay for the Fund's share at the time of the Fund establishment.

Article 10

(1) The investor must sign three copies of an application, of which one belongs to the investor. The registration of shares may be done via an authorized person, but exclusively on the basis of the power of attorney that is verified by a public notary and enclosed along with other copies of the application that shall be left with the Company.

(2) The application must include the following:

- name and surname, address and the unique personal identity number of the investor and the authorized person,
- basic information about the Company, the publication of the Fund prospectus,
- statement signed by investor stating that shares shall be paid for in accordance with the conditions defined in the prospectus,
- proof that the investor delivered the coupon with the defined number of privatization points and paid for the registered shares with the coupon,
- signature of the investor or authorized person,
- signature of an authorized member of the Company or institution where the shares are registered, with the Company's or institution's stamp.

For additional analytical, marketing, investment and business opportunities information, please contact Global Investment & Business Center, USA
(202) 546-2103. Fax: (202) 546-3275. E-mail: rusric@erols.com

(3) The Minister of Privatization may prescribe additional information to be contained in the application.

Article 11

The Company shall inform the Ministry about the number of shares collected by registration and payment and the number of points the company controls. The manner, content and deadline for delivering this information shall be prescribed by the Minister of Privatization within 15 days of this Law going into effect.

COLLECTION OF TRADING COUPONS FOR SHARES

Article 12

(1) The Ministry shall confirm and publish the amount of privatization points collected by each Company that participates in coupon privatization.

(2) A Company which does not collect at least a total of 100,000,000 (one-hundred million) privatization points (hereinafter the "Unsuccessful Company") may not establish a Fund, regardless of the number and value of the privatization shares that the Company collected by converting the privatization coupons in the coupon privatization process.

(3) Upon the completion of the procedure of trading privatization coupons for privatization shares, the Ministry shall hold an auction in order to collect registrations and privatization shares collected by Unsuccessful Companies.

(4) Companies that have collected enough points may participate in the auction. The Minister of Privatization shall prescribe the rules of the auction within 60 days of the Law going into effect.

(5) Registration and shares of individual Unsuccessful Companies shall be taken over by those Companies that during the auction offer to the Unsuccessful Company the highest compensation for the cost of coupon and share collection. A Company may not acquire only a portion of registrations and shares.

(6) If no one offers compensation for costs, then the registrations and shares shall be taken over by the Company that collected the greatest amount of points, however without compensation to the Unsuccessful Company.

(7) For each Company that collects enough points, the Ministry shall, after the auction is complete, present to the Commission a copy of the issued licence to participate in coupon privatization and the accompanying request with all appendices, and proof of collection of privatization points, registrations and privatization shares taken over from Unsuccessful Companies.

ESTIMATION OF THE VALUE OF COLLECTED SHARES

Article 13

(1) Within 30 days of the completion of the public auction, the Company shall be required to estimate the total value of all collected shares.

(2) The total value of all collected shares shall be estimated based on the principles of fair valuation by applying the International Accounting Standards and taking into consideration the decreasing rates of the nominal value of shares and the number of privatization points traded according to the rules and indices that the Commission shall prescribe.

INITIAL CAPITAL

For additional analytical, marketing, investment and business opportunities information, please contact Global Investment & Business Center, USA
(202) 546-2103. Fax: (202) 546-3275. E-mail: rusric@erols.com

Article 14

(1) The amount of the Fund's initial capital shall be the estimated value of all collected shares.

(2) The Fund may not change the amount of initial capital, except in the manner set forth in Article 42 paragraph (2) of the Investment Fund Law and Article 33 of this Law, until it is registered in the Court Register that the Fund shall continue to operate as a closed-end fund in accordance with the provisions of the Investment Fund Law.

ADOPTION AND CONTENTS OF THE BYLAWS

Article 15

Immediately after the amount of initial capital is confirmed in accordance with Articles 13 and 14 of this Law, the Company shall adopt the Fund bylaws which shall be in accordance with the established initial capital and the outline of bylaws specified in the prospectus.

Article 16

(1) The Fund bylaws must contain the information listed in Article 3 paragraph 4 except for items 5 and 6 and Article 41 of the Investment Fund Law, except for item 1. In addition, the bylaws must contain the following:

- the words "Privatization Investment Fund" in the name
- percentage of charges from Article 33 of this Law,
- provisions for increasing initial capital in order to establish the rights of the Company to transform the charges for managing the Fund into the Fund's shares in accordance with Article 35 of this Law.

(2) The Commission may prescribe additional required content for the bylaws.

APPOINTMENT OF THE FUND BODIES

Article 17

(1) Upon issuing the Fund bylaws, the Company shall appoint the Management Board and the initial Supervisory Board.

(2) The mandate of the Fund's initial Supervisory Board shall last until the first assembly of the Fund is held.

(3) Members of the Management Board must be employees of the Company.

ALLOCATION OF SHARES

Article 18

Upon the adoption of the Fund bylaws, the Company shall allocate the Fund's shares to each shareholder so that each shareholder receives a number of shares proportionate to the number of points which the shareholder invested in the Fund in the total number of invested points.

APPROVAL OF THE FUND'S ESTABLISHMENT

Article 19

(1) Within 7 days of estimating the total value of all collected shares, the Company must submit a request seeking approval from the Commission to establish and manage a Fund in accordance with Article 40 paragraph 2 of the Investment Fund Law.

(2) All disclosures provided for by Article 40 paragraph 3 of the Investment Fund Law must be enclosed along with the request referred to in paragraph 1 of this Article, except for the prospectus, registration draft and the report on the Fund's establishment.

For additional analytical, marketing, investment and business opportunities information, please contact Global Investment & Business Center, USA
(202) 546-2103. Fax: (202) 546-3275. E-mail: rusric@erols.com

(3) The establishment report must include all the information about the registration of and payment for the Fund's shares, the collected privatization shares, the estimate of their total value, and the allocation of the Fund's shares. The Commission may prescribe additional mandatory content to be included in the establishment report.

(4) The bylaws, prospectus and establishment report must include all the information that is required to be published when the Fund's shares are being listed on the stock exchange or regulated public market.

(5) The bank that directly or indirectly holds the Company's shares may not be the Fund's depository bank.

(6) If the request and appendices, the registration and payment of the Fund's shares, the collection of privatization shares and the estimate of their total value, the bylaws and the allocation of the Fund's shares are all in accordance with the law and correspond to the Fund's published prospectus, and if the request from the preceding paragraph has been complied with, the Commission shall grant approval to the Company for establishing and managing the Fund.

PUBLICATION OF BYLAWS AND ESTABLISHMENT REPORTS

Article 20
The Company must publish the bylaws and the establishment report in the same manner as the prospectus within 7 days of obtaining approval to establish and operate the Fund.

CONVENING OF THE FUND'S ASSEMBLY

Article 21
(1) It is not necessary to hold a foundation general meeting in order to establish a Fund.

(2) A Company is required to call a general meeting no later than six months after registering the Fund in the Court Register.

Article 22

(1) In addition to the registration in the Court Register of the Fund's establishment, the Company must also enclose the approval for establishing and managing the Fund.

(2) In addition to the information about the members of the Fund's Management Board and Supervisory Board, information about the fund management company shall be registered with the Court Register.

Article 23

A Company may not establish voting rights from collected privatization shares until the Fund is registered in the Court Register.

LISTING ON THE EXCHANGE

Article 24
(1) Within 30 days of the Fund's registration in the Court Register, the Company shall list the shares of the Fund on a stock exchange or regulated public market.
(2) The stock exchange or regulated public market must prescribe the conditions for a separate quotation of the Funds' shares.

For additional analytical, marketing, investment and business opportunities information, please contact Global Investment & Business Center, USA
(202) 546-2103. Fax: (202) 546-3275. E-mail: rusric@erols.com

(3) The Commission may prescribe the conditions under which the stock exchange or regulated public market is required to list shares of the Fund and the information that must be published upon listing.

(4) The Fund's shares shall be listed on the stock exchange or organized public market based upon the Fund prospectus, the bylaws, the establishment report, approval for establishing and managing the Fund, and the decision on the Fund's registration in the Court Register.

(5) The information on the content of the Fund prospectus, the bylaws and the establishment report, information on the issued license and registration in the Court Register must be published upon listing. It is not necessary for the Commission to grant special approval for publication.

(6) The Company must not in any way dispose of the Fund assets until the Fund's shares are listed on a stock exchange or organized public market.

GUARANTEE DEPOSIT

Article 25

(1) The establishment and management of a Fund shall be financed exclusively from the guarantee fund, in accordance with the financial plan on the distribution of funds in the guarantee fund, which is an integral part of the prospectus.

(2) The Company may invest a part of the deposited funds that are not indispensable for the immediate financing of the Fund only in short-term government securities that shall become an integral part of the guarantee deposit.

(3) The Fund's Management Board shall issue payment orders listed in the preceding paragraphs.

(4) The Company may not remove funds from the guarantee deposit until the termination of the Fund's life, except for the interest and income made from investment of the deposit funds.

(5) The funds in the guarantee deposit account and securities acquired by investing the deposited funds shall be property of the Company and exempt from seizure.

(6) After the Company pays the guarantee deposit, it may increase the deposit by additional payments only after being granted approval by the Commission and exclusively from sources that are not property of the Fund or in any way connected with the Fund, if the remaining funds are not sufficient for managing the Fund.

(7) After the Fund's termination or termination of the management of the Fund, the Company may withdraw its assets from the deposit only after the Commission approves the final calculation of the Fund management expenses and the withdrawal of funds from the deposit. An Unsuccessful Company may remove the remaining funds from the deposit after the Ministry approves the acquisition of registrations and collected shares.

PROPERTY OF THE FUND AND LIMITATIONS ON INVESTMENTS

Article 26

(1) The limitations referred to in Article 9 paragraph 2 and Article 10 paragraph 3 of the Investment Fund Law shall not apply to the Fund.

For additional analytical, marketing, investment and business opportunities information, please contact Global Investment & Business Center, USA (202) 546-2103. Fax: (202) 546-3275. E-mail: rusric@erols.com

(2) The Fund's structure must be brought within the limits established in Article 10 paragraph 1 of the Investment Fund Law at the latest within 180 days of the listing of the Fund's shares on a stock exchange or an organized public market.

(3) The provisions of Article 14, paragraph 1 of the Investment Fund law shall not apply to the fund. The Company shall calculate and establish the value of the Fund's assets in annual and quarterly reports. The methods of assessment and establishment of value must comply with internationally accepted standards and rules referred to in Article 13, paragraph 2 of this Law.

Trading in the Fund's Items of Assets

Article 27
Every sale, disposal or investment of securities from the Fund's portfolio must be conducted on a stock exchange or on an organized public market by way of quotation or public auction.

FUND'S TERM AND TRANSFORMATION INTO A CLOSED-END FUND

Article 28

(1) The Fund may operate for a maximum of five years from the day the Fund is registered in the Court Register.

(2) The Company shall be obliged to submit a request to the Commission for the continuance of the Fund's operation as a closed-end fund in accordance with the provisions of the Investment Fund Law, and to enclose a report on the balance of the Fund's assets no later than the expiry of the term referred to in paragraph 1 of this Article.

(3) Upon the expiration of the Fund's term referred to in paragraph 1 of this Article, the Company may not engage in any operations of disposing of the Fund's assets until the Commission approves that the Fund shall continue to operate as a closed-end fund in accordance with the provisions of the Investment Fund Law.

Article 29

(1) If the Company does not submit the request referred to in Article 28 of this Law, the Commission shall revoke the Company's approval for conducting operations.

(2) If another fund management company submits a request in accordance with Article 49 paragraph 5 of the Investment Fund Law, that request must include the request referred to in Article 28 of this Law.

Article 30

(1) If the Fund does not meet the conditions to operate as a closed-end fund in accordance with the Investment Fund Law, the Commission shall refuse the Fund's request to continue its operations, and the Company shall be required to carry out the liquidation of the Fund.

(2) If the Commission approves the continuation of the Fund's operations, the Company shall render decisions on the following:

- to increase initial capital, if conditions exist to do so, in accordance with Article 33 of this Law, and
- to bring the Fund's acts into conformity with the Investment Fund Law; if the decisions were made earlier, they shall be then put into effect.

For additional analytical, marketing, investment and business opportunities information, please contact Global Investment & Business Center, USA (202) 546-2103. Fax: (202) 546-3275. E-mail: rusric@erols.com

(3) Increase in initial capital and the continuation of the Fund's operation as a closed-end fund shall be entered in the Court Register based on the prior approval granted by the Commission.

Article 31

(1) The Commission may prescribe the mandatory content of the request for the continuation of the Fund's operation, the request for approval of increase in initial capital, and the request for approval of bringing into conformity of the Fund's acts, as well as of appendices enclosed to these requests.

(2) The Company may bring together the requests referred to in paragraph 1 of this Article in the request for the continuation of the Fund's operation.

Article 32

(1) The Company may submit the request referred to in Article 28, paragraph 2 of this Law before the expiration of the term referred to in Article 28 paragraph 1 of this Law.

(2) The Company may not engage in any operations of disposing of the Fund's assets after it has submitted the request referred to in the previous paragraph and before the Commission has rendered a decision on the request.

(3) If the Company submits the request in accordance with paragraph 1 of this Article, and the Fund fails to fulfil the conditions of operating as a closed-end fund, the Commission shall refuse to honour the request but may permit the Fund to operate according to the provisions of this Law until the final term of the Fund is terminated as set forth in Article 28, paragraph 1 of this Law.

THE COMPANY'S FEE

ARTICLE 33

(1) The Company has a right to a fee for managing the Fund which shall amount to no more than 30% of the difference between the average stock exchange price of all the Fund's shares in the last ninety days of the Fund's term and the second ninety days upon the listing of the Fund's shares on the stock exchange.

(2) The Company shall regulate the percentage of the fee in the prospectus for the collection of coupons and in the Fund's bylaws.

(3) The Company's fees shall not be paid out of the Fund's assets. After the Commission grants permission to the Fund to continue operating as a closed-end fund, the Company shall be granted the right to replace that claim or transform it into the Fund's shares.

(4) In order to exercise the rights referred to in the preceding paragraph, the Fund's initial capital shall be increased, and the Company shall be issued the Fund's shares that must be listed on a stock exchange or an organized public market.

CANCELLATION AND TERMINATION OF THE FUND MANAGEMENT

Article 34

(1) A Company may cancel its management of the Fund only with the approval of the Commission.

(2) In addition to providing notice of cancellation, the Company is required to submit to the Commission a report on the management of the Fund and a report on the use of the guarantee deposit.

For additional analytical, marketing, investment and business opportunities information, please contact Global Investment & Business Center, USA (202) 546-2103. Fax: (202) 546-3275. E-mail: rusric@erols.com

(3) The Commission shall only approve cancellation if a fund management company exists that is prepared to continue to manage the Fund.

(4) With respect to the guarantee deposit and the right to a fee for managing the Fund, the Company which continues to manage the Fund shall be the legal successor of the Company which made the cancellation. Mutual relations regarding the guarantee deposit and the company's fee shall be regulated by a contractual agreement between the two companies.

(5) The Company that continues to manage the Fund shall be responsible to the Fund for the Company's liabilities to the Fund that were incurred until the effective date of the cancellation.

(6) The Fund may not terminate the Company's management of the Fund until it is written in the court register that the Fund shall continue to operate as a closed-end fund in accordance with the provisions of the Investment Fund Law.

(7) The Fund's assembly may not render any decisions bearing upon the termination of the Fund until it is registered in the Court Register that the Fund shall continue to operate as a closed-end fund in accordance with the provisions of the Investment Fund Law.

Article 35

(1) If the right of the Company to manage the Fund ceases in any manner other than by cancellation, the right to dispose of the guarantee deposit shall be passed to the depository bank, and the Company shall have no right to a fee for managing the Fund. The Commission shall approve the final calculation for management of the Fund and allow the Company to withdraw all remaining assets from the guaranteed deposit only after the other fund management company establishes its guarantee deposit and is granted approval from the Commission to manage the Fund. The Commission may approve a lesser amount for the new guarantee deposit proportionate to the amount of time left in the term of the Fund.

(2) In the case that bankruptcy or liquidation proceedings have been started against the Fund, the Commission shall permit that funds be withdrawn from the guarantee deposit only after the fact of the termination of the proceedings has been entered in the Court Register.

RIGHT OF LIEN AND LIABILITY FOR DAMAGE

Article 36

(1) In order to ensure claims against the Company arising from the liability for damage incurred during the establishment and management of the Fund, the Fund and the Fund's shareholders have a legal right of lien on funds in the guarantee deposit and on shares issued in accordance with Article 32 of this Law; these funds, in turn, shall constitute a guarantee deposit, but not exceeding the amount of the claim, within three months of the issuing of shares until the termination of the legal proceedings instigated in the specified term.

(2) The Company, members of the Company's Management Board and members of the Fund's Management Board shall be held solidarily accountable to the Fund and the Fund's shareholders for any damage caused in the course of founding or managing the Fund.

PUBLIC RELATIONS

Article 37

(1) The Company shall submit to the Commission for approval all messages concerning the Fund's foundation and management that the Company intends to communicate to the public

For additional analytical, marketing, investment and business opportunities information, please contact Global Investment & Business Center, USA
(202) 546-2103. Fax: (202) 546-3275. E-mail: rusric@erols.com

through radio, television, newspaper, telephone, electronic mail, flyers, or other form of communication designed to reach more than one person.

(2) The Commission shall forbid the publication if it finds that the message:

- contains false or incorrect statements that may be important to investors,
- omits, does not reveal or does not contain facts that may be important to investors with a view to its content, or
- is misleading to investors

(3) If the Commission does not prohibit the publication within five business days, the Company shall be allowed to publish the message.

POWERS OF THE COMMISSION IN THE CASE OF IMPROPER MANAGEMENT

Article 38

If in managing the Fund the Company or its employees violate the provisions of this Law, the Investment Fund Law, the Law on Issuance and Trade of Securities or rules adopted on the basis of these laws, if the Company operates the Fund contrary to the bylaws, the prospectus or the contract on the Fund management, or if the Company gives false information in the process of establishing the Fund, the Commission may:

- revoke the approval for operation granted to the Company,
- issue an order to the Company to undertake certain actions or to bring the management of the Fund into conformity with regulations,
- invite other fund management companies to submit offers or requests to manage a particular Fund,
- suspend all withdrawals from the guarantee deposit account, or
- suspend disposal of the Fund's assets.

LIMITATIONS FOR NATURAL PERSONS CONCERNING THE FUND'S OPERATIONS

ARTICLE 39

Employees or members of the Management Board or Supervisory Board of the Company, Fund or depository bank may not, directly or indirectly, for their account, on their behalf or on behalf of a third party, do the following:

1. purchase securities or other assets of the Fund or any legal entity in which the Fund has a majority interest, except for the purchase of securities on a stock exchange or a regulated public market.

2. sell securities, things or rights to the Fund or any legal entity in which the Fund has a majority interest, except for the purchase of securities on a stock exchange or a regulated public market.

3. accept from any source any remuneration for brokerage concerning the Fund's operations or operations of a legal entity in which the Fund has a majority interest, unless the Fund's Supervisory Board judges that the remuneration amount does not exceed three average remunerations on the market for similar brokerage services.

4. conclude a contract with the Fund or a legal entity in which the Fund has anownership interest of 5% or more, unless the contract has been previously approved by the Fund's Supervisory Board.

For additional analytical, marketing, investment and business opportunities information, please contact Global Investment & Business Center, USA
(202) 546-2103. Fax: (202) 546-3275. E-mail: rusric@erols.com

5. take any opportunity presented to the Fund to purchase or sell securities for personal advantage or advantage of others.

(2) As defined in the preceding article, the Fund's assets shall also be privatization coupons and privatization shares collected by the Company before entering the Fund in the Court Register.

PENALTY PROVISIONS

Article 40

(1) The investment fund management company shall be subject to a fine of HRK 10,000.00 to 20,000 if:

1. it acts contrary to the provisions of Article 6 paragraph 3 of this Law,
2. it begins to subscribe shares before fulfilling the conditions referred to in Article 9 paragraph 2 of this Law,
3. it collects privatization coupons contrary to the provisions of Article 9 paragraph 4 of this Law,
4. it does not publish the bylaws and establishment report within the term and manner stated in Article 20 of this Law,
5. it does not convene the Fund's assembly within the term referred to in Article 21 paragraph 2 of this Law,
6. it disposes of Fund's property contrary to the provisions in Article 24 paragraph 6 of this Law,
7. it disposes of the funds in the guarantee deposit contrary to the provisions referred to in Article 25 of this Law, or if the management of the Fund is financed from the Fund's assets,
8. it disposes of the Fund's assets contrary to the provisions of Article 27 of this Law,
9. it begins conducting activities leading to the disposal of the Fund's assets contrary to the provisions of Article 28 paragraph 3 and Article 32 paragraph 2 of this Law,
10. it addresses a message to the public contrary to the provisions referred to in Article 37 of this Law.

(2) The depository bank shall be subject to a fine of HRK 20, 000.00 to 100,000.00 if:

1. it does not make available all necessary documentation on the transactions on the guarantee deposit account, or if it does not act under the orders of the Commission (Article 6),
2. it concludes a contract on the guaranteed deposit with a Company in which it directly or indirectly holds stakes or shares (Article 6 paragraph 4),
3. as a depository bank, it concludes a contract on the guaranteed deposit with a Company in which it directly or indirectly holds stakes or shares (Article 19 paragraph 5).

For additional analytical, marketing, investment and business opportunities information, please contact Global Investment & Business Center, USA (202) 546-2103. Fax: (202) 546-3275. E-mail: rusric@erols.com

(3) A natural person shall subject to a fine of HRK 4,000.00 to 20,000.00 if it acts contrary to the provisions of Article 39 of this Law.

(4) Member of the Management Board or a responsible person in the investment fund management company shall be subject to a fine of HRK 4,000.00 to 20,000.00 for committing the offence referred to in paragraph 1 of this Article.

(5) The responsible person in the depository bank shall be subject to a fine of HRK 4,000.00 to 20,000.00 for committing the offence referred to in paragraph 2 of this Article.

(6) The responsible person in the investment fund management company shall be subject to a fine for committing the offence referred to in paragraph 1 of this Article, and a protective measure shall be pronounced against him forbidding him to perform the activity for a period of two years.

FINAL PROVISIONS

Article 41
The minister shall be authorized to adopt regulations for the implementation of this Law.

Article 42
This Law shall enter into force on the eighth day of its publication in the Official Gazette of the Republic of Croatia.

THE STATE AUDIT ACT

I. GENERAL PROVISIONS

Article 1

This Act shall regulate the audit of public incomes and expenditures, the audit of financial statements and financial transactions of government units and local and regional self-government units, legal entities being partly or wholly financed from the budget, public enterprises, companies and other legal entities owned in major part by Republic of Croatia or local and regional self-government units, use of EU funds and funds of international organizations or institutions for financing of public needs.

This Act shall also regulate the audit of the procedures of transformation and privatisation in legal entities, which implemented such procedure pursuant to the (i) Act on the transformation of Socially-Owned Enterprises, published in "Narodne Novine" Nos. 19/91, 83/92, 84/92, 94/93, 2/94, 9/95 and 21/96 (hereinafter referred to as the "Transformation Act"), (ii) Privatization Act, published in "Narodne Novine" Nos. 21/96, 71/97 and 16/98, (iii) Social Capital Act, published in "Narodne Novine" Nos. 84/89 and 46/90 and (iv) special laws."

Under this Act, as government incomes and expenditures are understood all incomes and revenues, and expenditures being financed from the state budget or from appropriate funds at the national level, and from the budgets at the level of local and regional self-government units. Under this Act, as government units are understood all legislative, executive and judiciary bodies, as well as all agencies, institutions and other subjects at the level of the Republic of Croatia and at the level of local and regional self-government units, financed from the state budget or budgets of local and regional self-government units.

Article 2

Under this Act, audit is the examination of documents, deeds, statements, internal control and internal audit systems, accounting and financial procedures, and other records in order to determine whether financial statements truly reflect the financial activities in compliance with accepted accounting principles and accounting standards.

Audit is also a procedure of examining financial transactions which represent government incomes and expenditures in terms of legal utilizations of funds.

Audit also includes an assessment of the efficiency and effectiveness of activities, as well as an assessment of the efficiency in pursuing the objectives of a certain project.

For the purpose of this Act, the transformation and privatization audit means examining the documents, decisions, business records, contracts and acts pursuant to which the transformation and privatization was completed, as well as examining other documentation necessary to establish whether any violation of the provisions of the Restructuring Act, Privatization Act, Social Capital Act or special acts occurred in the procedure of restructuring and privatization.

Article 3

Under Article 2, Para (1), of this Act, audit shall be performed once a year on the state budget, funds at the national level, and budgets of local and regional self-government units.

Audit of the financial statements of government units, local and regional self-government units, public enterprises, companies and other legal entities owned in major part by Republic of Croatia or local and regional self-government units, shall be performed in compliance with the Annual Programme of the State Audit Office.

Audit, in terms of Article 2, Para (2) and (3), of this Act shall be performed as needed

The extent of auditing shall be defined in the Annual Programme of the State Audit Office.

II. AUDITING PROCEDURE

Article 4

The audit method and procedure shall be performed in compliance with the established INTOSAI Auditing Standards.

The audit standards referred to in Para (1) of this Article shall be published in the Croatian language in "Narodne novine" (Official Gazette).

Audit shall be performed by certified state auditors

A certified state auditor is an independent professional who is in holder of a certificate to this effect and who meets other requirements under this Act, employed with the State Audit Office.

As an exception to Para (3) of this Article, the State Audit Office can engage an expert for dealing with specific problems involved in an audit procedure.

Article 5

A legal representative of a legal entity where an audit is performed shall furnish the certified state auditor with complete required documentation, deeds, statements and other records, as well as provide other information needed for the audit work.

Article 6

A certified state auditor is not allowed to audit:

if he/she is a member of the supervisory committee or another body of the legal entity where the audit work is to be performed;

if he/she was involved in keeping business books or preparing financial statements of the legal entity where the audit work is to be performed;

if he/she is a spouse, a blood relative in the direct line up to the fourth kinship degree, or in the in-law line up to the second kinship degree, a tutor, an adoptive parent, an adopted child, or a foster-parent of one of the legal representatives of the legal entity concerned or of one of the members of the supervisory committee.

Article 7

After completed audit work, the certified state auditor shall prepare and sign the audit report. The audit report shall be prepared in conformity with the audit standards referred to in Article 4, Para. (1), of this Act.

For additional analytical, marketing, investment and business opportunities information, please contact Global Investment & Business Center, USA (202) 546-2103. Fax: (202) 546-3275. E-mail: rusric@erols.com

The audit report shall be submitted to the legal representative of the legal entity where the audit has been carried out, to the responsible minister and/or to the fund.
The legal representative of the legal entity where the audit work has been carried out can within 8 days make an objection to the audit report. The Auditor General shall decide on the matter within 30 days.

Article 8

The certified state auditor shall meet the following requirements:
that he/she is citizen of the Republic of Croatia,
that he/she is a graduate economist, graduate lawyer, graduate in IT or in other relevant profession.
that he/she has passed the examination for certified state auditor and acquired an authorized auditor's certificate,
that he/she has never been found guilty for criminal acts in the economy,
that he/she is an honourable and honest person who meets the requirements defined in the Code of Professional Ethics.
The Code of Professional Ethics must be in compliance with Code of Ethics of INTOSAI.
Admitted to the examination qualifying for a certified state auditor shall be those candidates who have at least three-year working experience in relevant profession.

Article 9

Examinations for a certified state auditor shall be taken according to the State Audit Office's programme.
Examination under para (1) of this Article shall be taken before a commission appointed by the Auditor General. Candidates who have passed the examination shall be given the certified state auditor's certificate by the Auditor General.
Prior to sitting for the certified state auditor's examination, candidates shall have passed the general part the civil service examination, unless exempt from this obligation according to the regulations related to civil servants.

III. THE STATE AUDIT OFFICE

Article 10

For performance of work under this Act the State Audit Office shall be established.
The State Audit Office shall be a legal entity.
The State Audit Office shall be directly responsible to the Croatian Parliament (Sabor).
The seat of the State Audit Office shall be in Zagreb.

Article 11

The State Audit Office shall perform the following duties:
planning and conducting of the audit work to an extent as envisaged in Article 2, Para (1) of this Act,
conducting of the audit work to an extent as envisaged in Article 2, Para (2) and (3) of this Act, according to the Annual Programme or as requested by the Croatian Parliament (Sabor),
conducting of the transformation and privatisation audit,
submission of an annual report on executed audits and its own work,
in particular cases of specific interest, submission of individual audit reports,
carrying the annual programme of work.
The report under Para (1), point 4. of this Article shall be submitted to the Croatian Parliament (Sabor), till the end of current year for the previous year.
The Charter of State Audit Office shall be approved by the Croatian Parliament (Sabor).
The State Audit Office shall also perform other duties defined in its Charter.

Article 12

The State Audit Office shall be run by the Auditor General.

The Auditor General shall be appointed by the Croatian Parliament (Sabor) for the term of 8 years and he/she can be reappointed.
The tenure of actual Auditor General is to be assumed as per its original appointment.

Article 13
The Auditor General shall be dismissed before expire of the tenure:
if he/she requests that,
when appointed to the other position with his/her consent,
if permanently looses the capability to carry out the duty, and
if found guilty for a crime which makes him/her unworthy to carry out the duty of Auditor General.

Article 14
After completing the tenure, the Auditor General has the right to be retired under the same legal provisions applicable to members of the Croatian State Parliament.

Article 15
The financial means necessary for the function of the State Audit Office shall be provided by the state budget..

IV. PENAL PROVISIONS

Article 16
For an economic offence a government unit or another legal entity shall be fined kn 3.500,00 to 40.000,00, if it:
fails to furnish the certified state auditor the documents, deeds, statements or other information required for audit (Article 2, Para (1)),
fails to provide or provides wrong information required for audit financial transactions (Article 2, Para (2)),
fails to provide or provides wrong information required for audit work intended to assess the efficiency and effectiveness of activity and/or to assess the efficiency in pursuing the objectives of a project (Article 2, Para (3)),
fails to make available the necessary documentation, fails to furnish, or furnish the wrongful, information needed to conduct the transformation and privatisation audit (Article 2, paragraph 4).
For acts under Para (1) of this Article a legal representative shall also be fined in the amount of kn 1.500,00 to 3.500,00.

TRANSITIONAL AND FINAL PROVISIONS

Article 17
The Social Accounting and Auditing Service (SDK) Act (Official Gazette No. 53/91) shall cease to be effective on the ninetieth day from the day of entering of this Act into force.
The State Audit Office
Tkalciceva 19
10000 Zagreb
revizija@revizija.hr

REGULATIONS CONCERNING BANKING SUPERVISION

REGULATORY CAPITAL

1.	Decision on the methodology for calculating bank's capital (National Gazette No. 32/1999)
2.	Decision on the amendments to the Decision on the methodology for calculating bank's capital (National Gazette No. 101/2004)

For additional analytical, marketing, investment and business opportunities information, please contact Global Investment & Business Center, USA (202) 546-2103. Fax: (202) 546-3275. E-mail: rusric@erols.com

3.	Decision on the methodology for calculating bank's capital (amended text, October 23, 2004)
4.	Instruction for the uniform implementation of the Decision on the methodology for calculating bank's capital (National Gazette No. 123/2004)
5.	Form JK1 - Liable Capital

CAPITAL ADEQUACY

1.	Decision on the methodology for calculating capital adequacy and risk-weighted assets of banks (National Gazette No. 32/1999)
2.	Decision on the amendments to the Decision on the methodology for calculating capital adequacy and risk-weighted assets of banks (National Gazette No. 101/2004)
3.	Decision on the methodology for calculating capital adequacy and risk-weighted assets of banks (amended text, October 23, 2004)
4.	Instruction for the uniform implementation of the Decision on the methodology for calculating capital adequacy and risk-weighted assets of banks (National Gazette No. 123/2004)
5.	Forms PA1, AK1 - Risk-weighted assets, Capital adequacy

	CLASSIFICATION OF PLACEMENTS AND BANK EXPOSURE
1.	Decision on the classification of placements and risky off-balance sheet items and assessment of bank exposure (National Gazette No. 32/1999)
2.	Decision on the amendments to the Decision on the classification of placements and risky off-balance sheet items and assessment of bank exposure (National Gazette No. 101/2004)
3.	Decision the classification of placements and risky off-balance sheet items and assessment of bank exposure (amended text, October 23, 2004)
4.	Instruction for the uniform implementation of the Decision on the classification of placements and risky off-balance sheet items and assessment of bank exposure (National Gazette No. 36/1999)
5.	Amendments to the Instruction for the uniform implementation of the Decision on the classification of placements and risky off-balance sheet items and assessment of bank exposure (National Gazette No. 123/2004)
6.	Instruction for the uniform implementation of the Decision on the classification of placements and risky off-balance sheet items and assessment of bank exposure (amended text, January 5, 2001)
7.	Classification Forms IK1, R, VIB, DIB, POB, SKO
8.	Instruction for keeping credit records

SPECIFIC RESERVES

1.	Decision on the amount and method of forming specific reserves to ensure against potential losses of banks (National Gazette No. 32/1999)
2.	Instruction for the uniform implementation of the Decision on the amount and method of forming specific reserves to ensure against potential losses of banks (National Gazette No. 36/1999)
3.	Amendments to the Instruction for the uniform implementation of the Decision on the amount and method of forming specific reserves to insure against potential losses of banks (National Gazette No. 123/2004)
4.	Instruction for the uniform implementation of the Decision on the amount and method of forming specific reserves to ensure against potential losses of banks (amended text, January 5, 2001)
5.	SR1 Forms - Specific Reserves

	CHART OF ACCOUNTS FOR BANKS
1.	Decision on the chart of accounts for banks (National Gazette No. 36/1999)
2.	Decision on amendments to the chart of accounts for banks (National Gazette No. 123/2004)
3.	Decision on amendments to the chart of accounts for banks (January 22, 2001)

LIMITING BANK INVESTMENT IN TANGIBLE ASSETS AND EQUITY PARTICIPATION

1.	Decision on limiting bank investment in fixed assets and equity participation (National Gazette No. 38/1999)
2.	Decision on the amendments to the Decision on limiting bank investment in fixed assets and equity participation (National Gazette No. 64/1999)
3.	Decision on the amendments to the Decision on limiting bank investment in tangible assets and equity participation (National Gazette No. 101/2004)
4.	Decision on limiting bank investment in fixed assets and equity participation (amended text, October 23, 2004)
5.	Instruction for the implementation of the Decision on limiting bank investment in fixed assets and equity participation (National Gazette No. 66/1999)
6.	Amendments to the Instruction for the implementation of the Decision on limiting bank investment in fixed assets and equity participation (National Gazette No. 123/2004)

SHAREHOLDERS HOLDING MORE THAN 3 PERCENT OF SHARES

1.	Instruction for completion of Form shareholders with more than three percent of shares (June 29, 1999)
2.	Amendments to Instruction for completion of Form shareholders with more than three percent of shares (January 15, 2001)

For additional analytical, marketing, investment and business opportunities information, please contact Global Investment & Business Center, USA (202) 546-2103. Fax: (202) 546-3275. E-mail: rusric@erols.com

3.	Form PD3

OTHER REPORTING

1.	Decision on the form and content of the application for granting the operating license for banks (National Gazette No. 99/1999)
2.	Decision on conducting supervision of bank operations (National Gazette No. 50/2004)
3.	Decision on the form, minimum scope and contents of an audit and reports on audits of banks (National Gazette No. 64/1999)

For additional analytical, marketing, investment and business opportunities information, please contact Global Investment & Business Center, USA
(202) 546-2103. Fax: (202) 546-3275. E-mail: rusric@erols.com

TRAVEL TO CROATIA

US STATE DEPARTMENT SUGGESTIONS

COUNTRY DESCRIPTION: Croatia is a moderately developed nation in transition to a market economy. Facilities for tourism are available throughout the country, and the Adriatic coast has traditionally been a popular tourist destination.

ENTRY REQUIREMENTS: A passport is required. For tourist or business trips of less than 90 days, a visa is not required for U.S. passport holders. Visas are required for all other types of stays and must be obtained prior to arrival in the country. Unless the traveler is staying at a hotel, all foreign citizens must register with the local police within 48 hours of arrival. Failure to register is a misdemeanor offense: some Americans have been fined and/or expelled as a result of their failure to register. Additional information on entry requirements may be obtained from the Embassy of Croatia at 2343 Massachusetts Ave., N.W., Washington, D.C. 20048, tel. (202) 588-5899, or from the Croatian consulates in New York City, Cleveland, Chicago or Los Angeles. Overseas, inquiries may be made at the nearest Croatian embassy or consulate. The Internet home page of the Croatian Embassy is http://www.croatiaemb.org.

DUAL NATIONALITY: The Government of Croatia does not recognize U.S. citizenship of persons who are citizens of both Croatia and the United States. This may hinder the ability of the U.S. consular officer to assist persons who do not enter Croatia on a U.S. passport. Dual nationals may also be subject to national obligations, such as taxes and military service. Travelers should contact a Croatian embassy or consulate for further information. Travelers may also wish to consult the Dual Nationality flyer posted on the Bureau of Consular Affairs home page on the Internet at http://travel.state.gov.

SAFETY/SECURITY: Though fighting in all parts of the country ended in 1995, the conflict over Croatia's independence led to the laying of land mines on Croatian territory, mostly along the former confrontation lines. De-mining is not complete; marking of mined areas is similarly incomplete. Travelers in former conflict areas should exercise caution and not stray from known safe roads and areas.

There are no known indigenous terrorist groups in Croatia. There are occasional attacks targeted at specific persons or property as a result of organized criminal activity or actions prompted by ethnic tensions residual from Croatia's war for independence. There were no reported terrorist actions in Croatia during the past 12 months.

CRIME INFORMATION: Croatia has a relatively low crime rate, and violent crime is rare. Foreigners do not appear to be singled out; however, as in many cities, displays of wealth increase chances of becoming the victim of a pickpocket or mugger. Such crimes are more likely to occur in bus or railroad stations. The loss or theft of a U.S. passport should be reported immediately to the local police and the nearest U.S. embassy or consulate. Useful information on safeguarding valuables and protecting personal safety while traveling abroad is provided in the Department of State's pamphlet *A Safe Trip Abroad*. It is available from the Superintendent of Documents, U.S. Government Printing Office, Washington, D.C. 20402, via the Internet at http://www.access.gpo.gov/su_docs or http://travel.state.gov.

MEDICAL FACILITIES: Health facilities in Croatia, although generally of Western caliber, are under severe strain due to serious budgetary problems. Croatian citizens using these services find that some medicines are in short supply in public hospitals and clinics. The number of private medical and dental practitioners is substantial, and pharmacies stock a variety of medicines not readily available through public health facilities. Because of the weaknesses in funding, Croatian health care facilities, doctors and hospitals may expect immediate cash payment for health services.

MEDICAL INSURANCE: U.S. medical insurance is not always valid outside the United States. The Medicare/Medicaid program does not provide payment for medical services outside the United States. Please check with your own insurance company to confirm whether your policy applies overseas, including provisions for medical evacuation. Please ascertain whether you will be reimbursed later for expenses that you incur. Some insurance policies also include coverage for psychiatric treatment or deposition of remains in the event of death. Useful information on emergencies abroad, including overseas insurance programs, is provided in the Deparment of State, Bureau of Consular Affairs brochure *Medical Information for Americans Traveling Abroad*, available via its home page and autofax.

OTHER HEALTH INFORMATION: Information on vaccinations and other health precautions may be obtained from the Centers for Disease Control and Prevention's hotline for the international travelers at 1-877-FYI-TRIP (1-877-394-8747), fax 1-888-CDC-FAXX (1-888-232-3299), or via their Internet site at http://www.cdc.gov.

TRAFFIC SAFETY AND ROAD CONDITIONS: While in a foreign country, U.S. citizens may encounter road conditions that differ significantly from those in the United States. The information below concerning Croatia is provided for general reference only, and it may not be totally accurate in a particular location or circumstance.
Safety of Public Transportation: Good
Urban Road Conditions/Maintenance: Good
Rural Road Conditions/Maitenance: Fair
Availability of Roadside Assistance: Fair

For specific information concerning Croatian driver's permits, vehicle inspection, road tax and mandatory insurance, please contact the Croatian National Tourist Office in Parsimony, New Jersey at tel. (201) 428-0707.

Since gaining independence in 1991, Croatia has seen an increase in the number of cars, leading to heavy congestion on major routes on weekends (towards the coast, for example) and in major cities during rush hour. Parking can be difficult and expensive in city centers. Drivers can be aggressive and, in Zagreb, motorists must also pay special attention to trams (streetcars). Primary roads are generally adequate, but most have only one lane in each direction, including roads going to and from the coast. Drivers traveling through former conflict areas should stay on paved roads to reduce the risk of encountering mines and unexploded ordnance left over from the war. Emergency road help and information may be reached by dialing 987. Additional road condition and safety information may be obtained from the Croatian Automobile Association (HAK) at tel. (385)(1) 455-4433.

AVIATION SAFETY OVERSIGHT: As there is no direct commercial air service by local carriers at present, nor economic authority to operate such service between the United States and Croatia, the U.S. Federal Aviation Administration (FAA) has not assessed Croatia's Civil Aviation Authority for compliance with international aviation safety standards for oversight of Croatia's air carrier operations. For further information, travelers may contact the Department of Transportation within the U.S. at tel. 1-800-322-7873, or visit the FAA Internet home page at http://www.faa.gov/avr/iasa/index.htm. The U.S. Department of Defense (DOD) separately assesses some foreign air carriers for suitability as official providers of air services. For information regarding the DOD policy on specific carriers, travelers may contact the DOD at tel. (618) 256-4801.

CUSTOMS REGULATIONS: Croatian customs authorities encourage the use of an ATA (Admission Temporaire/Temporary Admission) Carnet for the temporary admission of professional equipment, commercial samples, and/or goods for exhibitions and fair purposes. ATA Carnet Headquarters, located at the U.S. Council for International Business, 1212 Avenue of the Americas, New York. N.Y. 10036, issues and guarantees the ATA Carnet in the United States. For additional information, please call (212) 354-4480, or send e-mail to atacarnet@uscib.org, or visit http://www.uscib.org for details.

CRIMINAL PENALTIES: While in a foreign country, U.S. citizens are subject to the laws and regulations of the country in which they travel, which sometimes differ significantly from those in the United States and may not afford the protections available to the individual under the U.S. law. Penalties for breaking the law can be more severe than in the United States for similar offenses. Persons violating Croatian laws, even unknowingly, may be expelled, arrested or imprisoned. Penalties for possession, use, or trafficking in illegal drugs in Croatia are strict, and convicted offenders can expect jail sentences and fines.

SPECIAL CIRCUMSTANCES: Credit cards and traveler's checks are more widely used than previously, but they are still not accepted everywhere.

CHILDREN'S ISSUES: In general, foreign citizens may not adopt Croatian children. For more specific information on international adoption of children, international parental child abduction, and international child support enforcement issues, please telephone (202) 736-7000, or refer to the State Department's Internet web site at http://travel.state.gov/children's_issues.html.

REGISTRATION AND EMBASSY LOCATION: U.S. citizens are encouraged to register at the U.S. Embassy and obtain updated information on travel and security within Croatia. The U.S. Embassy in Zagreb is located at Andrije Hebranga 2, tel. (385)(1)455-5500, Internet home page: http://www.usembassy.hr. On weekends, holidays, and after hours, an Embassy duty officer can be reached at tel. (385)(1)455-5281.

TRAVEL AND TOURISM

The tourist trade in Croatia is more than 150 years old. Although inns and guesthouses were built throughout the country in the first half of the 19th century, the beginnings of tourism are linked with the construction of first hotels designed for tourists, such as those in Opatija (Grand Hotel, built in 1890) and Dubrovnik (Hotel Imperial, built in 1897), as well as with the foundation and activities of tourist societies, especially those on the islands of Krk (in 1866) and Hvar (Hygienic Society in 1868). Poreè and Pula had tour guides as early as 1845, while in Zagreb the first guidebook, called "A Guide for Natives and Foreigners", was published in 1892.

In 1950, 84,000 overnights of foreign tourists were registered in Croatia while in 1987 this number reached 59,000,000.

The largest number of bed nights was recorded in the 1986–1987 period, 68,000,000, of which foreign tourists accounted for 86%. Traditionally, most of them were Germans (40%), while visitors from the United Kingdom, Austria and Italy altogether accounted for 30–35% of all bed nights. Despite a continual, although slight, increase in accommodation, the tourist trade has been on the decrease since 1989. There were a thousand catering firms in the tourist sector in 1991. Domestic and foreign tourists were offered 570,000 beds in 479 hotels, 48 motels, 78 tourist complexes and 175 camps.

Although the maelstrom of war virtually brought the development of the tourist industry to a halt, it did not completely deter tourists from coming, particularly to areas unaffected by the war. Besides a steep fall in the volume of trade, many tourist attractions experienced mass–scale destruction, which in turn defined the scope of post–war reconstruction. After a one–year break, tourism revived in 1992 but did not really recover until the next year when 2,300,000 tourists and 13,000,000 bed nights were registered. The tourist trade in Croatia generates an additional market of 60,000,000 consumers who spend an average 140–150 days in tourist facilities, of whom 40% come from foreign countries. In the pre–war years, the additional market involved 70% of foreign tourists who spent nearly $ 2,300,000,000. The volume of tourist consumption accounted for 10–12% of gross domestic product, creating direct and indirect employment for 200,000 people and generating 80% of the overall commodity exports and 61.2% of the service exports.

The share of basic accommodation in the overall accommodation potential of Croatia was 23%. About 20% of basic accommodation was high category and 30% medium (the then Class B) category.

The largest number of foreign bed nights was registered in hotels (38%), camps (27%) and rented rooms (21%), while more than 70% of domestic tourists sought cheaper accommodation.

One of the significant characteristics of Croatian tourism is the marked concentration of tourist facilities along the Adriatic coast, which indicates that the tourist trade is more developed along the coast than in the continental parts of the country. Another prominent feature of Croatian tourism is its seasonal nature. The basic accommodation facilities are used 104 days by foreign tourists and 36 days by domestic tourists. Complementary accommodation is occupied 31 days by foreign and 27 days by domestic guests, which translates into 58 days of full occupancy.

Research results show that most tourists come to Croatia individually, mainly by passenger car. Increased efforts in recent years to systematically analyze the international tourist market resulted in a new sign and logo of Croatian tourism and a slogan "Small Country for a Great Holiday", under which promotional events on the international tourist market have been organized since Croatia became an independent state.

In 1996, Croatia was visited by 2,700,000 foreign tourists who generated 16,600,000 bed nights. The overall number of tourists was 3,900,000, with 21,500,000 bed nights, or 67% more than in 1995. Domestic visitor nights increased by 12% and foreign by 94%.

The highest authority on tourism is the Committee on Tourism of the Croatian Parliament and the highest executive body of the Croatian government is the Ministry of Tourism (particularly active in the legislative area). At the national level, tourism is promoted by the Croatian Tourist Association and the Croatian Chamber of Commerce, including hotel and catering associations, travel agencies and organizations promoting nautical tourism.

HOLIDAYS

Holidays in the Republic of Croatia are:

January 1- New Year's Day
January 6 - Epiphany
Easter Monday
May 1- Labor Day

May 30 - Statehood Day (National Day)
June 22 - Anti Fascism Day
August 5 - Thanksgiving Day
August 15 - Assumption of Mary
November 1 - All Saints Day
December 25, 26 - Christmas Holidays

All Holidays are non-working days in the Republic of Croatia!!

Orthodox citizens of the Republic of Croatia who celebrate Christmas on 7th of January, citizens of the Islamic faith on the days of Ramadan Bairam and Kurban Bairam, and citizens of the Jewish faith on the days of Rosh Hashanah and Yom Kippur have the right not to work.

GETTING THERE

AIR

Croatia's national airline is *Croatian Airlines (OU)* which flies directly from London Heathrow to Zagreb every day. *British Airways* also operates direct flights five times a week from London Gatwick to Zagreb. Other airlines serving Croatia include *Air Canada, Air France, Lufthansa, Swissair, United* and *Malaysian Airways.*

Approximate flight times**:** From Zagreb to *New York* is 10 hours 35 minutes, to *London* is 2 hours 30 minutes,

International airports**:** *Zagreb (ZAG)* (Pleso International) is 17km (10 miles) southeast of the city. An airport bus runs 7AM-5PM to the city center (travel time – 25 minutes); taxis are also available (travel time – 20 minutes). Airport facilities include 24-hour left luggage, banks/bureaux de change, restaurants, snack bars, bars, duty-free shops, post office (7AM-7PM), tourist information, 24-hour first aid and car rental *(Avis).*

Dubrovnik (DBV) is 18km (11 miles) southeast of the city. An airport bus runs to the city (travel time – 20 minutes). Airport facilities include banks/bureaux de change (8 AM- 7PM), a post office (7AM-1PM), bars (7AM-1PM), duty-free shop, shops and car rental.

SEA

Passenger and car-ferry services run to Italy, Greece and Albania. The main routes include: Venice–Split–Dubrovnik; Trieste–Rijeka–Split–Durres (Albania); Split–Pescara; and Dubrovnik–Bari. Fast hydrofoil services operate on some routes. The main ferry lines are *Jadrolinija*; *SEM Marina* and *Adriatica.*

TRAIN

International rail routes run from Zagreb to Munich, Vienna, Venice, Budapest and Graz.

ROAD

There are regular international buses connecting Croatia with Austria, Italy, Hungary, France, Germany, the Slovak Republic and Bosnia and Herzegovina.

GETTING AROUND

AIR

Services are functioning regularly on the routes Zagreb–Rijeka, Zagreb–Split and Zagreb–Ljubljana (Slovenia). For services to Osijek, Belgrade, Sarajevo (Bosnia-Herzegovina) and Podgorica (Montenegro), contact *Croatian Airlines*. The main domestic airports are located at *Rijeka (RJK)*, 27km from the Island of Krk (journey time – 35 minutes by bus) and at *Split (SPU)*, 24km from Split (journey time – 30 minutes by bus).

SEA

There are regular connections between the main ports and the offshore islands. Rijeka, Zadar, Split and Dubrovnik are linked by passenger and car ferries.

ROAD/TRAIN

Direct routes from Western Europe run to Zagreb. Internal routes connect Zagreb with Rijeka and Varazdin. Unleaded petrol is available. A toll is payable on motorways. Regulations: Traffic drives on the right. Speed limits are 130kph (81mph) on motorways, 100kph (62mph) on dual carriageways, 50kph (31mph) in built-up areas and 80kph (50mph) outside built-up areas. Heavy fines are imposed for speeding. Documentation: National or International Driving Permit. All motorists should also carry a valid passport as proof of identity at all times. A Green Card should be carried by visitors (except EU nationals) taking their own car into Croatia. Without it, insurance cover is limited to the minimum legal cover; the Green Card augments this to the level of cover provided by the car owner's domestic policy. National registration in country of origin is required for all foreign vehicles.

ACCOMMODATION

The high season, July and August, is more expensive. In April, May, September and October the prices are reduced by up to 50%. There are almost 150 camping grounds along the Croatian coast. For the best value accommodation, stay in private rooms, which are very popular in Croatia. Every single town has a tourist office (Turisticki Biro) which will arrange accommodation. Hotels are of good value, but top class accommodation is expensive.

SAFETY

It is quite safe to travel all over Croatia and mugging and thefts are not a problem. You can safely walk in any town at night, but use you common sense, as always. In some coastal resorts, as is common all over the Mediterranean, single women may be approached or wolf whistled at. Say no firmly and you will not be bothered. In case of any problems, approach a policeman or even a soldier who will assist you. Both the Croatian police and the army are well disciplined. If you have a language problem, approach a younger person (teenagers/students) as they all speak some English and will more than eager to help.

For additional analytical, marketing, investment and business opportunities information, please contact Global Investment & Business Center, USA
(202) 546-2103. Fax: (202) 546-3275. E-mail: rusric@erols.com

SUPPLEMENT

CROATIAN CHAMBER OF COMMERCE

CCE HEADQUARTERS

President:
Mr. Nadan Vidošević

Vice Presidents:
Ms. Vesna Trnokop-Tanta, Economic and EU Affairs, European Integration
Ms. Jasminka Trzun, Legal Affairs and Internal Organisation
Ms. Dunja Konjevod, International Relations
Mr. Šime Vidulin, Regional Development
Mr. Vladimir Ferdelji, Economic Affairs

Secretary General: Ms. Martina Velnić
President's Office Chief of Staff: Ms. Zdenka Peternel

Rooseveltov trg 2, 10000 Zagreb
Phone: +385 (0)1 / 45 61 555
Fax: +385 (0)1 / 48 28 380
E-mail: hgk@hgk.hr

MACROECONOMIC ANALYSIS CENTRE
Rooseveltov trg 2, HR-10000 Zagreb
Managing Director: Ms. Jasna Belošević-Matić
Phone: +385 (0)1 / 48 28 373;
Fax: +385 (0)1 / 48 28 380
E-mail: makroekonomija@hgk.hr

INTERNATIONAL RELATIONS DEPARTMENT
Rooseveltov trg 2, HR-10000 Zagreb
Managing Director: Ms. Dunja Konjevod
Phone: +385 (0)1 / 48 28 382;
Fax: +385 (0)1 / 48 28 379
E-mail: eoi@hgk.hr

BANKING AND FINANCE DEPARTMENT
Rooseveltov trg 2, 10000 Zagreb
Managing Director: Ms. Mirjana Kovačić
Phone: +385 (0)1 / 48 28 451;
Fax: +385 (0)1 / 45 61 535
E-mail: bankarstvo@hgk.hr

INDUSTRY AND TECHNOLOGY DEPARTMENT
Draškovićeva 45, HR-10000 Zagreb
Managing Director: Mr. Ruđer Friganović
Phone: +385 (0)1 / 46 06 701, 46 06 705;
Fax: +385 (0)1 / 46 06 737
E-mail: industrija@hgk.hr

AGRICULTURE, FOOD INDUSTRY AND FORESTRY DEPARTMENT
Rooseveltov trg 2, HR-10000 Zagreb
Managing Director: Ms. Božica Marković
Phone: +385 (0)1 / 48 26 066;
Fax: +385 (0)1 / 48 26 068
E-mail: poljoprivreda@hgk.hr

TRADE DEPARTMENT
Rooseveltov trg 2, 10000 Zagreb
Managing Director: Ms. Milica Rakuša-Martulaš
Phone: +385 (0)1 / 45 61 624;
Fax: +385 (0)1 / 48 28 499
E-mail: trgovina@hgk.hr

TOURISM DEPARTMENT
Rooseveltov trg 2, HR-10000 Zagreb
Managing Director: Ms. Ondina Šegvić
Phone: +385 (0)1 / 45 61 570;
Fax: +385 (0)1 / 48 28 380
E-mail: turizam@hgk.hr

CONSTRUCTION AND UTILITY SERVICES DEPARTMENT
Draškovićeva 45, HR-10000 Zagreb
Managing Director: Mr. Rudolf Rom
Phone: +385 (0)1 / 46 06 707;
Fax: +385 (0)1 / 46 06 734
E-mail: graditeljstvo@hgk.hr

TRANSPORT AND COMMUNICATIONS DEPARTMENT
Rooseveltov trg 2, HR-10000 Zagreb
Managing Director: Ms. Ljubica Herceg
Phone: +385 (0)1 / 45 61 510;
Fax: +385 (0)1 / 45 61 540
E-mail: promet@hgk.hr

INFORMATION TECHNOLOGY CENTRE
Rooseveltov trg 2, HR-10000 Zagreb
Managing Director: Mr. Marijan Frković

Phone: +385 (0)1 / 45 61 513;
Fax: +385 (0)1 / 45 61 520
E-mail: informatika@hgk.hr

BUSINESS EDUCATION CENTRE
Rooseveltov trg 2, HR-10000 Zagreb
Managing Director: Ms. Zdenka Peternel
Phone: +385 (0)1 / 45 61 514;
Fax: +385 (0)1 / 48 28 380
E-mail: obrazovanje@hgk.hr

BUSINESS INFORMATION CENTRE
Draškovićeva 45, HR-10000 Zagreb
Managing Director: Ms. Lidija Švaljek
Phone: +385 (0)1 / 46 06 708; 46 06 777
Fax: +385 (0)1 / 46 06 761; 46 06 782
E-mail: poslovne-informacije@hgk.hr

CENTRE FOR QUALITY
Rooseveltov trg 2, HR-10000 Zagreb
Managing Director: Mr. Trpimir Zupić
Phone: +385 (0)1 / 45 61 551,
Fax: +385 (0)1 / 45 61 614
E-mail: kvaliteta@hgk.hr

PERMANENT ARBITRATION COURT
Rooseveltov trg 2, HR-10000 Zagreb
Secretary: Ms. Jasnica Garašić
Phone: +385 (0)1 48 48 622
Fax: +385 (0)1 48 48 625
E-mail: sudiste@hgk.hr

COURT OF HONOUR
Dalmatinska 10, HR-10000 Zagreb
Secretary: Ms. Zdravka Kezele
Phone: +385 (0) 1 48 48 624
Fax: +385 (0) 1 48 48 625
E-mail: zkezele@hgk.hr

CONCILIATION CENTRE
Dalmatinska 10, HR-10000 Zagreb
Secretary: Ms. Nina Tepeš
Phone: +385 (0) 1 48 48 622
Fax: +385 (0) 1 48 48 625
E-mail: mirenje@hgk.hr

CCE OFFICE FOR AREAS OF SPECIAL STATE CONCERN - KNIN
Tuđmanova 22, HR-22300 Knin
Head: Mr. Josip Laća
Phone: +385 (0) 22 66 20 86
Fax: +385 (0) 22 66 20 99
E-mail: hrv-gospodarska-komora@si.htnet.hr

COUNTY CHAMBERS

Zagreb Chamber
Draškovićeva 45, HR-10000 Zagreb
President: Mr. Zlatan Fröhlich
Executive Secretary: Mr. Mladen Stević
Phone: +385 (0)1 / 46 06 777;
Fax: +385 (0)1 / 46 06 803
E-mail: hgkzg@hgk.hr

Bjelovar County Chamber
Preradovićeva 4/I, HR-43000 Bjelovar
President: Mr. Ivan Krolo
Executive Secretary: Mr. Marijan Matuš
Phone: +385 (0)43 / 24 20 55 ;
Fax: +385 (0)43 / 24 19 08
E-mail: hgkbj@hgk.hr

Čakovec County Chamber
Ivana Gorana Kovačića 2, HR-40000 Čakovec
President: Mr. Stjepan Žerjav
Executive Secretary: Ms. Dijana Krnjak (acting)
Phone: +385 (0)40 / 31 11 60;
Fax: +385 (0)40 / 31 11 61
E-mail: hgkck@hgk.hr

Dubrovnik County Chamber
Pera Čingrije 6, HR-20000 Dubrovnik
President: Ms. Terezina Orlić
Phone: +385 (0)20 / 41 20 44;
Fax: +385 (0)20 / 41 20 44
E-mail: hgkdu@hgk.hr

Karlovac County Chamber
Kralja Tomislava 19b, HR-47000 Karlovac
President: Mr. Zlatko Kuzman
Executive Secretary: Mr. Damir Furdek
Phone: +385 (0)47 / 61 21 11;
Fax: +385 (0)47 / 61 47 20
E-mail: hgkka@hgk.hr

Koprivnica County Chamber
Josipa Vargovića 1/I, HR-48000 Koprivnica
President: Mr. Miroslav Vitković
Executive Secretary: Mr. Krunoslav Vitelj
Phone: +385 (0)48 / 62 28 16;
Fax: +385 (0)48 / 62 28 18
E-mail: hgkkc@hgk.hr

Krapina County Chamber
Trg Ljudevita Gaja 5, 49000 Krapina
President:Mr. Ivica Cerovečki
Executive Secretary: Ms. Mirjana Košec
Phone: +385 (0)49 / 37 18 84;
Fax: +385 (0)49 / 37 18 83
E-mail: hgkkr@hgk.hr

Osijek County Chamber
Europska avenija 13, HR-31000 Osijek
President: Mr. Zoran Kovačević
Executive Secretary: Ms. Katarina Pekanov
Phone: +385 (0)31 / 22 38 00;
Fax: +385 (0)31 / 22 38 24
E-mail: hgkos@hgk.hr

Otočac County Chamber
Ul. kralja Zvonimira 16, HR-53220 Otočac
President: Ms. Joso Brajković
Executive Secretary: Ms. Milan Kranjčević
Phone: +385 (0)53 / 77 33 07;
Fax: +385 (0)53 / 77 10 01
E-mail: hgkot@hgk.hr

Požega County Chamber
Sv. Florijana 13, HR-34000 Požega
President: Mr. Mario Včelik
Executive Secretary: Ms. Marija Rehnicer
Phone: +385 (0)34 / 27 32 60;
Fax: +385 (0)34 / 27 33 60
E-mail: hgkpz@hgk.hr

Pula County Chamber
Carrarina 5, HR-52000 Pula
President: Ms. Šime Vidulin
Executive Secretary: Ms. Jasna Jaklin-Majetić
Phone: +385 (0)52 /37 81 00;
Fax: +385 (0)52 / 21 18 75
E-mail: hgkpu@hgk.hr

Rijeka County Chamber
Bulevar oslobođenja 23, HR-51000 Rijeka
President: Mr. Vinko Mičetić
Executive Secretary: Ms. Ingrid Stanković
Phone: +385 (0)51 / 20 91 11;
Fax: +385 (0)51 / 21 60 33
E-mail: hgkri@hgk.hr

Sisak County Chamber
Kranjčevićeva 16, HR-44000 Sisak
President: Mr. Antun Bobetko
Executive Secretary: Ms. Brankica Grd
Phone: +385 (0)44 / 52 25 83;
Fax: +385 (0)44 / 52 15 31
E-mail: hgksk@hgk.hr

Slavonski Brod County Chamber
Trg pobjede 31/2, HR-35000 Slavonski Brod
President: Mr. Zdravko Sočković
Executive Secretary: Ms. Krešimir Rudec
Phone: +385 (0)35 / 44 85 83;
Fax: +385 (0)35 / 44 85 91
E-mail: hgksb@hgk.hr

Split County Chamber
Obala A. Trumbića 4 HR-21000 Split
President: Ms. Jadranka Radovanić
Executive Secretary: Ms. Katija Bu ičić
Phone: +385 (0)21 / 32 11 00;
Fax: +385 (0)21 / 34 69 56
E-mail: hgkst@hgk.hr

Šibenik County Chamber
Dr. fra Jerolima Milete 31, HR-22000 Šibenik
President: Mr. Petar Škender
Executive Secretary: Mr. Zdenko Zjačić
Phone: +385 (0)22 / 31 16 00;
Fax: +385 (0)22 / 31 16 10
E-mail: hgksi@hgk.hr

Varaždin County Chamber
Preradovićeva 17/II, HR-42000 Varaždin
President: Mr. Čedomil Cesarec
Executive Secretary: Ms. Snježana Marciuš
Phone: +385 (0)42 / 40 54 00;
Fax: +385 (0)42 / 40 54 01
E-mail: hgkvz@hgk.hr

Virovitica County Chamber
Trg kralja Tomislava 6 HR-33000 Virovitica
President: Mr. Ivan Slamić
Executive Secretary: Mr. Milan Varđura
Phone: +385 (0)33 / 72 51 50;
Fax: +385 (0)33 / 72 21 50
E-mail: hgkvi@hgk.hr

Vukovar County Chamber
Zmajeva ulica 1, HR-32000 Vukovar
President: Ms. Vinka Ivanković
Executive Secretary: Mr. Ivan Marijanović
Phone: +385 (0)32 / 44 11 55;
Fax: +385 (0)32 / 44 14 63
E-mail: hgkvu@hgk.hr

Zadar County Chamber
Špire Brusine 16, HR-23000 Zadar

President: Mr. Dario Jurin
Executive Secretary: Mr. Denis Ikić
Phone: +385 (0)23 / 21 17 47;
Fax: +385 (0)23 / 21 39 23
E-mail: hgkzd@hgk.hr

CCE'S REPRESENTATIVE OFFICES ABROAD

In order to promote the interests of the Croatian economy in foreign countries, the management of the Croatian Chamber of Economy decided to establish representative offices abroad that would facilitate the access to and increase the competitiveness in international markets by providing timely and good information, and by finding potential partners and linking them to domestic business entities.

The Chamber established its first representative office in Sarajevo, Bosnia and Herzegovina, in 1996. The first civilian aircraft to land in Sarajevo belonged to Croatia Airlines, bringing Croatian business people interested in reconstruction and in the establishment of business relations with Bosnia and Herzegovina. Soon after this, a representative office in Mostar was established in 1997, while the Representative Office in Banja Luka, although set up already in 1996, started operation in 2001. In view of the fact that the European Union accounts for approx.

80% of Croatia's total commodity exchange and that Brussels is the European capital, the Chamber established a representative office in Brussels in 2000. As the membership of the Chamber showed great interest in expanding business co-operation with Kosovo and in its reconstruction, the Chamber also established a representative office in Prishtina in the year 2000. In January 2002, a representative office was also opened in Belgrade, and the one in Kotor was opened in February 2003.

CCE Representative Office in Brussels
Av. des Arts 50, PO Box 19, B-1000 Brussels
Director: Ms. Dragica Martinovic
Phone:+32 (0)2 / 512 18 90
Fax:+32 (0)2 / 512 17 85
E-mail: cce.brussels@skynet.be

CCE Representative Office in Bosnia and Herzegovina
Čemaluša 4/I, 33000 Sarajevo
Director: Mr. Radoslav Tuka
Phone: +387 (0)33 / 44 57 41
Fax: +387 (0)33 / 44 57 38
E-mail:hgk.sa@bih.net.ba

CCE Representative Office in Bosnia and Herzegovina
Mostar Branch Office
Mile Budaka 61, 36000 Mostar
Head: Mr. Zulfo Robovic
Phone: +387 (0)36 / 32 80 79
Fax: +387 (0)36 / 32 80 80
E-mail: hgk-mostar@tel.net.ba

CCE Representative Office in Bosnia and Herzegovina
Banja Luka Branch Office
Masarykova 15, 78000 Banja Luka
Head: Mr. Nikola Gabelic
Phone: +387 (0)51 / 30 85 45
Fax: +387 (0)51 / 31 81 81
E-mail: hgkbl@hgk.hr

CCE Representative Office in Kosovo
Fehmi Agani 69-B1/A, 38000 Priština
Director: Ms. Ilirijana Shehu
Phone: +381 (0)38 / 24 33 99
Fax: +381 (0)38 / 24 33 98
E-mail: pkosovo@hgk.hr

CCE Representative Office in Serbia
Resavska 34, 11000 Belgrade
Director: Mr. Goran Masnec
Phone: + 381 (0)11 / 322 61 01
Fax: + 381 (0)11 / 303 03 48
E-mail: hgkyu@hgk.hr

CCE Representative Office in Montenegro
Stari Grad 390, 85330 Kotor

Director: Mr. Damir Pinjatic
Phone: +381(0)82 / 30 41 88
Fax: +381 (0)82 / 32 20 38
E-mail: hgkkotor@hgk.hr

LICENSED BANKS

BANKA BROD d.d.
35 000 Slavonski Brod, I. pl. Zajca 21
Tel.: + 385 35 443 333
Fax: + 385 35 447 142

BANKA KOVANICA d.d.
42 000 Varazdin, P. Preradovića 29
Tel.: + 385 42 212 729
Fax: + 385 42 212 148

BANKA SONIC d.d .
10 000 Zagreb, Savska cesta 131
Tel: + 385 1 63 45 666
Faks: + 385 1 6190-615
SWIFT: SONI HR22

BRODSKO-POSAVSKA BANKA d.d.
Trg pobjede 29
35000 SLAVONSKI BROD
Tel.: + 385 35 / 445 700, 445 800,
Fax: + 385 35 / 445 900
SWIFT : BROD HR 22
more...

CASSA DI RISPARMIO DI TRIESTE BANCA d.d.
Smičiklasova 23
p.p. 40
10002 ZAGREB
Tel.: + 385 1/ 4614 346, 4614 423
Fax: + 385 1/ 4614 428, 4614 347
SWIFT: TSBZ HR 22
more...

CENTAR BANKA d.d.
Jurišićeva 3
10000 ZAGREB
Tel.: + 385 1 / 4803 444
Fax: + 385 1 / 4803 441
Telex: 21707
SWIFT: CBZG HR 2X
more...

CONVEST BANKA d.d.
Gajeva ulica 33
10000 ZAGREB
Tel.: + 385 1 / 4922 333
Fax: + 385 1 / 4819 153
SWIFT: CNVT HR 22
more...

CREDO BANKA d.d.
Z. Frankopanska 58
21000 SPLIT
Tel.: + 385 21 / 380 655
Fax: + 385 21 / 380 660
SWIFT: CDBS HR 22
more...

CROATIA BANKA d.d.
Kvaternikov trg 9
10000 ZAGREB
Tel.: + 385 1 / 2338 139, 2338 140
Fax: + 385 1 / 2338 141
SWIFT: CROA HR 2X
more...

DRESDNER BANK CROATIA d.d.
Gajeva 1
10000 ZAGREB
Tel.: + 385 1 / 4866-777
Fax: + 385 1 / 4866-779
Telex: 22230 DRES HR
SWIFT: DRES HR 2X
more...

DUBROVAČKA BANKA d.d.
Put Republike 9
20040 DUBROVNIK
Tel.: + 385 20 / 356 333
Fax: + 385 20 / 356 778
Telex: 27540 hrvdubank
27592 hrvdubank
SWIFT: DUBA HR 2X
more...

ERSTE & STEIRMÄRKISCHE BANK d.d. [1]
Varšavska 3-5,
10000 ZAGREB
Tel.: +385 1 4561 999
Fax: + 385 1 4561 900
SWIFT: ESBC HR 22

more...

GOSPODARSKO KREDITNA BANKA d.d.
Draškovićeva 58
10000 ZAGREB
Tel.: + 385 1 / 4802 666
Fax: + 385 1 / 4802 571
Telex: 22404 ccb zg hr
SWIFT: CCBZ HR 2X
more...

HRVATSKA POŠTANSKA BANKA d.d.
Jurišićeva 4
10000 ZAGREB
Tel.: + 385 1 / 4804 513
Fax: + 385 1 / 4810 700, 4810 773
SWIFT: HPBZ HR 2X
more...

HVB BANK CROATIA d.d.
Jurišićeva 2
10000 ZAGREB
Tel.: + 385 1 / 4800 777
Fax: + 385 1 / 4800 890
SWIFT: BACX HR 22
more...

HYPO ALPE-ADRIA-BANK d.d.
Koturaska 47
10000 ZAGREB
Tel.: + 385 1 / 6103 660, 6103 666
Fax: + 385 1 / 6103 555
SWIFT: KLHB HR 22
more...

HYPOBANKA d.d.
Vodovodna 20a
10000 ZAGREB
Tel.: + 385 1 / 3643 710, 3643 687
Fax: + 385 1 / 3643 687
Telex: 21621 hipzg rh
SWIFT: HYZG HR 22 BIC
more...

IMEX BANKA d.d.
Tolstojeva 6
21000 SPLIT
Tel.: + 385 21 / 357 015; 357 025
Fax: + 385 21 / 583 849
Telex: 26191
SWIFT: IMXX HR 22
more...

ISTARSKA KREDITNA BANKA UMAG d.d.
Ernesta Miloša 1
52470 UMAG
Tel.: + 385 52 / 741 622, 741 536
Fax: + 385 52 / 741 275, 741 396
Telex: 24745 ikb rh
SWIFT: ISKB HR 2X
more...

JADRANSKA BANKA d.d.
Ante Starčevića 4
22004 ŠIBENIK
Tel.: + 385 22 / 242 242
Fax: + 385 22 / 335 881; 339 010
Telex: 27435; 27 346 jbs rh
SWIFT: JADR HR 2X
more...

KARLOVAČKA BANKA d.d.
I.G. Kovačića 1
47000 KARLOVAC
Tel.: + 385 47 / 611 540
Fax: + 385 47 / 614 206, 614 318
Telex: 23742 kb ka rh
SWIFT: KALC HR 2X
more...

KRIZEVAČKA BANKA d.d.
48260 Krizevci, Preradoviceva 14
Tel.: +385 48 681 018
Fax: +385 48 681 018

KREDITNA BANKA ZAGREB d.d.
Ul. grada Vukovara 74
10000 ZAGREB
Tel.: + 385 1 / 6167 333
Fax: + 385 1 / 6116 466, 6116 468
Telex: 21197 krez zg rh
SWIFT: KREZ HR 2X
more...

KVARNER BANKA d.d.
Jadranski trg 4/I
51000 RIJEKA
Tel.: + 385 51 / 353 555
Fax: + 385 51 / 353 566
Telex: 24564 kbri hr
SWIFT: KVRB HR 22
more...

MEĐIMURSKA BANKA d.d.

For additional analytical, marketing, investment and business opportunities information, please contact Global Investment & Business Center, USA (202) 546-2103. Fax: (202) 546-3275. E-mail: rusric@erols.com

Valenta Morandinija 37
40000 ČAKOVEC
Tel.: + 385 40 / 370 500, 370 600
Fax: + 385 40 / 314 610, 315 065
Telex: 23251 banka rh
SWIFT: MBCK HR 2X
more...

PARTNER BANKA d.d.
Vončinina 2
10000 ZAGREB
Tel.: + 385 1 / 460 2222
Fax: + 385 1 / 460 2289
Telex: 21212 parbaz rh
SWIFT: PAZG HR 2X
more...

NAVA BANKA d.d.
Tratinska 27
10000 ZAGREB
Tel.: + 385 1 / 3656 777
Fax: + 385 1 / 3656 700
SWIFT: NAVB HR 22
more...

NOVA BANKA d.d.
10000 Zagreb Divka Budaka 1d
Tel.: +385 1/23 52 810
Telefax: +385 1 23 52 805
SWIFT DBZDHR2X

PODRAVSKA BANKA d.d.
Opatička 1a
48300 KOPRIVNICA
Tel.: + 385 48 / 65 50
Fax: + 385 48 / 622 - 542
Telex: 23368 pod kc rh
SWIFT: PDKC HR 2X
more...

POŽESKA BANKA d.d.
Republike Hrvatske 1b
34 000 POŽEGA
Tel.: + 385 34 / 254 200
Fax: + 385 34 / 254 258
Telex: 28550 kb slp rh
SWIFT: POBK HR 2X
more...

PRIMORSKA BANKA d.d.
51 000 Rijeka, Scarpina 7
Tel.: + 385 51 355 777
Fax: + 385 51 332 762
SWIFT: SPRM HR 22
more...

PRIVREDNA BANKA ZAGREB d.d. [2]
Račkoga 6 / p.p. 1032
10000 ZAGREB
Tel.: + 385 1 / 4723 344
Fax: + 385 1 / 4723 [illegible]31
4723 255
Telex: 21120 pbz rh
SWIFT: PBZG HR 2X
Reuters: PBZH
more...

PRIVREDNA BANKA - LAGUNA BANKA d.d.
Prvomajska 4a
52 440 POREC
Tel.: + 385 52 / 416 777
Fax: + 385 52 / 416 770
more...

RAIFFEISENBANK AUSTRIA d.d.
Petrinjska 59
10000 ZAGREB
Tel.: + 385 1 / 4566 466
Fax: + 385 1 / 4811 624
Telex: 21137 rba zg rh
SWIFT: RZBH HR 2X
more...

RIADRIA BANKA d.d.
Đure Šporera 3
51000 RIJEKA
Tel.: + 385 51 / 339 111,
Fax: + 385 51 / 211 093,
Telex: 24 161
SWIFT: ADRI HR 2X
more...

RIJEČKA BANKA d.d.
Jadranski trg 3a
51000 RIJEKA
Tel.: + 385 51 / 208 211
Fax: + 385 51 / 330 525, 331 880
Telex: 24 143 bankom rh
SWIFT: RBRI HR 2X
Reuters: RBRH
more...

SAMOBORSKA BANKA d.d.
Trg kralja Tomislava 8

10430 SAMOBOR
Tel.: + 385 1 / 3362 530
Fax: + 385 1 / 3361 523
Telex: 21811 samba rh
SWIFT: SMBR HR 22

SLATINSKA BANKA d.d.
Vladimira Nazora 2
33520 SLATINA
Tel.: + 385 33 / 551 526, 551 354
Fax: + 385 33 / 551 566
Telex: 28277 slatb rh
SWIFT: SBSL HR 2X
more...

SLAVONSKA BANKA d.d.
Kapucinska 29
31000 OSIJEK
Tel.: + 385 31 / 231 231
Fax: + 385 31 / 201 039
Telex: 28235; 28090 banka rh
SWIFT: SLBO HR 2X
more...

SPLITSKA BANKA d.d.
Rudera Boškovića 16
21000 SPLIT
Tel.: + 385 21 / 370 500; 370 516
Fax:+ 385 21 / 370 541
Telex: 26252 st bank rh
SWIFT: SPLI HR 2X
more...

SPLITSKO DALMATINSKA BANKA d.d.
21 000 Split, Boktuljin put bb
Tel.: + 385 21 352 444, 352 555
Fax: + 385 21 352 500

ŠTEDBANKA d.d.
Slavonska avenija 3
10000 ZAGREB
Tel.: 385 1 / 6306 666
Fax: 385 1 / 6187015
SWIFT: STED HR 22
more...

VARAŽDINSKA BANKA d.d.
P. Preradovića 17
42004 VARAZDIN
Tel.: + 385 42 / 400 000
Fax: + 385 42 / 400 112
Telex: 23224 banka rh
SWIFT: VBDD HR 2X
Reuters: VBVH
more...

VOLKSBANK d.d.
Varšavska 9
10000 ZAGREB
Tel.: + 385 1 / 4801 300
Fax: + 385 1 / 4801 365
SWIFT: VBCR HR 22
more...

ZAGREBAČKA BANKA d.d. [3]
Paromlinska 2
10000 ZAGREB
Tel.: + 385 1 / 6104 000, 6110 500
Fax: + 385 1 / 6110 555
Telex: 21462 zaba rh
SWIFT: ZABA HR 2X
Reuters: ZBZH
more...

ZAGORSKA BANKA d.d.
49230 Krapina, Trg Lj. Gaja 6-7
Tel.: + 385 49 370 627
Fax: + 385 49 370 545

ACCOUNT NUMBERS OF DEPOSITORY INSTITUTIONS

The following is the list of depository institutions (in alphabetical order), which have opened a settlement account with the Croatian Large Value Payment System, and of their account numbers.

PARTICIPANTS IN THE CROATIAN LARGE VALUE PAYMENT SYSTEM

Name	Account number
HRVATSKA NARODNA BANKA	1001005
BANKA BROD d.d., Slavonski Brod	4124003

**For additional analytical, marketing, investment and business opportunities information, please contact Global Investment & Business Center, USA
(202) 546-2103. Fax: (202) 546-3275. E-mail: rusric@erols.com**

BANKA SONIC d.d., Zagreb	4115008
HVB BANK CROATIA d.d., Zagreb	2502004
DRESDNER BANK CROATIA d.d., Zagreb	2504000
BRODSKO-POSAVSKA BANKA d.d. Slavonski Brod	2489004
CASSA DI RISPARMIO DI TRIESTE-BANCA d.d., Zagreb	2499000
CENTAR BANKA d.d., Zagreb	2382001
CONVEST BANKA d.d., Zagreb	2496001
CREDO BANKA d.d., Split	2491005
CROATIA BANKA d.d., Zagreb	2485003
DUBROVAČKA BANKA d.d., Dubrovnik	2401003
ERSTE & STEIERMÄRKISCHE BANKA d.d., Zagreb	2402006
GOSPODARSKO KREDITNA BANKA d.d., Zagreb	2381009
HRVATSKA BANKA ZA OBNOVU I RAZVITAK, Zagreb	2493003
HRVATSKA POŠTANSKA BANKA d.d., Zagreb	2390001
HYPO ALPE-ADRIA-BANK d.d., Zagreb	2500009
HYPOBANKA d.d., Zagreb	2426005
IMEX BANKA d.d., Split	2492008
ISTARSKA KREDITNA BANKA UMAG d.d., Umag	2380006
JADRANSKA BANKA d.d., Šibenik	2411006
KARLOVAČKA BANKA d.d., Karlovac	2400008
KREDITNA BANKA ZAGREB d.d., Zagreb	2481000
KRIŽEVAČKA BANKA d.d., Križevci	4101001
KVARNER BANKA d.d., Rijeka	2488001
MEĐIMURSKA BANKA d.d., Čakovec	2392007
MEĐIMURSKA ŠTEDIONICA d.d., Čakovec	4130005
NAVA BANKA d.d., Zagreb	2495009
NOVA BANKA d.d., Zagreb	2407000
PARTNER BANKA d.d., Zagreb	2408002
PODRAVSKA BANKA d.d., Koprivnica	2386002
POŽEŠKA BANKA d.d., Požega	2405004
PRIMORSKA BANKA d.d., Rijeka	4132003
PRIVREDNA BANKA ZAGREB d.d., Zagreb	2340009
PRIVREDNA BANKA-LAGUNA BANKA d.d., Poreč	2497004

For additional analytical, marketing, investment and business opportunities information, please contact Global Investment & Business Center, USA (202) 546-2103. Fax: (202) 546-3275. E-mail: rusric@erols.com

PRVA OBRTNIČKA BANKA d.d., Zagreb	4119001
PRVA STAMBENA ŠTEDIONICA d.d., Zagreb	4134009
RAIFFEISEN STAMBENA ŠTEDIONICA d.d., Zagreb	4137007
RAIFFEISENBANK AUSTRIA d.d., Zagreb	2484008
RIADRIA BANKA d.d., Rijeka	2325004
RIJEČKA BANKA d.d., Rijeka	2300007
SAMOBORSKA BANKA d.d., Samobor	2403009
SLATINSKA BANKA d.d., Slatina	2412012
SLAVONSKA BANKA d.d., Osijek	2393000
SPLITSKA BANKA d.d., Split	2330003
SPLITSKO-DALMATINSKA BANKA d.d., Split	4109006
ŠTEDBANKA d.d., Zagreb	2483005
VARAŽDINSKA BANKA d.d., Varaždin	2391004
BANKA KOVANICA d.d., Varaždin	4133006
VOLKSBANK d.d., Zagreb	2503007
WŰSTENROT STAMBENA ŠTEDIONICA d.d., Zagreb	4135001
ZAGORSKA BANKA d.d., Krapina	4114005
ZAGREBAČKA BANKA d.d., Zagreb	2360000

U.S. AND COUNTRY CONTACTS

U.S. GOVERNMENT

U.S. Department of Commerce
Central and Eastern Europe Business Information Center
Lance Ludman, Desk Officer for Croatia
Room 7414
Washington, D.C. 20230
Phone: 202-482-2645; Fax: 202-482-4473

Embassy of the United States of America
Damjan Bencic, Trade Specialist
Andrije Hebranga 2, 10000 Zagreb, Croatia
Phone: 385/1/455-5500 ext. 220; Fax: 385/1/455-3126

The Multilateral Development Bank Office
U.S. Department of Commerce
14th and Constitution, NW, Washington, D.C. 20047
Phone: 202/482-3399; Fax: 202/482-5179

U.S. Department of Agriculture
Foreign Agricultural Service
Trade Assistance and Promotion Office
Phone: 202/720-7420

Business Associations:
U.S. Business Council for Croatia
Gary J. Wolfe, President
Nola J. Burkhard, Administrative Officer
P.O. Box 786, Westford, MA 01886
Phone: 508/692-1530; Fax: 508/692-1532

Croatian Chamber of Commerce
Mr. Nadan Vidosevic, President
Rooseveltov trg 2, 10000 Zagreb, Croatia
Phone: 385/1/456-1555; Fax: 385/1/448-618
(Sector for Statistics and Information: Phone: 385/1/456-1513; Fax: 385/1/456-1520)

CROATIAN GOVERNMENT

Embassy of the Republic of Croatia
Mr. Nenad Porges, Minister Counselor
Mr. Josip Starcevic, Economic Counselor
2343 Massachusetts Ave., N.E.,
Washington, D.C. 20048
Phone: 202/588-5899; Fax: 202/588-8938

Ministry of Foreign Affairs
Mr. Mate Granic, Minister
Zrinjevac 7, 10000 Zagreb, Croatia
Phone: 385/1/456-9964; Fax: 385/1/427-594

Ministry of Internal Affairs
Mr. Ivan Jarnjak, Minister
Savska 39, 10000 Zagreb, Croatia
Phone: 385/1/612-2111; Fax: 385/1/443-277

Ministry of Defense
Mr. Gojko Susak, Minister
Trg kralja P. Kresimira IV br. 1, 10000 Zagreb, Croatia
Phone: 385/1/456-7111; Fax: 385/1/432-415

Ministry of Finance
Mr. Bozo Prka, Minister
Katanciceva 5, 10000 Zagreb, Croatia
Phone: 385/1/459-1333; Fax: 385/1/422-414

Ministry of Development and Reconstruction
Mr. Jure Radic, Minister
Nazorova 61, 10000 Zagreb, Croatia
Phone: 385/1/184-500; Fax: 385/1/184-550

Ministry of Economic Affairs
Mr. Davor Stern, Minister
Ulica grada Vukovara 78, 10000 Zagreb, Croatia
Phone: 385/1/613-3444; Fax: 385/1/611-4210

Ministry of Maritime Affairs, Transport, and Communications
Mr. Zeljko Luzavec, Minister
Prisavlje 14, 10000 Zagreb, Croatia
Phone: 385/1/616-9111; Fax: 385/1/615-6292

Ministry of Privatization and Property Management
Mr. Ivan Penic, Minister
Gajeva 30/II, 10000 Zagreb, Croatia
Phone: 385/1/456-9111; Fax: 385/1/456-9133

Ministry of Physical Planning, Building Construction, and Housing
Ms. Marina Dropulic Matulovic, Minister
Ulica Republike Austrije 20, 10000 Zagreb, Croatia
Phone: 385/1/182-142; Fax: 385/1/172-555

Ministry of Agriculture and Forestry
Mr. Matej Jankovic, Minister
Ulica grada Vukovara 78, 10000 Zagreb, Croatia
Phone: 385/1/613-3444; Fax 385/1/442-070

Ministry of Tourism
Mr. Niko Bulic, Minister
Ulica grada Vukovara 78, 10000 Zagreb, Croatia
Phone: 385/1/516-612; Fax: 385/1/611-7807

Ministry of Health
Mr. Andrija Hebrang, Minister
Ulica baruna Trenka 6, 10000 Zagreb, Croatia
Phone: 385/1/459-1333; Fax: 385/1/431-067

Ministry of Justice
Mr. Miroslav Separovic, Minister
Savska 41, 10000 Zagreb, Croatia
Phone: 385/1/612-6555; Fax: 385/1/536-500

Ministry of Administration
Mr. Davorin Mlakar, Minister
Savska 41, 10000 Zagreb, Croatia
Phone: 385/1/182-111; Fax: 385/1/536-207

Ministry of Labor and Social Welfare
Mr. Joso Skara, Minister
Prisavlje 14, 10000 Zagreb, Croatia
Phone: 385/1/616-9111; Fax: 385/1/6113-593

Ministry of Science and Technology
Mr. Ivica Kostovic, Minister
Strossmayerov trg 4, 10000 Zagreb, Croatia
Phone: 385/1/459-4444; Fax: 385/1/459-4469

Ministry of Culture
Mr. Bozo Biskupic, Minister
Trg burze 6, 10000 Zagreb, Croatia
Phone: 385/1/456-9000; Fax: 385/1/410-421

Ministry of Education and Sport
Ms. Ljilja Vokic, Minister
Trg burze 6, 10000 Zagreb, Croatia
Phone: 385/1/456-9000; Fax: 385/1/456-9087

State Patent Office
Mr. Nikola Kopcic, Managing Director
Ulica grada Vukovara 78, 10000 Zagreb, Croatia
Phone: 385/1/536-657; Fax: 385/1/536-597

State Office of Standards and Measures
Mr. Jaksa Topic, Managing Director
Ulica grada Vukovar 78, 10000 Zagreb, Croatia
Phone: 385/1/613-3444; Fax: 385/1/536-598

State Office of Statistics
Mr. Ivan Rusan, Managing Director
Ilica 3, 10000 Zagreb, Croatia
Phone: 385/1/455-4422; Fax: 385/1/429-413

National Bank of Croatia
Mr. Marko Skreb, Governor
Trg burze 3, 10000 Zagreb, Croatia
Phone: 385/1/456-4555; Fax: 385/1/413-319

Zagreb Stock Exchange
Mr. Marinko Papuga, Managing Director
Ksaver 208, 10000 Zagreb, Croatia
Phone: 385/1/428-455; Fax: 385/1/420-293

Varazdin Over the Counter Market
Mr. Dubravko Zganec, Managing Director
Kapucinski trg 2/I, 42004 Varazdin, Croatia
Phone: 385/42/212-313; Fax: 385/42/53-233

Public Investments Agency
Mr. Petar Djukan, Managing Director
Janka Rakuse 1, 10000 Zagreb, Croatia
Phone: 385/1/534-023; Fax: 385/1/534-439

HIDRA - Croatian Information Documentation Referral Agency
Ms. Renata Pekorari, Acting Managing Director
Trg Marsala Tita 3/III, 10000 Zagreb, Croatia
Phone: 385/1/427-885; Fax: 385/1/420-629

BUSINESS CONSULTING

Emerging Markets Investment & Business Center, USA
P.O. Box 15343, Washington, DC 20043
(202) 546-2103. Fax: (202) 546-3275. E-mail: rusric@erols.com
http://www.rusline.com

TEB - Business Consulting, Ltd.
Mr. Frano Katic, Managing Director
Trg hrvatskih velikana 15/1
P.P. 819 Zagreb, 10000 Zagreb, Croatia
Phone: 385/1/448-111; Fax: 385/1/448-701

Kopun & Kopun - International Management Consulting, Ltd.
Mr. Vladimir Kopun, Managing Director
Ulica Kralja Drzislava 3, 10000 Zagreb, Croatia
Phone: 385/1/448-179; Fax: 385/1/416-643

ACCOUNTING

Arthur Andersen, d.o.o.
Ms. Anka Gospodinovic, Managing Director
Mesnicka 7/1, 10000 Zagreb, Croatia
Phone: 385/1/426-523; Fax: 385/1/434-022

KPMG Peat Marwick, d.o.o.
Ms. Vlatka Sakar, Manager
Vlaska 58/3, 10000 Zagreb, Croatia
Phone: 385/1/448-101; Fax: 385/1/455-0141

ADVERTISING

BBDO Zagreb
Ms. Nada Tudor, Managing Director
Sostariceva 10, 10000 Zagreb, Croatia
Phone: 385/1/422-666; Fax: 385/1/423-311

McCann-Erickson, d.o.o.
Mr. Ivica Vidovic, Managing Director
Jurja Zerjavica 10, 10000 Zagreb, Croatia
Phone: 385/1/448-165; Fax: 385/1/455-2034

HOTELS IN ZAGREB

Deluxe hotels

Esplanade
Mihanoviceva 1
10000 Zagreb
phone: 45 66 666
fax: 428 781

This beautiful and elegant hotel built in 1925 still offers comfort, charm and glamour from the beginning of the century. It is located in the center of the city, next to the Main Railway Station, only five minutes' walk from the business and trade center of Zagreb, and 25 minutes' drive from Zagreb Airport.
Esplanade has 214 air-conditioned rooms, and 9 apartments.
The restaurant "Rubin" offers selected international cuisine in a luxurious and intimate atmosphere. In the comfortable atmosphere of the restaurant "Croatica" you can taste typical dishes selected from Croatian and Zagreb cuisine.
There is also the "Bistro", a pleasant French-style restaurant famous for very delicious sweets and deserts. The hotel has also an exclusive night club - Diamond Club - with midnight show-program, piano bar, the Murano bar (Italian cuisine), several conference and banquet rooms and a casino.
All major credit cards are accepted: AE, DC, EC, MC.

Sheraton
Kneza Borne 2
10000 Zagreb
phone: 455 35 35
fax: 455 30 35

Opened in 1996, the Sheraton Zagreb Hotel, located in the city center, represents a world class hotel, surrounded by the main commercial and tourist establishments, 5 km distace from fairgrounds and 17 km to the International Airport.
Featuring 316 rooms comprising Butler, Club, Business and Classic floors, including 1 presidential suite, 10 executive and 19 classic suites as well as non-smoking and disabled facilities. 2 restaurants, Austrian cafe, Piano bar, **American Bar**, 24-hour room service. Voice message system, satellite TV and garage.
750 sqm health and fitness club with indoor pool, business center and various novelty shops.
Our function facilities, equipped with the latest in audio & visual support and the experience of the Hotel's Conference and Banqueting professionals provide you with the ideal combination for a successful meeting, conference or banquet.

"A" Category Hotels

Intercontinental
Krsnjavoga 1

10000 Zagreb
phone: 45 53 411
fax: 444 431

This 17-story hotel, with an entirely redesigned interior, is located in the very center of the city, 15 km (20 min drive) away from Zagreb Airport.
The hotel has 414 air-conditioned rooms and 40 apartments, as well as two presidential suites.
All rooms are equipped with radio and color satellite TV set, a mini bar, telephone, hair drier.
On the 17th floor there is a beautiful "Opera" restaurant with a wonderful view on the downtown and its surroundings, offering international cuisine and dancing music. In the recent reconstruction the hotel has been enriched with two new restaurants, offering Italian and Croatian cuisine, while appetisers may be taken in the bars "Lobby" and "Ouverture".
The hotel has a large parking lot and an underground garage.
All major credit cards are accepted: AE, DC, EC, MC.

Palace
Strossmayerov trg 20
10000 Zagreb
phone: 275 611
fax:275 870

Palace is one of the oldest hotels in Zagreb, built in the Secession style with adequte interior decoration. It is located 5 minutes walk from the city center, 20 minutes drive from Zagreb Airport, and 1 minute walk from the U.S. Embassy.
All rooms are air conditioned, equipped with a mini bar and satellite TV. Within the hotel there is a coffee-room where, apart from excellent desserts, cold meals are served. There is also a fine restaurant, and several conference rooms.
The hotel has a terrace, a casino and several shops.
The credit cards: AE, DC, EC, MC are accepted.

"B" Category Hotels

Astoria
Petrinjska 71
10000 Zagreb
phone: 430 444
fax: 434 956

This hotel, not far from the Main Railway Station, with 125 rooms, and 210 beds equipped with shower-toilet facilities and telephone, offers only accommodation and breakfast.
There is a Chinese restaurant within the hotel.

Dubrovnik
Gajeva 1
10000 Zagreb
phone: 45 55 155
fax: 424 451

The hotel is located in the very center of the city. There are 269 rooms (450 beds) and 7 apartments. The rooms are equipped with a bathroom or shower-toilet facility, and telephone. The rooms in the new part of the hotel have also satellite TV. The hotel restaurant offers national and international cuisine.

Note:

Croatia Telephone Country Code = 385
Zagreb Area Code =

1 (from outside Croatia)
01 (within Croatia)

BASIC TITLES ON CROATIA

Title	ISBN
Croatia A "Spy" Guide - Strategic Information and Developments	1438711034
Croatia A "Spy" Guide - Strategic Information and Developments	1433008777
Croatia Air Force Handbook	1438711042
Croatia Air Force Handbook	1433008785
Croatia Banking & Financial Market Handbook	1433008793
Croatia Banking & Financial Market Handbook	1438711050
Croatia Business and Investment Opportunities Yearbook	1433008807
Croatia Business and Investment Opportunities Yearbook	1438711069
Croatia Business and Investment Opportunities Yearbook Volume 1 Strategic Information and Opportunities	1438776543
Croatia Business and Investment Opportunities Yearbook Volume 2 Leading Export-Import, Business, Investment Opportunities and Projects	1577519310
Croatia Business Intelligence Report - Practical Information, Opportunities, Contacts	1433008815
Croatia Business Intelligence Report - Practical Information, Opportunities, Contacts	1438711077
Croatia Business Law Handbook - Strategic Information and Basic Laws	1438711085
Croatia Business Law Handbook - Strategic Information and Basic Laws	1433008823
Croatia Business Law Handbook - Strategic Information and Basic Laws	1438769679
Croatia Business Law Handbook - Strategic Information and Basic Laws	1438769679
Croatia Business Law Handbook Volume 2 Investment and Trade Laws Volume 2 Investment and Trade Laws	1577518012
Croatia Company Laws and Regulations Handbook	1433069679
Croatia Constitution and Citizenship Laws Handbook - Strategic Information and Basic Laws	1438778783
Croatia Country Study Guide - Strategic Information and Developments	1438711093
Croatia Country Study Guide - Strategic Information and Developments	1433008831
Croatia Country Study Guide - Strategic Information and Developments Volume 1 Strategic Information and Developments	1438774214
Croatia Customs, Trade Regulations and Procedures Handbook	1438711107
Croatia Customs, Trade Regulations and Procedures Handbook	143300884X
Croatia Diplomatic Handbook - Strategic Information and Developments	1433008858
Croatia Diplomatic Handbook - Strategic Information and Developments	1438711115
Croatia Ecology & Nature Protection Handbook	1433008866
Croatia Ecology & Nature Protection Handbook	1438711123
Croatia Ecology & Nature Protection Laws and Regulation Handbook	1433073595

Title	ISBN
Croatia Economic & Development Strategy Handbook	1433008874
Croatia Economic & Development Strategy Handbook	1438711131
Croatia Energy Policy, Laws and Regulation Handbook	1433071355
Croatia Export-Import Trade and Business Directory	143871114X
Croatia Export-Import Trade and Business Directory	1433008882
Croatia Financial & Banking Law and Regulations Handbook	1433008890
Croatia Financial & Banking Law and Regulations Handbook	1438711158
Croatia Foreign Policy and Government Guide	1433008904
Croatia Foreign Policy and Government Guide	1438711166
Croatia Government and Business Contacts Handbook	1433008912
Croatia Government and Business Contacts Handbook	1438711174
Croatia Immigration Laws and Regulations Handbook - Strategic Information and Basic Laws	1438782403
Croatia Industrial and Business Directory	1433008920
Croatia Industrial and Business Directory	1438711182
Croatia Insolvency (Bankruptcy) Laws and Regulations Handbook - Strategic Information and Basic Laws	9781433085185
Croatia Insolvency (Bankruptcy) Laws and Regulations Handbook - Strategic Information and Basic Laws	9781433086229
Croatia Internet and E-Commerce Investment and Business Guide - Strategic and Practical Information: Regulations and Opportunities	1438711190
Croatia Internet and E-Commerce Investment and Business Guide - Strategic and Practical Information: Regulations and Opportunities	1433008939
Croatia Investment and Business Guide - Strategic and Practical Information	1438711204
Croatia Investment and Business Guide - Strategic and Practical Information	1438767390
Croatia Investment and Business Guide - Strategic and Practical Information	1433008947
Croatia Investment and Business Guide - Strategic and Practical Information	1438767390
Croatia Investment and Business Guide Volume 2 Business, Investment Opportunities and Incentives	1577518519
Croatia Investment and Trade Laws and Regulations Handbook	1433075687
Croatia Labor Laws and Regulations Handbook - Strategic Information and Basic Laws	1438780605
Croatia Land Ownership and Agriculture Laws Handbook	1438758871
Croatia Mineral & Mining Sector Investment and Business Guide - Strategic and Practical Information	1433008955
Croatia Mineral & Mining Sector Investment and Business Guide - Strategic and Practical Information	1438711212
Croatia Mining Laws and Regulations Handbook	1433077256
Croatia Privatization Programs and Regulations Handbook	1433008963
Croatia Privatization Programs and Regulations Handbook	1438711220
Croatia Recent Economic and Political Developments Yearbook	1433061198
Croatia Recent Economic and Political Developments Yearbook	1433061198
Croatia Recent Economic and Political Developments Yearbook	1433061198
Croatia Starting Business (Incorporating) in....Guide	1433065231
Croatia Tax Guide	1438711239

Title	ISBN
Croatia Tax Guide	1433008971
Croatia Taxation Laws and Regulations Handbook	1433079623
Croatia Telecom Laws and Regulations Handbook	1433081652
Croatia Telecommunication Industry Business Opportunities Handbook	143300898X
Croatia Telecommunication Industry Business Opportunities Handbook	1438711247
Croatia Transportation Policy and Regulations Handbook	143306524X
Croatia: How to Invest, Start and Run Profitable Business in Croatia Guide - Practical Information, Opportunities, Contacts	9781433083198

WORLD INVESTMENT AND BUSINESS GUIDE LIBRARY

Ultimate guides for business and investment operations in the country.

Price: $99 each

1. Afghanistan Investment and Business Guide
2. Aland Investment and Business Guide
3. Albania Investment and Business Guide
4. Algeria Investment and Business Guide
5. Andorra Investment and Business Guide
6. Angola Investment and Business Guide
7. Anguilla Investment and Business Guide
8. Antigua and Barbuda Investment and Business Guide
9. Antilles (Netherlands) Investment and Business Guide
10. Argentina Investment and Business Guide
11. Armenia Investment and Business Guide
12. Aruba Investment and Business Guide
13. Australia Investment and Business Guide
14. Austria Investment and Business Guide
15. Azerbaijan Investment and Business Guide
16. Bahamas Investment and Business Guide
17. Bahrain Investment and Business Guide
18. Bangladesh Investment and Business Guide
19. Barbados Investment and Business Guide
20. Belarus Investment and Business Guide
21. Belgium Investment and Business Guide
22. Belize Investment and Business Guide
23. Benin Investment and Business Guide
24. Bermuda Investment and Business Guide
25. Bhutan Investment and Business Guide
26. Bolivia Investment and Business Guide
27. Bosnia and Herzegovina Investment and Business Guide
28. Botswana Investment and Business Guide
29. Brazil Investment and Business Guide
30. Brunei Investment and Business Guide
31. Bulgaria Investment and Business Guide
32. Burkina Faso Investment and Business Guide
33. Burundi Investment and Business Guide
34. Cambodia Investment and Business Guide
35. Cameroon Investment and Business Guide
36. Canada Investment and Business Guide
37. Cape Verde Investment and Business Guide

38.	Cayman Islands Investment and Business Guide
39.	Central African Republic Investment and Business Guide
40.	Chad Investment and Business Guide
41.	Chile Investment and Business Guide
42.	China Investment and Business Guide
43.	Colombia Investment and Business Guide
44.	Comoros Investment and Business Guide
45.	Congo Investment and Business Guide
46.	Congo, Democratic Republic Investment and Business Guide
47.	Cook Islands Investment and Business Guide
48.	Costa Rica Investment and Business Guide
49.	Cote d'Ivoire Investment and Business Guide
50.	Croatia Investment and Business Guide
51.	Cuba Investment and Business Guide
52.	Cyprus Investment and Business Guide
53.	Czech Republic Investment and Business Guide
54.	Denmark Investment and Business Guide
55.	Djibouti Investment and Business Guide
56.	Dominica Investment and Business Guide
57.	Dominican Republic Investment and Business Guide
58.	Ecuador Investment and Business Guide
59.	Egypt Investment and Business Guide
60.	El Salvador Investment and Business Guide
61.	Equatorial Guinea Investment and Business Guide
62.	Eritrea Investment and Business Guide
63.	Estonia Investment and Business Guide
64.	Ethiopia Investment and Business Guide
65.	Falkland Islands Investment and Business Guide
66.	Faroes Islands Investment and Business Guide
67.	Fiji Investment and Business Guide
68.	Finland Investment and Business Guide
69.	France Investment and Business Guide
70.	Gabon Investment and Business Guide
71.	Gambia Investment and Business Guide
72.	Georgia Investment and Business Guide
73.	Germany Investment and Business Guide
74.	Ghana Investment and Business Guide
75.	Gibraltar Investment and Business Guide
76.	Greece Investment and Business Guide
77.	Greenland Investment and Business Guide
78.	Grenada Investment and Business Guide
79.	Guam Investment and Business Guide
80.	Guatemala Investment and Business Guide
81.	Guernsey Investment and Business Guide
82.	Guinea Investment and Business Guide
83.	Guinea-Bissau Investment and Business Guide
84.	Guyana Investment and Business Guide
85.	Haiti Investment and Business Guide
86.	Honduras Investment and Business Guide
87.	Hungary Investment and Business Guide
88.	Iceland Investment and Business Guide

89. India Investment and Business Guide
90. Indonesia Investment and Business Guide
91. Iran Investment and Business Guide
92. Iraq Investment and Business Guide
93. Ireland Investment and Business Guide
94. Israel Investment and Business Guide
95. Italy Investment and Business Guide
96. Jamaica Investment and Business Guide
97. Japan Investment and Business Guide
98. Jersey Investment and Business Guide
99. Jordan Investment and Business Guide
100. Kazakhstan Investment and Business Guide
101. Kenya Investment and Business Guide
102. Kiribati Investment and Business Guide
103. Korea, North Investment and Business Guide
104. Korea, South Investment and Business Guide
105. Kosovo Investment and Business Guide
106. Kurdistan Investment and Business Guide
107. Kuwait Investment and Business Guide
108. Kyrgyzstan Investment and Business Guide
109. Laos Investment and Business Guide
110. Latvia Investment and Business Guide
111. Lebanon Investment and Business Guide
112. Lesotho Investment and Business Guide
113. Liberia Investment and Business Guide
114. Libya Investment and Business Guide
115. Liechtenstein Investment and Business Guide
116. Lithuania Investment and Business Guide
117. Luxembourg Investment and Business Guide
118. Macao Investment and Business Guide
119. Macedonia Investment and Business Guide
120. Madagascar Investment and Business Guide
121. Madeira Investment and Business Guide
122. Malawi Investment and Business Guide
123. Malaysia Investment and Business Guide
124. Maldives Investment and Business Guide
125. Mali Investment and Business Guide
126. Malta Investment and Business Guide
127. Man Investment and Business Guide
128. Marshall Islands Investment and Business Guide
129. Mauritania Investment and Business Guide
130. Mauritius Investment and Business Guide
131. Mayotte Investment and Business Guide
132. Mexico Investment and Business Guide
133. Micronesia Investment and Business Guide
134. Moldova Investment and Business Guide
135. Monaco Investment and Business Guide
136. Mongolia Investment and Business Guide
137. Monserrat Investment and Business Guide
138. Morocco Investment and Business Guide
139. Mozambique Investment and Business Guide

140. Myanmar Investment and Business Guide
141. Namibia Investment and Business Guide
142. Nauru Investment and Business Guide
143. Nepal Investment and Business Guide
144. Netherlands Investment and Business Guide
145. New Caledonia Investment and Business Guide
146. New Zealand Investment and Business Guide
147. Nicaragua Investment and Business Guide
148. Niger Investment and Business Guide
149. Nigeria Investment and Business Guide
150. Niue Investment and Business Guide
151. Northern Mariana Islands Investment and Business Guide
152. Norway Investment and Business Guide
153. Oman Investment and Business Guide
154. Pakistan Investment and Business Guide
155. Palau Investment and Business Guide
156. Palestine (West Bank & Gaza) Investment and Business Guide
157. Panama Investment and Business Guide
158. Papua New Guinea Investment and Business Guide
159. Paraguay Investment and Business Guide
160. Peru Investment and Business Guide
161. Philippines Investment and Business Guide
162. Pitcairn Islands Investment and Business Guide
163. Poland Investment and Business Guide
164. Polynesia French Investment and Business Guide
165. Portugal Investment and Business Guide
166. Qatar Investment and Business Guide
167. Romania Investment and Business Guide
168. Russia Investment and Business Guide
169. Rwanda Investment and Business Guide
170. Saint Kitts and Nevis Investment and Business Guide
171. Saint Lucia Investment and Business Guide
172. Saint Vincent and The Grenadines Investment and Business Guide
173. Samoa (American) A Investment and Business Guide
174. Samoa (Western) Investment and Business Guide
175. San Marino Investment and Business Guide
176. Sao Tome and Principe Investment and Business Guide
177. Saudi Arabia Investment and Business Guide
178. Scotland Investment and Business Guide
179. Senegal Investment and Business Guide
180. Serbia Investment and Business Guide
181. Seychelles Investment and Business Guide
182. Sierra Leone Investment and Business Guide
183. Singapore Investment and Business Guide
184. Slovakia Investment and Business Guide
185. Slovenia Investment and Business Guide
186. Solomon Islands Investment and Business Guide
187. Somalia Investment and Business Guide
188. South Africa Investment and Business Guide
189. Spain Investment and Business Guide
190. Sri Lanka Investment and Business Guide

191. St. Helena Investment and Business Guide
192. St. Pierre & Miquelon Investment and Business Guide
193. Sudan Investment and Business Guide
194. Sudan South Investment and Business Guide
195. Suriname Investment and Business Guide
196. Swaziland Investment and Business Guide
197. Sweden Investment and Business Guide
198. Switzerland Investment and Business Guide
199. Syria Investment and Business Guide
200. Taiwan Investment and Business Guide
201. Tajikistan Investment and Business Guide
202. Tanzania Investment and Business Guide
203. Thailand Investment and Business Guide
204. Togo Investment and Business Guide
205. Tonga Investment and Business Guide
206. Trinidad and Tobago Investment and Business Guide
207. Tunisia Investment and Business Guide
208. Turkey Investment and Business Guide
209. Turkmenistan Investment and Business Guide
210. Turks & Caicos Investment and Business Guide
211. Tuvalu Investment and Business Guide
212. Uganda Investment and Business Guide
213. Ukraine Investment and Business Guide
214. United Arab Emirates Investment and Business Guide
215. United Kingdom Investment and Business Guide
216. United States Investment and Business Guide
217. Uruguay Investment and Business Guide
218. Uzbekistan Investment and Business Guide
219. Vanuatu Investment and Business Guide
220. Vatican City Investment and Business Guide
221. Venezuela Investment and Business Guide
222. Vietnam Investment and Business Guide
223. Virgin Islands, British Investment and Business Guide
224. Wake Atoll Investment and Business Guide
225. Wallis & Futuna Investment and Business Guide
226. Western Sahara Investment and Business Guide
227. Yemen Investment and Business Guide
228. Zambia Investment and Business Guide
229. Zimbabwe Investment and Business Guide

To order and for additional analytical and marketing information, please contacts International Business Publications, USA at:
P.O. Box 15343, Washington, DC 20003, USA. Phone: (202) 546-210 Fax: (202) 546-32
E-mail: ibpusa@comcast.net
Global Business Information Catalog: http://wwww.ibpus.com